Conversations on Russia

Conversations on Russia

Reform from Yeltsin to Putin

PADMA DESAI

OXFORD

UNIVERSITY PRESS

2006

OXFORD
UNIVERSITY PRESS

Oxford University Press, Inc., publishes works that further
Oxford University's objective of excellence
in research, scholarship, and education.

Oxford   New York
Auckland   Cape Town   Dar es Salaam   Hong Kong   Karachi
Kuala Lumpur   Madrid   Melbourne   Mexico City   Nairobi
New Delhi   Shanghai   Taipei   Toronto

With offices in
Argentina   Austria   Brazil   Chile   Czech Republic   France   Greece
Guatemala   Hungary   Italy   Japan   Poland   Portugal   Singapore
South Korea   Switzerland   Thailand   Turkey   Ukraine   Vietnam

Copyright © 2006 by Oxford University Press

Published by Oxford University Press, Inc.
198 Madison Avenue, New York, New York 10016

www.oup.com

Oxford is a registered trademark of Oxford University Press

Library of Congress Cataloging-in-Publication Data
Desai, Padma.
Conversations on Russia : reform from Yeltsin to Putin / Padma Desai.
p.   cm.
Includes bibliographical references and index.
ISBN-13 978-0-19-530061-1
ISBN 0-19-530061-0

1. Russia (Federation)—Economic policy—1991– .   2. Soviet Union
—Economic policy—1986–1991.   3. Privatizing—Russia (Federation)
I. Title.

HC340.12.D467 2006
338.647'009'049—dc22   2005020203

1 3 5 7 9 8 6 4 2

Printed in the United States of America
on acid-free paper

FOR   Abram Bergson
in fond memory
āchārya—devo bhava

TAITTIRĪYA UPANISHAD 1.11.2

Preface

Conversations on Russia: Reforms from Yeltsin to Putin is a collection of interviews that I conducted between late 1999 and early 2005 both with leading Russian and American policymakers involved in Russia's transformation from its Communist past, and with prominent analysts and intellectuals who commented on that process as it unfolded with dramatic twists and turns in 1992 under Boris Yeltsin.

Not surprisingly, the changes have prompted countless surveys, reports, and commentaries. These attempts at explanation, however, have failed to provide a systematic examination of the motives and objectives that underlay the many policy actions of the Russian reformers, with the principal architects speaking their minds. In addition, the concerns and objectives of the leading academics and analysts who commented on the reformers' decisions also call for a careful dialogue. I therefore decided on the novel format of interviewing both sets of participants in the reform process.

This project turned out to be a gigantic enterprise requiring a firm grasp of the unfolding scene in Russia and of its complicated past. I needed to understand fully the policymakers' decisions and the interviewees' writings and pronouncements in order to converse with them and ask them appropriate and incisive questions. Fortunately my scholarly engagement of nearly four decades with the Soviet experience and subsequently with the tumultuous events in Russia under Mikhail Gorbachev and Yeltsin provided me with the necessary background. My book-length studies, articles in scientific journals, and commentaries in the press and the media came in handy for the task at hand.

I introduce this book with a substantial story and analysis of the evolution of Russian reforms, starting from Boris Yeltsin's colorful and remarkable appearance on the Russian scene and ending with Vladimir Putin's orderly but disquieting consolidation of federal authority. My story weaves into itself several nuances and insights that the interviews in the volume provide, giving it an authenticity and flavor that, I hope, will make the volume a unique contribution to understanding recent developments on the Russian scene. There is no substitute for reading my introduction. Nonetheless, I provide here three insights that emerged from the analysis, while stressing that my introduction offers a diagnosis of recent events rather than an approbation of where Russia is headed.

It is incontestable that Yeltsin's reformers, whom he calls his "kamikaze crew" in his interview, firmly and irretrievably planted the liberal idea in the land of Lenin and Stalin. They dismantled the Communist planned economy and the authoritarian political arrangements that had prevailed over nearly seven decades. But while their "demolition project" was successful, their success did not extend to what might be called the balancing "creative project": the establishment of institutions necessary to support a market-oriented economy. Markets have to be embedded in institutions that have evolved in capitalist economies over decades; the Russian reformers, by contrast, leapt across the chasm to the new regime. However, for the reforms to take hold, a bridge should have been built slowly and assiduously across the divide.

Yeltsin's reformers ended up paying insufficient attention to the politics of the reform process they unveiled. Their technocratic stance underemphasized both the need to work at getting public acceptance of their programs and the need to countervail the adverse distributional implications of some of the key reforms. In particular, while one can understand the rationale for speeding up privatization, the precise manner of privatizing Russia's state-owned assets was ultimately seen widely as inequitable and even as an "outright robbery." This dissatisfaction has in turn resulted in favorable Russian perceptions of the punitive actions of the Putin regime against some of the oligarchs. Rather than adopt a blanket reversal of the privatization outcomes especially in the energy sector, Putin also resorted to widespread positioning of Kremlin bureaucrats as managers in some units with a view to reining in oligarchic influence.

As the reform team stepped into uncharted territory and made decisions in a vacuum marked by lack of previous experience, they not only encountered Communist opposition and massive difficulties in implementation but also imposed severe hardships on ordinary Russians. This led to a decisive turn by the Russian voters against the Yeltsin-era reforms and the liberal reformist groups, a change of sentiment that was reflected in the December 2003 parliamentary elections. After four years under Putin, who was elected president in the spring of 2000, Russians have continued stating—in their approbation of Putin in repeated polls by substantial majorities—that they are ready to settle for a mild dose of authoritarianism that promises containment of the oligarchs and a return to stability and economic gains that they feel has eluded them for so long.

What does the future portend? There are two possible outcomes: An optimistic scenario (to which I subscribe) is that, given Russia's long history of authoritarian rule, the "poisoned chalice of history," the evolution of the liberal economic and political order will be haphazard, perhaps even hazardous at times. In the end, however, the reformers' legacy will prevail despite Putin's consolidating impetus. Perhaps because of the perceived threat, Russian reformist groups will unite and reinvigorate their liberal aspirations, and consolidate their political efforts as the December 2007 parliamentary elections approach.

The alternative, pessimistic scenario, which has gained prominence, is that Putin will increasingly consolidate his authority over the political arrangements and take Russia back to an illiberal system. This seems to be the burden of much of the criticism in the Western media today. I feel it is based on excessive pessimism and ignores the solid changes that Russia has experienced. In the estimation of former prime minister Mikhail Kasyanov and central bank chairman Sergei Dubinin, Russia and Russians have changed. Yegor Gaidar, who launched the reforms in 1992, remains wary of Putin's democratic credentials but does not "believe in the emergence of nondemocratic regimes in countries with educated, urban populations" such as Russia's.

Since the adoption of the Constitution in 1993, Russia had four parliamentary and three presidential elections. The reform momentum has slackened, but the reform issues—among them reining in corruption and slashing the bureaucracy, redesigning the pension and Soviet-era welfare systems, and restructuring the monopolies—are daunting challenges and time-consuming endeavors under the best of circumstances. The Russian voters may not have fully matured, but their middle-of-the-road responses to public opinion polls seem to rule out the extremes of either the restoration of fast-paced reforms or an excessive tilt toward further authoritarianism. Outside attempts at forcing the former to thwart the latter will have to contend with the Russian electorate's rejection of rapid-fire economic changes and their preference for steady economic benefits in the currently resurgent economy.

As for Putin's grooming of a successor of his choice, incumbent leaders around the world exercise that prerogative. Yeltsin chose Putin because, as he declares in his interview, Putin was not a "maximalist" and could act as a stabilizer by reining in the post-Yeltsin political disorder and public discontent.

Such revelatory gems pervade the interviews. The interviewees liven up their responses with interesting anecdotes, historical and literary references, and revealing stories. The Russian interviewees in particular are exceptionally frank, even courageous in their assessment of Putin's illiberal forays. Overall my conversations go beyond economic issues to discuss Russian foreign policy, history, society, and demography. I thank the participants for generously giving me their time and sharing with me their opinions on some of the most controversial and dramatic events of our times.

My project stretched over six years and involved frequent trips, especially to Moscow, where I benefited generously from my contacts in the Indian Embassy. I would like to thank Ambassadors Nirupama Rao, Krishnan Raghunath, and Kanwal Sibal for extending their hospitality during my frequent and extended Moscow stays. Emil Czechowski, Mariya Konovalova, Julieanne Sohn, and Keith Garrod and Ronald Meyer transcribed the interview tapes patiently and skillfully, sparing me countless exhausting hours. Financial support from the Harriman Institute of Columbia University covered some of the project's costs.

When I started the project in late 1999 with my first interview with Anatoly Chubais, the architect of Russian privatization, I was not aware of the effort, persistence, and resourcefulness I would need to push it forward. By the time I wound it up in early 2005 with my final interview with former prime minister Mikhail Kasyanov, I felt I had gained a clearer and richer understanding of the Russian reform process than I could have managed with the standard academic practice of reading and researching. I do hope that my readers feel equally rewarded by dipping into the conversations in this collection.

Contents

Participants

ANATOLY CHUBAIS, former minister of privatization and first deputy prime minister in the Yeltsin governments; currently CEO of United Energy Systems (UES), Russia's giant electric power company, and one of the leaders of the Union of Right Forces (SPS), Russia's leading reform party

SERGEI DUBININ, former chair of the Central Bank of Russia, under whose watch in August 1998 the ruble collapsed; currently deputy CEO of UES

YEGOR GAIDAR, acting prime minister in 1992; currently director of the Center for Transition Economies, Moscow, and one of the leaders of the SPS

BORIS JORDAN, founder of the Moscow office of Credit Suisse First Boston and of Renaissance Capital, currently Russia's largest investment bank; former general manager of NTV, one of Russia's leading television networks, from which he was fired by President Putin; currently CEO of the Sputnik Group, an investment-cum-financial group

MIKHAIL KASYANOV, prime minister from 2000 to early 2004 during President Vladimir Putin's first presidency; plans to run for president in the 2008 election

MARTIN MALIA (deceased), eminent historian of Russia; professor emeritus of history at the University of California–Berkeley

JACK MATLOCK JR., U.S. ambassador to the Soviet Union from 1987 to 1991 under Mikhail Gorbachev; author of *Autopsy on an Empire: The American Ambassador's Account of the Collapse of the Soviet Union*, and *Reagan and Gorbachev: How the Cold War Ended*

BORIS NEMTSOV, former governor of Nizhni Novgorod province and first deputy prime minister in the government under Yeltsin; founder and leader of SPS

RICHARD PIPES, eminent historian of Russia; professor emeritus of history at Harvard University; national security advisor in the Reagan administration

SERGEI ROGOV, director of the U.S.-Canada Institute, Moscow, a leading Russian think tank

NODARI SIMONIA, director of the Institute of International Economy and International Relations (IMEMO), Moscow, Russia's leading international policy institute

GEORGE SOROS, financier and philanthropist

STROBE TALBOTT, deputy secretary of state in the Clinton administration from 1994 to 2001; author of *The Russia Hand: A Memoir of Presidential Diplomacy*; currently president of the Brookings Institution

ANATOLY VISHNEVSKY, Russia's leading demographer and director of the Center for Demography and Human Ecology

OLEG VYUGIN, former deputy chair of the Central Bank of Russia and the chief architect of its monetary policy; currently chair of the Federal Financial Markets Service of the Russian Federation

GRIGORY YAVLINSKY, founder and leader of Yabloko, Russia's leading left-of-center political party; Russia's pro-Western, liberal politician with presidential ambitions

BORIS YELTSIN, former president of the Russian Federation

Conversations on Russia

Introduction

When Mikhail Gorbachev became general secretary of the Communist Party of the Soviet Union (CPSU) in March 1985, he faced daunting challenges from three directions. He had inherited an economy in crisis, a restive and costly East-Central Europe under Soviet control, and the Soviet state at home held together by an authoritarian ideology enforced from Moscow by the CPSU. By the time he resigned as president of the Soviet Union on December 25, 1991, East Central Europe had slipped away from Moscow's grip, and the Soviet Union had been dissolved as well. It officially divided into separate, independent states.

In January 1992 Boris Yeltsin assumed charge as the first president of the Russian Federation, the successor state. His primary goals were to end the authoritarian Communist political system and the planned economy—not to reform them, but to finish them. To accomplish this goal, as Yeltsin later recalled in an incisive October 2003 interview published in *Moscow News,* "What was needed was a kamikaze crew that would step into the line of fire and forge ahead, however strong the general discontent might be. . . . I had to pick a team that would go up in flames but remain in history."

Yeltsin's reformers clearly achieved their goal of ending the authoritarian political arrangements and the economic management in the style of Soviet Communism before they went up in flames. By the end of 1993, Russia had a federal constitution, an elected president as the head of state, parliamentary elections, an active electronic media, and a lively press. At the same time, its firms were no longer state owned; its people could own property and businesses, travel freely, and choose jobs; its government relied on taxes for collecting revenue; and its currency was traded on foreign-exchange markets. However, controversy over Yeltsin's economic reforms and political changes has raged ever since. With every disappointment or failure that Russia has experienced since 1992, questions arise as to whether a different path of political and economic reform might have worked better.

Yeltsin's reformers, however, were so successful in ending the old economic and political patterns of state control that Yeltsin began to be concerned about whether the government could exercise its legitimate powers effectively—especially in a country as vast as Russia with ostensible federal arrangements. His decision to anoint Vladimir Putin as his successor in late 1999 demonstrated his acute unease over the breakdown of political cohesion and the urgency of restoring stability in Russia. "He [Putin] is not a maximalist, and this is what set him apart from the others," Yeltsin responded in the October 2003 interview when questioned about his choice. Predictably, Putin set about the task of consolidating state authority and restoring order following his election as president in April 2000, which in turn prompted concerns as to whether Russia's nascent democracy was being undermined.

In September 2004, early in Putin's second presidential term, a group of terrorists attacked a school in Beslan, a small town in the Caucasus region of Russia, and more than 330 hostages, including scores of school children, were killed. Putin then proposed sweeping changes for consolidating presidential authority with a view to fighting terrorism. These raised a blitzkrieg of condemnatory reaction in the West. The Russian president, these critics said, was undermining Russia's evolution as a liberal state and reversing the progress on private ownership and media freedom his predecessor and mentor, Boris Yeltsin, had made.

Given the number of claims about what Yeltsin's reformers should have done and whether Putin is undemocratic, even autocratic, it is useful to find out what the Yeltsin reformers and Putin policy makers were actually thinking and doing. Thus, I undertook an interview project with key participants in Russia's reforms from 1999 to early 2005. I also interviewed U.S. policy formulators and analysts from the Reagan and Clinton administrations with a view to eliciting their judgments on Russia's political and economic issues. The interviews, with appropriate questions to members of both groups, went beyond economic issues and political changes to discuss Russian foreign policy, history, society, and demography.

The Russian interviewees consisted of three principal economic reformers under Boris Yeltsin and one under Vladimir Putin, three policy analysts, three banking professionals, and one demographer. The U.S. interviewees included three Reagan and Clinton policy advisors, one historian, and one financier-cum-philanthropist with Russian connections.

THE PARTICIPANTS

The Russian Interviewees

The highlight of the project included repeated interviews with the three principal economic reformers under Boris Yeltsin. Yegor Gaidar was acting prime minister for a year, until his resignation in January 1993. Gaidar was known as the author of the "shock therapy" approach to Russian economic reform, which involved the rapid elimination of price controls, as well as of military procurement and industrial subsidies from the federal budget. Anatoly Chubais was the architect of Russian privatization, an enormous task for an economy in which all means of production had been state owned. Chubais carried out a plan in which 150 million

Russians—every man, woman, and child—received vouchers for purchasing shares in privatized firms and in which two-thirds of all Russian workers were employed by privatized firms by 1997. However, enormous controversy has continued over the extent to which ordinary citizens benefited from the privatization and the extent to which shares of Russian industry ended up in the hands of a relatively small number of owners in the second phase of the privatization process. Boris Nemtsov was a liberal, pro-market politician who had served in a variety of roles since 1992: He was the young, innovative, reforming governor of Nizhny Novgorod, a region of about 4 million people; the key minister in charge of monopoly; the key minister in charge of energy; and a member of the upper house of Parliament (the Council of Federation) in the early 1990s. He was active in Yeltsin's government until its resignation in August 1998, when the Russian ruble was hit with a financial crisis.

Yeltsin, looking back in his October 2003 interview, described Gaidar as "logical, coherent, and clear in his mind insofar as economic matters were concerned"; Chubais as "closer to me in spirit than the others"; and Nemtsov as "the most elusive, . . . a bit of a guerrilla." In my assessment, Gaidar came across (in two interviews in 2000 and late 2004) as the scholarly conceptualizer and policy maker; Chubais (in one interview in mid-1999) as the brass-tacks designer and enforcer of the necessary privatization measures; and Nemtsov (in four interviews between 2000 and late 2004) as the politician with a deft sales pitch. Together they generated a powerful pro-market synergy, while Yeltsin in hindsight complained that their "maximalism" "exasperated" him.

Grigory Yavlinsky is the best known of the liberal academic economists who became involved in Russia's economic reform. Yavlinsky had been the head of the economic department of the USSR government. In 1989, he was a member of a prominent committee that designed a plan for transforming the economy to a market system in five hundred days. When the plan was not implemented, Yavlinsky resigned. Throughout the 1990s, he was a prominent figure in economic reform debates, including policy measures enacted under Nemtsov in the Nizhny Novgorod region and a number of tax, budget, and sectoral reforms. As the founder of the opposition Yabloko group, twice a presidential candidate, and a fierce critic of the Yeltsin reforms, Yavlinsky has made his mark as the permanent oppositionist of Russian politics. His mid-2002 interview offers a blow-by-blow assessment of the economic reforms of the 1990s. Yavlinsky presents a strong pro-Western, liberal, and reformist stance but nonetheless opposes what he perceives as the extreme pro-market thrust of the Yeltsin team in favor of a social democratic approach.

Equally vociferous in their criticism of Yeltsin and his agenda (in their mid-2003 and late 2004 interviews) were two eminent academic analysts with social democratic leanings. Sergei Rogov is director of Moscow's Institute of USA and Canada Studies. Nodari Simonia is director of the Moscow-based Institute for International Economy and International Relations. Rogov's institute is a leading think tank under the Russian Academy of Sciences, which provides advisory input on foreign policy, military, and economic issues to Russian government agencies. Similarly placed under the Russian Academy and the largest think tank in Russia, Simonia's institute undertakes research on social, economic, military, and foreign policy issues. Both institutes award undergraduate and graduate degrees.

Three banking professionals responded with interviews that were crisply analytical and refreshingly candid. Sergei Dubinin, former chair of the Central Bank of Russia, under whose watch the ruble collapsed in August 1998, discussed the problems of steering monetary policy in the late 1990s and of current monopoly restructuring in four interviews (between 2000 and early 2005). As a former deputy CEO of Gazprom, the world's largest natural gas monopoly, and current deputy CEO of United Energy Services (UES), Russia's electric power monopoly, Dubinin has personal experience in restructuring these gigantic companies. Oleg Vyugin, Dubinin's successor as Central Bank's deputy chair, gave a firsthand account of post-August 1998 monetary policy formulation (in a 2003 conversation). Boris Jordan, who helped set up the Moscow office of Credit Suisse First Boston (and later Renaissance Capital, currently Russia's largest investment bank), talked about his experiences (in mid-2003 and late-2004 interviews) as a trailblazer on the Russian financial and investment scene.

Six of these nine interviewees (all except Chubais, Yavlinsky, and Vyugin) corresponded with me in October 2004 with their view of how Putin's proposals might affect Russia's continuing evolution to a democratic system and a liberal market economy. Nemtsov and Rogov also discussed aspects of Russian foreign policy in the context of the reviving economy and Putin's consolidating impetus.

In December 2004 I interviewed Mikhail Kasyanov, prime minister in the government during the first Putin presidency, from 2000 to early 2004. A pro-market policy maker, he succeeded in having the Parliament adopt a series of reformist laws on taxation, land transactions, corporate governance, and judicial reform. He was fired by Putin in March 2004 on the eve of the presidential election, ostensibly for his probusiness leaning. He has declared his intention to run for president in the 2008 election.

Finally, in a December 2003 interview, Anatoly Vishnevsky, Russia's leading demographer and director of the Center for Demography and Human Ecology, provided a historical perspective with illuminating insights on Russia's emerging demographic crisis.

The American Interviewees

Strobe Talbott, deputy secretary of state from 1994 to 2001 in the Clinton administrations and author of *The Russia Hand: A Memoir of Presidential Diplomacy*, gave two interviews (in December 2000 and early 2001) that illuminate the critical policy choices driven by the personal chemistry between Clinton and Yeltsin. Later, in early 2005, he responded with his reaction to Putin's consolidating measures. Jack Matlock Jr., U.S. ambassador to the Soviet Union from 1987 to 1991, is the author of *Autopsy on an Empire: The American Ambassador's Account of the Collapse of the Soviet Union* (1995) and *Reagan and Gorbachev: The End of the Cold War* (2004). He assessed the impact of Putin's illiberal measures on Russia's nascent democracy and on U.S.-Russian foreign policy (in two interviews between 2003 and early 2005). Richard Pipes, professor emeritus of history at Harvard University and author of the classic *The Formation of the Soviet Union,* served as national security advisor in the Reagan administration. He provided a historical perspective on the current Russian situation (in two interviews in 2003 and late 2004). The late Martin Malia, professor emeritus of history at the University of California–Berkeley and author of the famous "Z" article, assessed Putin's policy decisions in the pre-Beslan phase in a refreshingly nuanced interview in April 2000.[1] Finally, in his December 2000 interview, George Soros, financier and philanthropist, provided details of his Russian philanthropic interests in the increasingly chaotic situation under Yeltsin.

While my questions were tailored to the participants' areas of expertise and interest, they were carefully designed to illuminate three principal aspects of Russia's halting progression to democracy and free markets.

First, what lessons might be drawn from the "poisoned chalice" of tsarist autocracy and seven decades of Soviet Communism for understanding Russia's current transition? From this distant past, how far has Russia traveled today? What were the economic and political features of the Soviet system that the reformers were bent on destroying?

Second, given their strategic objective of finishing off the Communist economic and political system, how did Boris Yeltsin and his reformers define their policy framework? How did their program differ from that of Mikhail Gorbachev? How did the U.S. policy makers react to the unfolding reforms under Gorbachev and Yeltsin? What role did the International Monetary Fund (IMF) play in the process? What did the reformers accomplish?

Finally, will Putin turn excessively authoritarian during his second term as president, which began in May 2004? What are the pressing reform issues of his second presidency? Will declining population affect economic growth and the reform momentum? How will the U.S.-Russian relationship evolve under his presidency?

First, for the history lessons.

From a historical perspective, current Russian events often raise the baffling question of whether Russia's future will be shaped by what John Stuart Mill called "the slavery of antecedent circumstances." I have outlined these past patterns in the minimum necessary detail with a view to focusing on their relevance for the current situation, rather than providing a full historical record.

Past Patterns of Economic Development

The transformation of the economy of predominantly agrarian Russia of the late seventeenth century into one with diversified industry required that the savings of the peasant households be invested to create urban factories.[2] Banks did not exist for channeling these funds into productive investments via lending to businesses, nor, for that matter, did business-savvy entrepreneurs. Under tsarist autocracy, to extract the necessary resources, the government dictated the speed and profile of industrialization by taxing the serfs.

From Peter the Great (1682–1725) to Stalin (1928–1953), Russian economic development took place in massive spurts followed by sharp declines. It lacked "balanced growth" sustained by adequate capital formation, technological changes, appropriate institutions, and entrepreneurial attitudes. These features advanced in eighteenth- and nineteenth-century Europe more or less together and much earlier than in tsarist Russia.

Industrialization Spurts and Military Objectives

Four major spurts have marked Russian history. The first occurred under Peter the Great.[3] The second took place in the 1890s under the energetic drive of Count Sergei Witte;[4] the third, under Piotr Stolypin's innovative reforms of the prewar, prerevolutionary stretch from 1907 to 1914;[5] and the last, in the longest and most painful decades, was initiated by Stalin in 1928 and extended to 1956, after which the annual growth rate began to decline. These surges were driven primarily by military objectives to be fulfilled under state direction and were financed by "primitive accumulation" involving the exploitation of the peasantry.

Historians agree that Peter the Great wanted to forge Russia into a naval and military power in the westernized mode. According to Malia:

> Russia has never existed in a political or cultural vacuum. It has always had to interact with other, neighboring countries, which, as it turned out from the very beginning, were all much more advanced culturally, economically, and politically than Russia was. . . . [T]he Russian nucleus of Muscovy developed as a poor frontier zone in a weak defensive position. Its only wealth was land, and serfs to work the land. Hence, the country became a very simple, military, serf-based autocracy. . . . All Peter needed to do in the early eighteenth century to be competitive with the rest of Europe was to create a standing army instead of a seasonal militia, which is what Russia had before; a navy; and enough education to make these two modern attributes work. Moreover, his Western models in the eighteenth century were almost all absolute monarchies.

Occasionally Peter was given to "flights of fancy" and attempted the production of "Venetian mirrors and French Gobelins," but Russia's empowerment through an educated, modern military and effective state direction was the sine qua non of the nascent industrial activity under his regime.[6]

A decisive policy shift by the government in favor of Russia's industrial development was to appear much later, in the 1890s under Count Witte. "It was as though a rotating stage had moved revealing an entirely new scene" of a vast industrial surge.[7] That, too, was influenced by the realization, following Russia's defeat in the Crimean War of 1854–1856, that the country was lagging behind in military preparedness.[8] The Stolypin economic program also followed another humiliating defeat for Russia in the Russo-Japanese war and the revolution of 1905, the latter marked by months of strikes, peasant outbreaks, and naval mutinies.[9] Then came World War I (1914–1918), in which Russia suffered a crushing defeat by Germany, followed by three years of civil war, during which foreign powers employed cat-and-mouse interventionist tactics. The British and the French set up a so-called government of the White faction consisting of the rightist remnants in Northern Russia, and the Japanese established a government in occupied Vladivostok that lasted until 1922. The humiliation cemented Stalin's resolve to orient the economy toward the military sector. Even so, the Red Army and the Soviet military machine were inadequately prepared to counter the Nazi invasion of 1942. Finally, the demands of the cold war under Nikita Khrushchev,[10] despite his peaceful coexistence rhetoric, and under Leonid Brezhnev,[11] egged on by the arms race with the United States, pushed the best resources of men and materials into military-related industries.

The military and foreign policy objectives of each phase influenced the financing and pattern of industrialization. The industrial spurts were originally financed from the state budget, but bank financing emerged in the 1890s and became significant under the Stolypin program. In 1914, on the eve of war, Russian banks had taken over the financing role of the retreating government. Next, the available funds—from the budget and increasingly from banks—were channeled to promote military needs, such as the production of machines and the development of the railroads as well as the iron and steel industries. Light industry was notably absent. Finally, the factories were large. Long before Stalin's planners launched "gigantomania" in integrated plants in metals and machine building, Russian industry was dominated by large units. Small businesses were few and far between. Banks had no interest in stretching their limited managerial and financial resources for promoting small activities. They also promoted mergers because these enhanced their profits. The industrial structure therefore remained skewed toward heavy industry and large plants, whose size was dictated by the available foreign technology, and limited local entrepreneurs, who were spread thinly in the plants.

A shortage of entrepreneurs impeded Russian industrialization in the second half of the nineteenth century, leading into the sudden growth of the 1890s.

Shortage of Entrepreneurs

Entrepreneurial activity was rejected in nineteenth-century Russia by the court nobility and the rural gentry, who ranked their pursuits under the tsars' patronage above all occupations; by the intelligentsia, who extolled the virtues of the simple life of the rural folk and lambasted the profane origins of wealth; and by the people themselves, who pursued the "Good Life which God intended for man to lead, tilling the land which belonged to God, and receiving the divine blessing of its fruit. The Good Life certainly did not mean craving for riches, did not mean laying up treasures on earth where moth or rust doth corrupt."[12] The Emancipation Decree of 1861 encouraged former serfs and their sons to build and operate merchant fleets on the Volga, but they proved to be exceptions to the negative attitude toward business pursuits.[13]

The prevailing opprobrium pushed the small number of entrepreneurial pioneers into devising their own conflicted behavioral norms. On the one hand, they made amends for their sinful activities by donating to the church via "graft payments to God." The "repentant merchant" Yermolai Lopakhin in Anton Chekhov's *Cherry Orchard* was evidently driven by this compulsion.[14] On the other hand, they lacked the norms of commercial rectitude of the European guild members. These medieval associations received their charters from the king and operated in cities as exclusive practitioners of their trade and craft, enjoying exemption from tolls and keeping outsiders at bay. They regulated members' wages and hours of work, as well as technical processes and trade practices, including product prices and the size of the workforce. Russian entrepreneurial practices, by contrast, lagged far behind. On the eve of the great spurt of the1890s, their "time horizon was often limited, their commercial customs backward, and their standards of honesty none too high."[15] Businesses declared fraudulent bankruptcies so routinely and public trust in commercial practices was so minimal that banks were unable to attract even the limited deposits that could be loaned out on a long-term basis. In any case, the financial needs of industry far exceeded the potential cash savings from the citizenry.

"The supply of capital for the needs of industrialization [in the1890s] required the compulsory machinery of the government which, through its taxation policies, succeeded in directing incomes from consumption to investment."[16] The only source of capital or savings was the agricultural sector, which could be taxed appropriately, requiring it to sell grain in order to pay the tax. The available grain would also meet the bread needs of the urban workforce and could be exported to pay for imports of better-quality machines. The higher the tax rate, the greater the involuntary extraction of savings from the rural incomes. Such primitive accumulation marked capital formation in the 1890s and later during Stalin's industrialization in the 1930s. The former was facilitated by the continuing arrangements of serfdom, despite a string of tsarist edicts intending to abolish it, and the latter by the enforced collectivization of farms.

Primitive Capital Accumulation under Serfdom

Russian peasants were strictly bound in servitude to the landowning gentry until the tsarist edict of 1861. That step, however, failed to convert them into either effective owners of land or landless laborers willing to migrate to urban centers as factory workers. That was hardly the purpose of the reform legislation. The abolition decree allotted strips of land to the peasants for which they paid rent to the gentry, who continued to own the land. However, it leased smaller holdings to the peasants than had been customarily assigned to them in the past. For their allotments, the peasants were also required to pay rents that were higher than the prevailing market price for land.

Despite these unjust provisions, the peasants did not flee the countryside. Rather, they stayed on because the emancipation procedures of the 1860s preserved and even strengthened the village communes (obshchiny), which were assigned a critical role in collecting taxes from the peasantry and, indeed, in controlling postemancipation village life. Despite the conquest of more territories under Catherine the Great, who added two hundred thousand square miles to her empire, the peasants could not escape to the distant regions that were their early sanctuaries.[17] "The very modernization of the state machinery under Peter meant that the government was much better equipped to enforce serfdom upon the peasant and to deal effectively with fugitives from serf status."[18] The institution of the zemskii nachal'nik (land captain), who was endowed with the powers of the local judicial authority, and further measures under Tsar Alexander III in the 1890s preserved the communes.[19] A member of the village commune working in a nearby town could be called back to the village. Permanent departure from the village required the permission of the commune and the household head. Because of the shortage of a permanent and reliable industrial labor force, factories deliberately adopted labor-saving devices. By contrast, farming continued to be hemmed in by traditional, labor-intensive practices. "Unlike the Prussian Junkers, the Russian gentry seldom showed much interest in technological innovation on their estates. The cheap labor discouraged them from introducing those improvements in the mode of cultivation which tended to have labor-saving effects and to increase the capital intensity of agricultural output."[20]

The primitive accumulation mode of industrialization via inordinate taxes on the peasants forced them to sell grain so that the urban population could be fed and advanced machines could be imported via grain exports. Ultimately, the exhaustion of the tax-paying powers of the rural population contributed to the end of the surge of the 1890s. That lesson was grasped by Stolypin, who initiated a string of liberating measures to free the serfs.

The Stolypin Reforms, War, and Revolution

The Stolypin reforms of 1906 and 1910 allowed the peasants to actually own their strips of land and form a single holding by exchanging them. Peasants could now sell the land, move to the city, and start small businesses, although the impact of the reform was slow and short lived since it was interrupted by war and revolution. The spurt between 1907 and 1914, however, chalked up significant positive accomplishments. Russian banks were more active, and entrepreneurs could be trusted. A permanent workforce had emerged. Wages had moved up, and working conditions had improved. The peasantry was less oppressed. In contrast to the 1890s, more bread grain was available per capita. If the war had not intervened and if the Bolsheviks had not seized power, the economic momentum and institutional improvements could have continued.

"The 1917 Revolution redeemed the ancient hopes of the Russian peasantry by letting them seize the lands of the gentry."[21] By the mid-1920s, the peasants also paid lower taxes, which allowed them more freedom in marketing grain. By contrast, most of the nonfarm sector, especially the commanding heights of heavy industry, was brought under state ownership and control. Industrial growth still depended on savings to be extracted from the peasants, who effectively regulated their flow by varying grain supplies. The great debates in the midtwenties raged over the issue of an ideal investment strategy for the postwar reconstruction and transformation of the Soviet Union. The group led by Bukharin emphasized balanced growth.[22] "The greatest sustained speed is achieved when industry develops on the basis provided by the rapidly growing agriculture."[23] In contrast, the left-wing opposition of Trotsky[24] and Preobrazhensky[25] argued that, in the prevailing Russian conditions, substantial economic growth could take place only if industry expanded at the expense of the peasantry. Ultimately, under Stalin, the investment program, with its emphasis on heavy industry, was implemented with a speed and ruthlessness that exceeded all formulations.

The industrialization drive presented challenges that far exceeded the boundaries of the earlier surges. The peasants had to be taxed and taxed heavily so that their diminished purchasing power would not strain the limited availability of consumer goods. The required tax payment would also force them to release substantial grain for feeding the urban proletariat. Such a scheme was to prove unworkable. Millions of Russian peasants, having finally acquired land at the end of the revolution and the civil war, were bent on exercising their discretion, unlike the docile serfs of tsarist Russia. Their dogged determination, however, failed to counter Stalin's forceful land seizures and collectivization, which were followed by a program of perpetual industrialization through a series of five-year plans.

"By reverting to a pattern of economic development that should have remained confined to a long-bygone age, by substituting collectivization for serfdom, and by pushing up the rate of investment to the maximum point within the limits of endurance of the population, the Soviet government did what no government relying on the consent of the governed could have done. . . . Economic backwardness, rapid industrialization, ruthless exercise of dictatorial power, and the danger of war [cold war] have become inextricably intertwined in Soviet Russia."[26] The final industrial spurt, which lasted until 1956, resulted in annual growth rates of 12–14 percent at its height, according to Western calculations.

These analytical nuggets from history's barrel throw light on the contrasts and the similarities with the current Russian situation.

History Lessons

In his pre-Beslan interview, Malia provided a nuanced contrast between the Westernizing and modernizing impulse in eighteenth-century Russia under Peter the Great and that currently under Putin:

> Since Russia was always a poor society even when it was a great empire, as under the eighteenth- and nineteenth-century tsars, in an exposed position, its natural form of organization was a monarchy, which means a strong leader. However, if conditions change in the future, there will not necessarily be a need for a strong leader. I think that conditions had changed by the end of the twentieth century: Putin cannot be Peter the Great because the twenty-first century is not the eighteenth. . . . All he [Peter] had to do was to call himself emperor and create a European, Versailles-like court, and he was modern. In the twentieth century, modernization or Westernization means much more than an army or navy.
>
> If Putin wants to make Russia strong, he must make it advanced technologically, and that means fostering education. Advanced technology and education mean an independent-minded, diverse, civil society. You cannot run a modern, technological, and educated society the way you run an eighteenth-century military monarchy. I think that Putin understands this, for he considers himself to be in the Petrine tradition. He's from Saint Petersburg. . . . it [Petrine] is a historian's word, and it connotes building a strong Russia internationally by creating a strong state internally so as to foster Westernization and modernization from above. But . . . Westernization in the twenty-first century does not mean the crude and simple thing it meant at the beginning of the eighteenth. It means creating a sophisticated, modern, technological society and market economy, and Putin understands that.

In his pre-Beslan interview, Talbott also referred to Putin's "Western vocation" by invoking the term *zapadnichestvo:* "*Zapadnichestvo* is actually a nineteenth-century word that was used by the [Russian] Westernizers, to be sure, and the way

I would translate it is 'Russia's Western vocation.' I was quite interested to discover, in the first several meetings that I had with Putin, that he uses it as part of his vocabulary, whereas both Gorbachev and Yeltsin didn't like to talk about the West because they thought the very word 'West' discriminated against Russia: Russia could never be part of the West. I don't think that is Putin's view."[27]

Leaving aside these broad insights, I now consider how current Russian practices have departed from the old arrangements, whereas in other areas they continue to resemble those of the past.

Departures from Old Arrangements

Despite Putin's post-Beslan consolidation measures, the current political system differs significantly from czarist autocracy and Stalinist repression. Yavlinsky is clearly unfair and widely off the mark in characterizing Putin's consolidating measures as "soft Stalinism." If Stalin were to revisit Russia, he would banish Gorbachev and Yeltsin to a distant gulag for reviving Russian anarchism with disastrous consequences—the former for destroying the Soviet Union and the latter for creating massive turmoil in the Russian homeland. Peter the Great would chastise Putin, a fellow St. Petersburger, for being a wimp in that he adopted, from Peter's perspective, only half-hearted measures for stabilizing post–Yeltsin Russia. In economic policymaking, too, the old model of primitive accumulation involving peasant exploitation has given way to the new possibility of extracting sizeable surpluses from the oil oligarchs via taxation. Stolypin would be thrilled by the new opportunity and marvel at the Russian tax authorities' recent tax-collecting record.

At the same time, a decisive break from the Soviet past has taken place with respect to the exercise of personal initiatives and free choices. Russians now have opportunities for choosing their means and places of livelihood. Russian businesses can seek out potentially profitable ventures and elect to take the risk of succeeding or failing in commerce. Of course, both groups continue to face massive limitations in an environment that carries substantial features from the past, but I believe that the rudimentary changes initiated by Yeltsin's reformers are here to stay and will progress over time.

The most significant departure from the tsarist and Soviet record has been the dramatic emergence in the past two decades of elite professional groups as policy makers and active participants in the reform process. By contrast, they played only a minor role as providers of independent policy input to the tsars or the Communist bosses. As opponents of tsarist autocracy or promoters of populist agrarian values, members of the Russian intelligentsia wrote and debated, argued and rebelled, and went into exile or were banished to Siberia, but they were hardly part of the policymaking apparatus.

The celebrated first Five-Year Plan of 1928, embodying a rigorous model in favor of heavy industry, was more an intellectual confirmation of the Stalinist policy line than an independent voice favoring capital goods over consumer goods. Under Brezhnev, academician Mikhail Suslov imparted a weighty glow to the CPSU's pronouncements by attempting to convert them into sensible policy guidelines.[28] Distinguished academics sought to justify the Soviet planners' resource allocation patterns by simulating their market economy variants. Fellow economists in the West viewed these exercises as intellectual puzzles. In marked contrast to the ceremonial nods to the past, the joint appointment by Gorabchev and Yeltsin in the summer of 1990 of an independent commission of economists, headed by academician Stanislav Shatalin, to formulate a market-oriented plan was a precedent-setting initiative that later brought professional economists into the government as policy makers. A concrete intellectual and professional underpinning of policy decisions, absent in Russian and Soviet experience in the pre-Gorbachev days, became a refreshing feature thereafter.

In response to my question, Chubais reminisced at length about the early days of the reform movement, which eventually led to the participation of its members in the Yeltsin government:

> It was difficult to find reasonable answers for the situation in the Soviet economy. Articles in textbooks and scientific journals discussed different ideas without clearly understanding them or how an economy worked. I had a clear understanding myself, and I found several people in St. Petersburg in the mideighties and later who had similar views. We got to work, started finding books that were forbidden in the Soviet Union, and established contacts with Western economists that were almost forbidden at that time. . . . We did not just discuss our ideas but also undertook solid work, prepared reports, researched the New Economic Policy of the early 1920s in the Soviet Union, and studied Hungarian and Yugoslav reforms. All of this was not easy to do in the Soviet Union. Our basic goal was to get a firm idea of the fundamental changes that needed to be undertaken. . . . When we started in 1989, in November 1989, we had a team consisting of fifteen, maximum twenty, people. . . . Of course, a number of alternative government think tanks were around, but all of those were Communist. It was simple: we or the Communists.[29]

Nevertheless, because they continue to be burdened by negative features, the task of overturning the old arrangements has been far from easy.

Similarities with the Past

Yavlinsky decried the Duma's adoption of a number of Czarist symbols:

> Russians still have the old mentality, the old habit of feeling comfortable with autocratic arrangements. One has to desire freedom strongly in order to be free. If you want to assess the current Russian situation with regard to the progress we

have made, look at some of our symbols. They tell you a lot about how strongly
we are tied to the past. Take the imperial, tsarist two-headed eagle. . . . I have
often wondered how a two-headed bird can live so long, but we have it in Russia.
Then we have the Soviet anthem. We pretend that we have a democratic flag. In
my view, it is not democratic, but we are made to believe that it is. That is my
answer to your question. We are unable to break away from the past. It is at best
a mixture with a heavy dose of the past, a sort of postmodernism.

Pipes wondered aloud why Yeltsin did not manage to banish the past by getting rid of old street names and Lenin's body:

I was in Perm recently, a city in the Urals, and all of the streets still have the old
names—Leninskaya, Oktyabrskaya, Komsomolskaya, Kuibysheva, and so on—
and you get the feeling there is really no break with the past. They don't quite
know where they are, as if they are between two worlds, in limbo. I think that
was a great mistake on Yeltsin's part. When he first came to power—he was elected
with a vast majority—he could have removed Lenin's body from the mausoleum.
He could have made these changes. He could have given orders—"within three
months all street names in Russia must abandon their Communist origins"—but
he didn't do that. Now it's too late. They are in limbo; they don't know where
they are or who the authorities are. The main thing they regret is the loss of the
great power status under the Soviet Union.

Beyond tsarist symbols and Soviet-era street names, the economy continues to
be hobbled by outdated, noncompetitive structures. Russian agriculture, no longer
exploited as it was in the past, is nevertheless still hampered by traditional practices.
Farm households, generally headed by retirees, have acquired ownership rights in
the former collective farms, but land deals are minuscule, and farming lags in productivity gains. Private farms numbered only 250,000 in 2004, slightly more than
1 percent higher than in 1999. Simonia described the situation thus:

The collective farm households, the *kolkhozniki,* were given the right to sell their
share and move off the farm. However, 90 percent of them have stayed put on
the farms, most of which are unprofitable. It was not enough to issue a paper
decree. The farms, especially the better ones, needed help to retain their workforce.
They needed technical input and matching credits. At the same time, some successful farms had their barns burned and their machinery stolen. Overall, the number of farmers has declined to 250,000 in all. Most of them are unprofitable units.
The situation is depressing. The fact is we do not have independent farmers in
Russia. We have kolkhozniki, who represent a totally different social phenomenon. . . . It is different because our kolkhoznik is not an Indian or a Chinese
peasant. Essentially the product of a modified slavery system, he was dominated
by the Communist Party organization in the past. The party bosses said, "You
must plant this and harvest now, and here is what you get as a reward from us."

But can that psychological makeup change because Yeltsin issued a decree assigning them formal ownership rights? The reality on the farms has not changed. The farm households still feel that it is dangerous for them to contribute to the farm's overall performance. . . . These small plots [attached to household dachas in the countryside] still provide 90 percent of all potatoes and other vegetables and most of the meat to city dwellers.

Industry is dominated by large monopolies in machine building, metals, and the energy sector. Manufacturing is less diversified, although the public can buy imported consumer goods that were not available in the old days. Small businesses are notably absent. The regulatory stranglehold of bureaucracy is extensive, and corruption is widespread. Russian entrepreneurs are notorious for breaking accepted corporate norms. Despite broad public aversion to their ill-begotten wealth, Russia's newly minted bourgeoisie display none of the conflict between acquisitive materialism and spiritual cravings that plagued their nineteenth-century forbears. The Central Bank of Russia, although effectively in charge of monetary policy, is nevertheless ineffectual in establishing its authority over the numerous commercial banks with dubious balance sheets and active money-laundering operations. Vyugin, the central banker, described the mid-2003 situation thus:

We need laws to initiate real changes in the banking sector. We talked about the urgent need for deposit insurance legislation, without which the Russian public will not deposit its savings in the banks. We also need laws to launch revisions in banking-sector licensing procedures. We have made changes on the basis of the regulatory authority available to us under current laws. We want to raise transparency in the banking sector, identify the genuine owners of the banks, and remove fake capital from their balance sheets. We published special instructions to combat this problem and found that some of the biggest Russian banks have fake capital. They get around this requirement via innovative schemes. We instruct them to show their genuine capital, to fill the gap if necessary, and in some cases to reveal in their published balance sheets that they have hardly any capital to back their assets. It is a serious problem and occasionally leads to tough fights. We try our best to make the Russian banking business transparent, healthy, and honest.

No wonder, then, that public savings are monopolized by the Soviet-era Sberbank, which controls 62 percent of public deposits and actively opposes the proliferation of Russian commercial banking. The question therefore arises: In what way have the economy's structure and its institutional underpinning advanced beyond Stolypin's energetic reforms, which were set back by war, revolution, and Communism? Can the Russian economy, which is about the same size as Portugal's, double by 2010? Or will it remain perpetually tied to the legacy of running a race against time? More to the point, will its growth performance depart from the volatile, boom-and-bust patterns I outlined earlier? The program Yeltsin's reformers launched in January 1992 ended with the financial collapse of August 1998. Will economic growth stabilize under Putin's leadership?

The chances of the Russian economy setting off on a stable growth trajectory in 1992 under Yeltsin were slim. The declared goal was to terminate the old Communist system rather than initiate steady growth. Indeed, the Soviet-era planned economy and its bureaucratized management were so antiquated and extensive from a market-economy perspective that their demolition was a monumental triumph. The planned model consisted of a plethora of targets handed down from above to the managers of farms, factories, and the service sector. The excessive administration manifested itself in the detailed role of the state apparatus in maneuvering the innumerable production, distribution, and financial transactions of an increasingly complex economy. Needless to say, the political arrangements underpinning the economic system were set out in painstaking detail from the center to the periphery under the vigilant direction of the CPSU. They were authoritarian and centralized.

The Soviet Planned Economy

The planning arrangements that Mikhail Gorbachev inherited in March 1985, when he became the Soviet leader, had been laid out six decades earlier under Stalin and had continued on a perpetual nonmarket treadmill under Stalin's successors.

Soviet industrial enterprises operated within the framework of a production-financial-technological plan assigned to them by state planners. The bonus the workers and managers earned depended on the fulfillment of this plan. The additional money was over and above the earnings based on payment scales set by the planners and distinguished by type of skill, the nature of the work, and the location of the factories. The main elements of the production plan were the output *(val)* targets, the allocation of the required inputs, and a wage bill.

What criteria did the planners use to decide that enterprise managers had fulfilled their assigned plan? The story here was that of a continuous hunt by the planners for the best rules. The reforms of 1965, under the initiative of Brezhnev's prime minister, Alexei Kosygin, introduced sales revenue and profits as additional criteria.[30] What was produced was now to be sold so that inventories would not accumulate. Moreover, profits, hitherto barred as a bourgeois contamination, could help raise productivity. Of course, profits of Soviet factories differed from the Schumpeterian market economy's "denizens of the world of a commercial society," which is determined by the free choices of consumers and producers. In any case, managerial bonuses (while related to profits) were still contingent on the fulfillment of the gross output target. As late as 1988, General Secretary Gorbachev referred to it somewhat exasperatedly in his speech at the Communist Party conference in June: "Oh, how many faithful followers we have of 'gross output'!"[31]

As a result of these arrangements, Soviet farms and factories had little genuine autonomy and few incentives in matters such as deciding what to produce, which raw materials to procure and from where, how much to sell, what prices to charge, which capacities to scrap, which new machines to install, and which new technologies to develop or adopt. There were two ways of coping with the strangulating system. Those at the top of the managerial hierarchy squandered their energies and talents in battling the maze of bureaucratic controls and devising networking mechanisms, often illegal, for circumventing the restraints in order to fulfill the plan targets. The majority at the bottom followed orders with a lackluster and frustrating handling of their chores, somewhat in the style of Nikolai Gogol's hero Akaky Akakievich.[32]

The result was predictable. More factories were built, but their output record was uninspiring. The workforce lacked the motivation to work hard and well. Besides, the growth of the labor force was slowing. Natural resources, coal and ores among them, were deteriorating in quality, and the best of them (oil in the wilderness of Siberia and beyond) were increasingly costly to extract. After a short-lived, postwar reconstruction boost, the Soviet economy began stagnating around 1956. The drag on output growth could have been countered by the Schumpeterian drive to innovate. However, except in the military and isolated industries, the Brezhnev-era (1965–1983) record on innovative breakthroughs and new product and process technologies and their successful adoption was scanty.

Yeltsin wanted this Kafkaesque system overturned. Under the new arrangements, market-determined prices and wages were to establish outputs and profits. The planners of Gosplan, the hallowed Soviet-era planning agency, had to be retired. In addition, factories and service outlets needed to be removed from state ownership so that the profit-making animal spirits could operate freely. In fact, the old economic structures had to be cleared so that a new social order could be created. But where was the old society mired?

The Social Order under the Planned System

In the final years of Brezhnev's leadership, the Soviet Union was by all accounts going downhill. The decay was visible on all fronts. While economists cited the declining growth rate of the economy as a surefire index of the malaise, others concentrated on recurring shortages, increasing corruption, and massive alienation.

The pervasive shortages gave a bizarre flavor to people's daily lives. Because the economy was overplanned and overadministered, the invisible hand of the market was nowhere to be seen. Since the production targets were handed down from above, what was produced had little relation to what was in demand. The economy was characterized by the paradox of accumulated inventories and persistent shortages. "The whole country is covered with blast furnaces," an exasperated friend told David Shipler of the *New York Times,* "but I can't get a table knife."[33]

Shortages bred disaffection. There was not much point in working hard if one could not spend the money on a color TV or a dishwasher. The Soviet social contract was aptly described as "They pretend to pay us, and we pretend to work for them."

Shortages bred corruption, too. The have-nots had to grease the palms of the haves—in the Soviet case, the party members who could procure almost anything in short supply: a Moscow apartment, an attractive job, a place for a child in a prestigious school, a better hospital for a sick relative (but at a price). Furthermore, there was nothing more alienating for the masses than the knowledge that those in power were corrupt. The legitimacy of the rulers—of the party in general and above all of the socialist system—became suspect. Life in the Soviet Union was so disheartening that it prompted this wry witticism: Religion comforts the masses by assuring them that there is life after death, whereas Communism does so by assuring them that there is death after life.

The New Social Order

The dismantling of the Communist economic structures, needless to say, brought its own trail of corruption and alienation. The breadlines disappeared, but the price increases, the massive nonpayment of wages following unsettled government and enterprise finances, and the capture of the prized economic assets by a few oligarchs contributed to alienation among the impoverished masses. According to Rogov, Yeltsin's overwhelming public support in 1991 disappeared over time, as the economic reforms imposed high costs on ordinary Russians: "There were enormous expectations. People came out by the thousands in the streets of Moscow, demanding immediate and fundamental changes. Later, people felt that they had been betrayed and manipulated by the government. There was frustration followed by societal fragmentation. Since the expectations were so high, the letdown was massive, too. Most Russians today [mid-2003] do not think they can do anything to bring about a positive turnaround. They have plainly retreated into a do-nothing pessimism. They do not believe the government wants to help them. . . . Russians have retreated into their homes, their family fortresses. 'Don't bother us. Leave us alone,' they are saying."

As for corruption, the rules of the game were to change as the planned economy disintegrated. In the old days, factory managers had created ingenious safety devices and informal adjustment mechanisms involving one another and the party bosses in order to fulfill the output targets the planners handed down to them. Managers padded their requirements of materials and built raw material inventories so that they could fight the uncertainties and delays of the state procurement system and continue receiving their bonuses.[34] They hired special operatives (tolkachi) who could be dispatched on a business trip (komandirovka) to Moscow with appropriate blessings: "Go to Moscow, my boy. All our hopes depend on you."[35] They used special connections and reciprocated favors via illicit economic activity (blat) by exchanging products and services. A tractor factory would change its product assortment plan and produce pots and pans, which could be exchanged in profitable blat operations.

The factory managers employing blat and tolkachi perhaps contributed to the "efficiency" of the planned economy by greasing its wheels. Their networking experience and longstanding connections with party *apparatchiks* (officials) in the system put them at the forefront of vast economic fortunes as old economic rules and entrenched party discipline began faltering under Gorbachev's liberating initiatives. At the same time, socialist commitments bordering on submissiveness and the involuntary egalitarianism imposed from above began weakening as Gorabchev sought to redefine the party's monolithic, all-pervasive role in the country's economic and political life. For anyone with potentially lucrative ties in the right places, it became open season to start making deals. Communist Party functionaries, factory managers, KGB operatives, Red Army generals, and budding entrepreneurs with vast money-making ambitions bought materials, metals, and oil at the prevailing fixed prices, exported them at higher world prices, and deposited the foreign exchange in offshore banks. They stripped factories and sold the assets or used them for private gain. With cash at their command, a few managed to buy the country's prized resources in the oil and metals sectors that were put up for privatization. The earlier Soviet-era corruption among the privileged few and the alienation of the masses paled before the brazen wantonness of Russia's nouveaux riches and the apathetic cynicism of the many who were left behind.

As the economic structures crumbled, so did the Soviet political system and ultimately the Communist Party of the Russian Federation, successor to the CPSU.

The Soviet Political Arrangements

The dominant features of the Soviet political arrangements were the commanding role of the CPSU and the party's control of the legislative and executive branches of the government across the USSR's territorial hierarchy. The reformers employed pro-market economic measures to weaken the hold of the party and its ideology on the economy. At the same time, in 1993 Yeltsin seized every opportunity to appeal directly to the public in order to dismantle party control of the legislative bodies (the soviets) and the governmental administrations. He accomplished this goal by managing the adoption of the 1993 constitution via a public referendum against the staunch opposition of the Communist legislators in Moscow.

Command and Control under the CPSU

The CPSU imposed tough ideological discipline on the economy as well as political control over the legislative and executive bodies by converting them into mere rubber-stamping agents of its policy directives. These directions emanated from the supreme body at the top of the party hierarchy, the Congress of People's Deputies. It met every so often, made important policy announcements, laid down major guidelines, and elected the Central Committee. The Central Committee, with more than three hundred members, was the policy-making body on a day-to-day basis. It was helped in its chores by the party secretariat and its various departments. (Gorbachev had once been in charge of agriculture in the secretariat.) The actual direction and control of policies was in the hands of the inner sanctum—the politburo. The party structure was repeated down the territorial line in regions, cities, and towns in both urban and rural districts.

Over the long historical stretch of six decades from Stalin to Yeltsin, the congressional sessions were marked by interminable speeches, sleepy delegates, occasional high drama, and acrimonious debates in the last phase before the entire paraphernalia of party and government organizations of the Soviet era was thrown out by the new constitution of 1993. Until then, the congress generated pivotal moments of lasting impact. On February 25, 1956, Khrushchev made his electrifying de-Stalinization speech before delegates of the Twentieth Congress.[36] On the occasion of the Twenty-seventh Party Congress, convened by Gorbachev on February 25, 1986, to coincide with the thirtieth anniversary of de-Stalinization, Yeltsin delivered the following thunderbolt before the party faithful: " 'Why, Congress after Congress, do we deal with the same problems over and over again?' Yeltsin asked. 'Why have we not been able to root out social injustice and abuse of power? Why is it that even now the demand for a radical change is bogged down, as in a swamp, in the inert layer of time-servers carrying the party card? . . . How many times can we make deities of certain party leaders?'"[37] On March 13, 1990, congress elected Gorbachev president of the Soviet Union on the basis of new rules that were adopted earlier to guarantee his continuing survival. His reform agenda could have been sabotaged if the election were undertaken by a handful of shifty members of the politburo.

With the disappearance of the Soviet Union in December 1991 and the emergence of Russia under Yeltsin as its legitimate successor state, the congress of the Russian Federation was smaller but still a contentious battleground often marked by Yeltsin's rousing oratory with direct appeals to the people and calls for Russia-wide referendums.

Thus, the Seventh Congress of People's Deputies, which opened on December 1, 1992, debated the draft of a new Russian constitution proposed by the proreform group that essentially required new election procedures, the establishment of a presidential republic, and the abolition of the congress and the privileges of party functionaries. When the congress rejected Yeltsin's suggestion of a constitutional referendum, he spoke directly to the Russian citizens, to whom he "owed" his presidency: "There is an authority above the congress and above the president: the people. . . . I am asking the people of Russia to decide who you are with, whose course you support: that of the president, the course of changes, or that of the congress, the course of curtailing the reforms."[38]

A frequent and consummate tactician of such populist offerings to the faithful, Yeltsin energetically marshaled two significant referendums over the objection of the Communist-dominated congress: the referendum of April 1993, seeking public approval of his presidency and his reforms, and that of December 12, 1993, aimed at the adoption of a post–Soviet Russian constitution. The former kept the reform momentum alive, and the latter introduced a presidential government, a parliament, elections, and multiple parties. The post-1993 Parliament consists of an upper house, the 178-member Federation Council, representing the elected governors (until the adoption of the new law of July 2003, authorizing the president to pick these members from the executive branch of the regions) and speakers of the legislatures of the eighty-nine regions of Russia. The lower house, the 450-member Duma, represents legislators elected every four years. On the basis of party lists, half of the Duma members are elected proportionately to their electoral votes, and the other half on the basis of single-mandate contests in constituencies throughout the country. (These single-member constituencies were abolished in early 2005 as a result of a presidential measure adopted by the Duma.) Among its important economic functions, the Duma adopts the budget and legislates reform. It can impeach the president and also remove the government after three no-confidence motions.

The constitution introduced elections to the Duma that the Communist Party of the Russian Federation managed to control until the December 1999 electoral vote. A well-organized party, it has continued to claim a steady voting allegiance among thirty-seven million Russian pensioners. Its vast network of party cells, however, became increasingly redundant when, in a series of daring moves in 1993, Yeltsin managed to break its hold over the legislative and administrative units. The dramatic severing of this Gordian knot, in sharp contrast to Gorbachev's halting measures, succeeded in overturning the Soviet-era, ideologically dominated CPSU control over the legislative and governmental policymaking.

CPSU Control over Legislative and Governmental Bodies

The cardinal features of the arrangements throughout the territorial hierarchy from the topmost level down to the village were a party committee and a legislative organization called the soviet. Your guess is right: The former dominated the latter. The party units were everywhere in the factories and farms, in educational institutions, in the army and the KGB, and in the offices. Their composition depended on the size of the establishment, but three or more Communists could form a party unit. One became the secretary, the second the deputy secretary, and the third constituted the membership.

Article 6 of the 1977 Soviet constitution describes these party units as "the leading and guiding force of Soviet society and the nucleus of its political system." Members were expected to spread Marxist-Leninist teachings, advance the cause of "Communist construction," and emphasize the vanguard role of the party both inside the establishment and outside. Because propaganda and persuasion ultimately had a limited appeal, party control was enforced via more effective methods. The top personnel of an establishment were invariably included in the party unit, and, in order to reach the top, one usually had to be a loyal Communist. One became a chief accountant, the story went, when one knew not that "two plus two makes four" but that "two plus two makes whatever the party boss wants it to make." As a matter of fact, party discipline was enforced by maintaining a list *(nomenklatura)* of critical appointments and dependable appointees. In the mid-1990s, when the industrial enterprises were formally converted into joint stock companies under the privatization program, they began to be managed by the nomenklatura, the old dogs of the communist era who found it difficult to switch to the new tricks of the marketplace.

The party committees dominated not only the production and service establishments but also the soviets, the legislative bodies mentioned earlier.

At the territorial level, the relationship between the soviet and the party committee was defined by the historical origin of the former. As workers' committees with a proletarian backbone, they spearheaded the revolutions of 1917. Indeed, in the brief interval between the February and October uprisings, the Petrograd (Leningrad) soviet, egged on by the Bolsheviks, was active in toppling the provisional government and usurping power.[39] Later, soviets sprouted up all over, and the Supreme Soviet, consisting of two houses with a membership of 750 each, emerged at the apex as the law-making body of the federal hierarchy. It met twice a year and gave legal stamp to the policies the party had already decided. Resolutions were unanimously adopted with a show of hands. Finally, the governmental organization also included executive bodies (councils of ministers) in the fifteen republics of the Soviet Union.[40]

The contentious relationship between the Communist legislators in the Supreme Soviet (later the Duma) and the Moscow reformist government led by Yeltsin was the hallmark of his presidency, from early 1992 to the end of 1999. During most of 1993, the "war of laws" between the Supreme Soviet and the government escalated into irreconcilable differences. The Supreme Soviet thoroughly revised the government's resolutions relating to defense spending and pension payments, pushing the budget deficit to 25 percent of GDP (gross domestic product). It suspended Yeltsin's decree designed to advance the privatization program and opposed Kremlin proposals to alter the Russian constitution, which was devised to augment presidential authority. At one point, Ruslan Khasbulatov, chair of the Supreme Soviet, called on all soviets to "intensify" their supervision of local executive bodies.[41] By contrast, Yeltsin insisted that the days of the soviets were numbered because they were "direct heirs" of the illegitimate bodies that had usurped power under the Bolsheviks. In his view, the soviets could not be reformed because they were incompatible with democratic practices. They therefore had to be abolished.[42] His position on the role of the soviets differed sharply from that of the die-hard Communists, who ultimately barricaded themselves in the parliament building and had to be flushed out with a military attack in October 1993. It was also at odds with that of Gorbachev, who believed that the soviets and indeed the party could be reformed by changing election procedures.

While Yeltsin's populist tactics, superficially resembling Jeffersonian invocations of "we the people," contributed to the weakening of the CPSU's hold over Russia's political arrangements, the policy framework his reformers designed also played a dismantling role. This structure was marked by four features that helped me steer the interview project.

THE POLICY FRAMEWORK OF THE INTERVIEW PROJECT

First, in January 1992, the reformist team's strategy was to launch fast-paced, pro-market *economic* measures in order to fulfill the *political* goal of retiring the Communist Party and its ideology. In contrast, in other reforming economies of Eastern Europe, the political authorities, few of them avowedly Communist, determined the pace and content of the economic measures. The process, in my view, was reversed in Russia. Economic measures, among them price decontrol, privatization, a market-determined ruble, and open foreign trade, were employed to unravel the commanding political role of the party and its ideology in these decisions. Malia agreed with my judgment: "[T]hey [the reformers] used the market reforms to promote political and social transformation by destroying the party. Since the party was the framework of the whole society, its destruction was necessary to clear the deck for a new society."

Not surprisingly, the Yeltsin team deliberately avoided a negotiating stance and instead engaged in a continuing collision course with the Communist left in the Duma. Their policy blitzkrieg, usually confrontational and at times calculated to outflank the adversary, also left the Communist Party in a defensive role, incapable of transforming its decaying ideology into a new vision and an alternative choice for the Russian electorate.

Second, the reformers were largely indifferent to the public's acceptance of their program and its distributional impact on the losers. Perhaps some pain from transforming the Soviet-era arrangements was inevitable. However, the urgency of minimizing the costs for the most vulnerable groups was not even articulated in the design of their policies, much less in the implementation. The Yeltsin team was out-and-out technocratic, and, perhaps not surprisingly, this led to its departure from active politics.

Third, the Yeltsin reformers neglected the inadequate institutional underpinning that was to transform the Soviet command economy into a market system. For example, Russia even now has a thin stock market, dominated by the oil industry. Although many firms are privatized in the sense that they are not state run,

Russia's industrial structure is dominated by monopolies in a largely unregulated environment rather than by competitive, rule-bound companies. Ultimately, Yeltsin's reformers ended up enacting bold market-oriented and democratic reforms with a view to finishing off the Soviet system rather than implementing them in a robust institutional environment.

Finally, the Russian voters decisively turned against Yeltsin-era reforms by defeating the liberal reformist groups and depriving Gaidar, Chubais, Nemtsov, and Yavlinsky of their Duma memberships in the December 2003 election. After four years under Putin, Russians were ready to settle for a mild dose of authoritarianism that promised further stability and steady economic gains, rather than opting for a Yeltsin-type liberal order that had aroused their expectations but largely excluded them from the hoped-for benefits.

Yeltsin, a confirmed anti-Communist, and his like-minded reformist team maneuvered tirelessly against the Communist Party. They largely succeeded, in the sense that the Communist Party's representation in the Duma declined in successive elections, and the party was virtually extinct after the December 2003 election. I build upon this policy framework and rely on the interviews to discuss the key elements of the process of economic reform that led to the decline of Communism, the shock therapy economic reforms, the controversial privatization plans, the end of popular support for Yeltsin, the steady popularity of Putin, and the prospects for rebuilding appropriate institutions and state power in Russia.

Who Killed Communism? Yeltsin versus Gorbachev

Yeltsin's reformist goal was categorical: "The [Soviet] political system had to be overturned, not just changed." In early 2000 Gaidar also summed up his assessment of the Communist Party:

> In Russia, even during Soviet days, the Communist Party of the Soviet Union was not really a Marxist party. It was an imperial party. And from the very beginning, the ideology of the Communist Party of the Russian Federation has been authoritarian and nationalistic. If you read the writings of Mr. [Gennadd] Zyuganov, the Communist leader, there is nothing Marxist about them, but there is much that resembles the writings of Hitler. . . . That is why they [the Communists] are dangerous. . . . The most dangerous moment in Russia's transition was the 1996 presidential election [when Zyuganov instead of Yeltsin could have been elected president]. Now everybody accepts the idea that the Communists will never come to power in Russia. . . . [T]hey will never rule Russia again.

Chubais was equally categorical in his pronouncement: "I do believe that everything that has happened in Russia in the last decade [of the last millennium] has been a fight between Communists and non-Communists to a greater extent than elsewhere in Eastern Europe—and on a much bigger scale, with more risk than in Poland or in East European countries. . . . Our strategy is to win. We have to win. I mean we *shall* win."

Nemtsov somewhat elliptically expressed his concern about the Communist opposition by drawing an outsider's contrast between Russian and American politics: "I wonder why people become politicians in the United States. Everything here, in contrast to Russia, is predictable. What will happen after the [2000] presidential elections here [in the United States]? Hardly anything. What will happen in New York City? Nothing earthshaking. But suppose Zyuganov becomes the Russian president. It will be a disaster."

Nevertheless, do Yeltsin and his team of reformers really deserve the credit for carrying out the radical changes that ended Communism? What about Mikhail Gorbachev's contribution to this demolition project? To what extent did Gorbachev's program of glasnost, literally "giving voice," and perestroika, implying economic "restructuring," begin undermining Soviet Communism?

Yavlinsky, Rogov, and Simonia, three Gorbachev supporters with solid social democratic orientations, were eloquent in their assessment of Gorbachev's contributions to weakening Soviet arrangements. According to Yavlinsky, Gorbachev "was a liberator in a very special sense because he liberated Russians from the system that existed here for more than seventy years. . . . He took initiatives and issued decrees in rapid succession that weakened the Communist administrative apparatus. I think you should compare the progress on this front under Gorbachev with the initial situation, in which the administrative structures under complete Communist Party control managed everything."

According to Rogov, "Gorbachev is a unique leader in Russian history because he initiated changes at a time when it was possible simply to continue. . . . Until Gorbachev, the majority of Soviet citizens never thought of alternative arrangements. His changes prompted people to start thinking about the possibility of a totally different system. That was a revolutionary move. People began searching for an ideal, transparent system because they knew that the Soviet system was a big lie."

Simonia was equally decisive in ranking Gorbachev's democratic credentials ahead of Yeltsin's: "That process [of democratization] started not with Yeltsin, but with Gorbachev. There was genuine freedom under Gorbachev. . . . Yeltsin gradually began to talk and act like a tsar, so he borrowed from the institutions of democracy, but in reality the essence was a traditionally Russian state of affairs." Simonia also provided a striking one-liner: "Gubernatorial elections under Yeltsin led to the feudal partitioning of Russia."

Jordan assessed the democratic beginnings under Yeltsin negatively:

The Yeltsin-era freedoms did not bring forth a democratic political system in Russia. I think the West saw several likable faces, heard familiar pronouncements, witnessed seemingly positive events, and took them as signs of a more developed democracy than actually existed—features such as elections, political parties, democratic rhetoric from businessmen and officials, massive privatization, a vocal private interest, and an outrageously open and bold press. A closer examination suggests that these were marks of a Potemkin democracy. . . . The most telling misperception centered around Yeltsin's 1996 election. It was hailed in the West as a major coup for democracy, although he and his policies had become unpopular by the time of the election, and the balloting process was acknowledged as flawed.

In my own view, Gorbachev did not intend to destroy the commanding role and ideology of the CPSU. He aimed at creating inner-party democracy within a single-party system by proposing political changes that focused on the role of party functionaries and the methods for electing them. Under his initiative, limited election procedures were begun. A so-called legislature, the Supreme Soviet, was elected in 1990 through a general and direct vote by citizens with the dominating participation of the Communists. However, the monopoly of the Communist Party in the political life of the land was an article of faith that Gorbachev found difficult to give up.[43] His proposed changes were also slow and zigzag because of his continuing apprehension that the Communist brass might remove him from office. Perhaps the most damaging mistake of Gorbachev's presidency, which I brought up in an unrecorded interview with him in the summer of 1999, was that he did not legitimate his authority by seeking to be elected president by a popular vote in the winter of 1990. As late as May 1990, public opinion polls indicated that Gorbachev was the most popular leader, ahead of Yeltsin. Instead, Gorbachev was elected president on March 13, 1990, by an indirect vote of the Congress of People's Deputies in the Soviet days, which was the supreme body at the top of the party hierarchy. Thus, Gorbachev lacked the legitimacy of a democratically elected leader (a handicap that he acknowledged in the interview), which would have enabled him to hold the Communist Party politburo at bay and perhaps to survive the power struggle with Yeltsin, who was elected president of the Russian Republic later in June 1991. While Gorbachev liberated Eastern Europe from Soviet control and introduced powerful winds of change in the Soviet Union, Yeltsin proved savvier by contesting and winning five elections in his political career, including the referendum of April 1993.

At a deeper level, Gorbachev's economic reforms failed because of his conviction that socialism, purged of its Stalinist aberrations, could promote economic efficiency under the openness of glasnost. Based on this belief, Gorbachev's orchestrated steps to loosen the Communist Party's political control remained ahead of measures to free the economy from administered prices, shaky budgetary management, and state ownership and management of productive resources. Gorbachev believed that he needed to draw from the positive aspects of Soviet history and ground economic restructuring in a vision of Soviet society that did not reject the "essential" correctness of its revolutionary past. He did not believe that he needed to walk over to Jeremy Bentham and Milton Friedman's corner, nor did he want to be seen doing so.[44]

Thus, Gorbachev's economic agenda from 1985 to 1991 was shot through with fundamental contradictions that went beyond policy muddles or technical lapses. For example, he thought that incentives could be created without private property and private ownership of the means of production. Soviet society would instead devise "socialist pluralism," "socialist competition," "socialist incentives," and the like.[45] He was an intellectual prisoner of the full-blooded socialist tradition, a mode of thinking that could not readily encompass the true functions of a market economy. Economic reforms under his leadership were piecemeal. The policies involved certain steps toward removing government economic controls, like leasing land to farmers, allowing some small, privately owned enterprises, and closing down some failing factories. However, perestroika also kept the economic planners fundamentally in charge.

At the same time, none of the policy makers—all operating in the socialist mindset—understood market reforms. Throughout Gorbachev's tenure, they thought in terms of raising prices via diktat rather than freeing them. Their approach to the problem of macroeconomic instability consisted of attempting to trim the fiscal imbalance. Consequently, they watched helplessly as budget deficits escalated.[46] Privatizing productive economic assets was beyond their consideration. In the end, Gorbachev greatly overpromised what perestroika could achieve, and by 1991 it proved a dismal failure at increasing output and improving living standards.

Perhaps Yeltsin did not comprehend the market economy, either, but he clearly wanted his firebrand reformers to purge it of the strangulating kit and caboodle of Communist economic arrangements. But could he and his team undertake fast-track economic reforms in Russia's chaotic political and economic environment of the 1990s? From launching the shock therapy economic reforms in January 1992 to the ruble's meltdown in August 1998, successive reformist teams in the Yeltsin government attempted to enact changes while they battled recalcitrant Communist legislators. Popular support for Yeltsin and his economic reform program, at its height in the referendum of April 1993, had collapsed to less than 5 percent approval when Yeltsin resigned in December 1999. My conversations brought out these dual aspects of the escalating legislative confrontation and the evaporating popular support as Yeltsin's reformers sought to push their policy agenda.

Before turning to an analysis of their program, to which the Yeltsin-Clinton rapport contributed, I highlight my American participants' view of the transforming roles Gorbachev and Yeltsin played on the Soviet stage.

Who Performed Better? Gorbachev versus Yeltsin

In assessing Gorbachev, Matlock combined his scholarly insights with his personal experience as U.S. ambassador to Moscow during Gorbachev's presidency:

> Presidents Reagan and Gorbachev, in effect, cooperated on a scenario, a plan of reforming the Soviet Union, which was defined initially by the United States. The plan was devised by the United States but with the idea that it should not be contrary to the national interests of a peaceful Soviet Union. . . . Gorbachev finally began to understand this in 1987. We know from the politburo records that, in effect, he adopted the U.S. agenda, which had been defined in Washington, without attribution, of course, as his own plan. He certainly had his own reasons for doing this when he began to see that the Soviet Union did need reform. As he moved along with these reforms, Reagan supported them. You may recall that when Reagan went to Moscow in May 1988, he was asked, "Is this still the Evil Empire?" He said, "No, that was another era, another time." Then someone asked, "Well, who is responsible?" And he said, "Mr. Gorbachev, of course. He is the leader of this country." One more question [to Reagan]: "Who won?" "Well, certainly, the Cold War ended on terms that had been set by the West, and specifically by the United States, and yet I think both sides won."

Thus the end of the Cold War, a joint Reagan–Gorbachev enterprise, contributed to the demise of Soviet Communism, which, in Matlock's view, was subsequently accomplished by Gorbachev.

In his *Formation of the Soviet Union,* Pipes had predicted the dissolution of the Soviet Union as far back as 1954. In his view, the collapse was inevitable because the union was not voluntary: "I had said that, if there was any trouble, any weakening in the center, the whole edifice would disintegrate, fall apart suddenly, because it had nothing to hold it together, really, except force. . . . It [the Soviet Union] was a unitary centralized authoritarian state such as the czarist state had never been. On the other hand, . . . by placing the national territorial principle as the base of the state's political administration, which it previously was not, the Communists gave constitutional recognition to the multinational structure of the Soviet population. . . . What I meant is that, by setting up these essentially spurious republics, they created a basis for the disintegration of the Union."

Pipes continued: "I would say that Gorbachev loosened the system to the point where it was ready to collapse, and then Yeltsin moved in and gave it a coup de grâce. . . . The trouble was he didn't know what to do with it afterward. He was not an administrator. I think he was essentially—the Germans have a word for it, *Krisenmensch*—a man for crisis situations. He was wonderful, courageous, brave, and imaginative, as he climbed on a tank. But after the battle was won and the situation had calmed down, he had to administer and work with people. He got bored with it."

Malia contrasted the two leaders in the following words: "He [Gorbachev] deserves credit for opening the windows, letting in fresh air, and permitting people to speak the truth. It was only this speaking of the truth that destroyed what Solzhenitsyn called 'the Lie,' the pretension of the system to be rational, just, egalitarian, and not coercive. Gorbachev deserves credit for that, but I don't think he deserves credit for the results that he produced because he did not intend to destroy the system and 'restore capitalism.'"[47]

According to Malia, Yeltsin was "part party boss and part democrat, even at times a demagogic politician, but I don't think that he ever gave up on his new, anti-Communist ends, namely, electoral politics, free markets, and free expression."

"Was Yeltsin a revolutionary?" I asked Malia. "In Russia there was indeed a transition from one era to another under Yeltsin, but the new era the Russian 'democrats' hoped to reach was simply self-government and the market, things that were hardly new in the human experience . . . . Nineteen ninety-one, therefore, [in Russia, under Yeltsin] was not a revolution in the same sense that 1789 had been [during the French Revolution]."

"Would you describe the Gorabchev-Yeltsin confrontation as the snake winning over the hedgehog?" I continued.

He replied, "I think it is an inapt comparison—and too unkind to Yeltsin. First, he was a craftier politician than Gorbachev, not a craftier apparatchik. Yeltsin's power was ultimately based not on his position as a party boss but on winning elections. . . . He did indeed devour Gorbachev, for in the end he drove him from the presidency. Yet comparing Yeltsin to a snake is inappropriate, for it implies a secretiveness and deviousness that are not central to his character. He is more a blustering Russian *muzhik* [peasant]." In the end, Yeltsin's choice of a kamikaze crew implied a decisive signal on his part that the transition to a market system had to ensure a destructive assault on the Communist economic and political structures.

Next I turn to a description of the so-called shock therapy reforms, the momentum they acquired from the Yeltsin-Clinton partnership, the controversial role of the International Monetary Fund in the policy choices until the collapse of the ruble in August 1998, and the factors leading to the reformers' retirement from active politics.

Shock Therapy Reforms in Russia: The Politics and the Economics

The key policy choices aimed at ending the Communist policies of economic planning were well known: decontrolling prices from their administered levels; slashing the inordinately high budget deficit; privatizing the state-owned means of production; and opening the economy via foreign trade and capital account liberalization under a unified, market-determined ruble. The question facing the Yeltsin reformers was whether to undertake these goals gradually and incrementally or in a quick and sweeping manner that became known as "shock therapy."

The argument in favor of shock therapy is that, during a time of extraordinary political upheaval, broad changes are politically possible and the public is more willing to endure the pain of higher prices and economic dislocation. By contrast, slow-paced reforms that wait for a political consensus can prolong the resulting costs and dislocations well after politics has turned "ordinary," giving opponents of reform a chance to regroup and counterattack—with the result that reforms may never actually occur.[48] Poland took the shock therapy approach to economic reform in 1989, seizing a window of opportunity that opened up after a decade of political struggle with the Polish Communist regime under the Solidarity banner and the country's liberation from the Soviet bloc. Yeltsin's reformers expected the collapse of the Soviet Union and the launching of the Russian Federation in 1992 to open a window, at least for a short time, for extensive reform. The economic decisions therefore had to be rapid-fire.

The shock therapy policy framework articulated by its prominent advocate, Jeffrey Sachs, included the following elements: Prices are freed, while an abrupt tightening of the money supply accompanied by large cuts in government borrowing from the central bank serves as a shield against inflation, the exchange rate is pegged to the dollar or some other hard currency, and massive amounts of foreign aid are marshaled to support the stabilization effort.[49] Defenders of the "big bang" tactics also emphasize that privatization is essential, even while acknowledging that it is complex and almost necessarily slow. On the other side, gradualists proposed escalating attacks on the budget deficit and inflation, supported by smaller and more realistic aid flows and without recourse to an early hard pegging of the exchange rate. Such a gradualist program also advocated gradual price decontrol and privatization of state-owned assets.[50]

When Yegor Gaidar launched the shock therapy economic reforms on January 2, 1992, he had hoped that presidential decrees backed by Yeltsin's personal authority would prevail over parliamentary recalcitrance. Prices were freed by decree. Gaidar then presented the Supreme Soviet with proposals that called for *eliminating* the budget deficit by the end of first quarter of 1992—a very aggressive step, given that Russia's budget deficit in 1991 had been 17 percent of GDP, according to IMF estimates. The proposed cuts in defense outlays, state-financed investments, and subsidies to consumers and industry were Soviet-style fiats: There had been no consultations with Parliament or the people, and there was no strategy of seeking a steady political majority within the Supreme Soviet, which was roughly divided into three equal factions: Communists, reformists, and an unsteady middle group that could float in either direction. The escalating rift between the government and the Supreme Soviet ended with a bang in October 1993, when troops loyal to Yeltsin stormed a group of diehard members who had barricaded themselves in the parliament building in Moscow rather than comply with the president's order to disband.

Starting with the shock therapy approach, Russian politics failed to settle down into a give-and-take mode. The politics of consensus building was ruled out by the Yeltsin crew's confrontational strategy, a pattern that continued up to the December 1999 Duma elections. Rogov, as a proponent of Gorbachev-style reforms, characterized the Yeltsin team's bare-knuckles approach in this way: "The so-called Yeltsin liberals went for the right-wing conservative ideology of the United States as an alternative to the Communist planned economy. They exchanged Marxism-Leninism for Friedmanism. For most of the post-Gorbachev period, the [reformist] Russian government was dominated by policy makers who would make the Cato Institute gang look like a Democratic outpost in Washington, D.C."[51]

In what way did Bill Clinton, a Democrat, and his policy makers contribute to this radical outcome?

Bill and Boris: The Personal Chemistry

Strobe Talbott, Clinton's "Russia hand" as deputy secretary of state in the administration, provided details of what became a mutual endeavor: "[F]or seven of the eight years that President Clinton was in office here, Boris Yeltsin was the president of Russia. He had, by virtue of his office, huge powers. He also had an extraordinarily strong and consistent commitment to certain principles and objectives that were in the interest of the United States. He was susceptible to the influence of only one man in the U.S. government, and that was Bill Clinton. Therefore, we decided early—President Clinton decided early—that he was going to concentrate his diplomacy on his Russian counterpart. I think that was absolutely the right thing to do. It yielded huge and lasting benefits to the United States."

Talbott continued: "Yeltsin felt a deep ambivalence about the United States. In some ways he regarded us as a beacon, a model, and a friend, and in other ways he regarded us as obnoxious as hell. . . . But the way he resolved that conflict, when push came to shove, was favorable, and that was largely because of the interaction between him and Clinton."

Finally, Talbott said, "I think there'll be a high degree of continuity in U.S.-Russian relations, but that doesn't go to the question of chemistry. Bill Clinton bonded with Boris Yeltsin. Big time. And he used that bond to get Yeltsin to do things that were hard for Yeltsin but important to us. That is the story of the last eight years more than any other single thing."

At one point, Clinton had reportedly summed up the interaction imperative in a memorable one-liner: "We can't ever forget that Yeltsin drunk is better than most of the alternatives sober."[52]

While the two presidents bonded, Russians were beginning to part ways with their president.

Declining Popular Support

Public discontent with the Yeltsin reforms materialized from three directions. The freeing of prices caused the costs of essential goods to rise dramatically, in a way that essentially wiped out the savings people had accumulated during the Soviet days. Bread lines disappeared, but bread prices climbed higher than wages. Second, price decontrol also destabilized enterprise balance sheets, forcing them to withhold wage payments to workers and tax payments to the government, and shortfalls in budget revenues created government defaults of wage payments to state-sector employees and pensions to retirees.[53] The pervasive withholding of wages from workers and nonpayment of pensions to retirees from 1994 to 1998 intensified the public's discontent. Finally, the voucher scheme did not buy enough stock to be of significant value to an average Russian, and voucher privatization led to uneven and unregulated ownership.

The human cost of the economic reform program could have been less if more resources had been available for subsidizing the losers and for supplementing wage and pension payments. According to Gaidar, however, the issue of "material support" from the West was not critical: "The problem [in 1991] was the absence of a clear, liberalization strategy in terms of which to define a policy framework in those days. . . . You could put in a lot of money and mess up the strategy. You could have less money and come out better." In his view, the name of the game was strategy, rather than the resource requirements for implementing its "policy framework" with less pain to the public. However, Gaidar's liberalization strategy seemed to have no component for addressing those without wages or pensions or for deciding who would win and lose as ownership of the means of production was transferred away from the state sector.

Both Talbott and Soros brought up the issue of generous and targeted support in response to my questioning. Talbott said, "I wish that we had invested much more money early on . . . but certainly at the beginning of the Clinton administration. We should also have invested it more wisely. The international support, which is to say, the economic stabilization programs, and particularly the social safety net programs, should have been more highly conditioned." Soros reminisced at length about his efforts to support Gorbachev financially: "I was advocating something along the lines of the Marshall Plan, only more intrusive. But then the idea simply didn't fly. I tried to push it in every way I could. I privately tried to reach Margaret Thatcher, but I never got past Paul, her personal assistant. I tried to reach George Bush [senior]. . . . I proposed it publicly at the East-West conference in Potsdam in the spring of 1989, when Potsdam was still in East Germany. I was literally laughed at. It was a rather embarrassing experience. I'd never been publicly laughed at. . . . Apparently the idea was simply not acceptable in Western public opinion."[54]

Soros, a strong Gorbachev supporter and a sharp critic of economic shock therapy, weighed in with more details: "Gorbachev counted on the United States to help him initiate economic reforms. He felt that he and his team were incapable of making the transition on their own. . . . Gorbachev visited the United Nations in 1987 and spoke about his new thinking. The U.S. leadership ignored it and instead set conditions, asking him to make concessions. When he made them, they asked for more. . . . To prove that it [direct cash payment] could be done, I established the International Science Foundation, which distributed $500 each to the top thirty thousand Russian scientists. . . . The cash they received is practically the only Western aid that Russians have actually received."

The foundation, however, became a casualty of the transition trauma. According to Soros, "I wanted the foundation to lead the way toward an open society in Russia. To some extent, it became embroiled in the transition. . . . We had the August 1991 putsch in Russia. We needed another one to clean the foundation of its Russian corruption. Instead of leading, the foundation became part of the process. That was the painful realization."

From the perspective of the Russian citizenry, the privatization of Russia's state-owned assets was not only inequitable but also an outright robbery, creating a potential and a continuing concern with regard to its reversal.

Russian Privatization

The privatization of Russia's state-owned assets came about in two stages. The first involved the distribution of vouchers worth ten thousand rubles to every man, woman, and child in Russia, including workers and managers of firms, that they could use to purchase shares of the privatized companies. In the second stage, the ownership shares of the Russian government in some of Russia's prized companies such as Norilsk Nickel were traded to a small number of oligarchs in exchange for loans to the state budget.

The first phase of the broad-based voucher plan, stretching from December 1992 to mid-1994, was spearheaded by the desire to provide a political counterweight in support of privatization that could beat the Communist majority in the Congress of People's Deputies. The voucher privatization was launched hastily, but it was very popular politically, and the distribution of vouchers worth ten thousand rubles to every citizen sounded to many people like a pathway to asset ownership and instant wealth. The voucher privatization program helped give a resounding "yes" to Boris Yeltsin and his reforms in the subsequent April 1993 referendum.[55]

In practice, however, many people ended up receiving very little for their vouchers. Information about the real worth of factories put up for sale to owners of vouchers was highly incomplete. An absence of electronic transactions meant that the voucher-based offerings took place in a rough-and-ready, sequential mode, which further contributed to uncertain and unequal outcomes for the voucher holders. Finally, domestic and foreign middlemen bought up the vouchers from cash-hungry citizens.

On both economic and political grounds, Anatoly Chubais defended the second phase of privatization, which involved loans by Russian oligarchs to the government in exchange for their eventual capture of state shares in Russian companies: "Politically, I was in a very complicated situation. . . . [T]he dilemma was simple: Either we will not sell state shares at all, or we will sell them via the controversial shares scheme, which would bring real money to the Russian budget. Don't forget that with the sale of Norilsk Nickel shares, we got the first $170 million. It was absolutely fantastic. It helped the federal budget a lot because the budget situation was critical."

Assessing the role of the oligarchs in the evolving political situation, Chubais said, "I strongly believe that the only way to prevent [the Communist leader] Zyuganov from becoming president in 1996 was to create big private business in Russia. Their [the oligarchs'] mentality differed from Soviet-style management. . . . They fought for improving economic efficiency. . . . That is the economic side of the story. At the same time, they became powerful and wanted to use their power according to their understanding of the political situation. The presidential election of June 1996 raised the question of Yeltsin or Zyuganov, and they [the oligarchs who bankrolled Yeltsin's election] definitely said Yeltsin. However, in the next phase, they thought they ruled the world and could do anything, so there are positive and negative sides to the story."

Nevertheless, Russian voters concentrated on the negative side of the story. Many of them had received little for their vouchers in the first place. They judged the loans-for-shares scheme as a corrupt maneuver to enrich the few while depriving them of their legitimate share in assets created collectively during the Soviet Communist period.

The privatization program succeeded in moving essentially all of Russia's formerly state-owned economy to the private sector. However, the Yeltsin team's economic reform program lacked an offsetting component to buy out the losers. For example, perhaps a fraction of the cash received from the oligarchs could have been set aside for welfare payments to poor people or pension payments to elderly citizens. According to Soros, "the same $15 billion [from the IMF] that provided balance of payment and budgetary support could have been earmarked for paying Social Security benefits [to pensioners]." Or perhaps legal titles to the apartments occupied by the worse-off city dwellers could have been turned over to them via a presidential decree at the start of the program. However, steps like these did not occur, and so, until the departure of the Yeltsin team from the Russian government in August 1998, the reformers had to face the entrenched Communist opposition in the Duma and eroding public support.

Institution Building and Policy Choices

Among the staggering institutional inadequacies inherited from the Soviet past, I focused on handicaps relating to monetary and budgetary problems during the period leading up to the financial crisis of August 1998.

At the start of the reform period in 1992, the Central Bank of Russia was under the leadership of Viktor Gerashchenko, who had also directed the bank during the final years of the Soviet Union. Jeffrey Sachs once memorably described Gerashchenko as the "world's worst central banker," and the Central Bank at this time was neither independent of the legislature nor in sympathy with the Yeltsin team's program. After a couple of interim chairs, Sergei Dubinin became the chair of the Central Bank in 1995, a position he held until the ruble collapse in August 1998. Then Gerashchenko returned to preside over the bank, and by mid-2000 it was mired in corruption scandals of having misused IMF funding. The Russian budgetary policy was also in shambles in the early 1990s. The Soviet government had offered automatic subsidies from its budget to loss-generating, state-owned enterprises, most of them massive monopolies. At the start of the Yeltsin reforms, these subsidies persisted as a result of the time-honored networking ties between party bureaucrats and factory managers. Moreover, budgetary management was hampered by a lack of transparent tax rules and rates involving the federal, regional, and local hierarchies and by a lack of effective tax collection.

In January 1992, Gaidar's adoption of economic shock therapy, combining price decontrol with a ruthless slashing of budgetary support to consumers and producers, was targeted to end the practices that routinely helped out inefficient factory managers with similar assistance. However, the traditional bailout practice reasserted itself in full force when the Central Bank, led by Gerashchenko, released a supply of money to meet managerial demands. At the end of 1992 inflation ran at 2,500 percent. At the same time, the Gaidar plan summarily transferred several entitlement outlays from the federal budget to the regions without matching resources.

"What would you do differently if you had another chance?" I asked Gaidar. Were he to be appointed acting prime minister again, he said, he "would handle a lot of technical issues differently." The technocrat reappeared in full measure: He would push oil price, foreign trade, and exchange rate liberalization faster, issues on which he had evidently "compromised" to placate the opposition. "I would be more certain of undertaking the right measures and less ready to make compromises, knowing well the high price one pays later for compromises." The policy shock that he introduced in early 1992 was, in other words, incomplete. A total earthquake was necessary because a limited one involved compromises. In hindsight, Nemtsov, too, minimized the importance of timing or sequencing of reform legislation. "The unfolding of the reform process is not the critical aspect. Absence of political will to undertake reforms is the main problem. The remaining issues are largely technical."

Revamping the tax and pension regimes with a view to improving the budgetary situation and converting the Russian Central Bank into a nimble policy-making body were clearly daunting tasks. They were hampered not only by the Communist intransigence in the Duma but also by a declining Russian economy through much of the 1990s. By the early 2000s, these impediments weakened. The December 1999 election diminished the presence of the Communists in the Duma, and Russia's economy began to revive, based in part on the ruble devaluation and oil exports, which together created a benign environment for institution building at the start of 2000. My interviews with Dubinin and Vyugin, who steered the monetary policies during these contrasting scenarios, brought out the acute problems the former confronted from 1995 to 1998 and the robust confidence of the latter in the last couple of years.

Dubinin, who succeeded Gerashchenko as director of the Central Bank in 1995, recalled the policy dilemmas that he faced leading up to the ruble's collapse in August 1998:

> The problem with the budget was lagging tax collections rather than cutting expenditures. . . . The joint decision of the government and the Central Bank was that we must continue our anti-inflation monetary policy and move forward on budgetary policy and structural reform. But every year we saw that progress in the latter sphere was missing. The gap grew wider and wider. . . . There were a number of mistakes. For example, the government attempted to handle the tax situation by trying to push the tax code, a massive document, in the Duma. It required a lot of time—months—to get it approved. [It was rejected by the pre-1999 Duma.] We needed changes in the tax system and the appropriate legislation in perhaps two months. The government worked on the tax code rather than on the concrete problems of taxation.

By contrast, in a mid-2003 interview, Vyugin came across as a policy maker in command of his role: "Our inflation rate is declining. . . . The Central Bank and the government together have set the 2003–2004 annual targets at 8–10 percent. . . . Public expectation is for inflation to steadily come down. People expect it to be lower in the foreseeable future." Describing the status of the Central Bank, he said, "We are independent. We have only one requirement. We must report to Parliament once a year. As far as the government is concerned, the Duma can pass a no-confidence motion. With us, it requires that we report to it once a year."

How did Russia's monetary and fiscal policies make the transition from dysfunction and chaos to the marked improvement and interaction starting in 2000 that Vyugin described at length? The International Monetary Fund figured prominently in this transition.

The IMF in Russia

When the International Monetary Fund stepped into Russia in early 1993, the four-digit inflation rate meant that the pressing concern was to salvage a building in flames, not to redesign its architecture. Thus, issues such as asserting control over monetary policy, or adopting rules to clean up the tax regime, or converting the Russian Central Bank into a model resembling the Federal Reserve received little attention. The IMF was a staunch advocate of speedy inflation control, buttressed by a strong exchange rate, and an enthusiastic promoter of free capital mobility. Thus, it supported a tight monetary policy, one that kept the Central Bank's discount rate at 25 percent and higher. This strategy was combined with an inordinately strong ruble. Finally, foreigners were allowed to buy short-term government bills so that the budget deficit at 7 percent of GDP from 1995 to 1998 could be contained.[56]

This policy mix brought down inflation, which fell to an annual rate of 70 percent by 1995 and to just 3 percent by the end of 1997. Nevertheless, the inordinately strong ruble exchange rate largely destroyed the competitive position of Russian industry in world markets. Also, the combination of extremely high interest rates and single-digit inflation meant that the Russian government and commercial banks went on a borrowing binge fed by speculative inflows that rushed in to earn a real return of 20 percent and more. Unsupervised and unconstrained by the Central Bank, Russian commercial banks borrowed short term in foreign-exchange markets and invested in government bonds that turned out to be worthless assets a year later. In Russia's institutional setting, the combination of high interest rates, a strong currency, and full capital account liberalization led to massive short-term speculative capital flows. The premature opening of Russia's economy to capital inflows was a colossal mistake that led to the Russian government's debt default, the collapse of the ruble, and another severe shock to Russia's economy in 1998.

The IMF could have reduced the risks of this outcome in several different ways. After tight monetary policy had succeeded in bringing inflation down to double-digit rates in 1995, it could then have encouraged a more gradualist approach to reducing inflation in the next few years. It could have opted for a selective opening of the economy focused on long-term capital inflows. The IMF could have supported temporary controls on outflows of funds from Russia toward the end of 1997, when foreign holders of government bonds, unnerved by the unfolding Asian financial crisis, went on a selling spree. However, given its policy commitment to free capital flows, that choice would have put the fund in the role of a clergyman renouncing his faith in the middle of a spiritual crisis. In Russia, the IMF stuck to its one-rule-fits-all-situations policy stance rather than craft a feasible mix of monetary control, exchange rate management, and capital mobility that would have worked with Russia's combination of an out-of-kilter tax regime and dwindling foreign exchange reserves.

Dubinin commented extensively on these issues from his perspective as chairman of Russia's Central Bank from 1995 to 1998: "The top-level IMF command team liked Russia. That was helpful, but it applied the same model in Russia as in other countries. For example, it insisted that we open up the market to foreign capital. When we decided to do so, it said the opening ought to be full and free, without restrictions."

He also sized up the Washington policy-making nexus in the following words: "In their assessment of the IMF, the U.S. Congress and the administration were influenced by political and even personal considerations. For example, it was absolutely clear to everybody that there was tension between the Fund and the U.S. Treasury. At the same time, the Treasury had a concrete role in negotiating a program for Russia. It insisted that our anti-inflation program, tax collection effort, and bankruptcy implementation be more severe."

While Dubinin and Vyugin assessed the IMF's policy-making role from a technical perspective, Gaidar put it in a broader political context. In 1990 and 1991, "an enormous, powerful empire [the Soviet Union] disintegrated, leaving anarchy in its wake. The existing institutions ceased to function, and new institutions could not be created overnight. . . . But what was the West's response to the new challenge? . . . Let us imagine for just a moment that the Fund was put in charge of restoring Europe after World War II. . . . It does not have the decision-making process and procedures and human resources to deal with this enormous problem, which requires political leadership rather than technical expertise to resolve. And so everybody is now wondering, Why is the Fund not up to handling the problem?"

Soros agreed with this assessment: "Basically the international lenders were not willing to put public resources and real money into the effort. . . . They gave the job of assisting the Soviet Union, and then Russia eventually, to the IMF, which was not the appropriate institution."

In the end, were Yeltsin and his team "up to handling the problem"? They succeeded in irreversibly planting the powerful *ideas* of democratic choices and free markets in the land of Lenin and Stalin. However, having experienced the inevitable turmoil of this transition, the public, in Gaidar's words, hankered for order and stability. The election of Vladimir Putin to the presidency in April 2000 was a predictable outcome. So was the resounding emergence of the pro-Kremlin United Russia group in the Duma following the December 2003 parliamentary election. Putin rode to a second, four-year presidency in March 2004, with full freedom to choose a government.

PUTIN AND STATE POWER

Following the Beslan school attack, Putin announced a series of measures in late 2004 that the Parliament later adopted. In the future, governors will be nominated by the president for subsequent approval by the regional legislatures rather than be elected by voters. The new laws will also eliminate the election of independent, single-mandate contenders to the Duma. Members will be elected solely on the basis of proportional votes garnered by party-list contestants to the exclusion of single-mandate constituencies. Moreover, a party must get 7 percent of the vote instead of the previous 5 percent in order for the winning candidates to gain eligibility as Duma members. Parties must have organizations in at least half of the eighty-nine regions of Russia in order to qualify for electoral contests. These tougher requirements are calculated to eliminate splinter groups and promote political party formation. My interviewees reacted with alarm to these measures abolishing popular gubernatorial elections and single-mandate electoral constituencies.

Gaidar assessed the presidential selection of regional governors from a historical perspective: "Russia was ruled like that from Moscow for centuries. . . . It did not prevent two revolutions, namely the end of the tsarist regime in 1917 and the breakup of the Soviet Union in 1991. . . . True, Russia is a young and unstable democracy. Therefore, voters tend to elect leaders who are far from the best. With greater experience, they will understand that local problems need to be resolved at local levels. They will realize that, in choosing regional leaders, they, rather than the president in Moscow, will decide how their regional problems . . . will be handled."

Dubinin saw a need for strengthening the state's authority but insisted that such control should be consolidated not only "vertically" but also "horizontally": "We need an independent courts and democratically elected municipal and regional administrations with adequate powers and responsibilities. The president's proposals suggest that he is ready to take on the responsibility of appointing the governors and their future decision making. Boldness is a solid quality of our president. But in my view, these steps represent a faulty orientation."

My American interviewees also reacted to the measure with concern. Talbott expressed it incisively: "If Russia is to survive as a unitary state, it must resume its development as a federal and a democratic state. The essence of democratic federalism is maximum self-government at the local and provincial level. People are most likely to respect and obey authority if they feel it reflects their interests and is invested in leaders they have chosen. Besides, Russia is vastly diverse, and federalism makes a virtue of diversity. The tsars and the commissars tried to impose unity and order by a more brutal version of the methods Putin is now applying. They failed and so may he."

As for the abolition of single-mandate electoral constituencies, Gaidar reacted to the Putin proposals with the force of his experience in government and as a former Duma deputy. Commenting on Putin's announcement to switch to a proportional, party-based election of Duma deputies, he said, "The Duma currently has a small but active group of independent deputies. . . . They are the ones who actively participate in meetings of key committees and plenary sessions. Their views have limited impact on decision making, but their voices are heard. They influence public opinion. If the presidential proposals are adopted, such independent deputies, who obtain entry via individual contests, will be absent from the Duma. The party loyalists will then take over. That, I think, is an alarming prospect."

Overall, Gaidar compared the evolving political arrangements in Russia to the one-party system under the Revolutionary Party in Mexico and to conditions in Italy and Japan between the end of World War II and the 1980s. Nemtsov argued that basing election to the Duma only on proportional representation along party lines would not jump-start a multiparty system in Russia because "financial resources for party formation are monopolized by the Kremlin; the electronic media are censored; the prospective parties, therefore, would be loyal to the Kremlin. It would destroy opposition because single mandate deputies were more independent and critical of government policies. According to Matlock, "The abolition of individual constituency elections for the Duma is, in my opinion, a dangerous step that can lead in practice to a one-party state. It also weakens the local institutions needed in a civil society." Pipes assessed the measure's impact on party formation from a historical viewpoint: "In a recent interview, a politician who is close to Putin said that political parties are fine as long as they cooperate with the government. This is the old tsarist mentality resurfacing: Tsarist statesmen like Pyotr Stolypin would have understood and concurred. The notion that political parties can express the interests of society is alien to Russian political culture. I don't see how you will develop parties unless you give them the maximum opportunity to act as a loyal opposition by giving them access to the media and so on."

These consolidation measures have raised a number of other questions. For instance, will they successfully fight terrorist attacks? Will they set back progress on Russia's fledgling democracy, property rights, and media freedom? Does the prosecution and severe jail sentencing of Mikhail Khodorkovsky, CEO of Russia's most successful oil company, Yukos, suggest a template for similar offenders? Will the political backtracking lead to a slowdown of pro-market economic reforms? How will the perceived retreat from a liberal order under Putin's leadership affect U.S.-Russia relations?

Why was the political tightening necessary? Putin has repeatedly advanced two arguments—the terrorist threat and the disorderly regional governance—both of which impede Russia's viability as a federal state.

Political Tightening and Terrorism Control

Russia's integrity as a state, in Putin's view, was threatened after the Beslan terrorist attack by the ethnic-religious faction of Islamic fundamentalism, which connects a string of small Muslim majority republics in the Caucasus region on Russia's southern border.[57] The rudderless handling of Beslan demonstrated to him the urgent need for a clear assignment of antiterrorism authority from the federal center to regional administrations.

Why the Terrorist Threat?

The two-stage, decade-old brutal war in Chechnya, a Muslim-majority republic in the Caucasus, intensified terrorist attacks on Russian territory. Under Yeltsin, the war of 1994–1996, which was calculated to thwart Chechen demands for self-determination, ended with a tenuous truce and the withdrawal of Russian forces.

Under Putin as prime minister, the second war began in late 1999, following an invasion of neighboring Dagestan by Shamir Basayev, a fundamentalist Chechen guerrilla leader, and his followers. Basayev's presumed goal of creating a Chechen-Dagestani Islamic nation posed a danger for the unraveling of the Caucasus region.[58]

What began as a small-scale regional skirmish escalated into a full-scale engagement by the Russian military, involved massive bombing, widespread destruction, and loss of life and created homeless refugees. The September 11, 2001, terrorist attack on New York City's twin towers tipped the balance in Putin's favor, in effect underwriting his claim that Russia's Chechen war was directed against Islamic fundamentalism and international terrorism. As a result, while direct criticism of the stalemate by the Western powers is muted, the Chechen problem continues to present a formidable challenge for Putin. Conceding genuine political decision making to moderate Chechen elements, assuming that they can be found, will in all likelihood convert Chechnya and the rest of the surrounding regions into radical, Taliban-type states. On the other hand, the current military control and the orchestrated installation of a pro-Moscow government, coupled with promises of economic reconstruction, are unlikely to contain the nationalist aspirations of the Muslim-majority Caucasus region, including Chechnya.

In the meantime, can the tightening of political authority across the chain of command ward off potential terrorist attacks? My interviewees provided multiple perspectives on this issue while wondering whether centralized political control can deal with terrorism.

Prospects for Terrorism Control

Gaidar distinguished between the two phases of the Chechen conflict and came up with a comparative point of view of the Chechen-Vietnam wars:

> The war of 1994–1996 was viewed in Russia in approximately the same way the Vietnam war was perceived here in the United States. Americans found it difficult to understand why they were there. . . . For Russians, too, the earlier war involved difficult questions about whether people have the right to be sovereign or whether the principle of self-determination should become subordinate to the overriding demands of the nation-state. But this issue should not be settled on the battlefield. That was the perception of the Russian public from 1994 to 1996. That is why Russians strongly opposed the previous war. . . . It was exactly the same as here in the United States: America had the resources to continue the war in Vietnam, but it did not have public support. But here the similarities end and the differences begin. The difference is geography. Vietnam is in a splendid location, twenty thousand kilometers from here. Americans could withdraw from Vietnam and more or less forget about it. Chechnya is in Russia. After the war, Chechnya became an increasingly serious problem for Russia with kidnapping, imprisonment, and trafficking in people for cash. . . . However, the situation

changed dramatically when we had a few thousand well-armed and trained people entering Dagestan from Chechnya. Of course, it is very difficult for the American public, which is not even aware of the existence of Dagestan, to understand what the aggression against Dagestan in August [1999] meant for Russia. Dagestan is part of our life, part of our country, and part of our reality. The Dagestani people do not wish to be enslaved by the Chechens. They took up arms, they asked for Russian military support, and then, of course, Russian public opinion changed drastically. The issue was no longer the Chechen people's right to self-determination. It was the question of whether Russian citizens should be protected by their own government.

Although thus defending the military offensive aimed at preserving Russia's integrity as a state, Gaidar doubted, however, that Putin's post-Beslan measures could effectively fight terrorism.[59] He explained, "I think this is a wrong decision. Russia was ruled like that from Moscow for centuries, but that did not end the corruption. That did not prevent terrorist acts, either, as the experience of the last decades of the tsarist regime demonstrated."[60] Rogov agreed with Gaidar's opinion of Russians' contrasting attitudes toward the Chechen war—their rejection of the first military engagement and their acceptance of the second—and reflected on the public's mood about the continuing stalemate: "Right now the public is in a 'leave us alone' mood with the Chechen war. 'If my family is not serving in Chechnya, then I wake up in the morning, drink my coffee, watch TV, and survive.' And you know the TV does not carry any news about Chechnya."

By contrast, Nemtsov was forthright in offering a solution for resolving the conflict:

To begin with, Putin should stop misleading the country and the world by claiming that Russia has been attacked by international terrorists. These attacks resulted from the Kremlin's continuing mistakes in the Caucasus, especially in Chechnya. Of course, the international terrorist organizations help their Chechen colleagues to the extent that the latter have a basis for undertaking terrorist activities. In truth, the Chechen problem needs to be resolved via political dialogue. Putin is able to mislead public opinion in Russia but not in the West. As a first step, therefore, media censorship should be removed so that the Chechen issue and its resolution can be widely and openly debated in Russia.

However, when questioned by pollsters about their readiness to part with their freedoms in order to rein in terrorism, Russians reacted overwhelmingly in support of the necessary restrictions. Toward the end of 2004, opinion polls dealing with terrorism revealed respondents' all-out willingness to surrender many freedoms in order to stamp out terrorism: As many as 57 percent were willing to let the secret services freely eavesdrop on telephone conversations and intercept mail, and a staggering 82 percent were willing to allow the police to check their documents on the street.

Russians, however, expressed their desire to preserve their basic political freedoms to protest, strike, and vote in elections.

Jordan and Matlock weighed in with their negative assessment of the Russian security agencies' potential for holding terrorism at bay. According to Jordan, "The biggest threat to Russia's security is corruption. No security policy will protect the country if it is undermined by corruption. . . . more direct measures to reform the police, the military, and the intelligence agencies should form the bulk of reforms aimed at improving security." In Matlock's judgment, "Russia will not be able to deal with terrorism effectively until it greatly reduces the corruption of its security organs. There is no easy solution, given what has happened [in Beslan] and the culture of revenge that is common in the region. Simply granting Chechnya independence will not work; the result would be more like Afghanistan under the Taliban than Algeria after the French left. It will be a long struggle that Russia can win only if most Chechens are convinced that they must oppose the terrorists."

Besides terrorism control, Putin provided additional arguments for enhancing presidential powers. The need arose from the danger posed to national integrity by a virtually nonfunctioning federal system that he had inherited as president in early 2000. In a series of interviews in Russia and abroad, he resolutely affirmed his belief that Russia will evolve into a liberal federal system at its own pace. Again, given the imperfect U.S. electoral procedures, U.S. leaders, he said, should stop lecturing to him.

The Nonfunctioning Russian Federation

The 1993 constitution formally designed Russia as a federal state. In practice, its execution fell short of genuine federal arrangements. The necessary checks and balances at the center were inadequate. Because the requisite institutions were missing, state authority across the hierarchy from the center to the periphery could not be exercised. At every level, rulers could not be held accountable because election procedures were less than perfect and legal safeguards could not be implemented. Again, while the Russian federation's political makeup at the time of Putin's election to the presidency in 2000 was disorderly, its economic management also lacked a uniform, legal infrastructure. A 2001 report by the Organization for Economic Cooperation and Development (OECD) characterized the situation thus: "There is no unified economic space, no 'level playing field' for businesses in Russia, because of the multitude of administrative barriers and obstacles encountered by investors, particularly at the regional level, often in contravention of federal legislation and regulation." Consequently, during Putin's first term as president and under Prime Minister Kasyanov's initiative, a spate of federal laws was enacted. These laws conformed to international norms, but Russian oligarchs created bottlenecks in their regional enforcement.

Laws and the Oligarchs: A Russian Conundrum

There is much evidence that the capture of prized assets (e.g., oil, automobiles, aluminum, and nickel) in strategic sectors in the mid-1990s contributed to regional noncompliance with federal laws: The oligarchs who seized these resources employed their financial clout to strong-arm government authorities, the judiciary, and the media at the regional level. They sought to undermine the federal laws as well. Thus, while Khodorkovsky developed Yukos as Russia's best-managed private oil company, his intrusive political blueprint extended to sabotaging the ongoing legislative houseclean-ing at the federal level, according to an October 15, 2004, interview in *Nezavisimaya Gazeta* with German Gref, trade and economic development minister and staunch pro-market, antimonopoly policy maker. While describing the federal prosecutor's Yukos investigation of charges of fraud and tax evasion as "cheap populism," Gref also highlighted Khodorkovsky's heavy-handed tactics for amending federal laws in favor of his business: "I don't think much of Khodorkovsky. He once said to my face: 'Sorry, but either you repeal this law, or we'll replace you. It's your choice.' "

Vyugin also referred to the government's inability to impose a "windfall tax" on the oil companies' profits according to IMF norms (before such a tax was even-tually imposed in 2003): "The government made two attempts without success. Why? Because some oil companies actively worked against the adoption of these bills by the Duma. This is one example. It is possible to find others as well."

Yukos: The Oil Oligarch versus the Russian State

Not surprisingly, the protracted trial of Khodorkovsky, which ended in June 2005, when he was sentenced to a nine-year prison term, was mounted in late 2003 to pre-empt the company's politically motivated strategy of influencing the December 2003 Duma vote. The winning slate of Yukos-led legislators could support the company's agenda (as Gref hinted) of low taxes on natural resources and of private ownership of oil and natural gas fields and pipelines. For example, should a new pipeline be con-structed to deliver oil to China (as Yukos would have liked) rather than to Japan (as the energy ministry preferred)? Shouldn't foreign-policy considerations be introduced in the decision making? Finally, the prosecution raised the ominous issue of whether the Yukos trial and its outcome would serve as a model for other offenders whom the prosecutors might choose to consign to the same category.

Yukos: The December 2003 Duma Election and the Company's Political Agenda

With vast financial resources at his command, Khodorkovsky was bent on in-fluencing the composition of the Duma resulting from the December 2003 elec-tion. His financial support extended to political parties and groups across the ideological spectrum, from the liberal Union of Right Forces led by Nemtsov, to the center-left Yabloko of Yavlinsky, to the Communist Party of the Russian Federation. At the same time, Khodorkovsky reportedly supported as many as seventy single-member constituencies.

In effect, the extravagant campaign financing by Yukos was predicated on a loophole in Russia's election law, which set limits on the overall campaign spending of contending parties and of single-mandate candidates and also restricted corporate contribution. Yet there were no restrictions on the number of parties or individual candidates that a corporation might choose to assist. Russian big business could thus manipulate election outcomes by spreading cash around in support of several parties and many candidates all at once. Yukos set out to do just that.

If even half of the seventy candidates under the company's banner were to win, that would qualify them under parliamentary rules to form a Duma group, which in turn had the right to elect its representatives in Duma committees and initiate legislation. Some might effectively stake their claim to inclusion in the future cabinet. Capturing these seats would therefore have given a strong institutional voice to Khodorkovsky in the Duma and perhaps in the government. In short, his tactics resembled the pre-1832 English-type "pocket boroughs," in which parliamentary representation was owed to a family or an individual.

At the very least, the prospective election hijacking by Yukos posed two challenges to Putin and his policy team. First, the winning slate of legislators could support the Yukos-led agenda on certain issues, such as no taxes on natural resources; private ownership of oil and natural gas pipelines; and the construction of new pipelines to deliver oil and natural gas to the United States, China, or Japan. Putin preferred to link decision making on some of these issues with foreign-policy considerations. Second, the resulting capture of the legislative agenda in the postelection Duma by a single corporation in a single sector, namely oil, threatened to create an out-of-kilter law-making body. The situation ran counter to the emergence of multiple Duma "lobbies" representing the interests of manufacturing, agricultural, or consumer groups, which could balance legislative deliberations.

The singularly uneven combat between the chair of Yukos and the president of Russia involved these complex economic, political, and legislative issues, which went far beyond the company's nonpayment of its tax liabilities. It was unlikely to be repeated in the case of other tax offenders.

Yukos as a Template

The tax authorities' claims of back tax payment by VimpelCom[61] and BP-TNK[62] raised concerns that the charges against these companies might take the Yukos trajectory. As I have argued, Yukos was dismantled to signal to the privatized companies that the state was not ready to let a single corporation in one sector influence legislation in favor of its business or to allow Russia's natural resources (e.g., oil and gas) to be controlled solely for private gain. The energy ministry reaffirmed that policy by announcing in March 2005 that only companies with 51 percent Russian ownership would in the future qualify to bid in auctions of oil and gas fields.

Furthermore, Gazprom, the natural gas monopoly, was converted into a 51-percent state-owned company, and its remaining stake was opened up for foreign and private Russian bidding. At the same time, the earlier "ring fence," in which the company's lower-priced domestic shares could be held only by Russian investors and the higher-priced American Depository Receipts on the New York Stock Exchange could be owned by foreign holders, was abolished. All in all, the fate of Yukos was tied with the establishment of state-imposed guidelines that defined the relationship between Russia's big business and state authority in the natural resources sector. The Yukos prosecution and the subsequent decisions in the energy sector established a decisive state presence, while allowing domestic oil companies and prospective foreign investors an active role in the sector.

At the same time, the privatized companies were ensured ownership of their assets. The Audit Chamber of the Duma, which investigated fifteen hundred companies, announced in late 2004 that their deprivatization was out of the question. Putin also declared in his State of the Nation address in April 2005 that the tax authorities' taxation powers would be brought under stricter legislative scrutiny. Throughout the long-winded Yukos prosecution, he had emphasized that Russian companies would remain privately owned. As early as April 2000, Gaidar had singled out Putin's adherence to private ownership while raising doubts about his commitment to a democratic order: "He does not have a good record in the field of democratic freedoms. . . . There are very few subjects in economic policy on which he is clear, but he has been clearest in his commitment to the protection of private property and his strong opposition to renationalization."

The State of the Media

The Russian president's controversial record in the field of media freedom has also raised concern. Putin's incomplete adherence to democratic norms was also evident in the government's establishment of selective control of the electronic media while leaving the printed press alone. Jordan provided details of his tenure as general manager of NTV, the television network, prior to his removal in early 2003 from that position. However, the excessive control and frequent intimidation of the media (as suggested by a *New York Times* editorial in December 2004) needs to be examined from a Yeltsin-era perspective. During the Yeltsin presidency, Russian TV networks and the press, strapped for money and lacking in advertisement revenues, turned to government bureaucrats and the cash-wielding oligarchs. The result? They became propaganda outlets for their sponsors, rather than independent information sources or competitive, rule-based businesses. According to the Russian Media Fund, a private U.S. media project, draconian Yeltsin-era laws constrained them from exploring avenues of financial sources and moving into the world of U.S.-style media culture. In particular, nonmedia oligarchs moved into the media business in order to take advantage of the tax exemption for profits enjoyed by media companies. Under Putin, the Yeltsin-era tax dodges have been eliminated, and advertising expenses have been made tax deductible, giving rise to more transparent sources of potential media support in an invigorated advertising market. While guaranteeing the security of past asset privatization with the exception of new rules for enhanced state ownership of energy resources, the government has selectively taken control of the three main TV channels and kept the freedom of the printed press intact.

All in all, the pace of the evolution of a liberal order in Russia, in Putin's view, will be dictated by the need to control terrorism and to guarantee compliance with federal laws in Russia's vast territory. Do the complicated maneuvers, especially the new presidential prerogative to appoint governors, violate the provisions of the Russian constitution?

How Flexible Is the Russian Constitution of 1993?

Articles 72 to 77 define Russia as a federal state that is based on the principle of people's sovereignty. The procedures for electing the executive heads of the eighty-nine constituent units of the federation are, however, unclear. Having energetically managed the adoption of the 1993 constitution, Yeltsin himself continued appointing governors until 1995. According to Putin, Russians will continue to elect their regional legislatures, which in turn will either approve or reject gubernatorial candidates proposed by the president. The procedural ambiguities of the constitution allow the federal executive this flexibility.

Will a lack of constitutional limits, combined with the escalating consolidation of political authority, convert Vladmir Putin, a former KGB operative and an avid judo master, into an absolute authoritarian leader? My interviewees expressed their concerns that the Russian constitution of 1993 lacked checks and balances. Rogov summed these up: "We adopted a constitution toward the end of 1993 that gave enormous authority to the executive without appropriate checks and balances. The legislative branch is weak and is dominated by the executive authority. The judiciary is not independent. . . . Yeltsin, the boyar, established democracy via the bureaucrats, who had no control from the legislative branch."

In particular, the constitution has a loophole that allows the executive to adopt critical measures via presidential decrees and government resolutions without involving the legislature. For example, Chubais pushed many decisions relating to asset privatization under Yeltsin in this manner with unusual speed and timing, occasional secrecy, and "dizzy with success" fervor, earning him the title of "neo-Bolshevik."[63] When the pro-Putin group, United Russia, gained majority power in the Duma in 2003, it effectively gave the executive initiative and control over the legislative process and government formation. In Yavlinsky's assessment, the current Russian government "is a technical department of the Kremlin. It is not a political institution."

Does Putin, however, need to justify his backtracking by introducing the imperfections of U.S. voting procedures?

Isn't the U.S. Democracy Less Than Perfect?

In this regard, Putin comes across as a tactical interlocutor wanting to score points in the transatlantic war of words. The U.S. presidential election process, in his view, is flawed because the popular vote is influenced by electoral college weights, thereby distorting the will of the people. The 2000 presidential election was again decided by the U.S. Supreme Court rather than the popular vote. In India, the world's largest democracy, governors, he said, are appointed by the center and not elected. However, his advisors overlooked the fact that the leading executives of Indian states are the chief ministers, who represent the winning party in the regional election rather than the governors.

In his interview, Rogov also brought up a comparative perspective by highlighting the less-than-linear progression of U.S. democracy: "[W]e must not make the mistake of . . . thinking that the West has always been democratic. If you take the United States, women were given the right to vote only eighty years ago. When I first went to the United States thirty years ago as a postgraduate student, I could see 'for blacks only' signs on benches and in buses in the South. . . . In the 1950s, U.S. democracy was different from what it was in the 1990s." In a later interview, Rogov also expressed a no-holds-barred view of Bush's current agenda of spreading democracy around the globe: "I have serious reservations about the standards of democracy Bush proclaimed and how he plans to apply them in Saudi Arabia, Pakistan, and Egypt. . . . There is a wide gap between the rhetoric and the reality in Bush's position."

Nemtsov was forthright in his emphasis that Russia does not have to copy the norms of the U.S. model: "Russia has a totally different history. The government structure should reflect Russia's specific features. We must, however, live by the Russian constitution, its division of powers along the federal hierarchy, the free press, and political competition. These basic principles enshrined in the constitution of 1993 should be protected."

Simonia illustrated the U.S.-Russian contrast by emphasizing the tax-evasion practices of Russian oil companies: "There is no point in borrowing the U.S. model of private ownership of oil and not enforcing the U.S. model of tax payment, right? Oil companies here effectively pay a 15–20 percent corporate tax, which is lower than the rates that U.S. corporations pay."

While these comparisons with other countries raise tricky issues, Putin would be on surer ground if he were to justify his post-Beslan initiatives in terms of the vastly different U.S.-Russian historical contexts. Whereas in the United States, "We, the People" willingly surrendered some of their freedoms to the state, in Russia, the people must extract their political freedoms and economic choices from an authoritarian state of almost three centuries. The transformation of an empire into a republic is more arduous than the voluntary U.S.-style contract of citizens parting with some of their liberties in exchange for state protection. Again, the U.S. emphasis on the "rule of law" implies the protection of individual rights via due process and fair hearing, whereas Putin's emphasis in his early days on a "law-based state" *(pravovoye gosudarstvo)* and "dictatorship of laws" *(diktatura zakonov)* suggests that he wants the Russian state to be different from its arbitrary tsarist and Soviet makeup, under which offenders could be exiled to Siberia or the gulag.

Putin can also argue his case by relying on his significant popularity rating and invoking the support of the Russian people rather than of U.S. policy makers and analysts. How have they reacted to the political tightening?

The People and the President

On this issue—which encompasses Putin's political authority relating to gubernatorial elections, political party formation, terrorism control, and the excessive regulation of Russian businesses reflected in the protracted prosecution of Yukos— the majority of Russians express opinions that are decidedly middle-of-the-road and mature. Thus, in a late September 2004 poll, 55 percent opposed appointments of mayors and governors by higher authorities, warning their president against "tugging the administrative blanket" in his direction. According to an early November 2004 poll, more than 50 percent believed that Russia needed a robust opposition party; 30 percent were ready to vote for a united liberal party in the 2007 Duma election—a signal to Russia's squabbling liberal groups to set aside their personal differences and unite as a single party. Finally, in a December 2004 poll, 54 percent regarded Russian business as socially irresponsible but objected to Yukos-style "show trials" of corporations. Russians want their business groups to clean up their act, and they want Kremlin-backed law enforcers to curb their prosecutorial zeal.

These opinions, combined with Putin's favorable rating, suggest that, while Russians want their leader to exercise his power (бласть) as an authority figure, they desire that he remain fair and reasonable. The dialogue between the president and the people expressed in these polls is qualitatively different from the nonpaternalistic connection between elected leaders and the electors in Anglo-Saxon democracies.

In the midst of the controversies relating to the likely damage from the political tightening on democratic evolution, property rights, and media freedom, a serious concern has emerged with respect to its negative impact on economic reforms.

Has the reform momentum slowed under Putin's second presidency, which began in 2004? Have the Yukos prosecution and the enhanced role of the state in the energy sector irreversibly damaged the investment climate and prospective foreign participation in the Russian economy? How can the slowdown of economic growth in 2005 be arrested?

The Economy: Performance, Reform Slowdown, and Prospects for Foreign Investment Flows

The Russian economy emerged from the financial collapse and debt default of August 1998 with robust GDP growth in 2000, accompanied by solid macroeconomic health and reduction in household poverty.

The Performance of the Economy

During the five-year stretch from 2000 to 2004, the Russian economy improved remarkably on several fronts.

POSITIVE FEATURES The GDP growth rate, averaging 6–7 percent annually, placed Russia behind China and India among the fastest-growing global economies.[64] Government finances improved steadily over the period. Part of the surplus in the consolidated government budget was set aside in a stabilization fund, registering $35 billion in mid-2005. At that time, the foreign exchange reserves of the Central Bank of Russia amounted to $145 billion. Foreign debt had ceased to be a problem since the government had prepaid $15 billion of the $43 billion Soviet-era sovereign debt owed to the Paris Club creditors.[65] In 2004, the Moscow stock exchange rose by 8 percent, demonstrating a positive portfolio investment environment, and both Moodys and Standard and Poor's lifted their Russian investment rating that same year. Thirteen initial public offerings (IPOs) were earmarked to be made available to the public in 2005, in contrast to eight in the previous decade. At the same time, direct foreign investment flows rose from $6.8 billion in 2003 to $9.4 billion in 2004, moving into construction, retail businesses, the auto industry, and consumer goods, including processed foods.

There are, however, troubling negative features continuing into 2005 that fall into four categories.

TOO MANY POOR PEOPLE Although the relative share of poor people has steadily come down from its highest point at 30 percent to a current World Bank estimate of 17.8 percent, they remain deprived even by Russian standards. The poverty line is currently defined at monthly wages of 2,451 rubles (88 dollars). Again, the income gap is widening, with the top 10 percent of wage earners making nearly fifteen times as much as those in the bottom 10 percent in 2004, in contrast to the norm of less than five times in developed countries.[66] In the interest of poverty reduction, Putin's agenda of economic growth faces arduous challenges from a comparative perspective. Russia's per capita GDP is only about one-quarter that of the United States.

Second, monopolies dominate the economy to the exclusion of middle-level and small businesses.

TOO MANY MONOPOLIES, TOO FEW SMALL BUSINESSES Monopolies in the energy, metals, banking, and railroad sectors dominate the economy as they did in the past. A mere twenty-three businesses control one-third of output and one-sixth of employment in Russian industry. According to the latest Forbes listing, Russia has twenty-seven billionaires, third in global rank after Germany with fifty-seven. The related concentration of ownership threatens the tax authority's ability to raise revenue and the judiciary's clout in handling corporate misdeeds. Until antimonopoly and antitrust laws are successfully implemented, Russian big businesses will continue to exercise inordinate political influence. Again, small businesses have long played a minor role in employment and output creation. By September 2004, the number of small businesses employing no more than one hundred workers had risen by 10 percent—to 946,000,. However, companies of this size generated only 10–12 percent of the Russian GDP (in contrast to 50–60 percent in developed market economies) and provided employment to 19 percent of the workforce (in contrast to almost 70 percent in some European economies). At the same time, regional and local regulations and meddlesome bureaucrats, as in the days of the tsars and the Soviet-era Communists, have stifled the small business environment.

Third, the resurgent economy, buoyed by vast export earnings from the oil, energy, and metals sectors, is unbalanced.

THE NATURAL RESOURCES VERSUS THE REST OF THE ECONOMY The Russian infrastructure is crumbling. The transportation and railroad rolling stock, the ports and bridges, and the electric power generators and turbines of Soviet days need to be replaced, which calls for massive investments. The strong ruble has put the Russian manufacturing sector at a disadvantage because it buys more items denominated in weaker foreign currencies and attracts imports. At the same time, the Central Bank's emission of rubles, in exchange for its acquisition of foreign exchange, has added to inflationary pressures. In fact, lowering the annual inflation rate from its current 10–12 percent and moderating the real appreciation of the ruble are the twin policy challenges facing the Central Bank. In his budget message to the Parliament, Putin singled out inflation control as one of the top governmental priorities.

The final negative feature is linked with the Yukos prosecution and the associated excessive tax claims. Have they irretrievably damaged the investment climate?

YUKOS PROSECUTION, TAX COLLECTION, AND INVESTMENT FLOWS The rate of investment in the economy has slowed down—from 17 percent in 2000 to 11 percent in 2004. At the same time, capital outflows have risen—from $3–5 billion in 2003 to $8–12 billion in 2004. Some capital undoubtedly moved out in search of higher returns abroad. In his final interview, Dubinin underscored the emerging imbalance between the falling investment rate and the strong consumption demand. Kasyanov worried about the loss of investor confidence, which he had bolstered during his tenure as prime minister: "From 2000 to 2004, as prime minister, I had worked hard to create a proinvestment environment. Potential foreign investors wondered why they were being asked to invest in Russia when domestic investors were holding back. We managed to induce local businesses, especially in the oil sector, to expand their investment. That in turn attracted foreign investors. That process has virtually stopped."

The lower investment and GDP growth rates, the latter a disappointing annualized 4.5 percent in the first quarter of 2005, are worrisome. The economy must grow at 7 percent plus in order to realize the presidential target of doubling it within a decade (by 2010).

The Yukos trial, the escalating tax demands, and the enhanced role for majority-owned Russian companies in the energy sector have evidently combined to dent domestic and foreign investor confidence. Yukos was set to wind down in 2005, but the expropriation of the company's minority foreign shareholders without compensation sent potential investors who were looking for gainful opportunities elsewhere. In addition, the negative impact of rising tax claims on investment activity brought some tax dodgers to their senses and raised the compliance level. Speaking at a London press conference in mid-December 2004, Russian finance minister Alexei Kudrin, another pro-market government member, clarified the situation: "Strict tax demands on Yukos and others influenced many companies operating in the black market economy to start operating legally in the past two years. A mass exodus from black market operations is under way. This will considerably lower the number of tax claims in the next two to three years."

According to the London-based Center for Economic Policy Research, stricter tax enforcement prompted companies to disclose their financial position accurately, forcing them to clean up their balance sheets, adopt Western accounting standards, close opaque subsidiaries, and occasionally list their shares on international stock exchanges. In his budget message to the Russian parliament in May 2005, Putin also extended an olive branch to tax defaulters. He suggested adopting legislation that would provide tax payers a government grant of deferment or installment payment of their tax liabilities following approval by the tax authorities. The reform of the renegade tax code will contribute positively to the tax enforcement environment.

Will foreign investors, especially the super majors, step into Russia's energy sector in a minority role?[67] Around the world from the Middle East to Nigeria,

Mexico, and Venezuela, oil and natural gas fields, energy companies, and their related pipelines have increasingly come under state ownership and management. At
the same time, the Russian energy sector badly needs new technologies and management expertise, which foreign private investors can supply only if the rules of
engagement are stable, predictable, and transparent. Lacking such rule-based participation, Gazprom converted into a 51-percent state-owned behemoth and will
likely remain a corruption-prone, bureaucratized black box. According to Gaidar
and Dubinin, it needs to be cracked open.

These energy sector maneuvers, combined with Putin's political tightening,
have raised the bigger issue of whether economic reforms have slowed down.

Economic Reform Momentum: Is There a Slowdown?

Yes, according to former prime minister Kasyanov, whose government introduced a series of pro-market reforms during Putin's first term as president (2000–
2004). For example, Kasyanov's government successfully steered measures through
the Duma related to the adoption of a tax code (which had a uniform personal tax
rate of 13 percent and lowered the corporate tax rate from 35 to 24 percent), a land
transactions bill, a criminal code, and a joint stock company law. These pro-market
initiatives were, however, combined with a handful of reversals in the existing
constitutional provisions. The upper house of the Parliament, composed originally
of elected governors, was converted into a rubber-stamping body of presidential
appointees;[68] Kremlin-vetted loyalists were appointed in seven sectors of Russia
with a view to making regional laws conform to federal norms; media restrictions
went into effect on the eve of the December 1999 Duma election. These illiberal
political measures were later supplemented by the parliamentary adoption of the
post-Beslan proposals.

Despite Putin's consolidating impetus, which had already begun in 2000, Malia
provided a perceptive argument in support of Putin's pro-market orientation in his
pre-Beslan interview:

> To speculate a bit on the basis of very little evidence, I would say that one of the
> traumatic experiences of Putin's life must have been his experience in East Ger-
> many, for while there he witnessed the complete collapse of the Soviet system, a
> system in which he believed when he joined the KGB in 1975. This could only
> have impressed on him the extraordinary vulnerability of that system and the con-
> trasting dynamism of its rival, which he had always been taught to hate as "capital-
> ism." . . . Putin could only have concluded that what he had been brought up to
> believe was progress for Russia—that is, socialism—was in fact a burden. The cor-
> ollary of this was that Russia had to chuck the old Muscovite ways of Stalin and
> adopt the new modern ways of the so-called capitalist world. So, when he returned
> to St. Petersburg after having lost his job in East Germany, he joined the reformers.

In contrast, Yeltsin's leading reformers, Gaidar and Nemtsov, argued that, with political tightening, the pace of economic reforms had slackened. According to Nemtsov, Putin believes that Russia needs a healthy market economy, but, "unfortunately, he doesn't believe that Russia also needs a democracy. It is difficult to explain to someone with a KGB background that a connection exists between democracy and competitive markets. That is the real difference between Putin and Yeltsin. Yeltsin believed in this connection in his very soul, especially after he visited the United States and went to a supermarket. 'I am for democracy, and I am for private business,' he said. He kept that pledge to the end of his career."

In his October 2004 interview, Gaidar had this to say: "In my opinion, the Russian government carried out a series of extremely important economic reforms between 2000 and 2002 under presidential initiative. Unfortunately, events in 2003 and 2004 suggest that economic reforms have slowed down just as the consolidation of political power has increased." Nemstov supported this position in his later December 2004 interview by emphasizing that "pension system reforms and restructuring of the energy complex have stopped. . . . The continuing consolidation of political power under Putin, on the other hand, has expanded the role of the bureaucracy without generating any positive benefits." In contrast, Jordan argued that Putin needed tighter political control to limit bureaucratic corruption: "I'm not sure that Putin views the consolidation of political power as necessary for promoting economic reform. I think he views the consolidation of control over his own bureaucracy as vital to promoting economic reforms. In fact, short of abolishing interventionist bureaucrats, control over the bureaucracy is vital for enforcing any policy whatsoever. The president's lack of control of the bureaucracy, by the way, is another reason this president can never become a Stalin even if he wanted to. The ground under him is very soft—wherever he steps, it gives way under corruption."

In my view, the challenges of economic reform facing Putin and his government during his second presidential term remain complex and have become more demanding. Budgetary management cannot be streamlined unless the Soviet-era real entitlements are converted into monetary payments that would affect as many as forty million recipients, including pensioners, veterans, and people with disabilities. These constituencies form a solid group that invariably turns up to vote in elections in favor of the Communist Party. Continued economic growth will also require head-on engagement with several powerful lobbies, including the entrenched bureaucracy, big business, and the military.

RECONSTRUCTING THE SOVIET-ERA SOCIAL WELFARE CONTRACT In January 2005, the governmental measures to monetize free travel allowances and medical benefits, which were to be followed by reduced subsidized utilities and housing, brought protests in Russian cities. As with the shock therapy reforms, the proposed changes were launched without public discussion. The cash payments for travel and medical benefits from the federal treasury to the regional distribution points were either delayed or inadequate. However, they were subsequently speeded up and suitably adjusted after the president publicly chastised the prime minister and the government ministers.

Further reforms of rent and utility charges by households are planned and will move forward with parliamentary approval. They represent a bold and desirable transformation of the Soviet-era social contract, the changes resembling the much-debated Social Security overhaul in the United States. Western media and analysts have concentrated their critical firepower on the public protests rather than assess them as sound economic initiatives. In pushing them forward, the government must balance the public's demands for higher monetary payments against the inflationary impact of more generous cash benefits. Having decided to concentrate on these issues, the government postponed the pension and education reforms, which would also have required increased budgetary allocations. In his May budget address, Putin suggested that the stabilization fund should not be used for monetary disbursements because they would add to inflationary pressures. The cabinet, on the other hand, raised the 2005 budget appropriations by 11 percent, a third of the additional allocation earmarked from the stabilization fund. The IMF, in turn, lifted the 2005 inflation rate from the current 10–12 percent to 13 percent. Vyugin aptly described the Russian budgetary process as a battleground for political fights.

Reforming the bureaucracy represents another intractable challenge.

REFORMING THE SOVIET-ERA BUREAUCRACY With regard to bureaucracy, Yavlinsky exhibited a chart with a Byzantine maze of more than forty regulatory agencies that must be cleared by Russia's small and medium units before they can set up shop. Russian bureaucracy grew unabated from 1994 to 2004, which includes the years of the Yeltsin presidency, from about 1.0 million to 1.26 million. A federal commission ruled that as many as 4,000 of the 5,300 activities of the federal government were essential. Kasyanov argued for the elimination of bureaucratic controls and the provision of infrastructural support to small businesses on transparent, competitive terms:

> Government funding can provide the necessary infrastructure in a transparent, predictable fashion with equal access to everyone. For example, if someone wants to start up a car repair shop, he can readily access the power and gas companies for electricity and heating. Right now, he does not feel sure of securing a bank loan for the purpose because the infrastructure support is missing.
>
> Then there is the problem of government regulations and countless inspections. The fire safety inspector suddenly appears and orders the unit closed. The health inspector raises problems, too. Everybody wants cash under the table. Corruption has exploded to unimaginable levels.

The new government formed in April 2004 slashed the number of federal ministries from twenty-four to fourteen, but many of them were absorbed as committees in the new structure. According to Nemtsov and Rogov, eliminating the bureau-crats' control of economic decision making will test the new government's com-mitment to generating growth and employment via small businesses.

In growing economies, low- and middle-level bureaucrats get absorbed in lucrative businesses, including stores, restaurants, and laundries, as well as numer-ous activities in the service sector. Such absorption calls for decisions about which activity to step into, how to raise the needed capital, where to locate the unit, whom to team up with—all demanding experience, networking skills, and the savvy for uncovering opportunities. The process caught on in China, Vietnam, and the East-ern European countries, in which the planned economy drive had left small busi-nesses more or less under private initiative, but not under the Soviet arrangements, in which complete state ownership and management of all activities had precluded the nurturing and accumulation of private-enterprise traditions and skills. The elimi-nation of a few ministries at the top, therefore, cannot jump-start the process of slashing the extensive bureaucracy.

Restructuring the monopolies, among them Gazprom, United Energy Ser-vices (the electric power company), and the railroads, represents another daunt-ing challenge.

REFORMING THE MONOPOLIES The process involves three major decisions. First, should the corporations be broken up into separate units before they are privatized? For example, should the electric power company be separated into separate power-generating units before these are sold off? Dubinin, in charge of the process as the company's deputy CEO, provided details of the momentous challenges he and his team face. Second, should the prices of the services these monopolies provide be decontrolled before they are broken up? The prices of passenger and railway freight and of natural gas and power for industry and households have gradually been raised, each time creating a blip in the price level, yet Gazprom charges its Russian cus-tomers 10 percent of world prices. Despite substantial earnings from its foreign hard-currency sales, the company is heavily in debt.

The profitability of these companies continues to be low because their charges remain below world prices. As a result, the minority foreign stakeholders in the electric power company, for example, vigorously object to the privatization of the power-generating units because they remain underpriced and may be captured by Russian bidders. Finally, the restructuring of the three companies is predicated on their division into natural monopolies on the one hand and the rest of the units on the other. For example, the power-generating units will eventually fall into private ownership, but the transmission lines involving huge fixed costs can stay under state management with respect to pricing to the ultimate buyer. Similarly, the rolling stock of the railroads needs to be separated from the tracks and other installations. Russian monopoly reform, which has become a buzzword for hasty commenta-tors, involves complicated decisions because of the excessive physical integration of the companies under Stalinist planning, as well as the internecine turf wars among the decision makers in the Kremlin, the relevant ministries, and the companies.

PROBLEMS OF MILITARY REFORM   The Russian military also needs to be reformed, and Russian policy makers are bent on improving the pay and technology of the military. As yet, however, there is no consensus on how this should be done. Nemtsov pointed out the difference between the plan for military overhaul proposed by his reformist group, the Union of Right Forces (SPS), and the alternative, Soviet-style changes favored by the generals: Putin "supports the top-level military bureaucracy by wanting to retain its privileged position in the military and combining it with Soviet-style military service at the lower, nonofficer level. The recruits must serve for two years with an additional year thrown in. . . . We in the SPS believe that the armed forces must be completely voluntary and well paid from the bottom up. The financial problems of higher pay scales [for the soldiers] . . . can be managed." These decisions will affect both the government's budget situation and the prospective labor market alternative for young men.

Finally, Russia is faced with a demographic crisis that will have damaging consequences for the long-term growth prospects of the economy. A clear immigration policy that can compensate for the decline in the natural population growth is missing.

THE DEMOGRAPHIC DILEMMAS   The numbers suggest a looming catastrophe. Russia's population declined by 1.8 million in 2003 and 2004, to 145 million by the end of 2004. The net inflow of immigrants in 2004 was a mere 40,000 in contrast to 840,000 in 1994. In his nuanced and persuasive interview, Vishnevsky painted a worsening long-term situation that defies standard solutions. The current decline in the birthrate, as in all developed countries, cannot, in his view, be arrested by incentives aimed at increasing family size: "The current contraction, the fourth since 1913, differs significantly from the previous three, which were caused by extreme social shocks—World War I and the civil war, famine, the repressions and purges of the thirties, and World War II. In contrast, the current loss is conditioned by stable changes in the demographic behavior of Russians. That is why one should not expect that it will be transitional and that a positive natural population growth will be reestablished in the near future, leading to an increase in the number of the country's residents. The Russian population will continue to decline in the future. All of the demographers agree on this prediction."

At the same time, the high mortality rate, especially among working-class men, which can be traced to "external causes" such as alcoholism, accidents, and suicide, cannot be countered by merely refurbishing the antiquated health care system. In Vishnevsky's view, the problem goes back to Soviet times: "Excessive mortality due to external causes is a Russian problem, but it is also an old problem. The gap between Russia and the Western countries has been increasing for decades. . . . In the last twenty-five years of its existence, the Soviet Union lagged behind the rest of the developed world in enforcing measures for fighting mortality. As a result, Russia began its transition in 1992 as a laggard. That was its Soviet heritage. To this day, no changes have occurred to alter the situation, so high mortality and low life expectancy continue to be predetermined by the strong inertia of the Soviet days."

In Vishnevsky's judgment, the solution calls for newfangled measures designed to raise workers' awareness and personal accountability via counseling and behavior modification. Russia's AIDS problem also needs to be tackled similarly.

Can the natural decline in population be countered by immigration? Vishnevsky provided the numbers: "In order to keep the population at 146 million people, the count at the turn of the current century, Russia would need to accept, on average, more than 700,000 immigrants on a net basis and gradually increase the inflow to 1.2–1.3 million by 2035. These are, of course, ballpark figures." Russians, however, do not support an active strategy for encouraging immigrants, even Russians from the neighboring states. Indeed, the fear of losing jobs to outsiders, including Russians, is reflected in Russia's citizenship law. It is so strict that few of the 20 million Russians left in the surrounding states would qualify for a Russian passport. According to Vishnevsky, "The locals see the outsiders as potential competitors in the labor market. Perhaps reflecting public sentiment, the Law on Citizenship passed on May 31, 2002, [and] imposed severe restrictions on applications for Russian citizenship. It was amended on November 11, 2003, and restored fairness with regard to former citizens of the Soviet Union. In reality, though, it acknowledges only that they can serve as stopgap additions for countering the shortages inherited from the breakup of the Soviet Union. Nothing more." In the long run, however, this diaspora could provide a solid solution for arresting the decline in natural population growth.

Not surprisingly, public reaction to immigrants from China and the Caucasus region tends to be xenophobic. That, too, cannot be remedied immediately. According to Vishnevsky, Russians have limited experience in dealing with the problems of cultural assimilation facing immigrants or in assessing their contribution to the economy. A poll taken on May 23, 2005, illustrates their negative reaction: Of sixteen hundred representative respondents, 63 percent believed that immigrants contributed to crime and corruption; 40 percent desired stricter immigration laws; and 60 percent believed that they take away jobs from local workers.

The influx of Chinese immigrants, especially in the Far Eastern province of Russia, poses a special problem. Pipes reminded me that the phrase "yellow peril" was coined in the late nineteenth century by the philosopher Vladimir Soloviev, who referred to the Chinese as the "yellow hordes." Nemtsov, Yavlinsky, and Vishnevsky wondered about the possibility of Chinese immigrants coming in massive numbers and staking claims on Russian territory. These fears are exaggerated. Chinese immigrants in Siberia, numbering some 200,000, come in temporarily as workers selling their low-wage services or as traders carrying cheap Chinese goods and then move back to China. Chinese entrants numbered only 20,000 in 2004, according to Chinese statistics. The official Russian policy stance, focused on regulating Chinese immigration, is robustly pragmatic and aims at resolving border disputes, furthering trade in military items, and exploring energy deals with China. Russian and Chinese military units carried out their first joint exercises in August 2005.

In contrast, U.S.-Russian relations, despite shared concerns over a number of issues, have been overtaken by marked inertia and mounting opposition over Putin's political consolidation.

Putin's Political Backtracking and U.S.-Russian Relations

These interactions have entered a different phase marked by converging interests and conflicting pressures. With the end of the Cold War, the demise of the Soviet Union, and the near oblivion of the Communist Party, the superpower ideological and military confrontations on a global scale seem to have receded into the past. These have been replaced by U.S.-Russian intrusive foreign-policy maneuvers in the new independent states in Russia's neighborhood. These interests diverged in Ukraine and Georgia but mostly converged in Kyrgyzstan and Uzbekistan, thereby testing the policy makers' judgments and tactical skills.[69] Russia, however, has become economically stronger, politically more stable, and diplomatically more visible. As a result, the greater Russian assertiveness under Putin has made the bilateral dialogue and decision making slow and at times contentious because Russian input has become relevant and, on occasion, indispensable.

Terrorism control, nonproliferation of nuclear armaments and weapons of mass destruction, and advancing U.S.-Russian nuclear parity are the major areas of common concern. Occasionally the negotiations tend to involve several countries around the world. The European Union stepped forward in helping the United States counter Iran's presumed plans for converting reactor fuel into nuclear material. Six negotiators, including the United States and Russia, are engaged in forestalling North Korea's program of advancing its nuclear capability. A UN conference on nuclear nonproliferation in late May 2005 failed to produce an agreement. In view of their massive nuclear arsenals and the rivalry surrounding the bilateral nuclear parity issue, neither the United States nor Russia, the participants insisted, could serve as exemplars of nuclear nonproliferation. Nevertheless, while the current problems will at times pull in many participants, their ongoing resolution will be driven by U.S. and Russian security interests.

In this context, the new fly in the ointment is the question of whether Putin's consolidation of political authority will revive the mistrust of the Cold War days and intensify U.S. moves to contain potential Russian adventurism in its neighborhood. Even the more tractable trade issues run the risk of being defined in political rather than economic terms. Russia's entry into the World Trade Organization (WTO), which requires bilateral U.S.-Russian agreement and abolition of the Jackson-Vanik Amendment by the U.S. Congress, made scant progress in 2005.[70]

Despite this caveat, the give-and-take will be driven by the mutual concern for terrorism control, which ranks at the top of U.S.-Russian cooperation.

Terrorism Control

The 9/11 terrorist attack on U.S. soil and the subsequent U.S. military operation in Afghanistan, resulting in the defeat of the Taliban, freed Russian armed forces from their long and arduous operation across the border from Tajikistan. It also transformed the Chechen war from a regional Russian conflict into an international terrorism arena, cementing U.S.-Russian relations on the issue. Indeed, the establishment of the U.S. air base near Tashkent in Uzbekistan was welcomed not only by the Uzbek president, Islam Karimov, but also won a nod of approval from Putin. The overthrow of the autocratic regime of former president Askar Akayev in Kyrgyzstan in April 2005 by a group of opposition politicians, as well as the subsequent bloody killings by Uzbeki armed forces on May 13 in the city of Andijon in Uzbekistan's Fergana valley, raised the specter of similar disturbances spreading into central Asia. The threat of Islamic fundamentalists replacing the autocratic Soviet-era presidents in these states and destabilizing the region pulled the U.S. and Russian presidents into closer cooperation. It will perhaps dampen the U.S. administration's mission of spreading democracy beyond Ukraine and Georgia for fear that the domino dynamics of a democratic order may instead morph into more repressive autocracies or Islamic regimes in central Asia.

Terrorism control also spills over into U.S. concerns about the safety of Russia's nuclear facilities despite Rogov's bland assertion that Russia does not have "loose nukes." These facilities remain inadequately guarded. Guards "protect" them without loaded weapons, turn off alarm systems, and leave security doors open.[71] By late 2004, about 60 percent of Russian nuclear installations, including an estimated sixteen thousand warheads, had undergone U.S.-funded upgrade.[72] Beyond the upgrade, Russian defense ministry officials object to joint U.S.-Russian oversight of these facilities. In their view, current Russian legislation prohibits such a procedure. U.S. concern that the safety procedures are not accident proof and that nuclear material might fall in terrorist hands due to human error remains an irritant in the relationship.

The Russian perspective holds that safeguarding existing nuclear facilities is a separate subject from developing new systems. This distinction complicates progress in resolving the issue of bilateral nuclear parity.

Whither Nuclear Parity?

Russian defense specialists wonder whether Russia is included as a target in the "axis of evil" floated by the Bush administration.[73] While the technological parameters and economic costs of developing a missile defense system are debated in the United States, Russians fear that it might be used against Russia.[74] Despite their consistently steadfast liberal credentials, Nemtsov and Yavlinsky argued that bilateral nuclear parity must be negotiated without demands for undue concessions from the Russian side. Safeguarding strategic security interest is every politician's primary concern across Russian party lines. New and advanced missile systems will therefore continue to be developed. Indeed, from the Russian perspective, these weapons of last resort can serve as the ultimate, "just-in-case" guarantors of protection against a variety of dangers, real or imagined: a unilateral, U.S. military move, as in Iraq; NATO's military incursion in Russia's traditional area of interest; possible Chinese claims on Russian territory; an Islamic nuclear threat; and so on.

The exaggerated perception of external threat and the overreaction to safeguard Russian security by developing advanced weapons systems are often associated in the Russians' view with the defeat and humiliation that followed the dissolution of the Soviet Union. Every defeat on the battlefield after the Crimean War of 1854–1856, the Russo-Japanese War of 1904–1905, and the two world wars was followed by a military buildup and a determination to start anew. Reflecting on the combined U.S.-European consensus directed against Putin and Russia, Rogov noted the "siege" mentality: "It is clear that Russia is not a superpower now. In the last fifteen years, Russia faced the predicament of a country that had lost a war—the Cold War. Therefore, it must play according to the rules of the victors, we are told. Russia's interests should not be taken into account. Russia is not ready to accept this, however. It does not want to be told, as was the case in the 1990s, what economic policies Russia should adopt and how it should conduct its relations with neighboring states."

Putin's recent characterization of the dissolution of the Soviet Union as "the greatest geopolitical disaster of the twentieth century" also symbolizes this subjective Russian view of the defeat, loss, and humiliation associated with the event to his deliberate exclusion of reference to the repression imposed by Soviet rule both inside the country and out.

However, with the protective nuclear umbrella in place, Putin's operational mode consists of stabilizing Russia's interests by accepting the fait accompli when inevitable; sorting out border disputes; and promoting bilateral economic interests, rather than flexing military muscle. In any case, he does not have the numbers. The size of the armed forces has declined from four million at its height to a little more than a million. Its upkeep is poor and its morale is low. The Russian economy, despite its recent upbeat performance, has a lot of catching up to do. The line of least resistance reflects Putin's pragmatic assessment of these limitations.

Promoting Russian Interests in the Neighborhood—Nonmilitarily

NATO's continuing eastward expansion to include the Baltic states is a case in point. In due course, Ukraine's admission to NATO will bring the alliance to Russia's doorstep. In early June 2005 opinion polls, less than 20 percent of Ukrainians voted in favor of NATO entry. Moreover, the Ukraine constitution disallows such an alliance. However, the constitution will be changed, and NATO propaganda can be counted on to overcome voter resistance. Given this inevitability, Putin's response is to make the most of the opportunities afforded by the antiterrorism military cooperation under NATO.[75] For example, joint U.S.-Russian military exercises can diffuse the Russian military's misgivings and fears over encirclement of Russia by a string of newly admitted NATO members. One has to be a Cold War–era hawk to justify NATO's advance as a defensive military alliance for preempting Russian military adventurism or territorial excursions in the former Soviet satellite countries. On the other hand, Ukraine's NATO membership may have prompted Putin's accommodating maneuvers designed to resolve neighborhood disputes. For example, the border conflicts with the Baltic countries are to be settled bilaterally via negotiations. The early June 2005 agreement to pull out the Russian military base from Georgia in 2008 follows a similar approach. Settlements were also reached to exchange border territories with China.

These accommodating decisions complement continuing efforts to seek out economic and trading opportunities in Ukraine, Georgia, and the Baltic states. Kazakhstan and the central Asian states also figure as competitive arenas for Russian and Western companies. The historical ties, the neighborhood factor, the supply of natural gas and power via existing pipelines and transmission grids, and the continuing presence of Russian as a common language give Russian businesses an edge. According to Kasyanov, "Russia will continue to be a global player, especially in the regions where, because of its history and geography, it has continuing interests and responsibilities." In the Soviet days, the Moscow-based Academy of Science specialists characterized the economic activities of U.S. multinationals in Latin America as "neocolonial exploitation." Russia's economic forays in the neighborhood will open up opportunities for similar investigations by concerned Western analysts. Chubais fired the first salvo providing such analytical fodder when he suggested that Russia should operate as a "liberal empire" in its neighborhood.[76]

Russian businesses would acquire a powerful pro-market nudge both inside and out if Russia were admitted to the World Trade Organization. Membership in the WTO would impose obligations on Russia but would also create trading and investment opportunities. What are the prospects for Russia's entry into this world body?

Russia and WTO Accession

Indeed, Russia's entry into the organization, which requires bilateral support from the United States, has taken on overtones of a contentious political issue as a result of mounting opposition in the U.S. Congress associated with Putin's illiberal measures. Senators John McCain, a presidential contender, and Joseph Lieberman, a former vice presidential candidate, have called for Russia's expulsion from the G8.[77] Prior to the politicization of the issue, the major bilateral bone of contention was the U.S. demands for the protection of intellectual property rights (IPR) in

Russia. Although the Duma has passed an IPR law, its implementation is weak. Piracy of foreign films, CDs, DVDs, and pharmaceuticals in Russian markets is widespread. According to Russian specialists, however, such violations pale before the brazen piracy practices in China, already a WTO member.

Besides, with each negotiating phase, Russia is being held to stricter standards. For example, Russian negotiators regard the demands that Russia scale back its protective regime for its agriculture as unfair not only because the United States and the EU subsidize Russia's agriculture but also because agricultural protection automatically declined substantially in the 1990s as Russia's federal budget suffered massive deficits. While the WTO's working groups are sorting out the economic issues, political pressures remain paramount in the U.S. Congress. Congress is unlikely to revoke the Jackson-Vanik Amendment to the Trade Act of 1974, which linked the granting of the most-favored-nation trade status to Russia with Jewish immigration. Its abolition could pave the way for Russian membership in the WTO and adherence by Russian businesses to international practices that Vyugin talked about in his interview: "WTO membership is useful in creating psychological confidence at various levels. Foreign investors know that a WTO member must follow internationally accepted norms and rules. They may not be stringent, but a member country has accepted established codes of conduct in foreign trade, global finance, and the like. It may not produce tangible results right away, but outside investors feel that a WTO member will not suddenly go off a policy track. From that perspective it is useful."

Everything considered, U.S.-Russian relations have reached a stalemate if not a dead end. In contrast, the shared interests under the Reagan-Gorbachev and Clinton-Yeltsin presidencies transformed the bilateral negotiations into an energetic joint enterprise. Under Putin, on the other hand, despite the common interests, the United States has lost the decisive edge. George W. Bush drove Vladimir Putin's car on the Kremlin grounds, but he is no longer in the driver's seat in navigating the bilateral policy agenda.

U.S.-Russia Relations in Limbo

The new circumstances raise two fundamental issues. Bad as the situation is under Putin from the U.S. perspective, what should the immediate U.S. policy stance be? Second, what are the long-term prospects for a liberal order in Russia?

The Short-Term Scenario

The short-term response from the U.S. policy makers requires a clear understanding of how extensively and in what way Russian society changed under Yeltsin, who further cemented the new freedoms Russians began experiencing under Gorbachev.

- According to Kasyanov, "Russians today are a different people, despite the fact that a majority lived in the Soviet Union and remember the old times. It is a different country. In fact, it is a different society." Dubinin supported that assessment fully. Russians can choose their jobs, select their place of residence, own property, travel, strike, and protest. Under Putin, despite the consolidating political measures, including selective media restrictions, these freedoms have remained intact.
- Yeltsin and his reformers, however, failed to establish the institutions of a liberal democracy and a free market economy. Despite the state's enhanced role in the energy sector, Russian industry, including the oil sector, remains in private ownership.
- Progress in economic reform is slow, but the new challenges that I noted earlier are tougher. The government is proreform, especially Finance Minister Alexei Kudrin, Trade and Development Minister German Gref, and Anatoly Chubais, who is still in charge of the electric power company.
- The daunting challenge facing this reformist team is to revive investors' confidence in the midst of the receding Yukos fallout and to rein in inflation pressures. These pressures arise as the Central Bank issues rubles against its acquisition of petrodollars and as the government uses tax money, collected from the oil industry, to pay cash to the public in order to replace the Soviet-era real entitlements. Given the double whammy, the need of the hour is clear: The tax claims should be properly assessed and moderated, and foreign investment should be facilitated across the board via clear, stable, and predictable signals in order to keep economic growth on track. Putin's recent pronouncements call for the tax authorities and the government to make the necessary policy shift.
- In general, Putin comes across as a pragmatic leader, fully aware of the complexities of operating in the international arena and conscious of the critical voices emanating from Europe and the United States. He will host the G8 summit in St. Petersburg in the summer of 2006. At the same time, he is fending off pressure from the *siloviki,* from Russian nationalists eager to restore the past glory of the homeland, and from the Russian masses bent on improving their lives.[78]
- As the United States moves forward with the development of missile defense technology, Putin, however, has the full support of both the military and my Russian interviewees on maintaining Russian nuclear parity with the United States and developing new strategic weapons. Subject to this caveat, Putin's accommodating stance reflects his calculated attempts to promote Russian interests in the context of the country's current weaknesses.

The question then is, What guiding principle should U.S. negotiators follow so that bilateral cooperation in areas of mutual interest remains on track?

As a watchful insider, Rogov viewed the current situation with concern: "We are struggling with the historic issue of whether Russia can become a mature liberal state in isolation from other developed democracies. Russia must meet certain norms if it wants to belong to that group, but it cannot accomplish that goal in isolation. I am seriously concerned about the escalating attempts to throw U.S.-Russian relations back to the Cold War days. These voices are vocal not only in the United States and in Europe but in Russia as well. It can become a self-fulfilling prophecy."

Talbott firmly disagreed with Senators McCain and Lieberman, who called for Russia's expulsion from the G8. Instead, he suggested a Skinner-type incentive-cum-penalty stratagem so that Putin can continue to pursue a liberal course: "[T]he [G8] group is due to gather . . . in St. Petersburg in the summer of 2006. Putin's desire for an upbeat meeting gives the other seven some leverage. If they close ranks behind George W. Bush and Tony Blair and acknowledge that the Group of Eight has a Putin problem, they can use the next sixteen months for a campaign of quiet, calibrated diplomacy. If Putin allows adverse trends in Russia to continue, his guests in St. Petersburg will go public with their disappointment. They would provide an incentive for him and his successors to keep Russia on a reformist course."

I asked Matlock how he, as a seasoned diplomat, assessed the intensely personal relationship between Bush and Putin as a negotiating template. Commenting on the "self-serving rhetoric" of "looking into the soul and the eyes of a foreign leader," he brought up the theme of the positive effect that the "brutal" private frankness of Reagan and Bush Sr. had on Gorbachev. Nonetheless, as he noted, "Once the relationship developed, they were less so in public, but they refrained from saying anything terribly misleading. So I think we should encourage our presidents to develop close personal relations. We do not gain anything from open hostility of the kind that occurred between George W. Bush and Jacques Chirac. When things get to that point, they are bad for both countries. At the same time, it is important to define our interests, prioritize them, and trade off a minor concession to protect a critical advantage. Such tradeoffs may offend some bureaucrats who are used to focusing on a specific objective rather than balancing several of them. However, that's what we elect our presidents to do, rightly or wrongly, and that's what we pay them for."

In 1988, Ronald Reagan provided an operational rule for dealing with Gorbachev in order to advance U.S. interests: "Doveryay, ny proveryay," meaning "trust, but verify." Currently, the trust is damaged, so the rule needs to be inverted: "Proveryay, ny doveryay," meaning "verify, but trust." At each stage of negotiating a shared interest, it is important to first verify all of the relevant parameters, offer feasible tradeoffs, formulate an agreement, and trust the process to work.

The more demanding question relates to long-term U.S.-Russian relations in the context of Russia's evolution to a democratic order.

What Are the Prospects for a Transition
to a Liberal Political Order?

My interviewees suggested that Russia's progress toward a liberal political order will sometimes continue to appear endangered, certainly by the standards that apply to an advanced liberal order of the U.S. or European variety.

Rogov was quite articulate about the need for an appropriate perception of the unfolding political order in Russia. "Of course, we have limited experience with democracy. For a millennium or more, Russia was an autocratic country with imperial authority or Soviet-style ideology. . . . I think that democracy here will take longer to mature than I would like."

While lamenting the slowed pace of economic reform, Gaidar remains optimistic about the progress already achieved.

> There is a definite consensus among Russian society and the elite that Russia needs a market economy. However, arguments persist over policy choices with a view to improving the standard of living of the thirty million Russians who live below the governmental poverty level. Nobody argues about the need for market prices, a convertible ruble, and private property. These are firmly and irreversibly in place. By contrast, our struggle to form a robust, functioning democracy has not brought decisive results. On the other hand, its long-term prospects are positive. I do not think that the educated, urban populations in large countries such as Russia can put up with undemocratic regimes for long.

Matlock made two broad observations: "While Russia under Putin is regressing in terms of democracy, I never really understood why some thought it would be easy or automatic for Russia to suddenly become a democracy. When I was in Moscow in the eighties and nineties, I was asked by Russians how long it was going to take for them to become a normal country. They didn't then say 'a democratic country' but rather 'a normal country.' I would respond by saying, well, at least two generations. They are a little more than halfway through the first. I also think that the United States has very little leverage over the current internal developments in Russia. The Russians themselves will decide how to manage the process."

In managing the end of Soviet Communism, the Yeltsin team went up in flames, but it earned a place in history for implanting the powerful ideas of democracy and markets in an inhospitable environment. Viewed in a historical context, it is a monumental achievement. Despite the consolidating impetus under Putin, the kamikaze crew's liberal legacy will ultimately prevail because Russians are changing. Nevertheless, can a fully democratic Russia become a U.S. partner? According to Rogov, it would be difficult for Russia to be a "junior partner," reminding me that, in the old days, Bulgaria used to be the Soviet Union's junior partner. Russia will eventually embrace liberal values and gain economic stability. However, unlike Europe and Japan, it will have geopolitical interests in its neighborhood—along its southern borders and in the Far East. While subscribing to U.S. values, Russia's leaders might choose to define their interests independently. Ironically, the years under Gorbachev and Yeltsin, during which these principles and interests coincided, turned out to be rewarding for the United States as well, but brief. In my view, the future does not guarantee a bilateral identification of shared values and interests. The United States will remain an economic and military front-runner, but sorting out the geopolitical issues with a reconstructed Russia will keep the U.S. leadership fully engaged in demanding win-lose dialogues and "verify-but-trust" decision making.

NOTES

1. Martin Malia (Z), "To the Stalin Mausoleum," *Daedalus* 119 (Spring 1990): 295–344. In the article, Malia argues that Gorbachev's limited measures, aimed at reforming the CPSU, were unlikely to bring democracy or free markets to the Soviet Union.

2. In developing these ideas, I draw from the insights provided by Alexander Gerschenkron, my former teacher at Harvard University.

3. An absolute monarch, Peter the Great enhanced the power of the state and subordinated the church. He created a modern, educated military, including the navy. The building of St. Petersburg under his rule was a massive investment project carried out under state direction.

4. Under tsars Alexander III and Nicholas II, Count Sergey Yulevich Witte oversaw Russia's whirlwind industrialization as minister of finance from 1892 to 1903 and subsequently as prime minister from 1905 to 1906.

5. Count Piotr Arkadevich Stolypin, Witte's successor as prime minister from 1906 to 1911, launched agrarian and educational reforms by executive decrees after dismissing the second Duma in 1907. As governor of Saratov from 1903 to 1905, he had repressed the peasant rebellions in the revolution of 1905.

6. Alexander Gerschenkron, *Economic Backwardness in Historical Perspective: A Book of Essays,* 148–49.

7. Ibid., 125.

8. The Crimean War pitted Russia against the Ottoman Empire, France, and England over Russian possession of the Crimean peninsula and parts of the Ottoman Empire and its intent to take over Constantinople (present-day Istanbul). Despite its opponents' high casualties and lack of supplies, Russia was defeated.

9. The Russo-Japanese War (1904–1905) was fought over conflicting interests by the two adversaries in Manchuria and Korea and resulted in a surprise victory for the Japanese. The United States negotiated a peace treaty in which Russia did not lose much territory but suffered a humiliating loss of face at home and abroad.

10. Nikita Sergeevich Khrushchev served from 1953 to 1964 as first secretary of the CPSU and as premier of the USSR. He was deposed from the latter position in 1964 for his foreign-policy faux pas, destabilizing agricultural measures, and erratic personal behavior. His de-Stalinization speech at the Twentieth Party Congress in 1956 was his lasting contribution.

11. Leonid Ilich Brezhnev was general secretary of the CPSU from 1964 to 1982. His tenure was marked by economic stagnation. He formulated the "Brezhnev Doctrine," which asserted that the Soviet Union could intervene in any Soviet bloc country if Communist rule there were threatened.

12. Gerschenkron, *Economic Backwardness in Historical Perspective*, 60.

13. The Emancipation Decree was released on February 19, 1861, under the reign of Emperor Alexander II. The document formally outlined the serfs' rights of personal freedom, trading, and social movement.

14. The long tradition of merchants and industrialists contributing to the church had, by the late nineteenth century, turned to the promotion of arts and education. Thus, Pavel Tretyakov, the successful merchant, converted his art collection into the famous Tretyakov Gallery. According to Gerschenkron (60–61), the religious and social activity of nineteenth-century Russian businessmen, "repentant noblemen" all, was motivated by the fact that, by the accepted norms of the time, theirs was a sinful life. Lopakhin emerged from a similar conflict between acquisitive materialism and spiritual emptiness.

15. Gerschenkron, *Economic Backwardness in Historical Perspective*, 126.

16. Ibid., 20.

17. Catherine the Great, Russia's "enlightened" monarch, ruled from 1762 to 1796. Born Princess Sophia Augusta Frederica Anhalt-Zerbst in Stettin, Prussia, Catherine was involved in a plot to kill her husband, Emperor Peter III, whom she succeeded.

18. Gerschenkron, *Economic Backwardness in Historical Perspective*, 135.

19. Alexander III, the second son of Alexander II, became heir to the throne after his brother, the crown prince, died in 1865. He became emperor in 1881, following his father's assassination. He is credited with a strict autocratic rule and Russia's early industrial revolution.

20. Gerschenkron, *Economic Backwardness in Historical Perspective*, 121. The Junkers (from German "young lord") were the landed aristocracy of Prussia and Eastern Germany from the nineteenth century through the Weimar Republic. After 1871, the land-owning Junkers were the "rye" in the famous "alliance of iron and rye," with big industry as the "iron." The alliance pursued protectionist, proindustrial policies that led to Germany's technological development.

21. Ibid., 142.

22. Nikolay Ivanovich Bukharin, a revolutionary and Communist theorist, was editor of *Pravda* in the early 1920s. As a full member of the politburo in 1924, he opposed Stalin's call for rapid industrialization. The defeat of his faction led to his repression, subsequent public trial, and execution.

23. Erlich, *The Soviet Industrialization Debate, 1924–1928*, 10.

24. Leon Trotsky, born Lev Davidovich Bronstein, was a key figure in the Bolsheviks' seizure of power in Russia in 1917. He built the Red Army during the civil war. Second in command to Lenin, Trotsky was to be his successor but lost out in a power struggle with Stalin. In 1937 he was exiled to Mexico, where he continued to criticize the Soviet leader, advocating a more democratic and global Communism. In 1940 he was murdered in Mexico.

25. Evgeny Alekseevich Preobrazhensky, despite lacking higher education, became a leading economic theorist and a regional party official. By 1926 he favored a gradual move to industrialization, aligning himself with Trotsky and Bukharin. He was excluded from the CPSU in 1927 and died under Stalinist repression.

26. Gerschenkron, *Economic Backwardness in Historical Perspective,* 29.

27. Russian Westernizers *(zapadniki)* were nineteenth-century Russian intellectuals who believed that Russia should orient itself to Western Europe and follow its model of development and ideals, especially in abolishing autocracy. By contrast, the Slavophiles *(slavyanofily)* argued that Russia and the Slavic people were unique and must develop according to unique Russian and Slavic attributes. Russia's famous Westernizers include Peter Chaadaev and Alexander Herzen. Putin's "Western vocation," however, does not qualify him to be a Western-style liberal democrat as Talbott suggested in his later, post-Beslan interview.

28. Mikhail Aleksandrovich Suslov, CPSU secretary under Brezhnev, was the chief ideologist and "gray cardinal" under Khrushchev and Brezhnev. He taught economics in the 1920s but was a party official most of his life, supervising regional purges and "relocations" under Stalin. Despite his background as a party functionary, he was known as academician Suslov.

29. The New Economic Policy (NEP) introduced by Lenin in 1921 combined elements of the market and socialism. As a result, the ownership of land stayed with the peasants, whereas the "commanding heights" of the economy, among them heavy industry, transportation, banking, and foreign trade, were kept under state ownership. However, the management of industry, especially light industry, was freed from administrative controls, and private trade was restored. The NEP provided the framework for an impressive recovery of the economy until 1928.

30. Alexei Nikolaevich Kosygin was Soviet premier from 1964 to 1980, when Brezhnev was first secretary of the CPSU. With a background in manufacturing and as minister of light industry under Stalin and chair of the Central Planning Committee under Khrushchev, Kosygin argued for a move from the military-industrial complex to light industry. He was, however, increasingly overshadowed by Brezhnev's growing authority.

31. *Pravda,* June 29, 1988.

32. Nikolai Vasilevich Gogol, Russian writer during the first half of the nineteenth century, wrote powerful satires concerning his native Ukraine, the bureaucracy, the church, and class differences. Akaky Akakievich, the hero of his short, satirical novel, *The Overcoat,* is a "little man," lonely and alienated, who saves for months in order to buy an overcoat for the winter. The coat is stolen and he dies. Thereafter, a ghost wanders through St. Petersburg, attacking those who wear overcoats.

33. David K. Shipler, *Russia: Broken Idols, Solemn Dreams,* 173.

34. Joseph S. Berliner, *The Innovation Decision in Soviet Industry,* 96–97.

35. Ibid., 210.

36. William Taubman, *Khrushchev: The Man and His Era,* chap. 11.

37. Leon Aron, *Yeltsin: A Revolutionary Life,* 140.

38. Ibid., 501–503.

39. The provisional government *(vremennoye pravitelstvo)* was the coalition government that, under the leadership of Aleksandr Kerensky, attempted to rule Russia between the antimonarchical rebellion in February and the Bolshevik Revolution of October 1917.

40. Below the republics were executive committees rather than councils of ministers, and the soviets were essentially administrative rather than legislative bodies.

41. Aron, *Yeltsin,* 510.

42. Ibid., 511.

43. Padma Desai, *Perestroika in Perspective: The Design and Dilemmas of Soviet Reform;* Padma Desai, "The Soviet Bloc and the Soviet Union: Why Did They Fall Apart?"

44. Desai, *Perestroika in Perspective.*

45. Mikhail Gorbachev, *Perestroika: New Thinking for Our Country and the World;* Desai, *Perestroika in Perspective.*

46. Desai, "Perestroika, Prices, and the Ruble Problem."

47. For writing anti-Stalinist remarks, Aleksandr Isaevich Solzhenitsyn, Soviet writer, historian, scientist, and 1970 Nobel prize winner for literature, was imprisoned under Stalin, rehabilitated under Khrushchev, exiled under Brezhnev, and ultimately restored to his homeland upon his return in 1994.

48. Anders Aslund, "The Importance of Democracy for the Economic Transformation of Post-Communist Countries."

49. Padma Desai, "Aftershock in Russia's Economy."

50. Ibid.; also Padma Desai, "Ease Up on Russia," and Padma Desai, *Going Global: Transition from Plan to Market in the World Economy.*

51. The Cato Institute, a nonprofit public policy think tank with strong libertarian leanings, was founded in 1977 in San Francisco by Edward H. Crane. It is headquartered in Washington, D.C.

52. Strobe Talbott, *Russia Hand: A Memoir of Presidential Diplomacy,* 185.

53. Padma Desai and Todd Idson, *Work without Wages: Russia's Nonpayment Crisis.*

54. Formally known as the European Recovery Program, the Marshall Plan was an initiative sponsored by the United States to rehabilitate the economies of seventeen Western and Southern European countries (1948–1951). The plan was advanced by U.S. secretary of state George C. Marshall in 1947.

55. Padma Desai, " Russian Privatization: A Comparative Perspective"; Maxim Boycko, Andrei Shleifer, and Robert Vishny, *Privatizing Russia.*

56. Padma Desai, "Why Did the Ruble Collapse in August 1998?"

57. Ingushetiya, Dagestan, Karachayevo-Cherkessiya, Kabardino-Balkariya, and Adygeya are the Muslim majority republics in the Caucasus in addition to Chechnya. North Ossetiya, where the Beslan terrorist attack occurred, is not Muslim majority but is significantly Muslim.

58. The film *The Assassination of Russia,* financed by the exiled Russian oligarch Boris Berezovsky, suggests that the bombings of numerous apartment buildings in Moscow and other Russian cities were engineered by the Russian security agency, the Federal Security Bureau (FSB). These staged bombings prompted Basayev and his partners to invade Dagestan, which in turn provided a solid ground for the Russian military to begin the second war in Chechnya. The conspiracy theory caught on because the FSB never really finished its investigation of the bombings.

59. I interviewed Gaidar in Columbia University's Altschul Auditorium in front of a couple of hundred students. Some of them later expressed surprise at his defense of the military offensive. By contrast, Nemtsov has consistently opposed the military engagement and argued in favor of a political solution.

60. In the 1870s the wave of terrorism under the tsars was sponsored by several political movements, especially by the People's Will. In 1881 the assassination of Czar Alexander II in St. Petersburg was followed in 1883 by the murder of the tsar's chief of security, Lt. Col. Georgy Sudeikin. Richard Pipes has written a book about the killer, who later ended up as a mathematics professor in South Dakota.

61. VimpelCom is a leading provider of telecommunication services in Russia and Kazakhstan.

62. BP-TNK is Russia's third largest oil company. It was established in September 2003 as a result of the merger of two Russian companies—TNK (Tyumen Oil Company) and SIDANCO—with the majority of BP's Russian oil assets. Ownership of the company is shared equally by BP and a group of prominent Russian investors, among whom are Alfa Group and Access Industries.

63. "Dizzy with success" is a phrase with strong connotations for Russians because it was Stalin's description of his overzealous Bolshevik commissars, who got carried away in their program of collectivizing Russia's privatized farms in the early 1930s.

64. Most of the information in this section was generously provided by Blake Marshall, executive vice president of the U.S.-Russia Business Council.

65. The Paris Club is a group of lender states who coordinate and work to solve the payment difficulties of debtor nations through rescheduling and reduction of their sovereign debt obligations. The nineteen permanent members of the Paris Club are the largest creditor states, including Russia.

66. Erin E. Arvedlund, "Russia's Billionaires Club Now Totals 27 Members," *New York Times,* May 7, 2005.

67. The super majors are the seven Western private oil companies.

68. Before July 2000, the 178 seats in the Federation Council, two for each of the eighty-nine federal administrative units of Russia, were occupied by the highest officials, one each from the executive and legislative branches of the federal regions. Among the former were the regional governors or republic presidents, and among the latter, the speakers of the regional legislatures. In July 2000, the Duma adopted a Putin-supported law that denied governors their membership in the council. Since then, members representing the executive half are appointed (often by the president), and members of the legislative half are elected by the regions.

69. The elections of the proreform, pro-European Viktor Yushchenko in December 2004 in Ukraine and of Mikheil Saakashvili in Georgia in January 2004 resulted from a broad-based popular support for both. The transitions from the old regimes were also eased by the institutionalization of the process by experienced politicians and party groups. The European and U.S. support to the movements and the presidential candidates, in my view, played a marginal role. By contrast, Kyrgyzstan and Uzbekistan lack such institutionalization and further carry the serious destabilizing threat of leadership takeover by Islamic fundamentalists.

70. This amendment to the 1974 Trade Act denies favorable U.S. trade relations to specific countries with nonmarket economies and restricted emigration. Russia no longer fits the profile, but the U.S. Congress has not revoked the amendment.

71. Details are in Matthew Bunn and Anthony Wier, "Securing the Bomb 2005: The New Global Imperatives," Belfer Center for Science and International Affairs, Harvard University, 2005.

72. Ibid.

73. The phrase "axis of evil" first appeared in President Bush's 2002 State of the Union address. It encompassed states that support terrorism and promote weapons of mass destruction. In his address Bush included Iraq, Iran, and North Korea in the list.

74. The unilateral withdrawal by the United States from the Antiballistic Missile (ABM) Treaty in December 2001 eliminated the restrictions imposed by the treaty on U.S. deployment

of space weapons such as lasers. Despite the complex technical and cost problems of space missile defense, the program, which offers a civil and military competitive edge to the United States, is likely to continue.

75. Russia cooperates with NATO through the NATO-Russia Council established in 2002. The council provides a basis for Russia and NATO member states to cooperate on security and defense policy issues, crisis management, joint military training and exercises, and technological development. Russia, however, does not formally participate in NATO decision making. Direct military cooperation between Russia and the United States in security and intelligence sharing, joint peacekeeping exercises, and a program with Norway to reduce environmental damage by the military also continue.

76. In interviews with *Komsomolskaya Pravda* in August and September 2003, Chubais expressed the need for Russia to become a "liberal empire.". He recycled the concept in 2004 during an interview on Vremya (Russian satellite TV): "[W]e must be frank and straightforward and assume this mission of leadership, not just as a slogan but as a Russian state policy. I believe this mission of leadership means that Russia is obliged to support in every way the expansion of its business outside Russia."

77. In 1998 Russia joined the G7 (Group of Seven), which consists of the world's leading industrialized countries, as a full member to form the G8. Other member states are Canada, France, Germany, Great Britain, Italy, Japan, and the United States. The European Union participates in G8 events as a nonmember.

78. Putin's closest allies are the *siloviki,* who are the select few from the security service and the military. They provoke continuing speculation among analysts about their influence in policymaking. For example, FSB director Nikolay Petrushev is Putin's classmate from his high-school days. However, the economic reformers in the government are also Putin's associates from his St. Petersburg days.

REFERENCES

Aron, Leon. 2000. *Yeltsin: A Revolutionary Life.* New York: St. Martin's Press.

Aslund, Anders. 1994. "The Importance of Democracy for the Economic Transformation of Post-Communist Countries." Paper presented at the *Journal of Democracy* conference on "Economic Reform and Democracy," Washington, D.C., May 5–6, p. 4.

Berliner, Joseph S. 1976. *The Innovation Decision in Soviet Industry.* Cambridge: Harvard University Press.

Boycko, Maxim, Andrei Shleifer, and Robert Vishny. 1995. *Privatizing Russia.* Cambridge: MIT Press.

Desai, Padma. 1989. "Perestroika, Prices, and the Ruble Problem." *Harriman Institute Forum* 2(11) (November): 1–8.

———. 1990. *Perestroika in Perspective: The Design and Dilemmas of Soviet Reform.* Princeton, N.J.: Princeton University Press.

———. 1993. "Ease Up on Russia." *New York Times,* December 10, op-ed, A35.

———. 1994. "Aftershock in Russia's Economy." *Current History* 93(585) (October): 320–23.

————. 1995. "Russian Privatization: A Comparative Perspective." *Harriman Review* 8(3) (August): 1–34.

————. 1997. "The Soviet Bloc and the Soviet Union: Why Did They Fall Apart?" *Harriman Review* 10(2) (Summer): 1–11.

————, ed. 1999. *Going Global: Transition from Plan to Market in the World Economy*. Cambridge: MIT Press, 1–94.

————. 2000. "Why Did the Ruble Collapse in August 1998?" *American Economic Review: Papers and Proceedings* 90(2) (May): 48–52.

————, and Todd Idson. 2000. *Work without Wages: Russia's Nonpayment Crisis*. Cambridge: MIT Press.

Erlich, Alexander. 1960. *The Soviet Industrialization Debate, 1924–1928*. Cambridge: Harvard University Press.

Gerschenkron, Alexander. 1962. *Economic Backwardness in Historical Perspective: A Book of Essays*. Cambridge: Belknap Press of Harvard University Press.

Gorbachev, Mikhail. 1987. *Perestroika: New Thinking for Our Country and the World*. New York: Harper and Row.

Malia, Martin (Z). 1990. "To the Stalin Mausoleum." *Daedalus* 119 (Spring): 295–344.

Matlock, Jack F., Jr. 1995. *Autopsy on an Empire: The American Ambassador's Account of the Collapse of the Soviet Union*. New York: Random House.

Sachs, Jeffrey. 1994. "Russia's Struggle with Stabilization: Conceptual Issues and Evidence." Paper presented at the Annual World Bank Conference on Development Economics, Washington, D.C., April 28–29.

Talbott, Strobe. 2003. *The Russia Hand: A Memoir of Presidential Diplomacy*. New York: Random House.

Taubman, William. 2003. *Khrushchev: The Man and His Era*. New York: W. W. Norton.

PART I

Reform Maximalists

CHAPTER I

Boris Yeltsin

The Wrecking Ball

Moscow News, OCTOBER 22–28, 2003

In place of the Soviet political system, a democratic one had to emerge. The administrative command economy had to be replaced by a market economy, and freedom of speech had to replace censorship. . . . What was needed was a kamikaze crew that would step into the line of fire and forge ahead, however strong the general discontent might be.

I had to pick a team that would go up in flames but remain in history.

Within a short period of time, the prices rocketed to thirty times their previous levels. Yet foodstuffs appeared on the counters that had sported nothing but gray wrapping paper. Or take privatization. . . . If I hadn't launched it, we would still be saddled with a ruined economy. Was it easy? Of course not. But these things never are.

I purposely selected those with a minimum of Soviet-time experience. People without mental, ideological blinkers. People who did not have the ingrained habit of resorting to command methods but habitually used arguments, facts, and figures to achieve their goals.

Former Russian Federation president Boris Yeltsin granted the first interview after his surprise resignation on the eve of the millennium to Lyudmila Telen, first deputy editor of Moskovskiye Novosti *newspaper.*

THE CHOICE OF 1991

TELEN: What was the reason for your risky choice in 1991 in favor of little-known, but ambitious, politicians?

YELTSIN: I had a perfectly clear idea of the task to be solved. The political system had to be overturned, not just changed. In place of the Soviet political system, a democratic one had to emerge. The administrative command economy had to be replaced by a market economy, and freedom of speech had to replace censorship. I realized that the transition could not be painless. That meant that unpopular measures were inevitable. What was needed was a kamikaze crew that would step into the line of fire and forge ahead, however strong the general discontent might be.

TELEN: Did you realize that that job might cost them their political future?

YELTSIN: Of course. They had to do the job and then leave.

TELEN: Weren't you sorry for them?

YELTSIN: I was. I am now, although I do not believe they have dropped out of the running. Some of them may still rise. Time passes, everything gradually calms down, and many things fall into place. Judgments on what happened in the early 1990s are changing. Recently I have felt a certain warming toward myself. I have just come back from Rostov. Can you believe it—crowds of people came out to welcome me there, mostly young people. Neither Gaidar nor Chubais are welcomed like that. Not yet, no, but who knows what may happen in the future? In the early 1990s, though, I had no other option. I had to find men capable of tackling the knottiest problems without a thought for their own political future. I had to pick a team that would go up in flames but remain in history.

TELEN: Were they prepared to go up in flames?

YELTSIN: We did not discuss that subject.

TELEN: Didn't you mention at all the fact that they might soon have to go?

YELTSIN: No, that couldn't be done. They had to work at full throttle. And that was exactly the way they worked. By the way, so did I, twenty hours a day, with four hours for sleep.

TELEN: Isn't that an exaggeration?

YELTSIN: Not at all. We already seem to be forgetting the scope of the tasks that had to be solved then. Take price liberalization in January 1992. Within a short period of time, the prices rocketed to thirty times their previous levels. Yet foodstuffs appeared on the counters that had sported nothing but gray wrapping paper. Or take privatization. "Yeltsin would have been a great president," I recently read, "if he hadn't launched privatization." That is not true. If I hadn't launched it, we would still be saddled with a ruined economy. Was it easy? Of course not. But these things never are.

This year I visited Japan and met the prime minister there. "What is going on in Japan, Mr. Prime Minister?" I asked. "Why don't you launch the reforms you promised to launch?" He had made certain promises at election time. "Mr. President," he says, "I cannot ram them through the bureaucracy. I announced a five-point program, and I cannot make a breakthrough on any of those points, including a new stage in privatization." Now, with the crew that I picked, we did manage to make a breakthrough. We made a breakthrough on privatization, price liberalization, and trade freedom.

TELEN: Could it be that you did not wish to foist all of those disagreeable tasks onto the backs of the politicians that were closer to you and had been tested during several years of working together?

YELTSIN: They would not have been able to solve those problems. New people were needed to cope with the job. I purposely selected those with a minimum of Soviet-time experience. People without mental, ideological blinkers. People who did not have the ingrained habit of resorting to command methods but habitually used arguments, facts, and figures to achieve their goals. Young, knowledgeable, talented people. Others would not have coped with the task.

THE CHOICE OF 2000

TELEN: Who brought Yegor Gaidar to you?

YELTSIN: Various people mentioned him. Then I read some of his articles, and I invited him to come and talk. We talked a long time, mostly about his vision for the future of Russia.

TELEN: How did your closest associates receive the news of your choice of Gaidar's team? With relief?

YELTSIN: On the contrary, there were attempts on all sides to dissuade me.

TELEN: Was there anything about these knowledgeable and talented people that exasperated you?

YELTSIN: Their maximalism. Sometimes I just could not restrain them. Even in situations where we argued till we were blue in the face, they stood their ground.

TELEN: Just a year later you yielded to the Supreme Soviet's pressure and consented to Gaidar's resignation.[1] Did your relationship sour?

YELTSIN: I am on friendly terms with all of the ex-premiers. Even with Primakov, after a cooling-off period.[2] . . . With Gaidar? Well, maybe just after the resignation there was a sort of shadow. I saw that he was hurt.

TELEN: Did you warn him of your decision, or was it a complete surprise to him?

YELTSIN: I took him aside in an empty hall and said, "Let's decide this together. I have this feeling about the people's mood. Chernomyrdin will get the vote, and you won't."[3] He agreed with that decision.

TELEN: Do you know that Gaidar was against your running for president in 1996?

YELTSIN: He wasn't the only one. So was my family. I had my own doubts, too. But then I realized that Zyuganov was next in line, and no one but me could bring him down.[4] Can you imagine Zyuganov as president of Russia? I said to Gaidar, "Which one of you can beat Zyuganov? Go on, propose a candidate." There were no candidates. After that, Gaidar supported me, too.

TELEN: Why not Nemtsov?[5] Which of the new generation of politicians did you find the hardest to work with?

YELTSIN: Nemtsov was the most elusive, I suppose. He was a bit of a guerrilla.

TELEN: In what sense?

YELTSIN: He would often force his way regardless, spouting ideas that he didn't bother to discuss with me. The differences weren't strategic, just minor things. . . . Like his idea of making all officials use only domestically made cars. A kink, it was.

TELEN: Still, you publicly named him your successor.

YELTSIN: I did, but then I took a good look at him and realized he was not ready to be the country's president. But I still believe in Boris [Nemtsov] and have hopes for him.

TELEN: Why not Chubais?[6] When did you first meet Anatoly Chubais?

YELTSIN: Around the time I met Gaidar. That team was selected all at the same time.

TELEN: Is it true that Chubais talked you into taking part in the 1996 election?

YELTSIN: He was for me the whole time, but I was the one who talked myself into running.

TELEN: Still, Chubais did try to persuade you, although he knew you were not exactly a robust man.

YELTSIN: That is putting it mildly. I had five heart attacks during the presidency, yet I was never laid up at the hospital. There were times when I came home and wasn't strong enough to go upstairs, so my wife moved an armchair right into the hall. I would come home from work and drop into it.

TELEN: Back then, in 1996, you had to choose between Alexander Korzhakov and Anatoly Chubais, both of whom, up until that moment, had been members of your inner circle.[7] How prepared were you to make that choice?

YELTSIN: It was not easy. After all, Korzhakov had long stood by me, and I valued him as a loyal person, but at a certain point he made me wonder. He started foisting documents on me: Appoint so and so, remove so and so. Apparently he had started putting together some sort of a group, but I caught on to what was going on.

TELEN: What politicians of this generation did you find the easiest to deal with?

YELTSIN: This may sound strange to some, but it was Chubais. He was closer to me in spirit than the others, and he still is. Recently he and his wife visited us at our home, and then last Saturday we returned the visit.

TELEN: You don't find him difficult?

YELTSIN: I don't. I find him interesting. Moreover, we mainly see eye to eye, even on the reform of the power sector. Lately we have been discussing it in detail.

TELEN: Why not Stepashin?[8] Before Vladimir Putin became prime minister, you nominated Sergei Stepashin, and everyone immediately concluded that he was going to be your successor.

YELTSIN: I feel a little bit embarrassed recalling what happened then, but soon after Stepashin was appointed prime minister, I realized that I had made a mistake.

Incidentally, I told him so in so many words: "Let's admit that we both were wrong. I was wrong to offer you this position, and you were wrong to accept it without feeling sure that you were really suited for it."

TELEN: Did he admit to that?

YELTSIN: No, he disagreed with me, took it to heart. For a while our relationship cooled. Now it's all right.

TELEN: What were your complaints against him?

YELTSIN: I'd rather not list them now. It's not that he had any shortcomings: He is a talented and well-educated person. It was just that he did not have all it takes to be prime minister and then become president.

TELEN: Why not Nikolai Fedorov?[9] In the early 1990s there was someone in the Gaidar cabinet who stepped down long before the cabinet was dismissed en bloc. Justice minister Nikolai Fedorov disagreed with a draft decree granting you even broader powers. How do you see this now?

YELTSIN: I greatly respect Nikolai Fedorov. He is not only a good legal expert but also a very decent, tactful person. I was sorry to see him go, but at that time my opposition to Parliament was a matter of principle.

TELEN: Did you accept his resignation without qualms?

YELTSIN: I did, but then I backed his candidacy for Chuvashia president, and I think that I was right. There are so many problem regions today, but Chuvashia has done well. We often talk on the phone.

TELEN: Why not Yavlinsky?[10] At one time you believed in the five-hundred-day program. Is that right?

YELTSIN: That's right. I was vacationing in Jurmala; Yavlinsky came a bit later, and we discussed the program for several days. He convinced me. After that, I met with Gorbachev and said, "Here is a program that I suggest you accept." Gorbachev embraced it. True, he did not see it through to the end. Of course, today, in hindsight, you realize that much in that program sounded naive and that a civilized market cannot be put in place in 500 or even 1,000 days. But we were all charged with the spirit of the time: We wanted to get things done quickly. I greatly valued Yavlinsky at the time and so appointed him Silaev's deputy in the Russian government.[11] He did a good job.

TELEN: Why, in selecting a prime minister in 1991, did you place your bet on Gaidar, not on Yavlinsky, whom you had actually worked with?

YELTSIN: I thought that Gaidar was more logical, coherent, and clear in his mind insofar as economic matters were concerned. He is probably more discerning.

TELEN: Why Putin? Whom do you meet most often today?

YELTSIN: Gaidar, Chubais, Voloshin, Chernomyrdin, Kasyanov, and many others we have not mentioned today.[12] I keep in touch with the governors and presidents of our republics—also with the CIS presidents, of course.[13]

TELEN: What about President Putin?

YELTSIN: We meet, of course.

Telen: Do you deliberately shun publicity?

Yeltsin: I think that since I stepped down, I have no right to remain a public politician. I vowed not to comment on the incumbent's performance. What I like or don't like I tell him personally, one on one.

Telen: But you do tell him?

Yeltsin: Yes, I do. Plurality of opinion is vital to society. This is also what I told Putin.

Telen: How did you decide on your successor?

Yeltsin: I had studied him for a very long time—not only from his dossier. I had a pretty good understanding of his performance in St. Petersburg, under Sobchak.[14] And when he moved to Moscow, I started watching him especially closely. I could see that he was not just an intelligent and well-educated person but also decent and self-controlled.

Telen: But why did you choose him rather than one of those you brought into politics in the early 1990s?

Yeltsin: No one from that team would have been supported in an election. We've already discussed why.

Telen: Did Vladimir Putin have certain qualities that other politicians of his generation did not have?

Yeltsin: He is not a maximalist, and this is what set him apart from the others.

Telen: When did you decide on Putin, then?

Yeltsin: Before I offered him the position of prime minister.

Telen: You think you did right?

Yeltsin: I do.

Telen: Are you basically a good judge of character?

Yeltsin: When I took my first job at an industrial company straight out of college, I refused to be a foreman. I thought I first had to learn to size up people. Eventually I did. You know, I don't remember a single personnel mistake that I made at the company.

Telen: What about the Kremlin?

Yeltsin: In the Kremlin I did make mistakes.

Telen: You overestimated people?

Yeltsin: That's not the point. I simply did not know them well enough. Life was so turbulent that there was no time to study someone thoroughly. But as I said, it was different with Vladimir Putin.

Telen: Did you consult anyone in your entourage?

Yeltsin: No, it was my personal decision. I did not talk to anyone. Absolutely no one. Incidentally, when I visited China later on, Jiang Zemin said to me, "I like what you have done. I've also decided to step down before serving out my term."[15] Then he added in a whisper, "You are the first person I've told this. No one else knows." And he did.

Telen: Why did you step down six months before elections?

YELTSIN: I had to give Putin enough time.

TELEN: To score points?

YELTSIN: To give people a chance to see, understand, and appreciate him. He was a bit of a dark horse until then. And you have to hand it to him, he used that time well, showing himself to advantage.

TELEN: Was your choice accepted by all of the Kremlin denizens at once?

YELTSIN: No way. Staff officials would break into my office shouting, "Boris Nikolaevich, you've gone mad!" But I would say, "Save your breath. I'm already turning things over."

TELEN: Did Putin readily accept your offer?

YELTSIN: I talked to him twice. At first he refused. "Think about it—we'll revisit the matter," I said. About two weeks later I called him in again, and then he agreed.

TELEN: Do you remember what you told him at the time?

YELTSIN: "I've picked a hard lot for you."

TELEN: Does he remember it?

YELTSIN: He does—and often reminds me of that incident.

TELEN: Did you set any terms for your successor?

YELTSIN: None for myself. I did not ask for anything at all.

TELEN: What about for somebody else?

YELTSIN: We talked a good deal about the policy that the country would need in the future. Of course, we could not have anticipated everything at the time. The situation is changing, and it is a president's right to adjust his policy line, but there have never been disagreements of principle.

THE CHOICE OF 2008

TELEN: Will this generation of politicians be able to successfully run for the presidency in 2008?

YELTSIN: I do not rule this out. Actually, I have a pretty good idea about who the favorite candidate is going to be.

TELEN: Are you going to tell us?

YELTSIN: I am not.

NOTES

1. In December 1992 Yegor Gaidar tendered his resignation after the Supreme Soviet refused to confirm his appointment as prime minister.

2. Yeltsin sacked Prime Minister Primakov in 1999 and named Sergei Stepashin acting premier.

3. Viktor Chernomyrdin was appointed prime minister in 1994.

4. Gennady Zyuganov ran for president on the Communist Party ticket in 1996.

5. Boris Nemtsov served as Yeltsin's representative in the Nizhny Novgorod region from 1991 to 1994, where he implemented the so-called five-hundred-day regional reform program in 1992. From 1993 to 1996, Nemtsov was a member of the Federation Council; in 1997 he became a member of the Security Council and deputy prime minister in charge of monopoly and social policy.

6. Anatoly Chubais was minister of privatization and first deputy prime minister in the governments under Yeltsin.

7. Alexander Korzhakov was chief of Yeltsin's security service, State Duma deputy, and a retired lieutenant general.

8. Sergei Stepashin, appointed interior minister in 1998, was made prime minister in May 1999, a position he held until August, when he was replaced by Vladimir Putin, the future president.

9. Nikolai Fedorov became justice minister in June 1990 and held that position in Gaidar's cabinet after November 1991, resigning in March 1993 to protest Yeltsin's intention to dissolve Parliament. Fedorov was elected president of Chuvashia in December 1993. He has strongly criticized Putin's intention to abolish the direct election of governors.

10. Grigory Yavlinsky is the founder and leader of Yabloko, Russia's leading left-of-center political party; Russia's pro-Western liberal politician with presidential ambitions; and former member of the Russian Duma. He was one of the authors of the five-hundred-day program (1990) designed to implement the transition to a market economy.

11. Ivan Silaev resigned from his post as prime minister of the Russian Soviet Federated Socialist Republic (RSFSR) on September 27, 1991.

12. Alexander Voloshin was Yeltsin's chief of staff. Mikhail Kasyanov was prime minister of the Russian Federation from May 2000 to February 2004 and former deputy minister of finance.

13. The Commonwealth of Independent States (CIS) was created in December 1991 with the following members: Armenia, Azerbaijan, Belarus, Georgia, Kazakhstan, Kyrgyzstan, Moldova, Russia, Tajikistan, Turkmenistan, Ukraine, Uzbekistan.

14. Anatoly Sobchak (1937–2000) was mayor of Leningrad/St. Petersburg from 1991 to 1996. Putin was Sobchak's former student and political protégé.

15. Jiang Zemin was general secretary of the Chinese Communist Party and president of China from 1993 to 2003.

CHAPTER 2

Anatoly Chubais

The "Neo–Bolshevik" Privatizer

We were the only team in the country who could discuss—and not just discuss but also make—changes. . . . Of course, a number of alternative government think tanks were around, but all of those were Communist. It was simple: we or the Communists.

No one thought that we would immediately get economic growth in Russia by distributing vouchers.

Let us understand that the oligarchs are a big private Russian business with both positive and negative features they bring to Russia. The fact is that this private business was the major political resource for preventing Communist leader Gennady Zyuganov from becoming president in 1996.

I do not believe that Russia will fall apart.

Our strategy is to win. We have to win. I mean we *shall* win . . . and . . . if we lose, we will just disappear physically. There is no doubt about it.

MAY 1999

DESAI: You are a very committed believer in the market economy. How did your commitment start?

CHUBAIS: My belief in the market economy has a long history. It began long before the market economy started in Russia. I graduated from the St. Petersburg engineering economics school. It was clear to me that the Soviet economy was in terrible shape and was headed toward disaster. It was difficult to find reasonable answers for the situation in the Soviet economy. Articles in textbooks and scientific journals discussed different ideas without clearly understanding them or how an economy worked. I had a clear understanding myself, and I found several people in St. Petersburg in the mideighties and later who had similar views. We got to work, started finding books that were forbidden in the Soviet Union, and established contacts with Western economists, that were also practically forbidden at that time.

DESAI: Can you remember some of the books?

CHUBAIS: Yes, the works of Janos Kornai, Milton Friedman, Hayek, and others. We also established contact with Yegor Gaidar's team in Moscow. We did not just discuss our ideas but also undertook solid work, prepared reports, researched the New Economic Policy of the early 1920s in the Soviet Union, and studied Hungarian and Yugoslav reforms. All of this was not easy to do in the Soviet Union. Our basic goal was to get a firm idea of the fundamental changes that needed to be undertaken.

DESAI: It seems that there was a group of young people who thought like you and believed that there should be a market economy in Russia.

CHUBAIS: Yes, but I would say that we did not have a common belief, a clear understanding from the very beginning. We tried to find solutions stage by stage, and we found the answers in terms of basic changes such as private properly, competition, and free prices. All of this came from prolonged discussions. We did not accept it at the very beginning.

DESAI: There is a view here that almost all of the USAID [U.S. Agency for International Development] funding was given to the group of reformers Chubais led and that the fund givers from this end did not seek out other groups and encourage pluralism in Russia. You must be aware of this. How would you react to it?

CHUBAIS: You know, that is a very simple question. When we started in 1989, in November 1989, we had a team consisting of fifteen, maximum twenty, people. We were the only team in the country who could discuss—and not just discuss but also make—changes. At that time, our problem was that there was no alternative. Grigory Yavlinsky was with us at that time. He was a member of the team that prepared the five-hundred-day program.[1] But the fact was that there were no other teams. Before 1991, I myself spent years trying to find individuals everywhere in the country—in Novosibirsk, in Moscow institutes, in St. Petersburg, Odessa, and Ukraine, in Minsk and Sverdlovsk, and several Russian cities. When we became part of the government in 1991, everyone who was able to contribute something was invited. They came to the government, everybody except one or two people. Of course, a number of alternative government think tanks were around, but all of those were Communist. It was simple: we or the Communists.

DESAI: You emerged as a reformer explicitly in 1992 with your privatization program, voucher privatization in particular, and I believe that this move was motivated by ideological considerations. You wanted Russian industry removed from state ownership and control, converting industrial units into joint stock companies with diversified ownership. Would you agree with that view?

CHUBAIS: Absolutely.

DESAI: Private ownership promotes economic efficiency via incentives, but that was not your primary motive. The decision to issue vouchers to every man, woman, and child, worth ten thousand rubles each, was a populist measure. It was a huge political gambit that pushed the reform momentum forward and kept it alive. Would you agree with that analysis?

CHUBAIS: Yes, I think it was clear from the very beginning that a simple and transparent means of privatization did not exist, so some would gain and others would lose. A number of people would be unsatisfied with the outcome, but the fundamental problem was, will it happen or not? From an economic point of view, voucher privatization—the voucher itself was not the best way to achieve privatization. More to the point, it was clear that the voucher was a substitute for money, and if you issue a voucher, you will not get money from privatization by selling state properties, but that was the price. It was the only way to make it doable.

DESAI: Ultimately, the public felt cheated, and factories have remained in the charge of Soviet-era managers, who have failed to retool them. So what are the gains of privatization in your view?

CHUBAIS: I did not hear the question.

DESAI: Well, in the end, the public felt cheated. Gen. Alexander Lebed said later that the voucher would not even buy an iron.[2] And most of the factories have not been restructured. So what do you think the gains from privatization are?

CHUBAIS: Well, let's separate the goal from what was not the goal. No one said that the goal of voucher privatization was to restructure private property, to restructure companies, to attract investments, to speed up economic growth, or to increase the standard of living because it was clear that the process would require several stages. Voucher privatization was just asset distribution, leading to the next stage of property concentration, resulting in new investments, finally leading to enterprise restructuring. There are at least four or five stages.

DESAI: So you had some sequencing in mind?

CHUBAIS: Yes, General Lebed and Mayor Yuri Luzhkov of Moscow also stated that voucher privatization would not attract investments. No one thought that we would immediately get economic growth in Russia by distributing vouchers.

DESAI: The harshest criticism was leveled against the loans-for-shares program, as a result of which a few bankers advanced credits for supporting the government budget and bankrolling President Yeltsin's June 1996 election. Eventually they came to own a sizeable share of Russia's lucrative industrial units. Would you repeat that plan again—loans for shares?

CHUBAIS: No, that idea could not be repeated. There is no need for it. Loans for shares began in 1995. Up to that time, we did not get even a small amount of cash from privatization because it was a property sale for vouchers. In fact, no one believed that we could get real money from the sale of state property in exchange for vouchers. The plan was controversial at the time. Politically, I was in a very complicated situation—I was under serious attack from several branch ministries, from the railroad and transport ministries, from the Duma, and from certain governors. So the dilemma was simple: Either we will not sell state shares at all, or we will sell them via the controversial shares scheme, which would bring real money to the Russian budget. Don't forget that with the sale of Norilsk Nickel shares, we got the first $170 million.[3] It was absolutely fantastic. It helped the federal budget a lot because the budget situation was critical.

DESAI: But you don't think that, as a result of this strategy, you brought into being Russia's oligarchs as powerful lobbies? Also, in the spring of 1998, Sergei Kiryienko, the young reformist prime minister, was battling the left wing of the Duma, which was led by the Communists, and the oligarchs on the right, so he was dealing with two opponents at the same time.

CHUBAIS: Well, let us decide whether the oligarchs are good or bad. Let us understand that the oligarchs are a big private Russian business with both positive and negative features they bring to Russia. The fact is that this private business was the major political resource for preventing Communist leader Gennady Zyuganov from becoming president in 1996. I strongly believe that the only way to prevent Zyuganov from becoming president in 1996 was to create big private business in Russia. Their [the oligarchs'] mentality differed from Soviet-style management. They were mainly younger people who were attracting hundreds of thousands of new employees in their companies while restructuring them, which began with Norilsk Nickel and Yukos, the oil company. They started capital investment. They began attracting foreign investment. They fought for improving economic efficiency. These were the goals of privatization in its next phase. That is the economic side of the story. At the same time, they became powerful and wanted to use their power according to their understanding of the political situation. The presidential election of June 1996 raised the question of Yeltsin or Zyuganov, and they [the oligarchs who bankrolled Yeltsin's election] definitely said Yeltsin. However, in the next phase, they thought they ruled the world and could do everything, so there are positive and negative sides to the story.

DESAI: Do you think that the influence of private business, the so-called oligarchs, has been crippled as a result of the financial meltdown of August 1998?

CHUBAIS: No doubt about it. Of the seven big names in 1996, half of them no longer existed in 1998.

DESAI: Let's move forward in time. Why did the president fire Prime Minister Yevgeny Primakov?[4]

CHUBAIS: It was for the political compromise that Primakov managed. The price of the political compromise that Primakov achieved was increased Communist influence. This role grew constantly, and in the next phase, it could have become a powerful political force in the country.

DESAI: But you don't think the president removed him because Primakov was becoming increasingly popular with the public? He fired Prime Minister Viktor

Chernomyrdin in March 1998 because Chernomyrdin was beginning to have presidential ambitions.[5]

CHUBAIS: I know this president. Let me answer this question in a simple way. The president is now going to find his successor. so it should be clear to everyone that the president will not run in the presidential election next year. It is clear that he needs to find someone. The problem is not that Chernomyrdin or Primakov gets too much public support. The problem is that President Yeltsin accepts neither one as a successor. That is the reason for firing Primakov.

DESAI: He would not accept them as successors?

CHUBAIS: No, no.

DESAI: Do you think he has a successor in mind? I don't want any names, but does he have a successor in mind?

CHUBAIS: I know that this is one of his main priorities.

DESAI: What's your assessment of the new prime minister, Sergei Stepashin?[6] Even if he forms a credible government, can he manage to overcome Communist opposition and the continuing opposition of the Yavlinsky Yabloko group, which has declared its opposition?

CHUBAIS: Well, I think that Stepashin, despite his background and the unfavorable perception of him in the West because of his KGB past, the Chechnya war, and things like that, is absolutely reasonable, a representative of the new generation of Russian politicians. He will be able to build a wide political bloc, including Yavlinsky's group. He could build a genuine rapport with the Russian people because he is good at public policymaking, he is good at administrative functions, he is good with journalists, he is good with the Duma, and he is good with the governors. So he is respected by the Russian power elite and has the real support of the Russian population.

DESAI: So you are hopeful—more than hopeful—that the Duma will pass the legislation that the IMF is asking for before it releases the $4.5 billion funding?

CHUBAIS: No, I don't think so.

DESAI: They won't pass it?

CHUBAIS: No, no.

DESAI: So what will happen then?

CHUBAIS: I think that the Duma, after the failed impeachment of the president and the overwhelming support of the people in favor of impeachment, will seek an opportunity to express its objections, and the best opportunity will be to cancel this IMF package. Zyuganov said a week ago that he supported the government-IMF agreement, but I am sure that, in a week, he will say that this agreement is antipeople, that it undermines Russia's sovereignty, and things like that. I am sure that the Duma will be against it. I think this is a serious problem. The Stepashin government, the IMF, and the World Bank should sit down, analyze the whole list of problems they have, consider those that the Duma could support, and let go of the rest.

Desai: Do you think the current government will be a caretaker government until the Duma elections in December 1999? That's what Yegor Gaidar said yesterday.

Chubais: Let me tell you my assessment of the government. I do not think that Stepashin will immediately undertake major political steps and economic transformation. He does not need to do that. I do not think it is necessary now. In my view, the next stage of the Russian economic reforms will not start before the next Russian presidential election.

Desai: What are your best guesses about the composition of the new Duma as a result of the December 1999 elections?

Chubais: I don't think that something really radical will happen. The Communists will still be number one, but I do hope they will lose the majority. But there is a risk—the extreme leftist Communists will overcome the required 5 percent barrier because of the Yugoslav NATO bombing. The party of Luzhkov, the mayor of Moscow, will definitely gain entry into the Duma and be number one or two.

Desai: You met with a variety of business groups in the United States. You met with the IMF and treasury officials. In the old days, the general view was that the IMF, pressured by the treasury, would always support Russian reform because Russia has so many nuclear warheads that it cannot be allowed to go bust. Do you think they have now changed this position?

Chubais: In all of the discussions with the IMF that I have had since 1995, I have never discussed political positions. We discussed the IMF program itself, the growth rates of money supply and money demand, foreign exchange reserves, and things like that. We discussed the institutional and structural changes that must be made. They expressed their understanding, and we expressed our understanding. The discussions were very tough, but I never used the argument that if you include specific measures asking us to overhaul, say, the Russian railway ministry, and if we do not implement them, then the Communists will return or our nuclear forces will become unmanageable. Such things are not discussed with the IMF or the treasury.

Desai: Well, you do not discuss them explicitly, but they discuss them among themselves.

Chubais: I don't know.

Desai: My big question is, do you worry about Russia falling apart?

Chubais: No.

Desai: Why not? People here begin to worry about it as soon as something goes wrong with Russia.

Chubais: A number of concerns that people have here are absolutely unrealistic. On the other hand, serious problems in Russia that are extremely dangerous are not understood here. I do not believe that Russia will fall apart. With the increasing awareness of the need for a strong ruble, with the adoption of the 1993 constitution, and with the elections in the Russian regions, the chances of Russia's dissolution, in my view, are nonexistent. It was an issue in 1992 and 1993, in our relations with Tatarstan. Currently, the remaining problem that needs to be resolved is Chechnya.

DESAI: Dagestan?

CHUBAIS: Dagestan? No.

DESAI: My final question: When I consider your breathtaking career as a reformer, I feel that you regard the reform process as an ideological battle between the reformers and the Communists. I think you are a brilliant strategist who believes that every strategy has pluses and minuses but that the pluses must dominate and that the process must move forward as a result. You also do not want to distinguish between ends and means. You believe that you are dealing with a ruthless adversary, and therefore all means are acceptable.

CHUBAIS: I do believe that everything that has happened in Russia in the last decade [of the last millennium] has been a fight between Communists and non-Communists to a greater extent than elsewhere in Eastern Europe—and on a much bigger scale, with more risk than in Poland or in Eastern European countries. That is the essence of what is going on in Russia. It is clear that after several generations of Communist life, we could not leave it behind in a single year. At the same time, I believe that the strategic choice must be pragmatic. This does not mean that there are no moral limits. It does not imply that *any* means can be used for achieving these goals. At the very least, if immoral steps are used, they will immediately be used by the opponents.

DESAI: For example?

CHUBAIS: I cannot think of an example. I am trying to explain our strategy. Our strategy is to win. We have to win. I mean we *shall* win, but I do not think we can use any means for the purpose, even with the understanding that the game we are playing is quite serious and that if we lose, we will just disappear physically. There is no doubt about it. So we are paying the price that nobody in the West has paid. That is why it is a very serious game, but that does not mean that we can use any conceivable means for reaching our goal.

DESAI: Don't you feel tired sometimes? Don't you want to just throw in the towel sometimes?

CHUBAIS: All of us feel tired sometimes. I have been feeling tired for ten years.

NOTES

1. Grigory Yavlinsky was one of the authors of the five-hundred-day plan to boost the Soviet economy under Gorbachev (1990). The plan was never approved for implementation.

2. In the mid-1990s Gen. Alexander Lebed, an Afghan war hero, turned to politics and won a seat in the lower house of the parliament in 1995. He ran for president in 1996.

3. Norilsk Nickel is the world's largest producer of nickel and palladium and one of the largest producers of platinum. In 1994, shares in the company were distributed in accordance with privatization plans. More than 250,000 people bought shares in the company.

4. Having appointed Primakov prime minister in September 1998, Yeltsin fired him in May 1999 for "failing to rescue" the Russian economy. He then named Sergei Stepashin acting premier. The timing coincided with the impending hearings mounted by the Communist majority to impeach Yeltsin in the State Duma.

5. Viktor Chernomyrdin served as prime minister from 1992 to 1998. Yeltsin dismissed Chernomyrdin's entire cabinet in March 1998 and installed a new leadership to deal with economic reforms.

6. Sergei Stepashin, appointed interior minister in 1998, was made prime minister in May 1999, a position he held until August, when he was replaced by Vladimir Putin, the future president.

CHAPTER 3

Yegor Gaidar

The Shock Therapist

[The Russians'] desire to support a functioning government is the most important factor behind Putin's popularity.

A large part of the Russian public, especially the younger and better educated, is suspicious of the United States. On the other hand, they do not want another cold war.

There are very few subjects in economic policy on which [Putin] is clear, but he has been clearest in his commitment to the protection of private property and his strong opposition to renationalization.

The IMF is in the situation of a whipping boy. . . . The IMF is not bad, but it is an organization that was created to deal with currency crises, and then it took on the management of budgetary crises.

[W]e did not start the reforms because somebody promised to support us. We started the process because there was absolutely no other way.

[Putin] does not have a good record in the field of democratic freedoms.

[Yeltsin] was the first popularly elected president of the Russian state.

I would like to live in Europe but not leave my own country and [still be able to] speak Russian.

It is strange, but it will take enormous efforts to make "reform" and "democracy" bad words in Russia.

[The Communists] will never rule Russia again.

Russia is a young and unstable democracy. Therefore, voters tend to elect leaders who are far from the best. With greater experience, they will understand that local problems need to be resolved at local levels.

[P]olitical control in the final decades of tsarist rule did not prevent terrorist acts by dissidents.

I do not think that educated, urban populations in large countries such as Russia can put up with undemocratic regimes for long.

[Gazprom] is a black box.

[Putin's] foreign policy is pragmatic, realistic, and oriented toward safeguarding Russia's national interests.

April 2000

DESAI: Do you think that President Putin will turn authoritarian, even anti-Western, in view of the nationalistic surge related to the war in Chechnya, which contributed to his election?[1]

GAIDAR: Here in the United States and in the West and even in Russia, the connection between the Chechen war and Putin's victory is misunderstood and oversimplified. What we have now in Russia is not a strong nationalistic wave. It is something else. Having experienced eight years of an extremely difficult transition, after the collapse of the earlier regime, of the empire and ideology of the past, we are a country that has passed through a revolution—largely a peaceful one but still a revolution, and rebellions are unsettling. During this period of dynamic and difficult change, we had successive governments that were weak because governments tend to be weak during times of revolutionary change. Those who had a chance to live through the uprising found it trying though romantic. But after every revolution, whether in France or Mexico or Britain, people begin to think, "Well, splendid, but we are tired, we need peace and order, we need a predictable government, we need a government that functions, one that will deliver on its promises. We need a person who can be tough, make decisions, and implement them." Such feelings are strong after any revolt.

My friend and colleague Vladimir Mau has published a book with Oxford University Press on the social and economic theory of revolution.[2] He expressed similar views with regard to the Russian situation as early as five years ago. The Russians are tired. They need a government that will take the opportunity and deliver on its promises. Yeltsin was very smart in choosing someone who could make decisions and implement them. In this decision-making process, Chechnya was partly an accident. It was not the reason [for choosing Putin]. Russians are not very enthusiastic about the Chechen war, but their desire to support a functioning government is the most important factor behind Putin's popularity.

DESAI: What brought about the dramatic change in your position on the Chechen war, which you opposed from 1994 to 1996?

GAIDAR: It was the change that took place in Russian society in general. The Russians' attitude about this war differs from that about the previous war. This is another story because it is a different war.

The situation, as it is perceived in Russia, is quite different from what it was from 1994 to 1996. If you look at the polls, you will notice that the best educated, the young, and the most articulate groups in Russia strongly support the continuation of the current war. Exactly the same groups strongly opposed the previous war. What was the original situation? It is difficult to understand the difference if you are not familiar with the events. Russians cannot be crazy in being so vehemently against that war and so strongly in favor of this one. What happened? The war of 1994–1996 was viewed in Russia in approximately the same way the Vietnam War was perceived here in the United States. Americans found it difficult to understand why they were there. It was a faraway place involved in a nasty, dirty war to which they sent their sons to die. For Russians, too, the earlier war involved difficult questions about whether people have the right to be sovereign or whether the principle of self-determination should become subordinate to the overriding demands of the nation-state. But this issue should not be settled on the battlefield. That was the perception of the Russian public from 1994 to 1996. That is why Russians strongly opposed the previous war. That is why they practically pushed the Russian authorities to end the war, leaving them no choice but to terminate it in the summer of 1996. It was exactly the same as here in the United States: America had the resources to continue the war in Vietnam, but it did not have public support.

But here the similarities end and the differences begin. The difference is geography. Vietnam is in a splendid location, twenty thousand kilometers from here. Americans could withdraw from Vietnam and more or less forget about it. Chechnya is in Russia. After the war, Chechnya became an increasingly serious problem for Russia with kidnapping, imprisonment, and trafficking in people for cash. Journalists and American friends of Russia do not understand why the Russian press, so supportive of Chechnya from 1994 to 1996, has given up supporting it. But remember how many Russian journalists were kidnapped in Chechnya in the past three years and sold for money to their employers. Take the example of Elena Masliuk, a reporter for NTV.[3] She was extremely pro-Chechen and brought out the suffering of the Chechens, allowing them to express their opinions. After the war she was kidnapped, kept for half a year in horrible conditions, and finally sold to her TV station. Of course, this episode changed the attitude of Russian journalists. But still public opinion in Russia remained manageable. People said, "Let's keep them at a distance. Let's not interfere, and maybe somehow the situation will settle down. Maybe they will be able to stop the kidnapping and even organize themselves."

However, the situation changed dramatically when we had a few thousand well-armed and trained people entering Dagestan from Chechnya. Of course, it is very difficult for the American public, which is not even aware of the existence of Dagestan, to understand what the aggression against Dagestan in August [1999] meant for Russia. Dagestan is part of our life, part of our country, and part of our reality. The Dagestani people do not wish to be enslaved by the Chechens. They took up arms, they asked for Russian military support, and then, of course, Russian public opinion changed drastically. The issue was no longer the Chechen people's right to self-determination. It was the question of whether Russian citizens should be protected by their own government. It was not simply the problem of pushing the Chechens back to Chechnya from Dagestan and worrying about which regions would come under attack in the future, but rather of putting an end to such a possibility. That brought about the radical change before the current war actually started.

DESAI: Will President Putin be able to hold at bay the anti-Western, anti-U.S. sentiment among the Russian people who feel that the West and the United States misunderstand Russia's policies on Chechnya?

GAIDAR: First of all, I do not like the changes in Russian public opinion toward the United States and the West in the past two years, and the process started even before the Chechnya war. The turning point occurred with the events in Yugoslavia. I tried explaining to many of my American friends, including those in high positions, that the Yugoslav operation will have a serious, long-term effect on the Russian public with regard to the United States and NATO. It was very difficult to explain because the perception was that Russians have their own domestic worries. They have low living standards and wages that are in arrears. Why should they genuinely worry about Yugoslavia? Again, do you really think that they are seriously interested in eighteenth-century ties with Yugoslavia and the orthodox church? This has very little to do with historical ties and the orthodox church. If you ask an ordinary Russian whether he knows the difference between the Karadjordjevic and Obrenovic families and which of the two was sympathetic to the Austrians and which to the Russians, I doubt that he will be able to answer your question.[4]

The problem that really bothered ordinary Russian citizens was Russian security, rather than Yugoslavia. At the time of the decision regarding NATO's eastward expansion, which was not the best possible idea, my colleagues and I tried to ease Russian concerns by offering a variety of arguments: You see, we argued, NATO is a coalition of democratic nations, very predictable, operating within a framework of international law. It could not do something unpredictable and drastic, it would not start a war against other nations, it is a defense organization, and so on. Then, in the spring of 1998, the United States and NATO, outside the United Nations, outside international law, and outside their own territory, decided that the Yugoslav regime was bad. Maybe it is bad. I have seen a lot of bad regimes in the world.

And then they started bombing Yugoslav cities. So the Russians began thinking, "Maybe, sometime in the future, they will decide that our regime is also bad. So what is the guarantee that they will not do in Oryol and Vladimir what they are doing in Novi Sad and Kragujevac?"[5] This fear, of course, does not enhance the public's admiration for the United States and the West but instead fuels enthusiasm for expenditure on Russian defense. So that is the real problem. Of course, the Russian public has lost the enthusiasm it had for the United States and the West in the early 1990s. A large part of the Russian public, especially the younger and better educated, is suspicious of the United States. On the other hand, they do not want another cold war. A division between Russia and the rest of the world is not popular in Russia. So if Putin responds to public perception and pressures, his policy will be more skeptical of the West, more cautious about the West, and more oriented toward Russia's national interests but also not unrealistic and not anti-Western. It is entirely counter to Russian interests to create an anti-American alliance. It is a crazy idea.

DESAI: Does the January election of Gennady Seleznov, a Communist, as the speaker of the Duma—the result of an alliance between the Putin-backed Unity bloc and the Communists—bother you, a liberal reformer?

GAIDAR: I would not be telling you the truth if I said that I was enthusiastic about this partnership. I see a few simple explanations for the alliance as well as some limitations. The move was clever, tough, and cynical but also wrong. Well, what were the goals that the Unity bloc and the Kremlin were achieving by creating this alliance? First, they were preventing a potential collaboration between [Yevgeny] Primakov, also elected a member of the Duma on the basis of the Fatherland–All Russia bloc, and the Communists, an alliance that was discussed in the previous Duma. Second, they installed as speaker of the Duma a politician who was extremely weak politically. He had given up St. Petersburg, his own constituency. He had lost the election in the Moscow region. He is easy to manipulate and easy to work with. Third, Putin's main competitor in the presidential elections is Gennady Zyuganov, the Communist leader. The source of Zyuganov's support is the traditional protest electorate, those who hate the past eight years and the current regime. The coalition could undercut some of the traditional support for Zyuganov. Having made a deal with Putin, Zyuganov has begun his election campaign against Putin's terrible imperialistic regime—not a very good strategy to start a presidential campaign. Finally, you are delivering cars and dachas to the Communists in the Duma committees, but the key Duma committees are still controlled by people who are easy for the Kremlin to deal with.

Thus, the alliance is pragmatic and very clever, but it was still a mistake from two perspectives. First, strong support of a non-Communist electorate is crucial for Putin to win the first round of the presidential election, and the deal with the Communists is not the best possible way to garner support among the non-Communist electorate. Second, the Putin government will have a huge reform agenda to push through the Duma. It is easy to make a deal with the Communists on Seleznov's selection as speaker of the Duma but difficult to work with them on steering legislation on private property and land privatization. The government will have to turn to the factions that were isolated from the deal making. So the agreement was tactically very clever, but strategically it raised a lot of questions.

DESAI: Turning to economic reforms, does President Putin favor the introduction of state controls in the economy?

GAIDAR: There are very few subjects in economic policy on which he is clear, but he has been clearest in his commitment to the protection of private property and his strong opposition to renationalization. I do not take too seriously the various economic policy declarations he made during the presidential campaign. Everywhere, including here, policy declarations in presidential campaigns are not meant to be carried out. They are meant to signal concern for the electorate and various groups. I do not think that we will have a really good understanding of Putin's economic policies before he nominates his prime minister for confirmation before the Duma and initiates his legislation.

DESAI: Do you think that exchange controls can stop the outgo of as much as $20 billion a year in capital from Russia?

GAIDAR: I am absolutely certain that combating it with exchange controls is not efficient. They give short-term results. In about three months, private foreign exchange earners adapt themselves to the controls and find ways to circumvent them. Capital outgo is a key concern in Russia, and its reversal should be the top priority of a sensible Russian government. In that case, three basic problems affecting capital flight—political instability, poor protection of property rights, and a poor tax system—need to be dealt with. There is no other way of reversing capital flight.

DESAI: Do you think the extent of money laundering with regard to the Bank of New York scandal was exaggerated in the U.S. press?

GAIDAR: Yes, it was exaggerated. Money laundering and capital flight are two distinct issues. The problem of money laundering is connected with drug money and drug trafficking. That is a much bigger problem in the United States than in Russia. A similar market does not exist for this kind of activity in Russia. If you want to discuss the problem of money laundering seriously, you will have to discuss it with respect to the U.S. economy.

Capital flight, on the other hand, is a serious Russian problem. From that perspective, it was difficult to comprehend the story of the scandal surrounding the Bank of New York. I have not met a single person with an understanding of Russian problems who is unaware that we have had a serious problem with capital flight during the past eight years. It would be difficult to imagine that the prolonged, sizeable capital outgo from Russia could have taken place outside the world banking system—the big banks, including U.S. banks. So I do not understand the commotion over the Bank of New York scandal.

DESAI: On the reform front, what should the Russian government's immediate concern be?

GAIDAR: Three issues should be of immediate concern. First, the government must be a functioning administration, one with fewer state employees who are better paid. It must be prepared to seriously lighten the federal agencies' control over the federal structures in the regions. It must be prepared to remove the regional governments' influence on the judicial system. If and when courts rule in favor of property rights, their rulings must be implemented, not just endlessly discussed. The government must show an awareness of the corruption in a few structures that every Russian knows about. It must realize that overregulation of the economy is a source of corruption and an obstacle to creating new enterprises. In other words, it must demonstrate that it is serious about restructuring the state.

Second, the government must deal with the issue of property rights. We need new legislation to support property rights in the country. A land code, which is the first priority, was unable to be pushed through the Duma for eight years because of the Communist majority. It is now possible, for the first time in Russian history, for the government to adopt normal, civilized legislation relating to the investment climate, agricultural reform, and land mortgages. We need several changes in the basic legislation connected with property rights. The existing laws are not bad; they are good laws that need to be redesigned in light of the experience we have accumulated. We know that property rights should be protected better in Russia than in a functioning market economy with a long tradition of private property. We need to change certain articles in the civil code in order to remove some compromises that were included as a result of Communist pressure. We must improve the protection of property rights by changing the joint stock company law and the contract law relating to affiliated companies. A significant amount of legislation aimed at improving the protection of property rights needs to be adopted.

The third issue concerns tax reform. Focusing on tax reform does not imply that other important items in the reform program, such as the social protection of the population, pension reform, budgetary reporting, health care financing, and interbudgetary relationships, should be set aside.

DESAI: How do you view the role of the international financial institutions, especially the International Monetary Fund, in the process?

GAIDAR: Those who know British history are aware of the presence in British schools of the boy who would take beatings. If the Prince of Wales did not do his homework, he would be spanked.

DESAI: You mean the whipping boy?

GAIDAR: The IMF is in the situation of a whipping boy. When we discuss the problem of punishing the whipping boy, we need to find out whether the Prince of Wales did not do his homework. What happened in 1990 and 1991 in the Soviet Union and Eastern Europe? An enormous, powerful empire disintegrated, leaving anarchy in its wake. The existing institutions ceased to function, and new institutions could not be created overnight. We had a severe economic crisis in the Soviet Union because the former regime, the former system, stopped operating, and the new arrangements did not work. New states emerged, some of whom went to war, as in Yugoslavia. We were lucky to have prevented similar developments in the Soviet Union. These were times of enormous change and challenge that affected the fate of the world.

The Soviet Union of the Brezhnev era was more predictable and less dangerous, but what was the West's response to the new challenge? In the United States, the Bush administration faced presidential elections and opposition from the Senate and the House of Representatives. Germany wrestled with the problem of reunification. Japan was unable to provide leadership as in the past few years. Britain supported us, but it was economically weak. There was a lot of discussion, but everyone had problems. Of course, we had the International Monetary Fund. Let the International Monetary Fund resolve these problems. Let us imagine for just a moment that the Fund was put in charge of restoring Europe after World War II. The IMF is not bad, but it is an organization that was created to deal with currency crises, and then it took on the management of budgetary crises. It does not have the decision-making process and procedures and human resources to deal with this enormous problem, which requires political leadership rather than technical expertise to resolve. And so everybody is now wondering, Why is the Fund not up to handling the problem? The story of the whipping boy is still unfinished.

DESAI: Your friends in the fund must have been very pleased to hear your views.

GAIDAR: Yes, I had a chance to see those friends. I feel sorry for some of them who tried hard and had to answer for problems that were not within their sphere of competence.

DESAI: Did you expect more material support from the West than you asked for when you launched the reforms in January 1992?

GAIDAR: First of all, we did not start the reforms because somebody promised to support us. We started the process because there was absolutely no other way. If you take into account the way the socialist system actually worked, its actual condition in 1991, and how the August coup influenced the day-to-day working of the economic mechanism, then we can discuss the choice of alternative strategies. My book [*Days of Defeat and Victory*, 1999] deals with the practical limitations and actual factors that influenced our decision making and offers a limited corridor of possible policies. So in speaking of alternative strategies, I do not think about more money or less money. You could put in a lot of money and mess up the strategy. You could have less money and come out better. The problem was the absence of a clear, liberalization strategy in terms of which to define a policy framework in those days.

DESAI: What would you do differently if you had another chance?

GAIDAR: That depends on whether I were nominated tsar of Russia or whether I were nominated acting prime minister of the Yeltsin government with the pressures he faced, with the creation of the Commonwealth of Independent States, with the existing state machinery, with the Supreme Soviet [parliament] elected in the Communist days, and with the present constitution and its unclear division of state powers. If I were nominated tsar of Russia, I would do everything differently. On the other hand, if I were made acting Russian prime minister, I would handle a lot of technical issues differently. I would not wait until the spring of 1992 to liberalize oil prices. I would not introduce a complicated system of international economic controls in January 1992. I would not try to establish export controls in the autumn of 1992. If you have in mind broader aspects, then I would act approximately the way I did. However, I would be more certain of undertaking the right measures and less ready to make compromises, knowing well the high price one pays later for compromises.

DESAI: What kind of government do you visualize with Mr. Putin as president?

GAIDAR: I do not know, and frankly I do not think anyone knows. I doubt that Mr. Putin understands the composition of his cabinet. I know what the economic policy priorities are and which policies have a chance of being successful. I know the legislation that would be supported by this government because I know a few people in it. I hope it will be a government that pushes economic policies in the right direction.

DESAI: What about the role of the oligarchs in government formation?

GAIDAR: I see a number of problems with the Putin presidency, a lot of unpredictability. He does not have a good record in the field of democratic freedoms. He will have to prove his credentials as a genuine democrat. I hope that he will be smart enough to understand that democracy in Russia is a momentous achievement and that its nurturing is strategically important for the country.

The oligarchs' influence on Putin is a source of speculation. However, I doubt that they will exercise much control. It is difficult for me to imagine why Putin, unlike Yeltsin, needs the oligarchs around him.

DESAI: How would you assess Boris Yeltsin's legacy?

GAIDAR: Of course, he is a historical figure in the Russian political life of this century. He was the first popularly elected president of the Russian state. Sitting in the Kremlin, he had every opportunity to use his authority and operate as an autocrat. Instead, he chose to build a young democracy. That is his most important political legacy.

DESAI: Would you give some credit to Mikhail Gorbachev for initiating democratic freedoms in Russia?

GAIDAR: I give him credit for initiating democratic reforms in Russia. He is also a historical figure, but he started a process he ultimately failed to understand. He rapidly lost control and led the Soviet Union and Russia into complete anarchy. I did not recognize my country in December 1991. I know Russia now. Russian society and the economy have a lot of problems, but Russia has a functioning market economy and is a functioning democracy. And that was managed by Yeltsin, not by Gorbachev.

DESAI: Finally, what is your vision of the future Russia?

GAIDAR: I would like to live in Europe but not leave my own country and [still be able to] speak Russian.

DESAI: That is a lovely one-liner. Let us have questions from the audience.

Questions from the Audience

QUESTION: What is the motivation for Russia's union with Belarus, a much weaker economy?

GAIDAR: Perhaps you know that as the Union of Right Forces, we opposed the current plan to unite with Belarus in the December Duma elections.[6] We firmly believe that preserving the constitution in a young democracy is extremely important. Any union with Belarus will make an already complicated Russian constitution even more complicated and will inevitably increase political pressures inside Russia. If you are seriously talking about a union with Belarus, then you have to understand what type of regime must exist there.

We have [Alexander] Lukashenko, who has appointed himself the country's president for another term.[7] We have the only parliament in Europe that is not elected by the people but appointed by Lukashenko. If we proceed with this union, in a year or two, or five years, the Belarusan people will inevitably ask us, "With whom have you formed a union?" It is a bad idea for Russia. Of course, I understand the political motives of those who are not prepared to oppose this union because the Belarusans are close to Russians. The majority of Belarusans speak Russian. However, the idea of a union of Slavic forces is politically not a worthwhile one. We have to explain to the Russian people the reality of the situation.

QUESTION: Historically, was there political opposition from the regions or the Duma to your reforms?

GAIDAR: The reforms encountered a number of problems. Regarding the decontrol of oil prices, the opposition in the Supreme Soviet adopted special legislation in the spring of 1992 prohibiting governmental deregulation of oil prices. The regions strongly supported this parliamentary decision. The most serious problem in the early days of reform was the absence of a Russian state and a Russian constitution. The existing constitution could not provide answers to elementary questions such as who was responsible for what and whose decisions had priority. This mess was responsible for the weakness of policymaking between 1991 and 1993.

QUESTION: Contemporaneously, would you suggest that there are sufficiently strong economic interests of a liberal market that would allow you to live in the Russia of your choice?

GAIDAR: Which economic interests in Russia strongly support the Russia I want to live in? We can see the support of the population based on sociological polls. The young—under the age of thirty, well educated, and living in large cities—provided the core electorate for the Union of Right Forces. However, the development of Russian society will bring to the fore those who are young, those who are not connected with the socialist past, and those who are exposed to international economic and social ties, so we stand a reasonable chance.

QUESTION: What was the average Russian's reaction to President Putin's granting of full immunity with all the privileges it entailed to Yeltsin and his family?

GAIDAR: To be frank, it was the right move and prompted a normal reaction from the Russian people. It was a sensible, pragmatic decision. You have to remember that we are a young democracy, lacking two hundred years of democratic experience. Yeltsin was the first democratically elected president, and Putin inherited enormous powers granted by the Russian constitution. The president's voluntary relinquishment of power, bringing upon himself and his family the likelihood of prosecution from his successor, would have pushed Russia away from democracy for the next few years if immunity had not been granted. In the concrete Russian situation, it would be a mistake to copy other models. I think it was the right solution.

QUESTION: What are the chances of a continuation of reforms if, as you suggest, the Russian population is tired of them and is therefore looking for a strong man to control the situation?

GAIDAR: The Russian population is, of course, tired of a weak government but not of reforms per se. Somehow "reform" has not become a bad word in Russia. It is strange, but it will take enormous efforts to make "reform" and "democracy" bad words in Russia. You will not find a political party that says, we are against democracy and we will restore totalitarian rule. The people are exhausted by the radical changes that affect their way of life. They are tired of big government. These are the inevitable outcomes of the revolution. If the government is strong and efficient and prepared to deliver changes that do not control people's everyday lives—for instance, agricultural legislation that allows them private plots, creating conditions for further distribution of land or legislation that allows enterprises to attract investment—it will not create a social collision. These are different from the reforms of the early 1990s, which created cataclysmic changes in the day-to-day life of ordinary Russians.

QUESTION: In your book you distinguish between the Communist parties of Eastern Europe and Russia, stating that the Russian Communist Party was imperial and the rest were governed by democratic rules. What are the implications of this distinction for present-day party politics in Russia?

GAIDAR: The post-Communist Party in Poland is pretty much a normal, social democratic party, whereas the post-Communist Party in Russia is a branch of the national socialists with their anti- Semitic slogans. The Polish Communist Party never ruled Poland; it was a department of the Communist Party of the Soviet Union. The same situation applies to the Bulgarian and Hungarian Communist parties. After the end of totalitarian rule, after these countries became independent, radical nationalism was closed to them. They had nowhere to go except in the direction of social democracy. In Russia, even during Soviet days, the Communist Party of the Soviet Union was not really a Marxist party. It was an imperial party.

And from the very beginning, the ideology of the Communist Party of the Russian Federation has been authoritarian and nationalistic. If you read the writings of Mr. [Gennady] Zyuganov, the Communist leader, there is nothing Marxist about them, but there is much that resembles the writings of Hitler. Of course, a few members of the Communist Party of the Russian Federation are Marxists and Leninists. Some of them are genuine social democrats, but the bulk of their supporters are people with extreme nationalistic ideas. That is why they are dangerous. If they are less dangerous now, it is not because they have changed but because it is clear that they will not gain power.

We have seen the political dynamics of transition in the postsocialist countries. After the initial election, subsequent elections are usually won by the post-Communist parties. Transition is difficult everywhere because of social hardships. People all over the place have started supporting groups from the previous regimes. Then elections go in favor of people like [Aleksander] Kwasniewski in Poland, and nothing happens.[8] It was evident that this was no less true for Russia, but in Russia, the outcome would not be Mr. Kwasniewski but Mr. Zyuganov and Mr. [Albert] Makashov.[9] The most dangerous moment in Russia's transition was the 1996 presidential election [when Zyuganov instead of Yeltsin could have been elected president]. Now everybody accepts the idea that the Communists will never come to power in Russia. They could be close to power, behind power, a big faction in the Duma, a few governors in the regions, but they will never rule Russia again.

QUESTION: What is the main danger for the young Russian democracy?

GAIDAR: The major source of danger is the fact that it is young. It is not supported by traditions. It needs time and the ability to accumulate traditions—the security for the people that the next president of Russia will not abolish free speech and tell his countrymen that he will rule Russia himself and to hell with free elections. Russian society is now supportive of preserving democratic freedoms. You could find many people in Russia who are dissatisfied with democracy and who would answer positively when asked whether the government would be more efficient if democratic freedoms were limited. They would not be the majority, but they would be a very significant minority. However, if you then asked the same people concrete questions on censorship and the abolition of free elections, they would reject them. This means that democratic freedoms and institutions are still very young and respected, but we need time to stabilize them.

QUESTION: You explained the change of attitude among the Russian people toward the Chechnyan war as including the protection of Russian citizens in Dagestan and the removal of the possible harassment of Russian citizens in the future. I was not sure whether you agree with that policy. What is your opinion of the Russian policy?

GAIDAR: In general, I think the Russian government is doing what it has to do. It is unpleasant. Every war is dangerous and harmful for a society. This war is dangerous and bad for Russia because it is undermining democratic freedoms, but I do not see any other choice for the Russian government. If I were heading the administration, I would perhaps address several concrete and tactical problems differently, but I would not discuss them before an American audience. From 1994 to 1996, I had a clear notion: If I were heading the government then, I would have stopped the fighting and started negotiations, but now I am not in this position. However, I would not give the order for the troops to stop fighting.

QUESTION: I am British, and we are nearly over the loss of the empire. Have the average Russian citizens in the street reconciled themselves to the fact that Russia is now a second-rate power?

GAIDAR: We are moving in the right direction. I use the examples of the British and the French empires to explain to our people that we are not the first to go through this process. The problem here is that it was the result of a combination of several features. You know that the loss of the empire was not easy for the British to accept, but that loss, combined with the collapse of all of the past institutions and state structures and radical changes in the people's socioeconomic life, makes the Russian situation especially difficult and dangerous.

QUESTION: Given the current events in Chechnya, do you expect Russia to become more assertive in the former Soviet republics in the Caucasus and Central Asia?

GAIDAR: Of course not. In no way is it in our national interest. It is unfortunate that Chechnya is inside Russia and not one of the former Soviet republics outside it. Otherwise, we would have addressed this problem in December 1991, when we dissolved the Soviet Union. We are extremely interested in the stability of the Trans-Caucasian and Central Asian republics. We should not fret over the Balkans because they are far from our sphere of national interest. However, the Trans-Caucasian and Central Asian republics are in the Russian sphere of influence, but that doesn't mean in any way that Russia is interested in restoring imperial control over them. That would be a foolish move in the wrong direction.

QUESTION: It has been almost eight years since the start of privatization in Russia. What is your assessment? What was done well? What was done poorly? What would you have done differently in privatization?

GAIDAR: My answer is the same, regardless of whether I would have had to deal with the issue as a tsar or as a prime minister who had to work with the existing legislation, the Supreme Soviet in place, and a series of problems at the start of the process. I have not seen a single postsocialist country in which people are satisfied with privatization. I know of countries in which privatization was accomplished more successfully than in others. For example, I told an audience in Seattle that if I were the tsar of Russia, I would have approached privatization like our Hungarian friends did. I think they did a good job of it, but the Hungarians would disagree with me because they believe their privatization did not go well. When I brought this up in Seattle, a Hungarian professor said, of course, they would not agree, it was a terrible privatization because 80 percent of the assets are now in the hands of foreigners. So I do not know a perfect path to privatization after the collapse of socialism. And the Russian approach to privatization was not perfect, either.

However, in addressing privatization, you look for the most feasible and least harmful way rather than for the best way. For instance, not everyone knows that the legislation for privatization was elaborated three months before we started work in the government. Not everyone knows that the so-called second variant of privatization, through which 80 percent of Russian enterprises were privatized, was elaborated by the Communist faction in the Supreme Soviet in the spring of 1992. So there were a lot of compromises I would not have accepted if I had had the choice.

If you have in mind the highly interesting but different and complicated privatization at a later stage, the so-called loans-for-shares deals, then I must tell you that I had left the government by that time. But if you are speaking about the mass privatization of 1992–1994, then the choices were to either speed up privatization, given the circumstances under the rules we considered unfavorable, or try to stop it. That was the strategic choice. I was in favor of going forward as rapidly as possible even with bad rules because, after the collapse of socialism, it was better to have the property distributed and the property rights traded than to have the mess in property relations that was left over from socialism. That was an empirical question that you cannot answer from a theoretical perspective. So when I am trying to determine whether I was right or wrong, I must compare the civilian sectors of the economy that were privatized with those that were not. It is meaningless to compare the privatized Russian economy with the U.S. economy; instead, one should compare it with the nonprivatized sector of the Russian economy.

So, let us take two sectors, beginning with retail trade. We had two trading arrangements, the state retail trade in charge of the big cities and the consumer cooperatives, which, for a variety of historical reasons, were named differently. This massive system controlled retail trade in the small cities and the countryside. We privatized the state system, and that was a sound decision. You will notice that, in Moscow and St. Petersburg, the merchandise is of good quality and the service is not bad. As for the cooperatives, they have mostly disappeared. The system just collapsed because it was not privatized.

Take another sector, restaurants and food services, which was also privatized. You will find these businesses vastly improved. Contrast their performance with that of the hotel industry. Except for a few fancy five-star hotels, the hotels were left with the city administrations. One of the worst-functioning sectors in Russia is the hotel industry.

Let's take another area, the oil industry. There are several problems with the privatization of Russian oil companies. The best-run Russian oil company, Surgutneftegaz, is market oriented and efficiently run; it pays all of its taxes. The worst-run oil company, Rosneft, is the last big nonprivatized state oil company. So the results have to be judged on a practical basis rather than from a theoretical perspective. The decision to proceed with inefficient privatization even with the bad rules was correct.

QUESTION: How would you judge Russia's relations with the Baltic countries?

GAIDAR: Generally, there are no hard feelings in Russia toward the Baltic states because they have broken away from Russia. Russia accepted the fact that all of the previous Soviet republics were going to leave the Soviet Union. The problem with the Baltic states has to do with the minorities, especially the Russian-speaking ones. Of course, the Baltic minorities are not only Russians but also Ukrainians, Belarusans, and Jews—in a word, everyone who does not speak Estonian, Latvian, and Lithuanian. There was no problem with Lithuania because it accepted the rules protecting minority rights.

In contrast, Estonia and Latvia became a source of tension and disappointment in Russian society. I clearly remember how these states became independent, our discussions with their leaders beforehand, and their assurances at that time to the leaders of democratic Russia that the rights of the citizens of Russian origin would be fully protected. That promise was not kept. I see some progress in Estonia and modest progress in Latvia. I really think that the sooner these independent states understand that the protection of minority rights is important for the efficiency and stability of their democracies, the better it will be for them.

QUESTION: I liked your formulation of your wanting to be in Europe without leaving your country while speaking Russian. This is a new definition of "European in context and Russian in form." At the same time, you said Russia should not imitate or adopt foreign models. How do you see Russian capitalism or democracy differing from U.S. or European models?

GAIDAR: The Russian model has to be different because Russia has another history, its own problems, and distinct traditions. The United States had some of the features of a civil society before independence. It developed powerful traditions of contract enforcement, the rule of law, protection of property rights, and democratic procedures. If someone were to introduce the U.S. constitution and U.S. laws from A to Z in another society, that person would fail miserably. The U.S. model functions in the United States because of its history. We have another history, one that makes it enormously difficult to create a market economy and a working democracy. We have to keep in mind our history and our problems and not overestimate some aspects that can function efficiently in other societies with a better history.

For instance, we have an inefficient and corrupt bureaucracy. Even with the best intentions and efforts of the Russian government, this problem will not be eliminated for some time to come. You must not think that when regulations are eliminated, the new order will be implemented by perfect civil servants who are always concerned with the interests of the state. Even so, I think that liberal ideas and economic policies of the European variety are absolutely essential for Russia. I say this not because I am an ideological liberal but because I think they can be adopted under the conditions in Russia.

OCTOBER 2004

DESAI: How would you react to Putin's proposals to assign seats in the Duma based on proportional, party-contested election victories and to abolish the single-member constituencies in which the winner is elected on the basis of majority votes?

GAIDAR: Political scientists have endlessly discussed the merits of alternative arrangements of parliamentary elections, among them proportional and majority or a combination of both. It is impossible to say which one is ideal for contemporary Russia. Having said that, the latest proposals to reconstruct the electoral system in Russia have several features that raise concern.

First, Russian democracy is young. Therefore, stable electoral rules are important. I am at a loss to explain why these rules should be changed now and how the change will help fight terrorism.

Second, the proposed change suggests that, in order to qualify for proportional representation in the Duma via party-contested seats, the party or group must get at least 7 percent of the electoral vote.

DESAI: This qualifying limit is higher than the original 5 percent, right?

GAIDAR: Yes. The new number, in my view, is unusually high. In Turkey it is even higher. This does not contribute to the development of stable democratic arrangements. At the same time, the Duma will cease to represent the diverse views and positions of Russian society if individual contests—in which Duma membership is assigned on the basis of majority votes—are abolished. Finally, the Duma currently has a small but active group of independent deputies. By and large, these people have repeatedly won in their districts. They are politically astute and talented. They are the ones who actively participate in meetings of key committees and plenary sessions. Their views have limited impact on decision making, but their voices are heard. They influence public opinion. If the presidential proposals are adopted, such independent deputies, who obtain entry via individual contests, will be absent from the Duma. The party loyalists will then take over. That, I think, is an alarming prospect.

DESAI: How do you react to the proposal that the president select the regional governors, contingent on subsequent approval by the regional legislatures?

GAIDAR: As one who was active in the Russian government, I fully understand the reaction of Russian leaders who look at the mayhem committed by elected governors and dream of reinstating the practice of appointing them from Moscow. I think this is a wrong decision. Russia was ruled like that from Moscow for centuries, but that did not end the corruption. That did not prevent terrorist acts, either, as the experience of the last decades of the tsarist regime demonstrated. More to the point, it did not prevent two revolutions, namely the end of the tsarist regime in 1917 and the breakup of the Soviet Union in 1991.

DESAI: How do you ensure that better leaders are elected to run the regions?

GAIDAR: It is not clear to me why it is necessary to solve the issue of gubernatorial election in one fell swoop. True, Russia is a young and unstable democracy. Therefore, voters tend to elect leaders who are far from the best. With greater experience, they will understand that local problems need to be resolved at local levels. They will realize that in choosing regional leaders, they, rather than the president in Moscow, will decide how their regional problems, such as providing heat or collecting garbage, will be handled. A de facto appointment of governors from the center would entail reverting to a system in which collecting garbage in Uryupinsk and providing heat in Tambov once again end up as the Kremlin's responsibility.

DESAI: Are these consolidating measures necessary for fighting terrorism?

GAIDAR: I am not an expert in fighting terrorism, so I must refrain from making specific suggestions. I don't think there are any simple solutions, but how the tightening of political control can help in the struggle is beyond my comprehension. As I argued earlier, political control in the final decades of tsarist rule did not prevent terrorist acts by dissidents.

DESAI: Grigory Yavlinsky says that Putin's proposals smack of "soft Stalinism." What is your reaction?

GAIDAR: That is not a helpful choice of words. I would not use that phrase. What is happening in Russia today is a different phenomenon, significantly different from the events under Stalin in the Soviet Union from the 1930s through the 1950s.

DESAI: Do you think that Putin regards the consolidation of political power as a necessary precondition for promoting economic reforms?

GAIDAR: In my opinion, the Russian government carried out a series of extremely important economic reforms between 2000 and 2002 under presidential initiative. Unfortunately, events in 2003 and 2004 suggest that economic reforms have slowed down just as the consolidation of political power has increased.

DESAI: How does Putin's model differ from that of Pinochet in Chile and of the Communist leadership in China? Any other historical parallels?

GAIDAR: Russia's political analysts invoke these countries for comparison, but the parallels are obviously vague. The comparisons need to highlight the political similarities and the economic features as well. Keeping that in mind, the current Russian mix resembles Mexico under the single-party domination of PRI. Japan, from the end of World War II to the onset of the 1980s, was similar. So was Italy during the same time span.

DESAI: Does it make sense to apply the norms of a fully formed U.S.-style liberal order in order to assess Russia's evolving transition?

GAIDAR: I think it is incorrect to use U.S.-style norms of a liberal order to assess the effectiveness of transition processes in postsocialist economies. That is obviously a mistake. Most of these countries are moving ahead toward a liberal order at their own speed and according to their ability to shake off the accumulated burdens—economic, political, and institutional—of their socialist past. The important consideration is whether they will stay the course.

DESAI: From that perspective, do you think the long-term prospects of Russia continuing to evolve to a liberal political and economic system remain robust despite Putin's illiberal forays?

GAIDAR: There is a definite consensus among Russian society and the elite that Russia needs a market economy. However, arguments persist over policy choices with a view to improving the standard of living of the thirty million Russians who live below the governmental poverty level. Nobody argues about the need for market prices, a convertible ruble, and private property. These are firmly and irreversibly in place. By contrast, our struggle to form a robust, functioning democracy has not brought decisive results. On the other hand, its long-term prospects are positive. I do not think that the educated, urban populations in large countries such as Russia can put up with undemocratic regimes for long.

DESAI: How do you assess the prospects for the formation of the unified Gazpromrosneft company?[10]

GAIDAR: I do not see anything wrong with the merger of two state companies that work in the Russian gas and oil sector. In fact, several arguments can be advanced in favor of such a decision. The main problem is not the merger but the lack of progress in the reform of the natural gas sector and the total lack of transparency in the workings of Gazprom. It is a black box.

DESAI: How do you view Putin's foreign policy?

GAIDAR: His foreign policy is pragmatic, realistic, and oriented toward safeguarding Russia's national interests.

DESAI: Will he seek a third presidential term?

GAIDAR: I can only say one thing: I do not know.

NOTES

1. The question refers to Russia's second war with Chechnya (1999–), as opposed to the first, which was waged from 1994 to 1996. The second war has witnessed a dramatic increase in Russian nationalism as a result of terrorist acts (e.g., the bombing of apartment buildings) and, most recently, the Beslan tragedy of September 2004.

2. Vladimir Mau and Irina Starodubrovskaya, *The Challenge of Revolution: Contemporary Russia in Historical Perspective* (New York: Oxford University Press, 2001).

3. NTV is a Russian TV company that was brought under state ownership and control in 2003.

4. Karadjordjevic and Obrenovic are rival Serbian dynasties.

5. Novi Sad and Kragujevac are Serbian cities in Yugoslavia.

6. The Union of Right Forces, or the Soyuz Pravykh Sil (SPS), was formed in August 1999 as an electoral coalition. According to the party's manifesto, the SPS stands for "liberal goals and values, personal freedom and personal responsibility, freedom of speech and association."

7. Alexander Lukashenko has been president of Belarus since 1994.

8. In 1995, Aleksander Kwasniewski succeeded Lech Walesa as president of Poland.

9. Albert Makashov, former Soviet general, Russian Duma deputy, and hard-line Communist, has attracted much press for his outrageous anti-Semitism.

10. In the final act of the unification drama calculated to raise state control of Gazprom to 51 percent, Gazprom was set to acquire the private oil company Sibneft instead of the state-owned Rosneft.

CHAPTER 4

Boris Nemtsov

The Political Activist

You know, Putin is a lucky man in a happy situation. He can do whatever he wants with the State Duma.

I am sure [Putin] believes that Russia needs a healthy market economy. Unfortunately, he doesn't believe that Russia also needs a democracy. It is difficult to explain to someone with a KGB background that a connection exists between democracy and competitive markets. That is the real difference between Putin and Yeltsin. Yeltsin believed in this connection in his very soul, especially after he visited the United States and went to a supermarket. "I am for democracy, and I am for private business," he said. He kept that pledge to the end of his career.

Putin looks strong on issues such as Chechnya and flying an aircraft or visiting a submarine, but he is extremely cautious on economic and political decisions.

JUNE 2003

Because of the grim experience of World War II, during which millions perished, none of the grandchildren of the war veterans now want to join the army. At the same time, we have a huge demographic crisis. Russia's population is declining. Will the army disappear in Russia?

We have three million bureaucrats in the country. We live under a bureaucratic capitalism.

I think he [Putin] wants a loyal press. Like all politicians, he hates criticism. But a lot of politicians, including your president, the president of the United States, understand the meaning of freedom. Putin does not understand it, and that is the point.

Well, I think the main problem for Russia is to attract Russian investment, which in turn will promote growth. That is my position. I do not think foreign investment is crucial.

We [the reformers] stand not only for democratic arrangements and freedom of speech but also for a market economy based on genuine competition, transparent rules, and private ownership of assets.

Of course, we made a lot of mistakes. We were beginners. We had no experience.

Russians are not ready to work hard, take risks, and make money. . . . But Russians would rather count on their president, look into his eyes, and depend on him to give them cash without their having to earn it.

[O]ur biggest mistake was that we did not explain to the Russian public what we were up to. . . . [W]e thought that all we had to do was to stabilize the currency, fight inflation, and privatize companies and that the doors would open. The public would understand and support us.

You know, Putin is a lucky man. He has benefited from Yeltsin's reforms, among them the privatized economy. Again, the high oil prices, exceeding $30 a barrel, have brought him enormous gains. . . . Then again, Putin is a smart man. He understands the levers of power in the Kremlin. . . . The government has raised pensions for retirees and salaries for teachers and doctors. Russians support him for that. But the main reason for his popularity is the contrast with Yeltsin. Unlike Yeltsin, who reportedly got drunk during his U.S. visit, Putin is a teetotaler. Again, he is young and vigorous, and he enjoys swimming and horseback riding. Russians admire him for that. They are proud of their president.

Poverty will remain widespread because the poor have no more champions to advance their cause.

I'm afraid authoritarian modernization will not eliminate the strangulating bureaucracy, corruption, and the ruthless hold of the secret service and the military brass. Putin's methods cannot solve these problems.

Frankly speaking, we have a prime minister whose name is Vladimir Putin. The rest are his assistants, at best his advisors.

First, free speech must be restored. . . . Channels 1 and 2 of the Russian TV should be privatized. That will create genuine competition in information dissemination. Second, Putin should undertake a political dialogue with the Chechens. . . . Third, we need to get away from "managed democracy" and organize transparent elections in Russia.

Russian generals do not have political ambitions. The Soviet Union disappeared without the generals firing a shot.

As far as the reformers are concerned, we are in a serious crisis.

The critical area of foreign policy concern for Russia remains the former republics of the Soviet Union, which constitute the Commonwealth of Independent States (CIS).

As for the U.S.-Russia relationship, Putin is fortunate to have George W. Bush as the U.S. president because they are united in the fight against terrorism.

We know our leadership is concerned about China, and we hope that the Chinese will continue to be preoccupied with their serious internal problems.

As for Khodorkovsky, his future is unclear. Putin will be inaugurated president on May 7 [2004]. The tsars granted amnesty to prisoners when they were inaugurated, but that was a tsarist tradition. The KGB tradition is likely to be different.

Politics has ceased to be transparent in Putin's Russia.

I think markets will coexist in Russia without democratic freedoms, but what kind of society will we end up with?

Isn't it better to have a few oligarchs rather than the state, in the person of Putin, in charge of Russian TV? The oligarchs compete with one another. . . . Such competition is good for media freedom.

The government wants to control the private oil businesses by denying them the opportunity of owning pipelines. It is a political decision.

What we currently have in Russia is a contradiction between our laws and justice. Russians would rather have справедливость, that is, justice of any kind rather than law.

DECEMBER 2004

Without adequate representation in the Duma, regional economic interests will be neglected.

In truth, the Chechen problem needs to be resolved via political dialogue.

I do not think we need to move along the liberal U.S. trajectory, nor *can* we.

APRIL 2000

DESAI: I am going to take you back to the December 1999 Duma elections and then come forward in time. We would like to know at this end, as we face an election in this country, how you managed to get elected to the Duma as a candidate of the Union of Right Forces coalition. How did you campaign for the election? How did you raise the money?

NEMTSOV: Which is also relevant for financing U.S. election campaigns.

DESAI: Yes, but give us the flavor of your election strategy. What issues did you raise?

NEMTSOV: As you know, I represent the Union of Right Forces, or the SPS coalition. Public opinion polls in the summer of 1999 showed that the SPS had 1–2 percent of the electoral vote. If a faction or a coalition wants to get seats in the Duma, it must win at least 5 percent of the vote, according to Russian election rules. Quite a few observers inside and outside Russia doubted that the SPS had a chance to win seats in the Duma, but we did. We got 8.7 percent of the vote, and we have more than thirty seats in the Duma out of 450, which is not a small number. If we combine our seats with those of the Yabloko, Fatherland, and Unity blocs, we will have a majority, which is positive news from Russia, especially as we begin discussion on the ratification of the Start II Treaty in the Duma.

With regard to financing an election campaign, this is a special issue not only for Russia but also for the United States. I am aware of the discussion here of how the Democrats and the Republicans raise campaign monies. In that regard, the SPS had several advantages. First of all, the SPS election program included issues of concern to the business community. Among these were lower taxes, genuine and fair competition, the rule of law, law enforcement, a fair distribution of property, and transparent outlays from the budget. As a result, businessmen from around the country, in Moscow as well as the provinces, realized that it was cheaper to support the SPS than to pay bribes to everybody and to lose their jobs and their businesses day after day. We raised enough money to win. Unfortunately, I do not know, I really do not know the ultimate budget for the campaign, but it was sufficient for us to get 8.7 percent of the vote.

We won because we sent a concrete, transparent message to the voters. We realized that we had to interest the younger generation in political issues and social concerns. Unfortunately, as in several East European countries, only a small percentage of young voters is interested in politics and voting in Russian elections. That is terrible. So we organized rock-and-roll concerts to attract young voters all over Russia, in ten cities from Moscow to Irkutsk on Lake Baikal, in Novosibirsk, Samara, Nizhni Novgorod, cities in the Urals, and in Yekaterinburg and Perm. Our message to the electorate was that Russia has to have a new generation of politicians in the twenty-first century. One has to be clear about who will run the country. Only the young, energetic, and business-oriented community is ready to take the country forward, not the bureaucrats or the well-known tycoons. This is important because a lot of people, more than twenty million, are involved in new businesses. They provided a solid voting base for the SPS.

The coalition also focused on corruption deals. We suggested that immunity from prosecution be discontinued for Duma deputies, governors, mayors, and almost everyone in a position of power. Unfortunately, Russian laws protect Duma deputies and the powerful, but not the people. As far as I know, the United States does not have immunity for members of Congress on corruption charges, although they can make deals inside the Congress. But an investigation would immediately begin, should they undertake such activity outside the Congress. Russia has another problem. A number of criminals decided to seek power in order to avoid prison. Therefore, our promise to revoke the politicians' immunity from prosecution was attractive to those voters with liberal views and to those from the center and the Left. Our signals were clean and clear, and, as a result, we won.

DESAI: So it seems that you got a significant portion of the vote because of your appeal to the electorate via a clear message. But do you think that, in general, it was a fair election? How do you account for the defeat of the Fatherland–All Russia coalition of Moscow mayor Yury Luzhkov and former prime minister Yevgeny Primakov, who were ahead of you in the public opinion polls?[1]

NEMTSOV: I think that Fatherland lost a lot of seats in Parliament and failed in the campaign not because of huge mistakes made by Luzhkov and Primakov but because of the public relations campaign organized by Berezovsky's group and his media slayer, Sergei Dorenko.[2] He did a great job of getting rid of everybody he wanted to retire from politics. In 1997, for example, Chubais and I were engaged in similar activities. During the 1999 Duma election campaign, Dorenko appeared every week on national TV with concrete, credible remarks about Luzhkov, Primakov, and Nemtsov, according to Berezovsky's wishes. As a result, Fatherland lost its popularity, and Luzhkov his appeal. In fact, Luzhkov has lost an opportunity that he cannot reclaim by changing public opinion in his favor. For sixty years, Mayor Luzhkov was a happy man. Muscovites loved him, and our journalists refrained from criticizing him. They were excited about his renovation deals in Moscow, his business activities, his new family, his young wife, and so on. Finally, when he became a pensioner, a man called Dorenko appeared and started criticizing him at Berezovsky's bidding. What was Luzhkov's response? Well, I have been in politics for ten years. I have habits that can be criticized. I did not pay attention to that. But after Luzhkov and Primakov became pensioners, they were criticized by the press, correspondents, and journalists. They grew nervous and responded to the charges, and people felt they were not really strong. They were perceived as weak. Why should we vote for a weak politician? They lost the voters' support.

DESAI: So let's move forward. The December 1999 Duma elections are over, and President Yeltsin resigns on December 25. Were you surprised?

NEMTSOV: Yes, like you. You know I was surprised because I have known President Yeltsin for nine years. Life and power are the same for him. Did he want to kill himself by resigning? Where was the insurance for his survival if he resigned? What about his family? His health? The main problem was his immunity from future prosecution. I was so surprised that for a moment I did not believe it. It seemed like an April Fool's joke. But it was the end of 1999. Finally, I understood that he realized that it was impossible for him to continue in power. He was afraid that, if he did not resign, Putin would lose his popularity. And he did everything possible to give Putin a chance to be elected president. It seems to me that it was an act of genius on Yeltsin's part, absolutely out of character and unpredictable.

DESAI: So you do think it was a stroke of genius on the president's part?

NEMTSOV: Perhaps it was not his decision. I do not know. Perhaps it was Tatyana's [his daughter's] decision. Or maybe someone else's.

VOICE FROM THE AUDIENCE: How about Berezovsky?

NEMTSOV: Well, I know that Berezovsky is well known, not only in Russia but also here in the United States, but I do not think he played a role in the decision. I do not think Berezovsky can organize immunity from prosecution for the

Yeltsin family. In fact, I don't think that Yeltsin listened to him. Let me give you an example. When I was in the government, Chubais and I decided to fire Berezovsky, who was then the deputy chairman of the Security Council. We were young at the time. Berezovsky held a low official position. After all, he was not the chairman of the Security Council. Right now I do not know the name of the current deputy chairman of the council. Perhaps nobody does. So we went to Yeltsin's office in his dacha in the countryside, a fascinating place, and I said to him, "Boris Nikolaevich, it is impossible to continue in office fighting Berezovsky's bureaucratic wheeling and dealing. He acts like a bureaucrat, like a meddlesome politician." After about ten minutes, Yeltsin said, "What do you want, Boris?" I said frankly that I wanted to get rid of Berezovsky. "Where is the decree, Boris?" the president asked. I gave him the decree. He looked at it and said, "A decree is too much for Berezovsky. Let me instead sign a special presidential decision." Now, that is a low-level document, not a decree but an internal document. He signed it. Chubais and I were so excited that we tried to continue the discussion, but Yeltsin said, "Forget about it. This is not a subject deserving further discussion. Let's have a drink." We declined the president's invitation. This story illustrates the extent of Berezovsky's influence on Yeltsin. On the other hand, Tatyana and the president's wife, of course, and perhaps Alexander Voloshin, the chief of staff, understood that it was the right time for Yeltsin to resign and give his successor a chance to become the next president. The timing of the decision involved a political calculation that had to be made known to the president. That was a genuine achievement. But I don't think Berezovsky managed it. I don't believe that for a moment.

DESAI: Okay, let's get away from your favorite topic, Berezovsky. We'll talk about your next favorite topic, Vladimir Putin.

NEMTSOV: Oh, yes.

DESAI: He was elected president in April 2000 in the very first round. What was the reason for this? Was it because of the war in Chechnya or because the public wanted order, stability, predictability, or something else?

NEMTSOV: Well, let's first go back to 1991. Russians loved Yeltsin. They did not merely like him, they loved him. He was a strong leader, a true Russian tsar, perceived as honest, open, and warm. Within a decade Russians were so disappointed with Yeltsin, especially after the first Chechen war in 1994, that lack of trust in him became the country's biggest problem. By the end of the millennium, Russians wanted a new leader, one who was genuinely strong, honest, and incorruptible. They were once again ready to fall in love with someone, and they got their chance with Putin, mainly because he portrayed an ideal—a strong nation, a strong Russia—and he promised to solve the problems in the Caucasus and Chechnya. So he is popular because of Chechnya, unfortunately, and because the Russians desired a strong, honest leader.

Another source of Putin's popularity, paradoxically, is the fact that few people know him. A lot of people believe that Putin is a liberal. Some think that he will

revive the military. Others fear that he will curb the freedom of the press. Some
worry that he will damage the good relationship with the West. He is a black box,
and that is to his advantage. For example, compare Putin and Grigory Yavlinsky. I
think that Yavlinsky, who had the continuing support of 5–6 percent of the electorate, lost a lot of money during the presidential campaign. He should have saved
the money because the outcome was predictable. Everybody knew him. By contrast, Putin had an advantage—he was an unknown quantity. He was elected because he got votes from the Left of the political spectrum and from the Right as
well. Even now, a lot of people in the Duma think that he will support their ideas.
Perhaps after the inauguration and the appointment of the new government the
situation will become clearer.

DESAI: But the election results do raise some questions. Gennady Zyuganov,
the Communist leader, got 30 percent of the electoral vote, and Putin squeaked
through with about 52 percent, 2 percent more than the required 50 percent, right?
This is not a very strong mandate for Vladimir Putin.

NEMTSOV: It's enough for him to be the next president. If Governor Bush were
to get 52 percent of the vote in the U.S. presidential election, he would be thrilled.
It is a solid mandate for the Russian president. But Zyuganov represents a serious
problem, you are right. Thirty percent is a significant electoral vote. He got it not
because he is a charismatic leader and popular with the public but because there is
widespread poverty in the country. If you look at the Communist Party's gains in
recent elections, its electoral vote is close to the level of poverty. Currently, 30
percent of the population has an income below the subsistence level, the same percentage as the number of votes for Zyuganov. I am sure that if the poverty level
were less, say 20 percent, Zyuganov would have gotten fewer votes. Unfortunately,
this is the most painful problem the country has. And it can be resolved only through
concrete measures in the economic and social spheres.

DESAI: Do you think that, given the less-than-guaranteed mandate, the president will go for a coalition government? Will anyone from the Communist Party
be included in the government? What about someone from the Union of Right
Forces? What kind of structure do you see?

NEMTSOV: It seems to me that a more realistic scenario is a coalition between
the tycoons and the liberals. Currently three groups are vying for the president's
attention. The first represents liberal economists like Andrei Illarionov, who was
appointed advisor to the president yesterday, German Gref, and Yevgeny Yasin.[3]
This is the liberal group. The second team is formally headed by Voloshin, the chief
of the president's staff, and Roman Abramovich rather than Berezovsky, although
Berezovsky commands greater attention from U.S. specialists on Russia.[4] I think
that Abramovich plays a bigger role in current domestic politics than Berezovsky.

The third group is represented by members of the former KGB, people like
the chief of the FSB. Realistically, Putin can select candidates from the Abramovich
group, the reformist Chubais group, and perhaps from the secret service. The se-

cret service, in my view, does not currently play an important role because of inadequate finances. The secret service was privatized in the last few years like the Kremlin. The president might need to nationalize it. But seriously, the most difficult task for Putin is to be an independent president and change the country's economic and social infrastructure. You mentioned the Communists. Perhaps some of them will be invited, but not to hold key positions. Zyuganov failed in the election and lost seventy seats in the Duma. I doubt that the Communists will stick together. They are now left with fewer seats.

DESAI: It seems to me that the Duma's composition gives hope for a consensus between the government and lawmakers on reform issues. Would you agree with that?

NEMTSOV: The Duma is more liberal than before. I just said that the Communists lost a lot of seats, and I'm sure that the Start II treaty will be adopted tomorrow because of the absence of a majority for the Communists and the Left.[5] Besides, Putin holds an effective instrument in the Duma via the Unity bloc. Under the complete control of the president, it is the Kremlin's vote-getting machine. It has little scope for discussion or internal debate. It will vote against ratification if the president demands it. The current structure of the Duma is one-third Communist, one-third Unity, and one-third liberal groups. Everything depends on the group with which Unity chooses to join forces. If Unity votes with the Communists on an issue, it will be adopted. Gennady Seleznov from the Communist Party was elected chairman of the Duma as a result of this coalition. If Unity votes with us, the liberals, we can adopt the tax code, the Start II treaty, the land code, and private ownership of land. So Putin's total control of the Duma is unique and also a positive feature because it represents a genuine consolidation of federal power.

However, the president still faces the problem of consolidating his power vis-à-vis the governors. I know what it means to be a governor in Russia because I was one myself. First of all, governors have immunity from prosecution. It is impossible to dismiss them. They are elected. They are members of the senate. They have 50 percent of the budget allocation; the other half remains with the federal treasury. So the governors, occasionally criminal and sometimes stupid, are a powerful force. The critical problem for Putin is to exercise power vertically from the top. There are two ways of resolving the issue. The first is to cancel gubernatorial elections. In my view, that is not the correct approach. It is illegal because elections are part of the constitution. More critically, they are at the very heart of a democracy. There is an alternative route, proposed by the SPS, in the form of a special law to be passed by the Duma that provides for the dismissal of governors who violate the constitution or a federal law. This decision should be made by the constitutional court and not by the Kremlin or the White House [the government]. Such an arrangement will help us get rid of law-breaking regional governors. I think that such proposals will soon be discussed in the Duma.

DESAI: So you would be in favor of some strengthening and some consolidation of power by the center vis-à-vis the regions.

NEMTSOV: To take one example, the SPS has clear proposals about economic reforms involving the private ownership of land, lower tax rates, transparent budget expenditures, and the protection of minorities. We also need to undertake the reform of housing subsidies, which will be a painful business. Ten billion dollars—forty percent of the federal budget—has to be set aside every year for housing and heating subsidies. How can these subsidies be cut? You have to have political will and a mechanism to pressure governors and mayors to accomplish those cutbacks that are under their jurisdiction. The federal authorities are not responsible for implementing them. The president faces the serious challenge of consolidating his authority.

Raising the salaries of bureaucrats in order to deal with bribery and corruption is another issue. A general in the FSB has a salary of $250 a month, whereas an apartment in central Moscow rents for $2,000 a month. The only way out is a dramatic cutback in the bureaucracy and significant salary hikes for the remaining state employees. Putin has to find new ways of dealing with the situation, perhaps by attracting private individuals to government jobs.

DESAI: So these are the reform issues. I want to understand your role in steering the process through the Duma. You talked about Seleznov, who was elected speaker of the Duma as a result of the coalition between the Putin-led Unity bloc and the Communists. We also hear that Seleznov is not a heavyweight, and you are the deputy speaker of the Duma. I would like to think that you are a powerful politician in the Duma. Are you?

NEMTSOV: Not sufficiently powerful to make important decisions.

DESAI: How are you going to steer the reform legislation?

NEMTSOV: Let me briefly describe how the Duma functions. The Russian Duma is a madhouse. It's huge. On the one hand, we have your friend Berezovsky, who is a deputy. Then we have Yegor Ligachev from the other end of the spectrum.[6] Do you know who he is?

DESAI: Yes, the Soviet-era diehard Communist.

NEMTSOV: Very solid Communist. Then we have Abramovich, who was elected from Chukovskaya oblast. And then of course, Zhirinovsky, a colorful, historical figure.[7] This motley group will discuss the Start II and antiballistic missile treaties and tax and land reform. I am the deputy speaker of this organization. My responsibilities are education and pension reforms, both of which are critical issues. We have a genuine window of opportunity for reforming the pay-as-you-go pension system, which is currently inefficient and bankrupt. We need to switch to individual pension accounts as in the United States or Chile and some of the Latin American countries. We have a solid opportunity because our pension claimants were born during World War II, a smaller number than would otherwise be the case. We have a good chance to save outflows from the pension fund and reform the system. That is my responsibility. My third area is the relationship between the federal and the regional budgets, a very sensitive subject that Seleznov agreed to hand over to me. Now, if you have political muscle, you can do what you want in the Duma. Without it, you can accomplish little even though you may have some ideas and the necessary background and even though you may be the speaker of the Duma.

DESAI: But do you think that you have a chance of steering through some of the legislation that you, as first deputy prime minister, sought to pass toward the end of 1997 and which the pre-December 1999 Duma threw out?

NEMTSOV: Absolutely, absolutely! You know, Putin is a lucky man in a happy situation. He can do whatever he wants with the State Duma. The Duma will support all of his ideas. That's it. When Chubais and I were in the government, all of our proposals concerning tax reform and the deregulation of the energy sector were blocked, first in the Kremlin because the Kremlin operated as a family enterprise and then in the State Duma. By contrast, Putin has an enormous opportunity to push forward a speedy reform agenda.

DESAI: What is the most critical reform issue in your view? Stanley Fischer, the acting managing director of the IMF, who was in Moscow last week, mentioned a string of suggestions, among them land reform, industry restructuring, a revised bankruptcy law, pension reform, and patent law.[8] What in your view is the most critical item? How would you sequence the legislation?

NEMTSOV: The unfolding of the reform process is not the critical aspect. Absence of political will to undertake reforms is the main problem. The remaining issues are largely technical. Right now Putin can select a team consisting of liberals or radical liberals, but he is not interested in reforms at present. His main task is to consolidate his authority to push reforms forward, to create the infrastructure for reforms, if necessary, first of all, and to nationalize his power. As far as reforms are concerned, the most painful item, in my opinion, is the reduction in housing subsidies, which will affect nearly 148 million Russians. People will have to pay more. Not everybody, but millions of Russians will have to contribute to housing costs.

DESAI: How about privatizing agricultural land? We talked about this topic this afternoon at the Council on Foreign Relations.

NEMTSOV: I do not think that land privatization is a simple task that can be resolved quickly. It is a complicated management problem in the countryside. Unfortunately, Russia's young people do not want to be entrepreneurs outside the towns and cities. The quality of life is very poor in the countryside—no entertainment, no infrastructure, and serious risks for those who are enterprising. Of course, private ownership of land and agricultural tax reform are important, but we urgently need to upgrade management in the farm sector. Russia needs a new batch of 25,000 rural groups. The previous 25,000, who were organized by the Bolsheviks, had a concrete agenda—to liquidate private farmers and set up collective farms. Russia needs a similar program with absolutely different management groups with an understanding of farm business, agricultural operations, and risk taking. The state must support such programs of management training related to agriculture.

DESAI: How do you view the recent IMF decision to withhold credits to the Russian government? We had Yegor Gaidar talk to us, and he described the IMF as the whipping boy—мальчик для бцтья—of the West and the U.S. Treasury. Do you agree with that point of view?

NEMTSOV: I met with Stanley Fischer a few days ago in Moscow. Frankly, he didn't look like a whipping boy to me. He was a bit troubled about the state of economic reforms, the transparency of cash flows from the IMF to Russia, and some inside deals in the Central Bank, that's true. Unfortunately, this country asks only one crazy question about Russia: Who lost Russia? And then it gives the obvious answer: The IMF lost Russia. In my opinion, the Russians lost Russia.

I also believe the IMF will remain engaged in Russia, not only because it wants Russia to have an efficient economy but also because, even after the restructuring of Russia's commercial debt with the London Club creditors, Russia must make a debt repayment every year of $10 billion, which is 40 percent of the federal budget of $25 billion. The only way for the IMF to get its loans repaid is to continue extending funds to Russia in order to avoid bankruptcy not only for Russia but also for itself and to avoid having its policies judged as a failure. That's why, after the U.S. presidential elections in November 2000, the IMF will remain engaged in Russia. In my view, the IMF played a positive role there. Its advisors emphasized improved tax collection and transparent transactions in the budget and the Central Bank. These are important issues. That's why I think the IMF will continue its activities in Russia.

DESAI: Andrei Illarionov, the new presidential advisor, said yesterday that Russia should rely less on IMF funding.

NEMTSOV: There is one problem with that. How can the government pay $10 billion this year if the rest of the budget is only $15 billion? The suggestion would be all right coming from an economist but is inappropriate from someone in an official position. How can he say that? You know, $10 billion in debt payment represents official capital flight from the country. The amount of unofficial flight comes to a bit more. What does all this mean for Russia? Ultimately, Russia must improve the economy by itself, but I don't think that breaking the IMF connection now will help Russia.

DESAI: You talked about capital flight. How would you react to the idea of declaring an amnesty, no questions asked, for those who brought their capital back and paid their taxes?

NEMTSOV: Well, the problem with implementing amnesty is a lack of confidence. Suppose the Duma adopts a law declaring amnesty for those who bring back their capital. Who will trust the law? For someone living in Moscow, can there be amnesty without an investigation? I have my own idea on how to handle this problem.

DESAI: Tell us about your idea.

NEMTSOV: It is a very Russian idea without legal complications. Let us start with our favorite person, Berezovsky. Putin must invite him to his office and say,

"Mr. Berezovsky, I have information about all of your accounts outside Russia—in Swiss banks and in offshore deposits. I don't want to touch you now. ('Now' is important here.) If you are ready to invest in Russia in any activity of your choice—in hotels, construction, the auto industry, apartment buildings, real estate—go ahead and do so. We will watch you very carefully. You have to invest \$100 million." The next person will be Vladimir Potanin.[9] The president's office has to prepare a list of about twenty-five people and organize a public relations campaign about their proposed investment activity. I predict that these people will carry out their promises to Putin in order to show that they are not criminals, they are patriots, they are influential, and they have a direct link to the president's office. Such a scheme will set an example to others, who will then be induced to bring back their own capital. The arrangement can be combined with the idea of legal amnesty so that the cash starts flowing back into Russia.

DESAI: You prepared a similar list for former prime minister Stepashin. What happened with it?

NEMTSOV: I worked up a concrete proposal for Stepashin three days before his dismissal. Early one morning I visited him in his office in the White House and suggested the idea of the list and the need for a PR campaign to publicize the arrangement on channel 1 of Russian TV, which is owned by Berezovsky. We discussed the details of combining the plan with legalized amnesty. Stepashin was excited about the idea and considered implementing it the following week. After he resigned, he called me to his office and said, "You know, Boris, I had to resign because of your stupid list." However, now the situation is different. Putin is a president with enormous authority. He can implement this very Russian idea. If Russian businessmen realize that Berezovsky is being made to bring back his capital, they will follow his example. It may then be necessary to adopt an amnesty law a little later.

DESAI: Now I have a few big questions for you. You have been in Russian politics for a very long time as governor of Nizhny Novgorod province and subsequently as first deputy prime minister in the government. What is your view of Russian politics? What have you learned? How is it different?

NEMTSOV: My first priority for surviving in Russian politics is to remain honest. This sounds trivial but is absolutely necessary for political survival. Second, if I had been born in the United States, I would never have become involved in politics. I'll explain why. Russia is a totally unpredictable country, and Russian politics is wild. I wonder why people become politicians in the United States. Everything here, in contrast to Russia, is predictable. What will happen after the [2000] presidential elections here [in the United States]? Hardly anything. What will happen in New York City? Nothing earthshaking. But suppose Zyuganov becomes the Russian president. It will be a disaster. Just imagine my situation.

DESAI: There's no chance of his becoming president anymore.

NEMTSOV: Nevertheless, complete, airtight deals in politics cannot happen in Russia. That is why I am in Russian politics. You have to be honest and avoid telling lies day in and day out. For example, Yeltsin promised the people that he would kill himself if prices went up, and people remember it to this day.

DESAI: Let's talk about Putin as a politician and a political leader. There's concern here among U.S. policy makers that, given the surge of nationalist sentiment and anti-Western feeling in Russia, Putin will become authoritarian, perhaps anti-Western. Can he become a great figure like Peter the Great?

NEMTSOV: That's not a bad example. I'm sure he believes that Russia needs a healthy market economy. Unfortunately, he doesn't believe that Russia also needs a democracy. It is difficult to explain to someone with a KGB background that a connection exists between democracy and competitive markets. That is the real difference between Putin and Yeltsin. Yeltsin believed in this connection in his very soul, especially after he visited the United States and went to a supermarket. "I am for democracy, and I am for private business," he said. He kept that pledge to the end of his career. He never touched correspondents and the mass media. He never tried to press elected governors and mayors because he believed in his soul that democracy has a chance in Russia.

I don't think that Putin holds the same views. By pointing to the wealthy nations of the world, I can explain to him that it's necessary to nurture democratic development in Russia. They represent specific histories, of course. The United States has been a democracy for two hundred years, England even longer. Some countries are Christian, others are not, but the common feature of rich countries is that they are democracies. It is impossible to be a dictatorship and become wealthy. Unfortunately, the Russian mentality is different. A lot of Russians like Pinochet. Pinochet is a hero to Russians because he improved the Chilean economy and stamped out corruption. Russians tend to believe that a market economy can exist without democracy. I think this is the real trouble with Putin.

DESAI: So you would give tremendous credit to Boris Yeltsin for preserving democracy in Russia. How do you evaluate him as a historical figure?

NEMTSOV: I think he's a historical figure of immense stature.

DESAI: How about Gorbachev?

NEMTSOV: He played a role in Russia's transition. But Yeltsin broke Communism; he established democracy in the country and preserved it for a decade. That's precisely why a lot of Russians do not want to turn back. Therefore, Boris Yeltsin is a historical figure. Now, it is easy for me to say this because I am no longer in power, and I have no connection with Yeltsin. I don't have to flatter him.

DESAI: What is your vision of Russia in the future? We posed this question to Grigory Yavlinsky when he was in New York, and he said, "I want Russia to be a country of brave men, beautiful women, and happy children." When I asked Yegor Gaidar the same question, he answered, "I would like to live in Europe without leaving my own country and speak Russian." So what is your dream?

NEMTSOV: That is not a dream; that was our campaign slogan. Our slogan was "We want to stay in Russia, within Europe, sing Russian songs, love Russian women, and run our own businesses." I think it was a good message for millions of Russians, even for the Communists. The response to the idea of attaining a quality of life similar to that in Europe is always positive. "Do you want to join the European Union?" I asked Zhirinovsky, who has had a number of problems with visas. "It's a great idea, Boris. We can go in right away. We will vote for that immediately," he said. Unification with Europe is a welcome idea in Russia. Unfortunately, the European countries do not like it.

Now, about my dream. In conversations with Javier Solana, who was the president of the European Union, I suggested that Russia could become part of the European Union perhaps in 2020.[10] He thought it was a great idea. The Europeans seem to have come around to that possibility. It looks fanciful now, but it will become a reality some time in the future.

DESAI: Now I have a couple of fun questions.

NEMTSOV: You mean funny questions.

DESAI: Well, we say "fun" questions in American English for questions that are not quite serious but are not funny, either.

NEMTSOV: And "funny" questions is British English?

DESAI: It is English, too, with a different meaning. You were reported to have said that, under the new Russian president and his men, the country will turn into a gray land, but I think your president comes across as a daring fellow. He flew a fighter plane, he went skiing, and he spent a night in a nuclear submarine. With such a leader in charge, the Kremlin could become an exciting place, don't you think?

NEMTSOV: Well, I know why Putin did all of those things.

DESAI: Tell us.

NEMTSOV: First of all, he wants to prove that he is healthier than Yeltsin. Second, he wants to show that Russia is a great power, so he spends a night in a submarine. The response in Russian newspapers to all of these activities was negative.

DESAI: My final question is also a light-hearted one. I read that Russia's ministry of defense promoted almost one-fourth of the Duma members to higher military ranks on April 6. Berezovsky was made a captain, and Zyuganov and Fatherland–All Russia member Andrei Kokoshin were made colonels.[11] Did you feel left out?

NEMTSOV: On the contrary, we have a special internal decision-making procedure in the ministry of defense. They proposed upgrading my rank in the military, along with Zirinovsky's, to that of general. We are both colonels. They said, "Zhirinovsky can't be made a general if you remain a colonel," but I refused. The real reason is the Start II treaty, which Russian generals want to ratify because they don't have the money to support all of the missiles. Someone smart in the ministry of defense thought that, if the deputies felt more powerful with their higher ranks in the military, they would support the ratification of the treaty.

DESAI: So this turned out to be a serious question after all. We can take some questions from the audience now.

QUESTION: Why did Chubais undertake his privatization program? Because he felt he had no other way of accomplishing it? What was his agenda?

NEMTSOV: He did it because he wanted to kill Communism, and he believed that the only chance of destroying Communism in Russia was to privatize property since state property is the material base for Communism. In my view, he did it inefficiently, but he said, "Boris, it doesn't matter who becomes the owner and who controls the companies. The only solution is to separate the bureaucracy from property." That's why he didn't pay attention to the efficiency of privatization. He tried to solve only the political tasks, like politicians do. I know this because he is my friend. Second, I don't believe that he started privatization in order to take bribes. Forget about that. No, he strongly believed that privatization represented a real instrument for democracy and for future Russian development.

QUESTION: Do you see Russia ever becoming a threat to the former Soviet republics that are now independent countries along its borders?

NEMTSOV: Which do you mean, Chechnya?

QUESTION: No, Ukraine and the Baltic countries.

NEMTSOV: Well, I think that the decentralization and disintegration of the former Soviet republics will continue until Russia becomes stronger economically. The only chance for Russians and for Russia to attract the former republics as a magnet is to have a better standard of living and higher salaries. What do we have now? A few million Ukrainians are waiting for jobs in Russia. Illegal immigration in Russia is significant, and the standard of living in Moscow is higher than in Kiev, for example, but that's not enough. Russia needs real economic growth and solid signs of a better life. I am sure that other republics, even the Baltic countries, which depend on Russian markets, will find such a message attractive. Trade will grow rapidly. The Baltic states will refrain from anti-Russian activity. It is therefore important for Russia to be strong economically.

QUESTION: How long will it take for Russia to stabilize and grow economically?

NEMTSOV: I'd say that it will take a generation. That is nothing compared with seven decades of Communism. If we begin counting from 1985, when Gorbachev rose to power, then my daughter, who is here, will have a chance to live in a prosperous Russia when she becomes a grandmother.

QUESTION: How do you see the future of the Union of Right Forces and its relationship with Yabloko?

NEMTSOV: The situation has improved and continues to improve, especially after the results of the March presidential race. Yavlinsky understands now that it is not good for his future political career for him to remain alone. That's why he agreed to organize a coalition with us; perhaps he will be ready to form a common bond between the SPS and Yabloko. I think we are on the right track. My dream is to organize a united team before the next parliamentary elections of 2003. The positive signal from Yavlinsky, absolutely new for him, is that he does not want to be a single leader. Ten years of discussions between Gaidar and Yavlinsky have finally brought about the realization that we reformers have to work together.

QUESTION: You mentioned that one of the items in your SPS campaign was the rule of law. I understand that the Duma now has the opportunity to work with the Kremlin and pass the land privatization act. However, what about the enforcement of laws, business law, criminal law, the role of the judicial system, the government, the Supreme Court? Do you have a vision of how land reform, for example, would actually start functioning?

NEMTSOV: Law enforcement is a serious problem in Russia. The only solution is to transform the judicial system in every respect—increase judges' salaries, encourage public discussion of court decisions, and simplify the laws because they often clash with one another. Currently lawyers and bureaucrats apply whatever rules they want. This is at the root of the corruption and the bribes. The process will take time. It will also require funding from the budget. Russia has a liberal civil code, perhaps more liberal than in the United States; it was prepared with U.S. technical assistance. Law enforcement is still weak, although I must point out that, in the past two or three years, Russian businesses, big companies included, have begun to settle their disputes in the courts rather than with their bodyguards. That's progress.

QUESTION: Many people are concerned about Putin's ties with Berezovsky.

NEMTSOV: Putin depended on the Kremlin family before the presidential elections, and Berezovsky is a prominent member of that family. But look, Yeltsin started his presidential campaign in early 1996 with a 3 percent popularity, and Berezovsky promised to help him. Putin started his campaign with 60 percent. He ended up with 52 percent of the vote when he was elected president in March 2000. So how is Putin dependent on Berezovsky? He does not need him anymore.

QUESTION: How long will he wait?

NEMTSOV: Putin is in a tight spot right now. On the one hand, he is independent. On the other hand, the Kremlin was privatized, and he needs to nationalize it like all state agencies. This will take time, but he must resolve the situation quickly. He must find the funds to attract the right kind of people, but who will want to serve in the president's administration in the Kremlin for $200 a month and remain honest at the same time? This is the main problem in Russia and a complicated task for Putin. I am sure he wants to be independent of the tycoons, of Berezovsky, of Tatyana and Yumashev, of Abramovich, of the generals in Chechnya—that is why the war will be stopped.[12] He wants to be independent. But how can he be a genuinely independent president without an infrastructure that has a clean state?

QUESTION: My question is related to Putin's intervention in the St. Petersburg gubernatorial election, which does not provide a clear signal with regard to the handling of regional elections. How will he proceed in local elections in the future?

NEMTSOV: It seems to me that Putin fumbled in the St. Petersburg elections. He did not have his own candidate for the campaign. It was impossible for him to publicly support Yakovlev, who had succeeded Sobchak, because Putin had worked under Sobchak for a long time.[13] I listened to his speech at Sobchak's funeral, and I understood that the relationship between Yakovlev and Putin was not good. But he lost this election because he did not allow Stepashin to take part in it. That, in my view, was a mistake. After all, Putin is a beginner in politics. He started his political career with the presidential race. This was his first experience in public life. That's why he sometimes makes mistakes. One mistake was denying the candidacy of the St. Petersburg gubernatorial election to Stepashin. The second was to ask Matviyenko to run and then make her withdraw her candidacy because public opinion polls gave her a 15 percent rating.[14] This waffling created a bad impression among voters.

Putin looks strong on issues such as Chechnya and flying an aircraft or visiting a submarine, but he is extremely cautious on economic and political decisions. For example, he said nothing about the aluminum deals and the monopolization of the aluminum industry. Abramovich now controls 90 percent of the Russian aluminum industry, but there was no reaction from the Kremlin. He is a beginner in economic and political decisions; therefore, he is cautious. Regarding St. Petersburg, we need to collaborate with Yabloko and put up a single candidate for its constituency. Perhaps we should skip it altogether. Yakovlev controls the city's media, finances, and businesses, and they have become corrupted by the criminal element. As a result, politics has become risky, but the election results are quite predictable.

JUNE 2003

DESAI: Let's begin where we ended last time. How do you assess the performance of your favorite politician, Vladimir Putin? How is the economy doing? Are economic reforms on track? Is there a reform momentum?

NEMTSOV: The performance of the economy is improving. The GDP growth rate in the first half of 2003 was an annual 7 percent. As far as reforms are concerned, one must assess them on the basis of priority ranking. The restructuring of United Energy Services (UES) tops the list. The Duma adopted its restructuring package in the spring; in my opinion, this was a critical achievement for the government and the company itself. It was indeed a rare victory.

DESAI: This was the first step in overhauling the monopoly sectors, beginning with the electric power monopoly, right?

NEMTSOV: Correct. Down the road we will create a fully competitive market in electric power, reduced tariffs, and fresh investments in the energy sector. Reforming the railroad system is complicated. The railways have full freight monopoly, unlike the trucking system in the United States, and the entire infrastructure is publicly owned. As far as Gazprom, the natural gas monopoly, is concerned, there is no reform under way. It is a disaster. Gazprom is a black box. Its decisions are nontransparent. Next, the management team is essentially controlled by the Kremlin. Finally, it is the world's largest gas monopoly and a huge player in world markets, especially in the European markets, in which it is a critical supplier, but it lacks a vision, a long-term strategy.

One major reform item is the pension system, which we need to overhaul by introducing private pension fund holders, obtaining appropriate contributions from employees and employers, and making the funds available for our financial market. Unfortunately, we are far from realizing any such arrangements. On the other hand, we managed progress on other fronts. Take the flat personal tax rate of 13 percent, the cancellation of the turnover tax, and the reduction of the profit tax for companies from 34 percent to 25 percent. The wage payments also generally reflect employee performance. However, for the tax and wage reform momentum to continue, we need to reduce taxes on small and medium businesses and raise corporate taxes on the oil sector, which is making what might be called windfall gains because of the high oil prices in the world market.

Russia has enormous natural resources of oil, natural gas, and minerals, which give their companies an advantage far above those that small and medium-sized businesses have. The former have vast resources to grow, whereas the latter are struggling, so their tax burden must be reduced. Their growth will create a middle class in the far-flung regions of the country. Today we have massive tension between the oligarchs and the ordinary people. A huge potential exists for nurturing a middle class in Russia by putting a surcharge on the natural resources sector and using the revenue to promote small businesses. Unfortunately, our bureaucracy is a major hurdle in that regard. Naturally it opposes fewer controls and administrative deregulation at local levels. That is a critical problem. And I am afraid there has been no progress in administrative and bureaucratic reform.

DESAI: What about military reform? The president talked about it in his press conference. I heard him spell out the details at great length.

NEMTSOV: Oh, yes. He even invited suggestions from the SPS in designing military reform. In fact, however, he supports the top-level military bureaucracy by wanting to retain its privileged position in the military and combining it with Soviet-style military service at the lower, nonofficer level. The recruits must serve for two years with an additional year thrown in. Here is the big problem with his plan: Because of the grim experience of World War II, during which millions perished, none of the grandchildren of the war veterans now want to join the army. At the same time, we have a huge demographic crisis. Russia's population is declining. Will the army disappear in Russia?

We in the SPS believe that the armed forces must be completely voluntary and well paid from the bottom up. The financial problems of higher pay scales, which the president mentioned in his press conference, can be managed.

DESAI: So you do not think that financial resources are a problem in transforming the Russian armed forces into voluntary professional units?

NEMTSOV: Our calculations show that an additional billion dollars is necessary for upgrading the wage scales in the military. The current military budget is about $11 billion. The upgrading amounts to 10 percent of the military budget. However, Putin is under tremendous pressure from the military bureaucracy and the generals. He therefore favors a plan that incorporates involuntary Soviet-style features. Eighty-five percent of Russians support our plan, in contrast to 5 percent in favor of the generals.

DESAI: What is your plan?

NEMTSOV: We propose that monthly payments be fixed at higher levels from 2004 to 2006—$2,057 for sergeants, for example, which is 20 to 30 percent higher than most monthly salaries in the country. Next, after three years of active duty in the military, soldiers should be able to study free of charge at the universities. Finally, after five to seven years of service, they should be able to get a loan for building a home. These arrangements should be guaranteed by law. Our calculations and public polls show that young people would be ready to serve in the military under such conditions. Unfortunately, the generals do not want to invest cash in salaries, educational opportunities, and housing loans for soldiers. They want to upgrade the weapons systems and even build housing for the soldiers. This is a crazy idea certainly by U.S. standards. While Russian soldiers serve in the army and are in training, they will not have a chance to live in housing built by the generals. There may not be a good match in terms of choice and location. But the generals know that if they get into the business of constructing housing and apartments, they will get kickbacks from contractors. They also tend to steal cash allocated in the budget for payment to soldiers.

DESAI: Do you think the regulatory system has improved under Putin, resulting in better corporate governance, better tax collection, and less bureaucratic interference at the local level?

NEMTSOV: Good point. I think we now live in a unified Russia. That is a formidable achievement. Regional bureaucrats and politicians have fewer opportunities for violating the constitution and breaking laws, but there is a cost. The pressure from the secret service, the police, and other regulatory agencies has increased and reached dangerous levels. We have three million bureaucrats in the country. We live under bureaucratic capitalism, and the quality of our bureaucrats is abysmally low. Recently, a law was enacted, guaranteeing the current privileges of former KGB and military employees and thereby preventing the entry of professionals into these structures. We suggested three principles: competition to attract new people to the bureaucracy, contractual guarantees to raise their salaries, and the creation of a corruption registry. All of these suggestions were rejected.

DESAI: What about tax collection? Has it improved?

NEMTSOV: The economy is growing, the trade balance is positive, the Central Bank has substantial foreign exchange reserves, and the federal budget has a surplus, thanks to the tax revenue inflows, so tax collection is in good shape. But note that a few hundred large companies in the natural resources sector pay 80 percent of the taxes in the budget. The tax administration works with these large companies and ignores the remaining businesses. The improvement has not resulted from better enforcement of the rules or the creation of new investigative codes from the treasury department.

DESAI: Do you still worry about Putin's potential for democratic neutralization? You remember we talked about that in our last conversation.

NEMTSOV: I remember. I think he trusts capitalism, but he does not trust freedom. I'll give you an example. He started his presidential career when Russia had three independent federal TV channels. A few days ago, NTV went under. All of the central TV networks are under Kremlin control. We experience the heavy burden of censorship and the manipulation of the media. And then there was Putin's press conference.

DESAI: I watched it. What was wrong?

NEMTSOV: A reporter asked him about his response to the SPS proposals on military reform. He ignored the question. So the reporter repeated it. The president talked about the SPS but not about its military reform proposals. So there is censorship directly from the head of the state. I think this attitude is undemocratic.

DESAI: But Putin needs the press, doesn't he? He needs the press to talk about the forthcoming December 2003 Duma election in order to continue to increase his popularity rating, which incidentally exceeds 70 percent. So he has to strike a balance between how much freedom to give to the television channels and the print media and what kind of restrictions to impose on them. He cannot continue being a favorite of the press, the TV networks, and the public if he restricts the media too much.

NEMTSOV: I do not agree with you. I think he wants a loyal press. Like all politicians, he hates criticism. But a lot of politicians, including your president, the president of the United States, understand the meaning of freedom. Putin does not understand it, and that is the point. He wants to manipulate the press, the media, and public opinion so that they absolutely support his positions and ideas. Let me give you an example. The president of Lithuania visited Moscow in the summer. The SPS organized a demonstration against him and his discriminatory policies relating to ethnic Russians in Lithuania. None of the television channels showed our protests. Soon afterward, Putin signed an agreement with the president of Turkmenistan, the so-called natural gas in exchange for people. According to this agreement, Turkmenistan will buy excess Russian gas, but 150,000 Russians will have to give up their Russian citizenship.

DESAI: Why would they lose their citizenship?

NEMTSOV: Because the Turkmeni president wants Russians to be Turkmeni citizens. Otherwise, he will not buy Russian natural gas. I met with Putin and told him that the agreement was just plain wrong. We organized demonstrations in front of the Turkmeni embassy, but nobody took any notice, including the foreign TV networks. Putin said that he would try to change the agreement, but nothing happened.

DESAI: Really? And the Duma had nothing to say about it?

NEMTSOV: No, it was a scandal. That's why he responded by saying that he would change the agreement. They have a special commission consisting of Russian and Turkmeni foreign ministers. But when I asked him why the TV networks did not televise the SPS demonstrations, he said, "I have no idea. The TV is independent." However, the TV networks are under the control of the Kremlin at this point.

DESAI: Do you think that the Russian constitution makes the executive too powerful? Do you want to change it to a parliamentary system?

NEMTSOV: I don't think so. We do not have political experience of that sort. We are not Britain. It seems to me that Russia needs a strong executive, but we also need checks and balances. Nonetheless, power is concentrated in the executive, whereas the Duma's powers are limited; so are the powers of the upper house.

DESAI: So you think that the political arrangements lack adequate checks and balances.

NEMTSOV: That is true, but that does not follow from the constitution. First of all, Putin has used the constitution to concentrate his authority. He appointed regional representatives to rein in the regions. He has increased the size of the secret service. He has curbed freedom of speech. He has transformed our democracy into a managed democracy. You know, we had the same constitution under Yeltsin. Russia was a democracy under him. Putin's manipulations are possible because our civil society is weak.

DESAI: And increasingly the constitution is used to rearrange the political system.

NEMTSOV: Let me give you an example and illustrate the role of a strong civil society in preventing the manipulation of the constitution. The U.S. president cannot deprive state budgets of revenues or limit free speech because U.S. public opinion is strong, and civic groups would oppose such an attempt. Putin has concentrated his political power because our civic institutions are weak or nonexistent, because our Parliament is not sufficiently assertive, and because Russian society lacks experience with democratic practices.

DESAI: How will the reformist groups perform in the December elections?

NEMTSOV: Are you asking me, or do you know the answer?

DESAI: I don't know the answer. I'm asking you.

NEMTSOV: Let me first discuss the prospects of the SPS. It is a party of reform. It attracts the educated youth, who have benefited from the reforms and who want them to move forward. I will give you some numbers. Twenty million Russians own cars. Twenty million own homes and apartments. There are about thirty million cell phones in the country. Millions of Russian citizens travel around the world. Of course, these numbers overlap, but these are the SPS constituents.

DESAI: Do you think they will all vote for the SPS?

NEMTSOV: I am giving you the maximum possible numbers who will back the SPS. We will get votes from those who have gained from the reforms. The losers will back the Communists.

DESAI: The Communists still have the support of some thirty million, most of them pensioners.

NEMTSOV: That is approximately the number of losers. Our goal is to attract the support of the gainers. We expect to get a maximum of 20 percent of the vote; we will be happy if we get 10 percent.

DESAI: Ten percent of the electoral vote. Will you get over the conflict of personalities among the reformist elements and unite as a single reformist group?

NEMTSOV: What do you mean?

DESAI: I mean, will you consider joining forces with Yabloko?

NEMTSOV: Yabloko is not a reformist group. It is a left-wing party. They are social democrats. It is a party of the impoverished intelligentsia, just as the Communists are a party of poor people. Both are left-leaning parties. We are the liberal reformist group.

DESAI: But isn't Yabloko a liberal party politically?

NEMTSOV: It insists on democracy and political freedom, but it also wants higher taxes, a larger distribution of cash payments for budget entitlements, and additional social security. It wants some of the old practices to continue.

DESAI: Why don't you unite with the Unity group? You voted with them on all of the economic issues, right?

NEMTSOV: Let me explain. We voted together as far as economic issues were concerned, but we are totally opposed to their position on a whole set of political issues, such as Chechnya, freedom of the press, and human rights, including their stand on the terrorist seizure of the Moscow theater last October, when several hostages and some terrorists died as a result of special forces attacking the site with a special gas. We wanted to organize a Duma investigation of the tragic events and raise questions. It got nowhere. Unity would not support the idea. To this day we do not know why the tragedy happened, who was punished, and how it might have been avoided. But you are right. We worked together on economic reform issues.

DESAI: So why not make a tactical alliance with them?

NEMTSOV: Look, we are closer to Yabloko on political issues, but we disagree with them on their stupid economic policies. On the other hand, we agree with Unity on economic issues but part company with them on strategic political matters. We are completely opposed to their politics.

DESAI: Who are your financial supporters?

NEMTSOV: We have close to twenty-five big donors and a few hundred small supporters.

DESAI: Who among the oligarchs?

NEMTSOV: We are forbidden by law to take more than 10 percent of our campaign budget from one source. We have to diversify the sources of financial support in order to maintain some independence.

DESAI: What is your support from Yukos?

NEMTSOV: Mikhail Khodorkovsky, the chairman of Yukos, has promised us 7 percent of our campaign budget, but he has reportedly promised 100 percent to Yabloko, which has completely traumatized Grigory Yavlinsky, its leader. Among our other supporters is Alpha Group, with 7 percent support. Altogether we have twenty-five financial backers. The diversified assistance keeps us independent in our campaign politics, in contrast to Yabloko, which is completely controlled by Khodorkovsky.

DESAI: Will Putin be elected president next year? Will he be a forward-looking president in his second term?

NEMTSOV: Putin looks like a president of stagnation to me.

DESAI: President of stagnation with regard to what? The economy is growing, isn't it?

NEMTSOV: Not because of his policies, but because of high energy and mineral prices in world markets and because of the privatized and subsequently deregulated industry, beginning in 1995. He played no role in this. He must now recognize that Russia must move forward and not sit still. We absolutely cannot sit still.

DESAI: Do you have concrete suggestions to offer to him in that regard?

NEMTSOV: I have several concrete suggestions, among them measures to reduce and renovate the bureaucracy, reform the armed forces, lower taxes, demonopolize the natural gas industry and the railways, and provide more resources for health care and education. Russia can then move forward.

DESAI: I think Russia needs substantial direct investment from foreign entities to grow at 8 to 10 percent annually.

NEMTSOV: I do not think so.

DESAI: Why not?

NEMTSOV: Russian big businesses have enough cash for their purposes.

DESAI: But you need advanced technology and management practices to move into a high-growth trajectory.

NEMTSOV: Well, I think the main problem for Russia is to attract Russian investment, which in turn will promote growth. That is my position. I do not think foreign investment is crucial.

DESAI: What about foreign banks?

NEMTSOV: It doesn't matter. Russia has lot of cash. The Central Bank reserves amount to $65 billion. I do not think the problem is a lack of cash for investment. The problem is infrastructure—state infrastructure, institutional infrastructure. I mean communications, roads, everything, the rule of law, a functioning judicial system. Foreign investments cannot provide this. There is enough cash in Russia and with Russians. That is the point. How does one set up an infrastructure so that the investments move into the right sector? We do not know where to direct our cash. This is not a question for foreigners. It is a decision for our oligarchs to resolve.

DESAI: But even if they decided where to put the cash, the problem of management will remain unresolved.

NEMTSOV: That, of course, is a problem. We need to reorient our higher education and turn out modern managers. I also mean management in a broad sense, one that can promote productivity, raise growth, and generate demand. Again I would like to emphasize the need for creating a modern infrastructure not only of communication but also of an efficient bureaucracy and a modern court system. That is my view.

DESAI: What about U.S.-Russian relations?

NEMTSOV: They are better than during the Iraq War, but it seems to me that that is not enough.

DESAI: Does Putin have a long-term strategy for shaping relations with the United States?

NEMTSOV: Putin understands that the United States will help Russia in containing terrorism. He also understands that Russia faces the same problem as the United States with respect to a resurgent China. He wants the U.S.-Russian relationship to continue improving. Personally I feel that our anti-U.S. policy during the Iraq war was a mistake. Our oil companies lost contracts with their Iraqi partners. The nearly $8 billion debt that Iraq owed Russia has vanished.

DESAI: Do you think that Russia should have supported the United States during the Iraq war?

NEMTSOV: I think we should have remained neutral. It would have been wrong to support George Bush on this issue. Putin looks like a president of stagnation to me, just as some of the Central European countries did.

DESAI: What do you mean? I think they supported the U.S. position.

NEMTSOV: But not aggressively. They were very guarded in their support.

DESAI: In any case, you think Russia should not have cast its lot with Germany and France, right?

NEMTSOV: I understand the German position. Having won the election on an antiwar platform, the German chancellor could not have come out in support of the war. France opposed the war because it has a sizeable Muslim minority. So does Russia. The Russian public, including the Muslims, supported Putin's antiwar position, but had he taken a neutral position, that would have worked, too. That would have been more constructive for managing U.S.-Russian relations in the future, especially on the other issues we have talked about.

DESAI: How do you feel right now about being a Russian politician?

Nemtsov: I am on the run.

Desai: But you have been running all the time.

Nemtsov: More so now. I am getting ready for the December 7 [2003] elections.

April 2004

Desai: Why did the reformers lose the December 2003 Duma elections? Do you think they would have passed the required 5 percent eligibility limit of electoral vote for Duma representation if they had united?

Nemtsov: The Union of Right Forces [SPS] lost the election for specific reasons. If we had united with Yabloko, Yavlinsky's group, we would probably have gotten 10 percent of the vote. We lost because of the way Putin exercises state control over federal TV, the state-controlled channels 1 and 2. We could not function as a transparent, fearless opposition in the face of the restrictions he enforced four years ago. We failed because we could not deliver a clear message.

Needless to say, as leader of SPS, I made mistakes. I insisted that Chubais join our election campaign, and you know that his popularity is limited with the Russian electorate, at only 1–2 percent. One cannot cross the 5 percent electoral vote requirement with such a low popularity ranking. Besides, Putin's propaganda slogan was that everything was bad before Putin, and everything is swimmingly good under his presidency. And we were in charge before him, so we are responsible for Russian poverty and corruption, for Chechnya, and for mismanaging state power. I do not think that is true, but this has been the official propaganda during the last four years of his presidency.

However, turning to Yavlinsky, it is a mystery to me why he and his party, Yabloko, lost. We failed because we were responsible for bandit privatization, for corruption, for the loans-for-shares program, for Chechnya, for destroying the Russian armed forces, and for the oligarchs, among them Khodorkovsky, Gusinsky, and Berezovsky. You know the slogan was "Во всём виноват Чубайс" (Everything is Chubais's fault). It sounds like sputnik or perestroika, "Во всём виноват Чубайс." But for the life of me, I do not understand why Yavlinsky, who had no responsibilities for the last fifteen years, failed. That is a mystery.

Desai: So you were in power and he was not. But in the public mind here and probably in Russia, you are both known as reformers. What differences do you have with him? Why couldn't you bury the hatchet and form a coalition to campaign during the election?

Nemtsov: What are our differences? Yavlinsky suggested a five-hundred-day program to reform the Communist-planned economy, but his program, which is now a historical document, was radically different from the measures we implemented in the 1990s. We stand not only for democratic arrangements and freedom of speech but also for a market economy based on genuine competition, transparent rules, and private ownership of assets. Of course, the transformation was turbulent. For example, everybody talked about hyperinflation in 1992. Yes, at the end of the year we had an inflation rate of about 2,600 percent, but note that fourteen Central Bank branches of the former Soviet republics independently printed substitute currencies and coupons at the same time. The absence of a central currency-issuing center seems crazy, but it was real in 1992. In any case, the extreme inflation lasted only a year.

At that time I was governor of the Nizhny Novgorod region. My wife woke up early every morning to make sure we had milk. Everything was in short supply in the stores. Farmers organized protests and burned cars to make sure they had cigarettes and vodka, which were both in short supply. At that time, frankly, Russia faced a civil war. We had a historic choice between civil war and painful reforms. And Gaidar and Chubais, who were in charge of the government, decided in favor of painful reforms. In my view, it was the right decision.

Of course, we made a lot of mistakes. We were beginners. We had no experience. But look, the transformation from seventy years of Communism to freedom and markets has been painful everywhere. A lot of people lost everything. Poverty and corruption are widespread not only in Russia but also in Ukraine, Belarus, and other neighboring countries.

Yavlinsky insists that the reformers are responsible for these results, but, frankly speaking, Gaidar was prime minister for only nine months in 1992. For five years after that, Viktor Chernomyrdin, who is not a reformer, ran the cabinet and protected Gazprom, the natural gas company. I do not think that the loans-for-shares program, under which the oil and aluminum companies were privatized, was an altogether judicious measure although it had positive elements. Nevertheless, to say that the reformers are responsible for the current situation in Russia is incorrect.

DESAI: It's true that the reforms were painful and that, as a member of the reforming group under President Yeltsin, you took bold, aggressive measures. However, in the end you got political instability and a disillusioned public. Russians viewed the loans-for-shares privatization program as robbery, plain and simple. In their opinion, a few oligarchs got the assets jointly created under Stalin, whereas they were reduced to poverty. Don't you, therefore, think that the Duma elections of December 2003 represent the disillusionment of the Russian electorate with Yeltsin's reforms?

NEMTSOV: Well, I agree. SPS failed for that reason, but that does not explain Yavlinsky's electoral defeat. He was not responsible for the loans-for-shares program. Nevertheless, loans-for-shares privatization had positive results. When Norilsk Nickel, the world's largest producer of platinum and palladium, was bought by Vladimir Potanin, the company's workers, seventy-five thousand of them, were denied wages and salaries for six months. It looked bankrupt. Recently, it has boosted its sales revenue by 15 percent per year, and the average monthly salary of its workforce is 1,000 euros.

Or take Yukos, the oil company. When it was privatized, fifty thousand oil workers were denied their wages, and its production plummeted by 60 percent in the five years before its acquisition by Mikhail Khodorkovsky. In 2002, the company's oil output shot up by 20 percent, and the workforce salary averaged $1,000 a month. The company has U.S. and European managers, and its market capitalization has gone up six times in dollar values in the past three years. I agree that the company was sold at throwaway prices, but the results have been astonishing in terms of new management, transparent cash flow accounts, and the employment of foreign engineers and managers.

I do not think the loans-for-shares program has reduced Russians to poverty. The reasons are different. Russians are not ready to work hard, take risks, and make money. There are more opportunities in Moscow than here in New York City. There are more opportunities, there is less competition, a strong ruble, and a stable monetary situation. But Russians would rather count on their president, look into his eyes, and depend on him to give them cash without their having to earn it. Russia has abundant opportunities. Take Alpha Bank, for example. It has attracted U.S. bankers with salaries ten times higher than here. Why? Because competition is absent and opportunities are plentiful. But if Russians choose to wait for Putin's assistance, they will remain poor forever.

DESAI: Yes, Norilsk Nickel, Yukos, and Alpha Bank are success stories in Russia, but you have to be able to sell that to the Russian public and the Russian voters. How do they perceive it? Is there anything in the reform process that you would have done differently?

NEMTSOV: First, I would like to set the record straight. I was governor of Nizhny Novgorod for six years, from 1991 until 1997, when Yeltsin brought me to Moscow, so I was watching events in Moscow from a distance. But I do think that the reformers made several mistakes. After Yeltsin fired Gaidar at the end of 1992, the reformers lost their drive. At the same time, Chubais made a mistake in continuing with the Chernomyrdin government. He became everybody's "мальчик для бцтья" (whipping boy). I do not think that was a wise move on his part.

Second, I think we paid too much attention to the IMF. The decision to fill the budget deficit with short-term capital inflows from the outside was a mistake. The Russian financial system collapsed in August 1998 because of that.

Third, we did not set in motion the process for demonopolizing several sectors of Russian industry.

Finally, our biggest mistake was that we did not explain to the Russian public what we were up to. I was not very far from Boris Yeltsin when he was on top of that tank at the end of the August 1991 putsch. I believed that our main job then was to kill Communism. If we managed that, we thought we would live like the Americans, maybe in six months, perhaps nine months. I was not alone. Millions of Russians believed that the road to freedom was short, exciting, and without problems. We thought things would work out in a short time. Now I think we should have explained to the public that the road to prosperity is long and painful and that everybody has to work hard. Unfortunately, Gaidar, Chubais, and I thought that all we had to do was to stabilize the currency, fight inflation, and privatize companies and that the doors would open. The public would understand and support us. Our biggest mistake was our inability to talk to the people, take them into our confidence, and explain to them what we were up to. We failed to do that.

DESAI: So there was no communication between the reformers and the public at large. Do you think Putin is a better communicator? How do you account for his popularity?

NEMTSOV: Of course! Of course! Putin the Great!

DESAI: But please explain it to us. Why is he popular with the Russian electorate? Perhaps you knock off 10 percent from his popularity rating of 80 percent because he muzzled the media. You remove another 10 percent because he used state resources to campaign in the recent elections. You are still left with a 60 percent rating in his favor. We want to understand why the Russian public voted for him and his party, United Russia.

NEMTSOV: You know, Putin is a lucky man. He has benefited from Yeltsin's reforms, among them the privatized economy. Again, the high oil prices, exceeding $30 a barrel, have brought him enormous gains. When I was deputy prime minister, oil prices plummeted to as low as $8 a barrel in early 1998. Only $8! That also led to the collapse of the ruble in August 1998. Currently, oil prices are $25–35 a barrel, contributing to an annual trade surplus of $60 billion. The Central Bank's foreign exchange reserves are close to $100 billion.

Then again, Putin is a smart man. He understands the levers of power in the Kremlin. There are two: Russian TV and oil prices. Of course, oil prices depend on external factors. As for television, he realized that he had to control it, so he has established complete censorship of the electronic media. He has used the state TV channels as powerful instruments for increasing his popularity.

So what do we have now? GDP growth has averaged 7 percent a year in the last four years. The government has raised pensions for retirees and salaries for teachers and doctors. The Russians support him for that.

But the main reason for his popularity is the contrast with Yeltsin. Unlike Yeltsin, who reportedly got drunk during his U.S. visit, Putin is a teetotaler. Again, he is young and vigorous, and he enjoys swimming and horseback riding. Russians admire him for that. They are proud of their president. And finally, I think he is smarter than your president.

DESAI: That's not saying much.

(Laughter)

NEMTSOV: Sometimes, I would say. Do you think this will create problems for me with your immigration service?

DESAI: No, definitely not.

NEMTSOV: Let's be serious. The reason for Putin's popularity is the benefits associated with economic growth. People everywhere worry about their pocketbooks. From that perspective, Russia is a an attractive country.

DESAI: Your remarks contrasting Putin and Yeltsin remind me of a comment made by a Russian friend who said that Putin is popular in Russia because he is quite unlike Yeltsin, but Putin is not popular in the United States because he is so unlike Yeltsin. The contrast gives us something to talk about.

NEMTSOV: I think he is not popular in the United States because of the media censorship, his KGB background, and the war in Chechnya.

DESAI: We will come to that theme later, the U.S.-Russian relations. So Putin is lucky. The growth rate has picked up because of high oil prices pushing Russian exports and oil earnings. However, given that favorable outcome, he has provided stability, and the public appreciates that.

NEMTSOV: I disagree with you. Let me give an example of political stability.

DESAI: Go ahead.

NEMTSOV: What would happen to political stability in Russia if everything depended on the health of one person?

DESAI: What does the Russian constitution say in that regard?

NEMTSOV: In that case the prime minister will become the president.

DESAI: So what is wrong with that?

NEMTSOV: But look at Fradkov, the Russian prime minister . . .

(Laughter)

DESAI: I would not worry about that. Russia has talented people and enormous resilience. Let us go back to what we were talking about. Putin often talks about his goals for Russia, namely, economic growth, poverty reduction, and political stability. That position would garner widespread support. What is wrong with that in your view?

NEMTSOV: You have an ongoing election campaign here. John Kerry and George Bush also talk about economic growth, poverty reduction, and new jobs. You have to say the right things in order to be acceptable, even popular. But Putin's politics of "authoritarian modernization" is vastly different. Of course, it is not new. Several countries around the world—China, some Latin American countries, Malaysia among the middle-income countries—represent authoritarian modernization.

I will tell you what he will not be able to deliver. Of course, he can stabilize the ruble, adopt a surplus budget year after year, and promote economic growth, but will he win the fight against poverty? I doubt it. Look, the trade unions of Russia, the so-called guarantors of people's welfare, have joined United Russia, the party in power. How can they protect the people against the state and the capitalists? The Communist Party, the former champion of poor people, has been increasingly weakened and was finally destroyed in the December 2003 Duma elections. Poverty will remain widespread because the poor have no more champions to advance their cause.

Next, take corruption. He will not manage to root that out because of censorship and the lack of transparency and opposition in the country. Administrative reform has stalled. Firing one person and appointing another, changing names and titles, reducing the number of ministries but creating new agencies within the ministries—after all of this maneuvering, the size of the bureaucracy and the budgetary allocation for the purpose have increased.

Finally, for the same reasons, Putin is not ready to modernize the Russian army and the Russian secret service. Civilian control, genuine opposition, and freedom of speech are altogether lacking. Do you know what is happening in the Russian army? Last winter ten soldiers froze to death. And nothing happened. No general or colonel was charged with incompetence. Of course, monetary allocations to the military and the secret service have increased, but there are no signs of improvement. It is a bit like Soviet agriculture. The planners put money into it, but the country ended up importing grain from the United States.

I'm afraid authoritarian modernization will not eliminate the strangulating bureaucracy, corruption, and the ruthless hold of the secret service and the military brass. Putin's methods cannot solve these problems. That is why we are in the opposition.

DESAI: Let's sort out these issues one by one. Take poverty reduction. Finance Minister Alexei Kudrin has worked up proposals of additional surcharges on oil profits in order to support small businesses, which can generate more employment and alleviate poverty. What do you think about that idea?

NEMTSOV: We in the SPS support higher taxes on the oil sector, but we cannot raise more than $3 billion a year from that source.

DESAI: But it's a good start, isn't it?

NEMTSOV: I believe that reducing taxes on small businesses is critical. Prime Minister Fradkov's government has implemented measures to reduce social taxes on small businesses.

DESAI: Take the reduction of the enormous bureaucracy. You cannot make cutbacks in the bureaucracy via a top-down measure, such as reducing the number of ministries, ministerial appointments within ministries, and so on. It has to be a bottom-up process. Suppose you were in charge. What would you suggest? Do you think Prime Minister Mikhail Kasyanov was removed in a surprising move by Putin before the March 2004 presidential election because he did not proceed fast enough on bureaucratic reforms?

NEMTSOV: Let's talk about Kasyanov first. He was fired because Putin was afraid that Kasyanov might emerge as a presidential candidate in 2008. This is true.

As far as administrative reform is concerned, I think that, in an authoritarian country, the best course is to do nothing. A variant of Parkinson's Law operates under authoritarian regimes, which end up reforming their bureaucracies by increasing the number of bureaucrats. Administrative reform in authoritarian coun-

tries will fail because transparent, widespread discussion of overhauling the bureaucratic system itself is absent.

Moreover, Putin's state power is derived from bureaucratic support. Given his
KGB background, he opts for controlling the bureaucracy rather than reducing its
size. I do not think he is in favor of making a frontal attack on the administrative or
secret service personnel or, for that matter, modernizing the Russian military. He
has friends and supporters throughout the network. You cannot expect him to fire
his friends from his old days in East Germany and bring in new appointees. The
generals are his friends. Administrative reform will not start if you have a head of
state anointed as president of the bureaucracy.

DESAI: I agree that bureaucratic reform is complicated. Russia, India, and China
all have enormous bureaucracies. The only solution is for them to be gradually
coopted and absorbed into new business opportunities. That process is time consuming. Let's talk about military reform. I know that the SPS has its own proposals
for the purpose. How do they differ from Putin's ideas?

NEMTSOV: The SPS lost the December 2003 Duma elections. We do not count
anymore. The generals have taken over and decided that Russian students will serve
in the army. That is a disaster for higher education in Russia, and it will corrupt the
Russian army. My secretary has an eighteen-year-old son. She paid a colonel $3,000
so that her son could avoid serving in the army.

Putin made a serious mistake in making the generals responsible for reforming the armed forces. By contrast, military reforms began here in the United States
in the early 1970s, when President Nixon appointed a commission composed of
economists, sociologists, soldiers' mothers, experts from the U.S. Treasury, and
two generals. We have a group of twenty-five members, of which as many as
twenty-three are generals. The chances of military reform from such a group are
slim. At the same time, the military will get larger allocations from the government budget.

DESAI: How do you assess the credentials of the new government?

NEMTSOV: They have worked for only a few weeks, so it is difficult to assess
their performance.

DESAI: But you know some of them and their background.

NEMTSOV: I know Prime Minister Fradkov. Frankly speaking, we have a prime
minister whose name is Vladimir Putin. The rest are his assistants, at best his advisors. Every Monday and Tuesday Putin wakes up at 11:00 in the morning, arrives
at the Kremlin at noon, invites all of his ministers to his office, and tells them what
to do. I do not think the Russian government is an independent organization that
has its own proposals. It doesn't really matter who the prime minister is. As far as I
know, Fradkov is listening very carefully to what Putin wants.

DESAI: What reforms would you propose?

NEMTSOV: First, free speech must be restored. That is easy to undertake.

Channels 1 and 2 of the Russian TV should be privatized. That will create genuine competition in information dissemination.

Second, Putin should undertake a political dialogue with the Chechens. We have lost close to sixty-five hundred Russian soldiers and thousands of Chechen civilians in the war and spent millions of dollars fighting it.

Third, we need to get away from "managed democracy" and organize transparent elections in Russia.

These political changes are crucial for realizing the presidential goal of doubling the growth of the economy in the coming decade. However, Putin wants to repeat Russia's long history of an enslaved population without realizing that only a free people can be prosperous. I know he believes in free markets, but he does not believe in democracy. Perhaps many Russians share his contradictory philosophy. Of course, with oil going for more than $30 a barrel, anything will work, but free choice is the basis of a competitive economy. Putin does not value freedom. That's the point. Russians have limited experience with freedom, and they do not make the connection between free choice and prosperity. The prospering global economies, among them the United States, Canada, the European Union, Japan, Australia, and New Zealand, are all democracies. Russians fail to grasp that connection.

DESAI: In my opinion, the link between economic growth and democratic arrangements has not been established. I, however, value freedom as an end in itself. People should be free.

NEMTSOV: Sometimes I feel that our policy makers would realize the value of free choice and competitive pressure if the price of oil fell below $10. Take Saudi Arabia, for example. It is an autocratic, bureaucratized, corrupt regime, but the transforming pressures are minimal because the regime is rolling in oil money. Of course, Russia is not Saudi Arabia, but the link between oil revenue and Putin's consolidating politics cannot be overlooked.

DESAI: You talked about Chechnya. It seems to me that Russians do not actively discuss the Chechen war. Why not?

NEMTSOV: That is an interesting question. First of all, Russians are tired of the war. You know it has been ten years since the war began in 1994. There have been thousands of casualties and massive destruction in Chechnya. Second, because of censorship, people do not know enough about Chechnya. Third, the terrorists are mainly Chechens. Chechens carried out the recent Moscow terrorist incident, in which eighty Russians were killed. As a result, public opinion polls clearly suggest that the Russians hate the Chechens. That is one of the reasons for the popularity of fascist ideologies among Russians. Putin's policies will perpetuate these ultranationalist tendencies. Unfortunately, the Kremlin is not ready to start a political process in Chechnya. In fact, Putin has promised the Russians that he will "dunk the Chechens in a restroom"—"мочцть в сортире," in effect, liquidate them. You see, you need to be a strong leader, like Charles de Gaulle, who started negotiations with the Algerians. I do not think Putin is strong in that sense. For him, start-ing a war has been easier than negotiating an end to it.

DESAI: Will he consider granting Chechnya limited autonomy after he stabi-lizes in office the second time around? How will the Russian public react to such a suggestion?

NEMTSOV: It is difficult to predict how the Russians will react to such a pro-posal. I know that people are very tired of the war. In all likelihood, it will be a 50–50 vote.

DESAI: Let's talk about Putin's second term. Will he be able to keep the *siloviki,* members of the military, the bureaucracy, and the secret service, under control?

NEMTSOV: Well, he is one of them.

DESAI: Yes, but he has been elected president, and he is quite popular.

NEMTSOV: Take the military first. You know, Russia does not have a Latin American tradition. Russian generals do not have political ambitions. The Soviet Union disappeared without the generals firing a shot. They are not as adventurous as you academics think. They want to remain in military service. As for the secret service, they have been bought. The budget of the secret service and the special forces in the interior ministry has been increasing every year, so I do not think the siloviki will oppose him.

DESAI: So where will the opposition materialize from? The voters have rejected liberal groups like yours.

NEMTSOV: Right now, we have a single-party system in the country. United Russia, the Kremlin-backed party, controls more than two-thirds of the 450 seats in the Duma, 311 in all. From here on out, the political evolution will depend on economic performance. If economic growth remains on track, Putin will control the political process completely until 2008, when he will appoint his successor or manage to change the constitution, seek a third term, and remain in power. He is a young man.

On the other hand, if an economic crisis develops, opposition may materialize from the Left, from the nationalists, or even from the fascists, although these latter two groups are a small minority.

As far as the reformers are concerned, we are in a serious crisis. There is a regular mushrooming of liberal factions. Irina Khakamada has formed her group.[15] Yavlinsky still believes that he is the single savior of the liberal movement in the country. SPS is totally without a leader. Vladimir Ryzhkov wants to establish his own party,[16] but this does not mean that the reformist movement is dead. We have managed to organize the Committee of 2008 with Garry Kasparov, the chess champion, as the chair. The representatives of all of the groups have decided to be members of the committee. That is a healthy development. We may organize extensive public opinion polls at the start of 2007 and come up with a candidate for the presidency and a unified list of party candidates, based on the polls, for the parliamentary elec-tions. This proposal is supported by Yabloko, the SPS, Khakamada, and Ryzhkov.

I think we have a solid chance of creating a genuine democratic opposition early in 2007 before the election campaign begins for the December 2007 Duma elections.

DESAI: Let's discuss foreign policy. What do you think of Putin's foreign policy? Do you think that there's too much improvisation?

NEMTSOV: The critical area of foreign policy concern for Russia remains the former republics of the Soviet Union, which constitute the Commonwealth of Independent States (CIS). Russia is no longer a superpower. In my view, we do not have the resources to support an active role in the Middle East, Iraq, or even China.

Unfortunately, the Kremlin has little understanding of policy issues relating to these countries. Take Belarus, whose authoritarian president is a close friend of Putin's. Not long ago Belarus refused to pay for natural gas purchases from Gazprom. So what happened? President Lukashenko's popularity went up in Belarus because he snubbed the Russian bear. So much for the success of Putin's foreign policy foray into Belarus.

Take Ukraine, which is gearing up for presidential elections on October 31. The liberal candidate, Viktor Yushchenko, from the Our Ukraine group is pitted against former prime minister Viktor Yanukovich, who has been under investigation. Putin supports him because he is a friend of former president Leonid Kuchma. Yushchenko is more popular and better qualified to handle Ukraine's problems, ranging from the economy to the Russian minority in Ukraine and issues relating to the pipeline supplying natural gas to Europe via Ukraine. The Kremlin policy propagandists are against Yushchenko because he has an American wife, who, they think, has a link with the U.S. Secret Service.

Here's another example. The president of Turkmenistan recently decreed that property rights would be denied to foreigners, thereby forcing 150,000 Russians to give up their Russian citizenship. Russians who refused to become Turkmeni citizens could be evicted from their apartments. At the same time, Putin signed an agreement with the Turkmeni president facilitating the transporting of natural gas from Turkmenistan. Despite this concession, a few thousand Russians lost their apartments. When I discussed this issue with Putin, I told him that, in order to safeguard Russian interests in the neighboring states, he must promote democratic arrangements there so that minority rights could be protected. I got no response from him.

As for the U.S.-Russia relationship, Putin is fortunate to have George W. Bush as the U.S. president because they are united in the fight against terrorism. As a result, the U.S. administration ignores the issue of the erosion of democratic freedoms in Russia and the violation of human rights in Chechnya. Putin understands the advantage of this antiterrorism coalition. He has a free ride in Russia. If the current administration changes in the United States, perhaps a Democrat in the White House will pay more attention to the deteriorating political situation in Russia.

As for Europe, the inclusion of the Baltic states in the European Union and the expansion of NATO in their territory is of serious concern to Russia. That is a reality. Putin does not favor it, but he has no choice except to protest it.

I believe we must concentrate on resolving domestic issues and managing our relationship with the CIS countries, but the Kremlin lacks an effective strategy. Putin supported the separatist leader Abashidze in Azheria, who sought to establish a breakaway unit from Georgia. At the same time, he insists that Chechnya is an inseparable part of Russia. Such double standards smack of a muddled policy from the Kremlin so far as the neighboring states are concerned.

Desai: What about China?

Nemtsov: We sell weapons to China. That probably is a plus, but in our far eastern regions, we have as few as seventeen million inhabitants and unprotected borders, giving ample opportunities for the Chinese to settle there. We know our leadership is concerned about China, and we hope that the Chinese will continue to be preoccupied with their serious internal problems. The eastern part of China is prosperous, but the rest of the economy lags behind, and the Chinese Communist Party has its hands full. Putin's only policy signal with regard to China has been to deny it permission to construct an oil pipeline from eastern Siberia to China that Khodorkovsky was proposing. In my opinion, China offers a solid prospect for boosting Russian oil revenues. I do not understand Putin's opposition to the idea.

Desai: You have brought up Khodorkovsky and the Chinese pipeline and Khodorkovsky's support for it. He is once again in the news with yet another letter from his jail cell. What do you make of it?

Nemtsov: You know, I talked with Valeriya Novodvorskaya, who spent five years in a Russian prison.[17] She told me that one could write what one wanted from a Russian penitentiary. The conditions there are so terrible that one loses one's mental balance. Throughout Russian history, famous people under extreme stress have made similar pleas. Zinovyev, Kamenev, and Trotsky wrote to Stalin in a similar vein.[18] Pasternak wrote to Khrushchev with a view to continue living as a writer.[19] Not an exceptional demand. I do not think such an entreaty will work with Putin because he does not trust Khodorkovsky.

Desai: So what do you think will happen?

Nemtsov: Unfortunately, the decision to keep him in prison has already been made. Putin is afraid of Khodorkovsky because he has the financial resources to be a presidential challenger in 2008. You know that Khodorkovsky built a first-rate company, established contacts in the White House, and gained support from U.S. businessmen, who referred to "Yukosization" as a process of transformation from bandit capitalism to transparent business practices. All that is forgotten now. Russians need to look after their own interests. As for Khodorkovsky, his future is unclear. Putin will be inaugurated president on May 7. The tsars granted amnesty to prisoners when they were inaugurated, but that was a tsarist tradition. The KGB tradition is likely to be different.

Desai: My final question. You have been in politics for a long time.

Nemtsov: Yes. They have been the best years of my life.

Desai: How would you sum up your political career?

NEMTSOV: Politics has ceased to be transparent in Putin's Russia. I have three children to support, so I will go into business, make money, and reenter politics, perhaps in 2006.

DESAI: Would you like to come to the United States and give lectures?

NEMTSOV: No. Never. Occasional conversations at Columbia University are fine. You know that English is not my native language. I make mistakes.

DESAI: Your sparkle comes across despite your imperfect English.

NEMTSOV: On the other hand, I notice that U.S. campuses are full of Russian speakers. Once I began speaking in English in Boston, and a voice said, "Борис, хватит выпендриваться, говори по-русски" (Boris, quit showing off. Speak in Russian).

(Laughter)

I would like to answer questions if you have any—and in English.

QUESTION: You suggested that China has a serious problem holding together. Don't you think that Russia has a similar problem and might even disintegrate?

NEMTSOV: I do not think so. Market forces have sufficiently matured in Russia to hold the country together. Russia will remain united not because of the Kremlin in Moscow but because of the concentration of economic forces in Moscow. The Russian oligarchs operate from Moscow, except for Vladimir Bogdanov, who runs Surgutneftegaz, the oil and gas company, from Surgut. The rest, who are based in Moscow, control property all around the country. Their economic interests favor integration. I believe that capitalist countries do not disintegrate. Do you have a counterexample?

QUESTION: But don't you think the far eastern region of Russia may be interested in having closer economic ties with China or Japan rather than with Moscow?

NEMTSOV: I do not think that Russia's far eastern region would like to leave the Russian Federation because of increased trade with China and Japan. Such trade raises living standards for people in that part of the country.

DESAI: Perhaps I can help put an end to the discussion. In 1999, I asked Anatoly Chubais whether Russia might fall apart. He said decisively, as his is style, that during the final years of Gorbachev in 1990 and 1991, Russia faced a possible breakup because the Soviet Union itself disintegrated in December 1991. But that danger had passed.

QUESTION: But isn't it possible that Tatarstan and Bashkortostan or the Muslim-majority republics in the Caucasus region of Russia, for example, Chechnya and Dagestan, may want to secede?

NEMTSOV: This is a good question. Tatarstan and Bashkortostan, the two non-Caucasus republics, are important. The oil businesses in both need to be privatized. The local people need more initiative and opportunities. As for the Caucasus republics, Putin needs to combine military muscle with political dialogue.

QUESTION: How have your views on democracy and markets changed over time?

NEMTSOV: I think markets will coexist in Russia without democratic freedoms, but what kind of society will we end up with? How many people will remain below the poverty level? How soon will Russia create a middle class? Market forces need to be combined with political freedoms so that these problems can be handled, too. I know Russian businessmen who are totally lacking in social awareness. Their aggressive drive needs to be moderated in the interest of the weaker groups. We need to combine the economic choices of free markets with democratic freedoms.

DESAI: If you were a U.S. citizen, I think you'd end up being a registered Democrat.

NEMTSOV: Really?

QUESTION: Some time ago, members of the SPS were thrown out of Belarus . . .

NEMTSOV: Yes, Lukashenko threw some of us out, including Irina Khakamada.

QUESTION: Will Russia and Belarus form a union?

NEMTSOV: That will never happen so long as Lukashenko is president of Belarus. He does not want to give up power. Take his responses to a few suggestions. Can there be a common currency? Never, he says. Can the gas and oil pipelines be brought under a common management? Total silence. Russia ranks seventh as an investor in Belarus. The United States is at the top. Lukashenko wants cheap resources from Russia without giving up an inch of his hold on Belarus and its people. He does not want unification with Russia.

In any case, Russia does not need a monetary union with Belarus. An economic or trade union is something else. That perhaps is a more manageable idea than a monetary union. Above all, we need a genuinely transparent relationship with the Belarusian government. We do not want to subsidize the Belarusian economy as we did in the Soviet days.

QUESTION: You spoke about media censorship under Putin, but didn't the oligarchs Berezovsky and Gusinsky control the media under Yeltsin? What is the difference?

NEMTSOV: Isn't it better to have a few oligarchs rather than the state, in the person of Putin, in charge of Russian television? The oligarchs compete with one another. Berezovsky hates Gusinsky and vice versa. Such competition is good for media freedom, but do facts have a chance to emerge if the state controls the media? Facts about Chechnya? About the military? About corruption? About administrative reform? About Putin himself? A few oligarchs are better than one Putin. Of course, a hundred independent companies are the answer, but we are talking about Russia.

DESAI: Isn't the print media relatively free?

NEMTSOV: It depends. *Komsomolskaya Pravda* is under the firm control of the Kremlin. *Argumenty i Fakty* is relatively free.

QUESTION: At the start of the lecture, you said that you made a few mistakes in the reform process. Looking back, what would you do differently, especially about privatization?

NEMTSOV: I can talk about my own experience in Nizhny Novgorod province when I was governor. First we privatized small businesses, such as stores, restaurants, laundries, and trucks. Then we privatized the construction business, followed by agriculture. We moved up the scale from small to medium to large units. Such a progression is more effective than what Chubais did in Russia. I discussed it with him. He was more concerned with the political objective of getting rid of both state control and the Communist system itself than with the economic effectiveness of the process. But, of course, if you attempt something in haste, then you know "получается как всегда" (We wanted things to be better, but they turned out as usual).[20]

(Laughter)

QUESTION: Recently Prime Minister Fradkov stated that Russian oil pipelines will remain under state ownership. They will not be privatized. What is your position on this issue?

NEMTSOV: Putin wants the Russian GDP to double in a decade. A sure way of achieving this goal is to let Russian private businesses build oil pipelines. This will boost investments in the rest of the economy—in machine production, construction, chemicals, and the infrastructure by several fold. It will resemble the impact of railroad building on the U.S. economy in the nineteenth century.

Next, the construction of an oil pipeline from western Siberia to Murmansk in the north will allow Russian oil to be exported to the United States. It will reduce U.S. oil dependence on Saudi Arabia. Private Russian investors in the project are willing to concede that the state will own half of the stake and control the pipeline tariffs, but Fradkov has refused. The government wants to control private oil businesses by denying them the opportunity of owning pipelines. It is a political decision.

QUESTION: I have a follow-up question. How did you finance your December 2003 Duma election campaign?

NEMTSOV: I am proud that the SPS had cash assistance from a variety of sources. We had twenty-five sponsors. We had a rule prohibiting us from receiving more than 10 percent of our campaign budget from a single source. I brought in this rule as chairman of SPS. We did not allow Khodorkovsky or Mikhail Friedman of Alpha Bank to take over the SPS. As a result, we remained independent.

Currently the SPS is in a difficult situation. We are out of the Duma, and our influence has waned. I do not know how to raise money to support the SPS. At the very least, we need $1.5 million annually to fund our activities. Russian businesses may not want to support a coalition of SPS, Yabloko, and the Khakamada and Ryzhkov groups, of which I spoke earlier. The only way we have of raising substantial backing is to form a solidly united and democratic opposition. I think we have to wait and see how the situation unfolds.

DESAI: One final question.

QUESTION: This has been an interesting dialogue, but I have heard very little about laws. What is your view of legal reform in Russia? Rights cannot be guaranteed without that.

NEMTSOV: This is a serious and important question. What we currently have in Russia is a contradiction between our laws and justice. Russians would rather have справедливость, that is, justice of any kind rather than law. Therefore, the Kremlin gets away with extralegal ways of enforcing justice. That is very popular with the public. For example, sending Khodorkovsky to prison was a great decision. A half-Jewish billionaire was put behind bars.

(Laughter)

He built a private oil company, got to know Dick Cheney, and often traveled to Israel. Therefore, he had to be put in prison. Why worry about the legal implications? This is a serious problem and the major difference between Russia and the West. The Russian prosecutor general makes decisions that are popular rather than strictly legal. Anybody who has managed a business in Russia will agree with my observation. At every level, it operates most of the time from the bottom up.

I am reminded of a funny incident when I was governor of Nizhny Novgorod province. We had successfully built a road in the city, and as a gesture of celebration, I put a glass of vodka on the hood of my car and drove at a speed of 60 kmh. I promised that if the vodka did not spill, I would drink it with the city's chief of police and the construction engineer. It didn't spill, so I gave a personal order to the chief of police that drunk driving should be overlooked that day. The chief passed on the governor's rule throughout the department, and everybody loved it.

(Laughter)

I became immensely popular. Everybody was drinking because we had built a road. Nobody worried about accidents.

(Laughter)

I was young and unaware of the legal implications of my decision. We drank a bit of vodka because we had built a road. Thus everybody could do the same. That was it.

DECEMBER 2004

DESAI: How do you view Putin's post-Beslan proposal to retain only the party slate for the Duma elections and to abolish the single-member constituencies?

NEMTSOV: I believe that Duma elections based only on party lists will not help create a genuine multiparty system, including groups voicing their opposition, because financial resources for party formation are monopolized by the Kremlin; the electronic media are censored; the prospective parties, therefore, would be loyal to the Kremlin. It would destroy opposition because single mandate deputies were more independent and critical of government policies. Therefore, it does not make sense to compare these proposals with party-based election outcomes in countries such as Israel or the Netherlands.

Another danger is that most of Russia's regions lack the resources to build party organizations and finance election campaigns. Without adequate representation in the Duma, regional economic interests will be neglected. This will create massive imbalances between the center and some of the regions and [will result in] the impoverishment of their populations.

Finally, the abolition of single-member constituencies will destroy genuine opposition in the Duma. Independent opposition deputies, elected in single-member contests, are generally more critical of the leadership than party-affiliated members. Their voices will be silenced.

DESAI: Will the cancellation of gubernatorial elections and the appointment of governors by the president, to be subsequently approved by the regional legislatures, deprive voters of their rights to elect their regional leaders in a federal system?

NEMTSOV: I am opposed to this measure for several reasons. First, it violates the letter and spirit of the Russian constitution adopted in 1993. Second, the procedure is prone to corruption. Kremlin cronies may be selected as governors. Third, a Kremlin-appointed bureaucrat is not responsible to the voters and will fare worse in carrying out his obligations than an elected governor. Finally, the measure will transform Russia from a federal to a unitary state. Regional autonomy will disappear.

I admit that the gubernatorial elections were far from perfect and were marked by the domination of oligarchic groups. That called for measures designed to systematically control the financial clout of these groups rather than denying regional voters the right to elect their officials.

DESAI: Are these consolidating measures necessary to fight terrorism? What would you suggest?

NEMTSOV: To begin with, Putin should stop misleading the country and the world by claiming that Russia has been attacked by international terrorists. These attacks resulted from the Kremlin's continuing mistakes in the Caucasus, especially in Chechnya. Of course, the international terrorist organizations help their Chechen colleagues to the extent that the latter have a basis for undertaking terrorist activities. In truth, the Chechen problem needs to be resolved via political dialogue. Putin is able to mislead public opinion in Russia but not in the West. As a first step, therefore, media censorship should be removed so that the Chechen issue and its resolution can be widely and openly debated in Russia.

DESAI: Grigory Yavlinsky says that Putin's proposals smack of "soft Stalinism." What do you think?

NEMTSOV: I do not know what Yavlinsky has in mind. What is being established in Russia is "Putinism," not soft but solid. Putinism implies a denial of civic freedoms and federalism, of media censorship and control of the economy via monopolization and the growth of bureaucracy. It implies a move to a single-party system and Russia's political and economic stagnation. That is Putinism. I think it has only a marginal connection with Stalinism.

DESAI: Do you think that Putin regards the consolidation of political power as a necessary precondition for promoting economic reforms?

NEMTSOV: Economic reforms have stopped during Putin's second term. Pension system reform and restructuring of the energy complex have stopped. Government control of the pension fund implies a lack of momentum on the issue of pension reform. Gazprom, the world's largest natural gas monopoly, is corrupt to the core.

The continuing consolidation of political power under Putin, on the other hand, has expanded the role of the bureaucracy without generating any positive benefits. In this regard, Russia differs from Kazakhstan and China, whose authoritarian leaders can come up with arguments for denying civil liberties to their populations. Putin cannot provide such arguments.

DESAI: How does Putin's hybrid model differ from that of Pinochet in Chile and of the Communists in China?

NEMTSOV: The difference is that Chile under Pinochet and China under the Communists have managed to produce impressive economic results. These were in no way connected with accidental factors such as the current oil-led economic recovery in Russia. In contrast, Putin has frozen economic reforms.

On the other hand, Putin is not bloodthirsty. Russians are not killed as were Chileans under Pinochet and the Chinese under the Communists during the Tiananmen protests. I think Putin is closer to Salazar in Portugal because he has contrived a market authoritarian model devoid of significant structural reforms with gigantic power for a leader whom no one controls. Salazar also did not kill people.

DESAI: Does it make sense to apply the norms of a fully formed U.S.-style liberal order in order to assess Russia's evolving transition?

NEMTSOV: I do not think we need to move along the liberal U.S. trajectory, nor *can* we. Russia has a totally different history. The government structure should reflect Russia's specific features. We must, however, live by the Russian constitution, its division of powers along the federal hierarchy, the free press, and political competition. These basic principles enshrined in the constitution of 1993 should be protected. The state structures should reflect these specific features. For example, unlike in the United States, our educational system is organized along federal lines. The constitution also endows the federal executive branch with more authority than in the United States. We cannot copy the U.S. system.

DESAI: Despite Putin's illiberal forays, do you think that the long-term prospects of Russia's continuing to evolve into a liberal political and economic order remain robust?

NEMTSOV: I am not optimistic about Russia's democratic progression. I think we have passed the turning point. The significant question now is whether we will have the Duma elections in December 2007. The post-Beslan developments have put a damper on my hopes.

DESAI: Putin comes across as a nonideological, pragmatic leader who is interested in selectively pushing Russia's interests. How do you view his foreign policy?

NEMTSOV: Well, he has proclaimed solidarity with the U.S. president on the terrorism issue. He also actively cooperates with the European Union. I doubt that he, as an authoritarian leader, can be a full member of the community of democratic nations. On the other hand, as an autocrat, he can try manipulating public opinion in Russia and abroad to strengthen his domestic position. The xenophobic elements in Russia can also be exploited for the purpose, resulting in an extreme nationalistic tilt. Pro-Western attitudes cannot take root in such an environment.

DESAI: Do you view the proposed Gazpromrosneft merger favorably?[21]

NEMTSOV: The creation of Gazpromrosneft represents Putin's strategy to create a natural monopoly and increase the economic role of the bureaucracy. People who are loyal to Putin will direct and control this huge structure. That will promote corruption and inhibit managerial transparency. All of this implies that we are failing to move forward.

DESAI: Will Putin seek a third presidential term?

NEMTSOV: About six months ago, I would have said no, but now I think that the Belarusian experiment may be transplanted to Russia. If Putin successfully consolidates power and manages to appoint his candidates as governors, he can change the constitution and begin a third presidential term.

NOTES

1. A coalition of two separate parties, Fatherland and All Russia, was formed by the mayors of Moscow and St. Petersburg, Yury Luzhkov and Vladimir Yakovlev, respectively. Yevgeny Primakov topped the coalition's list of candidates for the parliamentary election.

2. Boris Berezovsky, Russia's most notorious oligarch, is living in exile in London, and Sergei Dorenko is a television journalist.

3. Andrei Illarionov has been an adviser to Putin on economic issues since 2000. German Gref has headed the Ministry of Economic Development and Trade since 2000. A staunch pro-market reformer, Yevgeny Yasin is currently a research supervisor for the State Higher School of Economics.

4. Roman Abramovich, one of Russia's most powerful businessmen, is listed by *Forbes* magazine as the second-richest man in Russia.

5. Start II, the Strategic Arms Reduction Treaty, was ratified by the Russian Duma on April 14, 2000.

6. In the 1980s, Yegor Ligachev (b. 1920), who had been a member of the Central Committee since 1966, advocated a conservative approach to perestroika.

7. Known for his attention-grabbing techniques with the press, Russian nationalist Vladimir Zhirinovsky (b. 1946) heads the Russian Liberal Democratic Party.

8. Stanley Fischer, former head of the Department of Economics at MIT, served as first deputy managing director of the International Monetary Fund from September 1994 to August 2001.

9. Billionaire Vladimir Potanin, one of the principal authors of the loans-for-shares program, has major holdings in Norilsk Nickel.

10. Javier Solana, former secretary general of NATO (1995–1999), became secretary general of the European Union in 1999.

11. Andrey Kokoshin, currently [2005] Chairman of the Duma Committee on CIS Affairs and Compatriot Relations, was from March through September 1998 the Chariman of the Federal Security Council. He served as First Deputy Minister of Defense from 1992 to 1997.

12. Valentin Yumashev, Yeltsin's chief of staff, supposedly worked closely with Berezovsky and Tatyana Dyachenko, Yeltsin's daughter.

13. In 1996 Anatoly Sobchak lost his bid for reelection as mayor of St. Petersburg to Vladimir Yakovlev.

14. Valentina Matviyenko, a deputy prime minister, dropped out of the St. Petersburg gubernatorial race. She is currently governor of the city. Russian cities situated within *oblasts* (regions) usually have mayors, and each region has its governor. The city of St. Petersburg, situated within the Leningradskaya Oblast, holds a special federal status, however, and has the rights and privileges of an oblast.

15. Irina Khakamada left SPS and ran for president in 2004. She launched her own party, "Our Choice" (Nash Vybor), in October 2004.

16. Vladimir Ryzhkov, one of the nineteen independents in the Duma, was elected as an independent member in the December 2003 Duma election. A prominent liberal, he is a Putin opponent.

17. Valeriya Novodvorskaya, Democratic Union leader, addressed protestors on May 21, 2004, from a cell similar to the one in which Mikhail Khodorkovsky was placed during his trial.

18. Lev Borisovich Kamenev (b. 1883), Grigori Evseyevich Zinoviev (b. 1883), and Stalin formed a triumvirate of successors on Lenin's death in 1924, excluding Trotsky. In 1936, Kamenev and Zinoviev were executed on charges of treason in the first big public purge trial. They were posthumously rehabilitated in 1988.

19. Boris Pasternak (b. 1890), author of *Doctor Zhivago,* was awarded the Nobel prize for literature in 1958. Rather than subject his art to the demands of the revolution and the dictates of the Soviet state, he treated social events only to the extent they affected the lives and destinies of individuals.

20. This is a remark attributed to former prime minister Viktor Chernomyrdin.

21. In the final act of the unification drama calculated to raise state control of Grazprom to 51 percent, Grazprom was set to acquire the private oil company Sibneft instead of the state-owned Rosneft.

CHAPTER 5

Mikhail Kasyanov

The Pro-Market Prime Minister

DECEMBER 2004

The economic situation seems stable now, but it is actually vulnerable and transitional. Economic growth cannot be sustained if property rights are questioned, businesses are taxed indiscriminately, and structural reforms are kept in a state of limbo.

From 2000 to 2004, as prime minister, I had worked hard to create a proinvestment environment.

In Russia, we have never had small businesses—not in agriculture, in industry, or in the service sector. We need a special program to fill that gap and encourage small businesses.

Russians today are a different people, despite the fact that a majority lived in the Soviet Union and remember the old times. It is a different country now. In fact, it is a different society.

Russia will continue to be a global player, especially in the regions where, because of its history and geography, it has continuing interests and responsibilities.

DECEMBER 2004

DESAI: How is the Russian economy doing?

KASYANOV: Let me take you back to August 1998, when the Russian economy underwent a deep financial crisis. The ruble declined precipitously, the Central Bank of Russia lost most of its foreign exchange reserves, and the government defaulted on its external and internal debt. The economy faced potential hyperinflation, and Russians suffered a massive loss in their real incomes. The picture was grim, and hardly anyone counted on a quick recovery. Today, six years later, the Russian economy has been growing for the sixth year in a row.

DESAI: Russia currently ranks as one of the world's fastest-growing economies, doesn't it?

KASYANOV: Absolutely. The GDP growth rate was 10 percent in 2000, 7.3 percent in 2003, and 7.1 percent in 2004. Inflation is down, almost in single digits. Real income growth is boosting consumption. Foreign exchange reserves have ballooned from $12 billion in 2000 to $130 billion currently. Federal budget revenues are high, and the federal budget has a significant surplus. The government's special stabilization fund for meeting unexpected emergencies already amounts to $20 billion.

DESAI: What were the reasons for this spectacular performance?

KASYANOV: Well, growth has been strongest in the extractive industries, mainly oil and natural gas. Of course, high oil prices contributed to GDP growth, but there is more to the story than just an external stimulus.

The principle contributory factor was the series of structural reforms that were initiated in 2000. The agenda covered budget, taxation, and pension reforms. The policies had to be supported by a number of structural and institutional changes designed to provide nondiscriminatory access to infrastructure in sectors such as energy, telecommunications, and transportation. Continuing privatization was aimed at supporting competition and promoting private investment. As we predicted, these factors became the main driving force behind growth. In constant dialogue with the business community, the Russian government set the rules of the game, which were acceptable to domestic and foreign businesses as well. Growing confidence brought immediate results, as Russian businesses started making long-term plans and investing in new production facilities.

DESAI: Does the economic resurgence that began in 2000, when you were prime minister, face new challenges?

KASYANOV: Of course. The most serious challenge arises from the need to diversify the growth. The manufacturing and processing industries need to grow faster than the extractive sector and take up a larger share of the economy. By the time I left the government in early 2004, we had made significant progress by providing incentives to manufactured exports, fine-tuning the tax regimes, and generally improving the investment climate.

DESAI: What about the recurring problems in Russian banks?

KASYANOV: I'm glad you brought that up. The financial sector as a whole has become a bottleneck that is impeding growth diversification. There are thirteen hundred undercapitalized banks in Russia. They are unable to provide financing to businesses, and they cannot attract deposits from the public even though we have deposit insurance in place. The domination of the state-owned Sberbank in capturing deposits undermines normal competition. This impediment needs to be corrected. The insurance and pension fund markets are also underdeveloped.

DESAI: I'm glad you brought up the pension system. How do you view the problems of the crumbling social welfare system in general?

KASYANOV: The government faces the daunting task of providing adequate social security, education, and medical services to the public. The benefits of the economic growth that I mentioned earlier have bypassed a sizeable part of the Russian population. The significant decrease in life expectancy has currently stabilized for Russian men at around sixty years. Pensions begin at that age. Further progress in pension reform is urgent because the current pay-as-you-go system cannot ensure a decent standard of living for retirees. The isolated schemes that have begun productively investing in Russian pension funds must gain speed. That will provide a solid impetus for modernizing Russia's economic growth.

Of course, high oil prices have provided additional revenues in the federal budget. In my view, these have not only made our policy makers complacent but have also distorted their priorities. The economic situation seems stable now, but it is actually vulnerable and transitional. Economic growth cannot be sustained if property rights are questioned, businesses are taxed indiscriminately, and structural reforms are kept in a state of limbo.

However, despite these recent reversals, I remain optimistic. I am confident that Russia will overcome these difficulties and become a modern, market-oriented economy.

DESAI: Let me go back to what you said earlier about the declining growth rate of the economy, even though oil prices remain high.

KASYANOV: The principal contributing factor is low and uncertain business expectations. Russian businesses, large and small, have stopped making investment plans. This means that the economy is currently getting returns from the investments, foreign and domestic, made earlier, at the start of the new millennium. From 2000 to 2004, as prime minister, I had worked hard to create a proinvestment environment. Potential foreign investors wondered why they were being asked to invest in Russia when domestic investors were holding back. We managed to induce local businesses, especially in the oil sector, to expand their investment. That in turn attracted foreign investors. That process has virtually stopped.

Of course, consumer demand has picked up. Lots of malls are being built in Moscow and other places. People are ready to spend cash, but the investment climate is depressed.

DESAI: If you were once more in charge, what would you do to improve the investment climate? What, in your view, are the much-needed policy measures?

KASYANOV: While Russia is making a transition to a market system, I firmly believe in the continuity of appropriate policy initiatives in order to maintain the reform momentum. Of course, the economy's macroeconomic fundamentals are robust. In fact, that should make Russia an attractive place for foreign investors. However, the cancellation and reversal of structural reforms send a negative signal. For example, the overhaul of Russia's energy company, United Energy Systems, was set to proceed in an orderly fashion. Now it is stopped in its tracks. The necessary legislation for restructuring the energy monopoly was adopted. It was a mistake to stop it in midstream. That was damaging to investor confidence.

A similar backtracking took place with regard to pension reform. The plan to invest the pension funds of a number of potential pensioners was shelved, too. That was a retrograde step. It set back the progress that had been made on reforming the pension system.

I would restart the reforms of the previous government. I would also put new items on the reform agenda, for example, restructuring the educational system, which I mentioned earlier.

Of course, the banking sector is a continuing headache. It is a huge bottleneck because the role of the state-owned savings bank, Sberbank, which is an unwieldy bureaucracy, has increasingly attracted deposits from the public. This is unfortunate because Russian businesses are now poised to seek out loans from banks. The banking sector can be an effective financial intermediary. In my opinion, private banks can effectively play that role. Banks with healthy balance sheets and adequate capital are missing from the scene.

DESAI: You emphasized the lack of progress on pension reform. How far and how fast can the Russian policy makers discard the pay-as-you-go arrangement and move into a privatized pension system? Is the public ready for that?

KASYANOV: All of the preparatory work for this plan was done by the previous government. We had extensive discussions in the Duma on the issue. We also had detailed discussions with public bodies. Russians had begun to understand the implications of the proposed changes. We had worked up a detailed and sophisticated package of reforms. You know, Russia really did not have a guaranteed system of pensions for its retirees under the old pay-as-you-go arrangement. If the pension fund was short of cash, the payments would stop. We had worked hard to convince the public that an alternative arrangement, in which the contributions could be invested properly, offered greater security. I believe that the population was ready for the change. In fact, we had placed some of the funds in secure investments. Now the process has halted.

DESAI: So you would say that pension reform is dead because of the lack of a decisive push from the leadership. Another issue: Why is Russia lagging seriously behind in the growth of small businesses?

KASYANOV: I think the reasons for that are a little different. First, Russia has never had a small-business tradition or culture. Russians do not have a memory of that to fall back on. In contrast, Hungary and Poland have had a long tradition of people owning small businesses even during the Communist period. In Russia, we have never had small businesses—not in agriculture, in industry, or in the service sector. We need a special program to fill that gap and encourage small businesses. We were unable to devise such a program in the government, and we bear the responsibility for that lapse. At the same time, we do not know what kind of program would be effective. I believe that we need to create a competitive environment in which potential business promoters can pick the right opportunity and develop it. Government funding can provide the necessary infrastructure in a transparent, predictable fashion with equal access to everyone. For example, if someone wants to start up a car repair shop, he can readily access the power and gas companies for electricity and heating. Right now, he does not feel sure of securing a bank loan for the purpose because the infrastructure support is missing.

Then there is the problem of government regulations and countless inspections. The fire safety inspector suddenly appears and orders the unit closed. The health inspector raises problems, too. Everybody wants cash under the table. Corruption has exploded to unimaginable levels.

DESAI: I was reminded of recent remarks by the U.S. ambassador, Ambassador [Alexander] Vershbow, who said that, in a city that he visited, a small business had to get permission from forty sources before it could open. The regulatory environment is suffocating.

KASYANOV: You're absolutely right. About two years ago, we managed to adopt legislation to slash licensed activities from 2,000 to 200, something approaching those numbers. We fought with a number of agencies, government bodies, and Parliament. In the end, we got this legislation. I personally had to put my reputation on the line because few ministers wanted to approve the changes. The legislation went through on the basis of my personal approval and stamp as prime minister. Barring a couple of members, the rest of the government, close to twenty ministers, stayed out of the matter. The situation has improved, but additional measures are badly needed.

DESAI: You talked about the striking growth of the natural resources sector in Russia. The United States would like to diversify its energy sources.

KASYANOV: That is a good idea.

DESAI: What role can Russia play? Can it be a swing supplier of oil in the U.S. market?

KASYANOV: We not only can be, but we already are major suppliers of oil and natural gas in Europe and elsewhere. Three years ago, we launched the so-called energy project with Vice President Dick Cheney, which was subsequently endorsed by the two presidents. Both sides need to explore the idea of constructing a pipeline from eastern Siberia to the Northern Sea and developing the deepwater port of Murmansk, so that oil and liquefied gas can be transported from there directly to U.S. ports on the Atlantic. This is a worthwhile and doable project. Russia will prove a reliable partner in the venture.

DESAI: President Putin seems to think that Russia's energy resources should be used to support its own interests rather than those of private oil companies in Russia. How would you react to that?

KASYANOV: I'm sorry, but that comes across as a populist position. I think natural resource exploration is a job that has to be undertaken by somebody, be it a state enterprise or a private company. It doesn't matter who owns the unit. It must, however, operate in a regulated environment. Above all, it must pay the appropriate taxes. With that end in mind, we brought down the corporate tax rate from 35 to 24 percent. We undertook a thorough investigation of how we might create an attractive investment climate for the purpose. The tax burden that we came up with is lower than in the UK, higher than here in the United States, and much higher than on oil producers in the Middle East. It doesn't matter who owns the enterprise so long as the investment climate is attractive and the country, by which I mean the oil producers, can sell oil at an appropriate market price and be a market maker in this area, so as to create benefits for Russia.

DESAI: So you want a predictable and stable regulatory environment for private oil companies in Russia. Starting from there, I want to ask you a broader question. I believe that certain features of a market economy have been firmly established in Russia, among them free prices, a convertible ruble, and private ownership of assets. Russians can choose their jobs. They can travel freely. So some of the features of a liberal economic and political order are firmly in place. Would you agree?

KASYANOV: Yes, I would. Nothing shocking has happened yet. However, if we continue moving rudderless without a free-market policy orientation in economic matters, the situation could deteriorate. Right now, all of the fundamental choices that you have mentioned, such as free travel, alternative jobs, and educational preferences, are firmly in place. But you know, no one can take them away from us. That is simply impossible. Russians today are a different people, despite the fact that a majority lived in the Soviet Union and remember the old times. It is a different country now. In fact, it is a different society.

DESAI: So Russia has changed a lot, but we have to watch how it develops down the road. I have a slightly personal question. Given your enormous role as a politician and a policy maker on the Russian scene, suppose a young Russian came up to you and said, "Mr. Prime Minister, I want to enter politics." How would you advise that person?

KASYANOV: I would say, "Splendid. Welcome to Russian politics."

(Laughter)

DESAI: That is very encouraging.

KASYANOV: We need young politicians with new ideas.

DESAI: We have a few minutes left. I would like Prof. Stephen Sestanovich to open the floor for discussion.

SESTANOVICH: I would like to ask the prime minister a question about the relationship between business and politics in Russia. Because of the lack of pressure from outside the government, reforms often lose momentum before they can be completed. As a result, the government loses interest. When President Putin came to power in 2000, he obviously thought that Russian businesses dominated politics. It is fair to say that he has managed to reduce this dominance, even more than just reduce it. Can you describe the situation now and tell us whether it is still possible for Russian business interests to push for policies that are in their interest and that they see as in Russia's national interest, to push for the kinds of reforms you are talking about? Are they a lobby for reform, and can they be effective politically, or has the Putin regime choked off that possibility?

KASYANOV: In my view, it is closer to the second alternative. Of course, Russian business groups can still sort out their position on an issue and relay it to the prime minister's office, for example, and the president will continue to have meetings with the captains and listen to their views. However, I am afraid they will not frankly and fully disclose their positions as they did several years ago because they don't quite understand just what the real policy is and whether their views are needed or whether their criticisms will be accepted. There is, therefore, a near vacuum in the communication between Russian businesses and the leadership at present. That is my opinion.

SESTANOVICH: There is obviously a big difference between having an appointment with the prime minister and making a suggestion and having a meeting with the president and making a request. The difference between that and being able to actively participate in politics is the ability, for example, to support opposition parties. Is it possible for businesses to do that any longer, or is the risk too great?

KASYANOV: I would say that I cannot disagree with you on the second scenario.

DESAI: When Putin recently addressed the Union of Entrepreneurs and Industrialists, he brought up two issues that I remember. He said, "Pay your taxes" and "Fear is unproductive." Since the tax authorities can be heavy handed, Russian businesses have reasons to be scared.

QUESTION: Mr. Prime Minister, what impact has a weak dollar had on the Russian economy?

KASYANOV: It has created problems for our policy makers. Russia imports consumer goods from the European Union, paying in the euro, which has become stronger with respect to the dollar, whereas it earns revenues in dollars by exporting oil and metals. The Central Bank has made the necessary adjustment by linking the ruble appropriately and jointly with the euro and the dollar. It has also raised its share of euros in the foreign exchange reserves at its command. At the same time, as the ruble has become stronger in real terms, it has hurt the competitiveness of Russian manufactured goods. The Central Bank must rein in this appreciation even as it must control inflation, which has been running at a higher rate than the annual 10 percent. The appreciating ruble and high inflation pose an unusual challenge for the Central Bank. We have faced this problem before but not to the same extent. It's like swimming in a fast river.

DESAI: When I go to Moscow, my Russian friends say, "You gave us the wrong advice." When I ask, "What did I do wrong?" they say, "Well, you told us to hold on to our dollars, and we did, and now we get fewer rubles for them for our purchases." So Russia has entered the global financial age. Russian households are worried about unstable exchange rates.

KASYANOV: That's right.

QUESTION: Mr. Prime Minister, my questions relate to small-business development and bank financing. Would it be possible to use some of the foreign exchange reserves of the Central Bank for setting up a Russian development bank for assisting small Russian businesses? Such a commitment from the government would induce commercial banks in Russia to seek lending opportunities to businesses and compete with the government agency. Does this make sense?

KASYANOV: I agree with you, although some members of the Russian cabinet may not like your suggestion. It would go against their predisposition for a tight budgetary policy because the government would have to incur additional outlays for funding the agency's capital. The extra spending by the agency would also add to inflationary pressures, so monetary policies would have to be adjusted accordingly. On the other hand, if the agency were set up as an independent unit and operated purely as a commercial body in its lending criteria, it could help finance badly needed infrastructure projects. The difficulty here is devising market-based criteria for selecting projects and applying them consistently. I think the significant foreign exchange reserves are partly a windfall that has arisen from favorable external circumstances, and they should be used for the general improvement of the national economy.

QUESTION: Are you in favor of adopting an industrial policy to improve Russia's economic performance?

KASYANOV: When I was in the government, I did not enforce industrial policies. On the other hand, we tried to create a level playing field for everyone, for all sectors of the economy, by affording them equal access to infrastructure and by creating a predictable environment so they could plan in advance. A potential entrepreneur would know what kind of service to expect from the state and at what price. Of course, the state itself could be an active player in defense production, for example. In that area, too, private producers may be allowed to participate. However, all of the rules should be transparent and provide equal opportunity to potential newcomers. They should be clear and conform to international norms and create a competitive environment.

DESAI: We have time for one more question.

QUESTION: What is your position on forgiving Iraq's debt to Russia? More generally, as Russia becomes strong economically, can it play a responsible role in global affairs?

KASYANOV: We support the U.S. initiative for reducing Iraq's debt burden in the interest of promoting its economic growth. All of the Paris Club creditors supported the initiative. Russia, of course, is Iraq's largest creditor and therefore will bear the maximum burden. As for a larger Russian role, I believe that Russia bears a responsibility for global security in the same manner as the United States. Russians also view the United States and Europe as their partners in this enterprise. Of course, there will be occasional differences and disappointments with the West. We understand that. Having said that, Russia's role in global affairs will be limited by its economic capacity and performance. As for our immediate neighborhood in the CIS [Commonwealth of Independent States], we have special interests and responsibilities. We have a long history of shared problems and common traditions, although the former Soviet republics are now independent states. I might say that we share common values with the states that are geographically closer to Europe.

Russia will continue to be a global player, especially in the regions where, because of its history and geography, it has continuing interests and responsibilities.

CHAPTER 6

Strobe Talbott

Bill Clinton's "Russia Hand"

NOVEMBER 2000

[F]or seven of the eight years that President Clinton was in office here, Boris Yeltsin was the president of Russia. He had, by virtue of his office, huge powers. He also had an extraordinarily strong and consistent commitment to certain principles and objectives that were in the interest of the United States. He was susceptible to the influence of only one man in the U.S. government, and that was Bill Clinton. Therefore, we decided early—President Clinton decided early— that he was going to concentrate his diplomacy on his Russian counterpart. I think that was absolutely the right thing to do. It yielded huge and lasting benefits to the United States.

Yeltsin felt a deep ambivalence about the United States. In some ways he regarded us as a beacon, a model, and a friend, and in other ways he regarded us as obnoxious as hell. . . . But the way he resolved that conflict, when push came to shove, was favorable. And that was largely because of the interaction between him and Clinton.

I wish that we had invested much more money early on . . . but certainly at the beginning of the Clinton administration. We should also have invested it more wisely. The international support, which is to say, the economic stabilization programs, and particularly the social safety net programs, should have been more highly conditioned. . . . I personally wish that I had paid more attention to Chechnya. It seemed literally like such a peripheral issue when it got started in 1994. We didn't focus on it enough. We didn't understand the ominous implications that it had for Russia's development as a state.

JANUARY 2001

He [Putin] has shown quite often in various ways that his instinct is, if not authoritarian, then at least tends toward the use of muscle rather than powers of persuasion and consensus building.

In fact, one of the reasons why I resist the simplistic labeling of Putin is that I think he is not ideological. Such authoritarian instincts [as] he has are more rooted in what he regards as pragmatism. That is how you get the job done. Now, they're also very much rooted in his desire to retain and consolidate personal power. But he has, for example, put together and kept in place the best team of economic reformers we've seen since 1992 and 1993.

Putin is all for multipolarity. And his dashing around is part of that.

I think there'll be a high degree of continuity in U.S.-Russian relations, but that doesn't go to the question of chemistry. Bill Clinton bonded with Boris Yeltsin. Big time. And he used that bond to get Yeltsin to do things that were hard for Yeltsin but important to us. That is the story of the last eight years more than any other single thing.

[I]t seems to me that Russia is trying to prosecute its end of a competitive and contentious relationship with the United States in accordance with the rules of normal international relations rather than fighting the Cold War.

MARCH 2005

I think Putin has used the Beslan tragedy to step up his five-year campaign to reestablish Russia as a highly centralized, vertical state with power concentrated in the Kremlin.

Putin's clampdowns have not much affected the lives of ordinary Russians.

If Russia is to survive as a unitary state, it must resume its development as a federal and a democratic state.

NOVEMBER 2000

TALBOTT: As I looked through your questions before you came in today, several points came forward with particular force, and those are the ones I want to concentrate on. I really think the Cox Commission is unworthy of serious attention, so I will not comment on that.[1]

The key thing that I think goes to the heart of one of the issues you're obviously grappling with is shock versus therapy. If I could take back any line that had come out of my mouth—you ask me at one point what I would have done differently—well, one thing, I wouldn't have made the wisecrack in December 1993 about more therapy, less shock, not because it was less true, but because it was a wisecrack and because it lent itself to misinterpretation. Even accurately quoted, it discouraged the good guys; it was seen as a distancing of U.S. policy from the reformers, which it was not intended to do. If at some point in your project you are interested in my giving you a detailed exegesis of what I meant to say, what lay behind the phrase . . .

DESAI: I'll invite you to a conference.

TALBOTT: We can sort it out then. But the real point is this: First of all, I think that Yeltsin and Gaidar made an early and correct decision to give priority to and take risks in dismantling as quickly and fully as possible the apparatus of the Soviet state, the Soviet system. And the demolition project was ugly, it was not very disciplined, [and] it was done without a lot of careful thought to consequences, but it was necessary.

DESAI: Of course, the old system had to go.

TALBOTT: Well, very good. So you obviously know the argument. But that was, first of all, what we believed was in their minds as we talked to them during that early period. And, second, we supported that decision, and we still support it. A lot of Monday morning quarterbacks are now saying that we should have counseled them to go slow and to take a more gradualist approach to the dismantlement of the old system until they had a clear idea of what they were going to put in its place, etcetera. I don't know how in God's name they could have done that. It was simply giving the old power structure more of a lease on life. That's point number one.

Point number two—and this is where the shock versus therapy line comes in—has to do with the connection between politics and economics. I spent more time on the politics. I hope you'll have a chance to talk to colleagues like Larry Summers, David Lipton, Carlos Pascual, Nick Burns, Nancy Lee, a lot of people who worked on the economics side.[2] But basically, sound economics for Russia meant hardship. There was no way around that. Hardship meant backlash. Backlash meant Reds and Browns. So there was, in the logic, the dynamics of the situation, almost an inevitability, I think, in the kind of radical reform that Yeltsin, Gaidar, and company carried out back in 1992 and 1993. The backlash would translate into the Zhirinovsky victory in 1993 and the Communist victory in 1995, and there was no way around it.

DESAI: Can I interrupt you? But does that mean that, in undertaking the demolition project, they did not distinguish between ends and means, that everything was all right for the good of the cause? Like the bombing of the parliament building in October 1993, for example.

TALBOTT: Well, I was going to come to that. That was actually the third point. At least in the way that you posed the question here, you have oversimplified, or missed the point of, the bombing of the parliament building.

DESAI: Tell me.

TALBOTT: Others can tell you much better, but the provocation mounted by Ruslan Khasbulatov and Rutskoi and those who occupied the White House, the Bely Dom, was very real, dangerous, and escalating.[3] Yeltsin's use of force against the Parliament did not come until after those who were occupying the parliament building broke out into the streets of Moscow [and] rioted in Smolensk Square. They went to Ostankino and to the mayor's office.[4] They used rocket-propelled grenades to blast their way into Ostankino. It was then that the crackdown came.

It was basically an armed insurrection against the constituted authority of the state and the government.

Second, if you do not [already] know it, you ought to go back and get the statement that Yeltsin made to the Russian people. I mean, it was hardly triumphal. He basically said that "this is a terrible thing that we have done to ourselves. There are no winners here." There was a deep sense of tragedy and even self-incrimination, starting with Yeltsin and on the part of everybody. So I don't think that you can take the willingness to use force against the Parliament as an indictment of Yeltsin and the reformers for having no regard for ends versus means.

DESAI: All right, so now let's take the new Parliament, which comes into play, as it were, after the 1993 elections up to the December 1999 elections: The Communists and the Left have a majority in the Parliament, in the Lower House, for about six years. No project, no reform legislation initiated by the reformist government could pass the Parliament dominated by the Communists and the Left. Is that why the Clinton administration sort of bypassed them?

TALBOTT: Bypassed?

DESAI: Bypassed in the sense that the relationship between Yeltsin and his young band of reformers at that end and the Clinton policy makers at this end was personalized.

TALBOTT: Bypassing, in effect, the powers that be in the Parliament . . .

DESAI: Not bringing the Russian legislators into the negotiating act . . .

TALBOTT: By us?

DESAI: Yes.

TALBOTT: Well, I don't want to put words into your mouth. This is a version of the criticism that we were Yeltsin-centric. Too much. We personalized the policy.

Desai. Yes.

TALBOTT: Let me refute that. First of all, I should acknowledge that, for seven of the eight years that President Clinton was in office here, Boris Yeltsin was the president of Russia. He had, by virtue of his office, huge powers. He also had an extraordinarily strong and consistent commitment to certain principles and objectives that were in the interest of the United States. He was susceptible to the influence of only one man in the U.S. government, and that was Bill Clinton. Therefore, we decided early—President Clinton decided early—that he was going to concentrate his diplomacy on his Russian counterpart. I think that was absolutely the right thing to do. It yielded huge and lasting benefits to the United States, which we can talk about. There are at least half a dozen examples of issues that could be resolved satisfactorily, from our standpoint, only at the Clinton-Yeltsin level, and that required a large expenditure of time and energy by our president.

Now, at the same time, we were dealing with a very broad spectrum of Russian politicians. Whenever Clinton went to Moscow, he always made a point of meeting with pretty much the full spectrum of the Russian Parliament, excluding only Zhirinovsky and the ultra-Browns. Gennady Zyuganov, Alexander Lebed, you

name it, the president met with those guys and talked with them. Ambassador Jim
Collins—and before that, Ambassador Tom Pickering—met on a regular basis with
opposition figures from, I guess we call it, the Left, so much so that Yeltsin at one
point complained to Clinton that our embassy was having too much contact with
the opposition. People like me, here in the department, would go to the Parliament when we would go to Moscow. I went to the old Bely Dom, I went to Staraya
Ploshchad, the new parliament building. When Vice President Gore went there,
he would visit the Parliament; he would meet with the speaker of the Parliament.
When those guys came here on Russian Parliament–Congress exchanges, we would
meet with them on a regular basis, so we had a lot of engagement.

DESAI: I missed something here. Why do you say that Yeltsin was susceptible
only to the president of the United States?

TALBOTT: Well, we had only two presidents that he dealt with. He dealt with
President Bush (senior), previously, of course, and to good effect there, too. President Bush, of course, took a little time to get used to dealing with President Yeltsin
because he was used to Gorbachev, whom he held in very regard and for very good
reasons. But my point is this, and we can go through the list: There was a range of
issues that came up between the United States and Russia which were highly contentious and where we were basically urging Russia to do something that was difficult. And in every case, the way in which we ultimately persuaded the Russian
government to amend, if not reverse, its policy in a way that supported our interests and objectives, was through the Clinton–Yeltsin relationship.

DESAI: What do you have in mind? Let me give you some examples: NATO's
eastward expansion, the Kosovo operation.

TALBOTT: You're missing one that goes back to 1993 and deals with your former
homeland, I believe: the Russian sale of rocket engines to India. Remember that?
I really stressed the importance of that. That was a key episode early on. If Russia
had not rescinded that sale [and] cancelled that contract, many other things would
not have been possible, including Russia's admission into the missile technology
control regime. It was a real bellwether issue. And then in 1994 there was the effort, ultimately successful, to get Russia to acquiesce, is the way I would put it, in
the use of NATO forces in Bosnia, which, of course, was critically important to
getting the Dayton Peace Accord because, as the cliché has it, we had to bomb
Milosevic to the table.[5] We had to come back and bomb him again subsequently,
as well. There were some smaller issues, like getting Russia, as a permanent member of the Security Council, to support the use-of-force resolution on Haiti. But
you cited the two biggest examples of all, and that is the NATO–Russia Founding
Act, so-called, on cooperation with NATO, and then Russian diplomatic support
for ending the Kosovo war on NATO's terms.

DESAI: Yes, but I do feel that Yeltsin did contain the anti-American, anti-
Western sentiment at the Russian end . . .

TALBOTT: In himself? Contained it in which sense?

Desai: "Contained" in the sense of not letting it get out of hand with regard to his people.

Talbott: I agree, but he contained it in another sense, too. He contained it in that he had it within himself. Yeltsin—and I saw this up close many times—Yeltsin felt a deep ambivalence about the United States. In some ways he regarded us as a beacon, a model, and a friend, and in other ways he regarded us as obnoxious as hell. And still, he had enough of the Soviet worldview and the Soviet experience in him to regard us as an enemy. He was always wrestling with that. But the way he resolved that conflict, when push came to shove, was favorable, and that was largely because of the interaction between him and Clinton.

Desai: Yes, but our policy makers at this end could not "prevail upon him" with regard to the Chechen operation.

Talbott: The second or the first?

Desai: Well, with regard to the first one, from 1994 to 1996, the Russians felt that it was an issue of the right of self-determination of an ethnic minority in Chechnya. So the Russian public was with the Chechen people; therefore, Yeltsin had to backtrack from Chechnya. This was the first episode, but now I am talking about the second conflict, when the Russian public sided completely with the bloody war that Yeltsin led them through because the Chechen leadership became a terrorist leadership and also because it invaded Dagestan.

Talbott: I'm going to start with the facts. The first Chechen war was basically from 1994 to 1996. That's number one. The second Chechen war started in 1999 and continues today. The first war was more or less a continuum. There were several ceasefires between the fall of 1994 and the end of the war in August 1996, but it was essentially one conflict. Yeltsin was sick a good deal of that time. The best reconstruction of it that I know is Anatol Lieven's book, which is called something like *Chechnya: Tombstone of an Empire*.[6] The domestic dynamics were the following, and I think you basically have it right: There was either indifference on the part of the Russian public or some support and sympathy for the Chechens for the reasons that you have mentioned.

Desai: I am giving you Gaidar's version.

Talbott: Well, Gaidar bears a lot of the responsibility for the Chechen war. When he was the acting prime minister back in 1992, he basically adopted a policy of what I would call, and what he thought [was], benign neglect. I am a great admirer of Gaidar, but I think this was a huge error. He essentially let Chechnya fester. It didn't get either supervision or help. It was just left to itself. As a result, it turned into this pit of criminality, terrorism, and misery that exploded in due course. Now, Yeltsin got out of Chechnya in 1996. He basically saw it as a political loser. He saw it as a threat to his own reelection campaign in 1996. He first put Chernomyrdin and then Lebed in charge of negotiating a settlement. They succeeded, and the war ended in August 1996. Horrible carnage up until that point, but they got out. Now Russia has the second Chechen war.

DESAI: Starting in 1999.

TALBOTT: I think you must see that more as Putin's war. Putin was already the prime minister. He had aspirations, encouraged by Yeltsin, that he would be succeeding Yeltsin. Several facts remain murky. It appears that, first of all, the criminalization of Chechnya had continued and escalated, and a lot of foreign elements had come in there, including from the Gulf area, from the Middle East. Some external talent was imported. The Chechens then, as you said, crossed the border from inside Chechnya into Dagestan and attacked Russian installations there, and that provided a pretext for what has followed. I think that has had resonance and support from the Russian people for exactly the reason that you say. It appeared to be a terrorist attack against the Russian state itself. And the bombings in Volgodonsk and in Moscow and elsewhere were pretty much confirmations of that.[7] Now there are Russians, as well as others today, who believe that those were provocations, that the Russian Special Services undertook these provocative acts. We have absolutely no evidence to support them, but that's the difference between the two wars. Yeltsin's generals' war—really Grachev's war, Stepashin's war, which is the way to look at the first one—followed by Chernomyrdin's and Lebed's peace, and then Putin's war, starting in 1999, continuing to today, which is not resolving into peace.[8]

DESAI: Before we come to Putin, let's wind down the Yeltsin years and your policymaking experience. What would you do differently?

TALBOTT: The short answer is "more." We should have done more.

DESAI: In what way?

TALBOTT: In particular, and this speaks to areas where you are truly an expert, I wish that we had invested much more money early on, going back to the Bush administration, but certainly at the beginning of the Clinton administration. We should also have invested it more wisely. The international support, which is to say, the economic stabilization programs, and particularly the social safety net programs, should have been more highly conditioned. We saw that particularly with the eruption of the scandal over the corruption in the Bank of New York business in September 1999.[9] We saw that there just weren't anywhere near enough strings attached. I think, going back to the G7 and G8 meetings of 1992 and 1993, we should have done more but had it conditioned more. As for bilateral assistance, which is to say U.S. economic assistance, we should have done a lot more in the way of exchange programs, technical assistance programs, institution-building programs, democracy support programs, and probably more in the way of humanitarian aid as well. We got, I think, $1.6 billion out of Congress in 1993, which sounds like a lot, but when you consider it against the backdrop of—people always compare it to the Marshall Plan—it was a drop in the bucket.

DESAI: What were the high and low points in your experience?

TALBOTT: You asked about Chechnya earlier. I personally wish that I had paid more attention to Chechnya. It seemed literally like such a peripheral issue when it got started in 1994. We didn't focus on it enough. We didn't understand the ominous implications that it had for Russia's development as a state. If we had laid down a marker on it earlier and had been consistent in doing so, it might have helped over time.

DESAI: Yes, but my feeling is that, in their military operations, the Russians paid no attention to the loss of life and property in Chechnya. They have also out-dated technology of warfare, of heavy bombardments from the air. They do not have modern, more surgical, technologies to deal with this kind of scenario.

TALBOTT: That's true, but you know there has been a fundamental change for the better in that regard. For example, I think that Yeltsin's decision to get out of Chechnya in 1996 had a lot to do with civil society taking form. It had a lot to do with Russian mothers agitating against their sons' fighting and dying in Chechnya. I remember going to Iceland in the fall of 1999. A large delegation of Russian women there from NGOs [nongovernmental organizations] and political groups were just raising hell with Putin about Chechnya. That's a force to be contended with. It depends on what you're comparing it to. If you're comparing it to a mature de-mocracy like ours, obviously it has got a long way to go. If you compare it to where it was fifteen years earlier, it is a huge improvement.

DESAI: So you must have gone up and down in your state of well-being as a policy maker. What were the high points, and what were the low points?

TALBOTT: Well, let's start with the low points, but then I want to make two general comments. The low points were certainly the events of early October 1993, culminating in the attack on the parliament building, when it looked as though Russia was on the brink of a civil war, followed by the Zhirinovsky group's vic-tory in the December Duma elections in 1993, the Communist victory in the December Duma elections in 1995, [and] Yeltsin's blowup at the Budapest summit in December 1994, which was then the lowest moment of the Kosovo war.[10] It looked not only [as though we were] not going to [be able to] budge Milosevic but [also as though] we were going to destroy U.S.-Russian relations as well. Those were the tough ones. We came through all of those. The high point, which has been sustained, has been the extraordinary resilience and consistency of the Rus-sian people's apparent commitment to democracy. They were given the vote, they liked it, they exercised it, they kept doing it. They had their elections. Yeltsin came very close to postponing or canceling the presidential election of 1996, but he didn't do it for a variety of reasons, which he actually describes in his new book, *Midnight Diaries*.

However, the other general point I want to make has to do with the long haul. We Americans are manic-depressive about foreign policy, perhaps about other things as well. We go up, we go down; it's like the Dow Jones: Are you buying or selling Russian futures today? That's not the way to look at it. We have to remind our-selves that this is a country that has had a thousand years of totalitarian and authori-tarian history. It never had the Enlightenment, it never had the Renaissance, it never had the industrial revolution. Some of my friends, including at Columbia, would argue that they did have the Renaissance, a little bit. All right. But the point is that, given the history of the political culture, not to mention the economic culture in that country, it is quite extraordinary that in the course of fifteen years—and that's what we're really talking about, we're going back to 1985 and Gorbachev's coming to power—they, not because they were defeated, but because they were fed up, they tore down this old system, and they started to put in place something that is at least on the right side of the great dividing line of the last fifty years in terms of governance and political values. But, look, it's a generational problem. It was a bloodless revolution. The old regime simply changed its rhetoric, its titles, its mode of operations and became the new regime in some ways. It's going to take the passing of that generation and probably another one before we can expect them to really stabilize. So, we speak of high points and low points. It's a fair question, but I do think that the ultimate high point, which is the fact that they are a functioning democracy today, has to be compared to the low point of where they were fifteen years ago.

JANUARY 2001

DESAI: We were talking about Yeltsin when you were whisked away to the White House. Let us talk about the political significance of Yeltsin resigning suddenly on December 31, 1999. Your reaction: Were you surprised by it?

TALBOTT: Big time.

DESAI: What did it signify? What was your reaction to the changes to come because he was the president with whom your president worked so well?

TALBOTT: Well, the political logic of it was not mysterious. I think an indisputable part of Yeltsin's strategy, no doubt strongly encouraged by Putin, was to ensure Putin's succession to the presidency. Yeltsin, as it were, was out of the way, and, of course, Yeltsin's popularity was below ground. This allowed Putin to campaign for the presidency with all of the benefits of incumbency and, as I say, without the "albatross" of Yeltsin around his neck. It was also important to Yeltsin that he handpick the heir to succeed him. We had a couple of reactions to it. One was, okay, it's constitutional; they are playing by the rules—good. On the other hand, they are playing a bit fast and loose with the rules—not so good. But you sort of grade on the curve where Russian democracy is concerned. I guess that's a quote I can live with.

DESAI: Grade on the curve.

TALBOTT: Grade on the curve. In other words, you make allowances when you're dealing with a transitional society. I mean, God knows, the IMF and the U.S. Treasury made allowances when it came to conditionality, and we had to make some when it came to Yeltsin's standoff with Parliament in 1993 and so on and so forth. In any event, it was another example of that. Strictly speaking, they were playing by the constitutional rules, and that was the bottom-line requirement for our support. On a more precautionary note, though, we had valued and used Yeltsin's special relationship with Clinton to advantage. The chemistry between the two was invaluable as the driving force for steadying what was otherwise a very rocky relationship. Clinton had met with Putin twice at that point, once in Oslo and once in Auckland. And while the relationship was okay, Clinton didn't feel that he had anything like the power of persuasion with Putin that he did with Yeltsin, so we knew we would pay a price. The third factor I would mention is Chechnya. Putin had ridden right to the top. We were against what Russia in general and Putin in particular were doing in Chechnya, so we knew we would have a more intractable Chechnya problem as a result of this change.

DESAI: So let's talk about Putin. Given his background, given the craving of the Russian people for law and order, do you think he might turn authoritarian by, say, curbing the press's freedom, or do you think that some of this is necessary in order to eliminate crime?

TALBOTT: Well, you've given me two choices, and I would actually say both are true. I think, on the one hand, there has to be a certain amount of correction. The pendulum has swung very very far in Russia, whether you are talking about street crime or the fragmentation of what is ostensibly a federal system. On the other hand, both because of who he is and what his background is and also because of the influences operating on him, we are not terribly confident that Putin will get the balance right. He has shown quite often in various ways that his instinct is, if not authoritarian, then at least tends toward the use of muscle rather than powers of persuasion and consensus building. So it just bears very close watching, and I think that's how most intelligent Russians view it as well. When Clinton saw Yeltsin in June of 1999, he made a rather moving speech to Yeltsin, which was clearly intended to try to use Yeltsin for whatever influence he has on Putin, so that Putin also feels democracy and civil society and freedom in his gut, but there is no evidence that Putin does.

DESAI: Yes, but some tightening of federal authority might give a push to the reform momentum, for example, practically getting rid of the federal council of elected governors, who are either incompetent or corrupt.

TALBOTT: Or both. No, you have a point. In fact, one of the reasons I resist the simplistic labeling of Putin is that I think he is not ideological. Such authoritarian instincts [as] he has are more rooted in what he regards as pragmatism. That is how you get the job done. Now, they're also very much rooted in his desire to retain and consolidate personal power. But he has, for example, put together and kept in place the best team of economic reformers we've seen since 1992 and 1993. I know you are close to Gaidar, and I don't know what Gaidar's view is on Putin's economic policies. I haven't talked to Yegor in quite some time, but my impression is that he would agree.

DESAI: Guarded, but, on the whole, positive.

TALBOTT: Yes, and who knows how long they'll last, either? You hear that Viktor Gerashchenko, the central bank chairman, is about to be ousted, and Mikhail Kasyanov, the prime minister, seems to be permanently on a banana peel. Nevertheless, they stay, and they do keep implementing policies that bring in, if not joy, then at least some comfort to the hearts of our economic policy makers.

DESAI: So let's talk about policies. I think if he [Putin] wants to build a strong state, he must open up Russia, globalize, and bring in foreign investments. When I view the Russian situation and talk with people, my guess is that, even if he brings about an orderly situation by tightening up the legal framework, there are numerous restrictions on foreigners owning equity in Russian companies. I feel that there is an implicit coalition between Russian businesses and Russian left-wing legislators, both of whom do not want foreign investors.

TALBOTT: Absolutely correct.

DESAI: Much like in India in the early days.

TALBOTT: Really?

DESAI: Yes.

TALBOTT: So you'll be doing some comparative transition economics?

DESAI: Well, not really. I make this point on Russia. Indian businesses didn't want foreigners to come in.

TALBOTT: So you need a bold reformer. What's the name of the former Indian finance minister . . . Singh?

DESAI: Manmohan Singh.

TALBOTT: Yes, Manmohan Singh. That's what they need, but they also need somebody who would vacuum, so I think that's right. I've had a number of glimpses into that problem and correctly diagnosed it. The counter to it, or the argument against allowing that to run amok, is that Russia simply will not attract foreign investment if this coalition, this unholy alliance between Russian businessmen, many of whom are crooks, and local and national-level left-wing legislators prevails. They just won't get it.

DESAI: Absolutely. This is what India did all these years, in my view.

TALBOTT: By the way, an interesting footnote, or a sideline for somebody to pursue—maybe you—is that, given the strategic partnership that supposedly exists between India and Russia, the new India might help the new Russia.

DESAI: I don't know. This is again a subject that I have not kept up with. However, the defense equation is very strong, and the trade equation lacks traction as it did in the past. Russians want to trade with the West, essentially for the goods and technologies they need.

TALBOTT: Well, we're now in a different era.

DESAI: That was the question I was coming to. Is Putin trying to counter U.S. hegemony and uphold a multipolar world by going to China, India, and Europe, or is he busy promoting sales of Russian military hardware to these countries, including Iran and Angola? What do you make of all of these initiatives?

TALBOTT: Again, I don't think it's an either-or proposition. There's no question that Putin is a believer in the French global ideology that the biggest threat to an equitable and prosperous world is a unipolar world. The Russians and the French make common cause around what I think is a pretty stupid proposition. I have a primitive knowledge of physics, but I've determined that in physics there is no such thing as unipolarity or multipolarity. There is bipolarity. That's how it works. That's how magnetism works, and that's how gravity works. So it is nonsense as a metaphor, and I think it's also nonsense in the way the metaphor is applied. That said, we all know what they mean by "unipolar" and by "multipolar." Putin is all for multipolarity, and his dashing around is part of that. The sale or leakage or assistance to these other states of dangerous high technology is a combination of good old-fashioned, short-term, short-sighted commercialism with a little bit of a geopolitical overlaying. I always felt, for example, dealing with Primakov, as I did for a couple of years on Iran sales, that part of what motivated Primakov was a desire to solidify Russia's relationship with Iran against the day that the United States got back into play in Iran and tried to elbow out Russia. On top of that you have this extremely decentralized set of baronies that are in it for the fast buck. So all of that's in there together.

DESAI: President Clinton's recent decision to postpone the missile defense directed against rogue states like North Korea followed Putin's trip to North Korea. Do you think that contributed ever so slightly?

TALBOTT: Ever so slightly. It was a combination of factors that led to the president's decision. [One was] the failure of the tests, which calls into question how promising the technology was, the vociferous resistance of the Chinese and the Russians, the high level of skepticism and discomfort on the part of the Allies, and then there were several things that suggested that North Korea might be somewhat less urgent a threat than we thought. One was the opening of the North and South, the overtures that Kim Jong-il put out,[11] and then there was Putin's trip just before the president and Putin saw each other in Okinawa. So all of these things were at play.

DESAI: The new president here. You said earlier that Yeltsin was susceptible to President Clinton. What can you say about Putin being susceptible to George W. Bush?

TALBOTT: I have no idea. First of all, I have no idea what kind of a president Governor Bush is going to make. I haven't had a chance to observe him for many years. I know some of the people who will be working with him, and they're a very confident and moderate group. I think there'll be a high degree of continuity in U.S.-Russian relations, but that doesn't go to the question of chemistry. Bill Clinton bonded with Boris Yeltsin. Big time. And he used that bond to get Yeltsin to do things that were hard for Yeltsin but important to us. That is the story of the last eight years more than any other single thing. Now you don't have Yeltsin, and you don't have Clinton. You've got a Russian president who made a point of being resistant to blandishments and bonding, and in Bush we don't know what we have.

DESAI: What do you make of Governor Bush's campaign slogan exhorting U.S. policy makers to keep away from nation building in foreign lands such as Russia? Will there be Russia bashing?

TALBOTT: To be honest with you, I don't take it terribly seriously. I don't think the Russians probably take it seriously, either. I think the Russians attach more importance to some of the strategic issues, and that will depend a lot on who emerges as the team in the Pentagon. I'll personalize it: If they get Steve Hadley as the driving force in these strategic issues, they will get reassured.[12] And if they get Richard Perle, they'll have their pants scared off.[13] So we'll just have to see.

First of all, nation building. Russians aren't very enthusiastic about it, either, so they're not going to lament a certain U.S. retreat in that regard. I'm a little bit skeptical about how much retreating the administration will actually do. I think that there are some new realities that they will quickly adjust to, so I'm really not a good predictor of where they'll come out. Condoleeza Rice will be one of the two or three key people I know quite well, and she figures rather prominently in the book that Michael Beschloss and I did eight years ago, so you might want to look at that and get a little feel for the way she talked back then.[14] Condi Rice deserves credit for having helped Bush Senior play a constructive role in the end of the Soviet Union and of the Cold War.

DESAI: Talking about security issues, do you think an economically revived Russia will be a security threat to U.S. interests down the road?

TALBOTT: I suppose so, but I'm rather more optimistic on that. I think that if Russia really does become economically powerful, it will become so in a way that will blunt the sharper edges of Russian political culture, which is to say, either Russia will revert to habits that caused the Soviet Union to be a failure, in which case it will not become economically powerful, or it will put its resources, human and natural, into having a vigorous economy that operates on market principles and is integrated with the outside world, in which case it will gain prosperity and economic strength, but it will neither have nor need the kind of muscle-bound military apparatus that made the Soviet Union both a failure and a threat.

DESAI: Final question: Russia's becoming a member of the European Union, say, in 2015. Does that prospect seem bizarre?

TALBOTT: Well, 2015 is fifteen years from now. Fifteen years ago it was 1985. In 1985, if you had asked me what the chances were that, fifteen years later, Russia would be cooperating in the Balkans and keeping the peace and that NATO would have taken in Poland, Hungary, and the Czech Republic, I would have said you should go back not to Columbia but straight to Bellevue. I mean, seriously. I would have said that is nuts. And 1985 was, of course, the first year of Gorbachev, so we already had reason to say, "Interesting new leader. Soviet reform," but it was Soviet reform.

DESAI: Yes, but when I talk with the young people there, and you have talked with some of them more than I have, they all passionately desire to be identified with Europe. Russia is a European country, apart from the Eastern world.

TALBOTT: Do you speak Russian?

DESAI: Yes.

TALBOTT: Do you know the word *zapadnichestvo*?

DESAI: A calling for the West.

TALBOTT: Well, *zapadnichestvo* is actually a nineteenth-century word that was used by the [Russian] Westernizers, to be sure, and the way I would translate it is "Russia's Western vocation." I was quite interested to discover, in the first several meetings that I had with Putin, that he uses it as part of his vocabulary, whereas both Gorbachev and Yeltsin didn't like to talk about the West because they thought the very word "West" discriminated against Russia: Russia could never be part of the West. I don't think that is Putin's view. And you're right, it is certainly the driving force of a generation of Russians who aren't yet in positions of power. And if we could just give them the time to get there without things getting too screwed up. The passion that you describe will end up being a major factor in Russian policy. It really already is in a lot of ways. I mean, one of the things I am grappling with is that, even with all of the troubles that we're having with Russia, it seems to me that Russia is trying to prosecute its end of a competitive and contentious relationship with the United States in accordance with the rules of normal international relations rather than fighting the Cold War.

MARCH 2005

DESAI: How do you assess President Putin's post-Beslan measure aimed at consolidating his personal authority by abolishing the direct election of regional governors?

TALBOTT: I think Putin has used the Beslan tragedy to step up his five-year campaign to reestablish Russia as a highly centralized, vertical state with power concentrated in the Kremlin. From now on, he will personally appoint governors. As a result, he calls into question Russia's self-designation as a federal state and raises new concerns about the fate of pluralistic democracy there.

A week after the Beslan hostage crisis, a Brookings delegation was traveling in Russia. On that visit, we found a combination of alarm and resignation among the Russians we met. In their view, Putin's latest move fitted all too logically with his ongoing effort to regulate and manipulate the dissemination of information. Russia no longer has an independent national television station. Journalists worry that censorship already extends to the print media and may soon reach the Internet. Remember Mikhail Gorbachev? His policy of glasnost, or openness, was crucial in ending the Communist system, the USSR, the Soviet empire, and the Cold War. Now more than ever, Russia needs glasnost and a free press, and, believe me, not least as an antidote to corruption of the kind that permitted terrorists to bribe their way past police checkpoints and into the doomed school.

DESAI: I want you to sort out a riddle for me. How do you account for Putin's continuing popularity with the Russian public despite these authoritarian instincts you describe?

TALBOTT: You are indeed raising an inescapable and complicating fact about the current situation. I have been visiting Russia since the sixties. As I absorbed the sobering, even ominous, impressions from my latest trip, I had to keep reminding myself that they did not mean that Russia had returned to Soviet times. Even though much of what I saw and heard was negative, Russia has come a long way from the monolith it was in Soviet times. There were significant, sometimes sharp, differences among the analysts, journalists, academics, and political figures we talked to. Some felt that Putin's firm hand is necessary to preserve public security and national unity from the twin threats of terrorism and secessionism. Others argued that the crackdown will do nothing to discourage corruption, nor will it necessarily improve the effectiveness of Moscow's governance of its far-flung regions.

DESAI: So there are vigorous debates among the influential and elite groups. But how has life changed for the people on the street?

TALBOTT: Putin's clampdowns have not much affected the lives of ordinary Russians. One of the few heads to roll after the horror at the Beslan school was that of the chief editor of *Izvestiya*. His sin was publishing vivid pictures of the carnage that brought home to the Russian public not just the horror of the crime but [also] the incompetence of the authorities who were supposed to prevent it from happening. But then, we were told, he would most likely land another good job. In other words, free-thinking intellectuals and hard-charging reporters are finding it more difficult to publish or broadcast their views, but all those we met during our visit told us that they could say what they felt without fear of arrest or dismissal.

DESAI: Hasn't the growing economy also contributed to his popularity?

TALBOTT: Of course, the Russian economy is doing well, earning support for Putin from a growing middle class and from Western businessmen, who have been investing in Russia for more than a decade. In their view, Putin has administered a corrective dose of stability and predictability to a country that seemed to be lurching toward chaos in the free-for-all 1990s under Boris Yeltsin.

Again, in economic policy, Putin still qualifies as a reformer. One reason is that he trusts the team of liberals who are advising him in that area. Indeed, Alexei Kudrin, the finance minister, and German Gref, the trade and development minister, are staunch, pro-market reformers. They also worked with Putin in St. Petersburg during his tenure in the city administration. He seems to be replicating those ties of personal loyalty in the political realm by appointing presidential proconsuls in the regional capitals.

DESAI: Do you think the political tightening is designed to push economic reforms systematically in the desired direction?

TALBOTT: Perhaps Putin is attempting a Russian version of the Chinese model, strengthening political controls while opening the country up to market forces. He—and Russia—may not be able to have it both ways. In my view, economic and political freedoms are inextricably linked. A genuine rule-of-law society, which is a precondition for economic progress, requires a system of checks and balances that is impossible when power is concentrated in one office.

If Russia is to survive as a unitary state, it must resume its development as a federal and a democratic state. The essence of democratic federalism is maximum self-government at the local and provincial level. People are most likely to respect and obey authority if they feel it reflects their interests and is invested in leaders they have chosen. Besides, Russia is vastly diverse, and federalism makes a virtue of diversity. The tsars and the commissars tried to impose unity and order by a more brutal version of the methods Putin is now applying. They failed and so may he.

DESAI: The proximate cause for the post-Beslan political consolidation is the decade-old war in Chechnya. How can that be resolved?

TALBOTT: Putin hopes to restore Moscow's writ over Chechnya and prevent other actual or potential secessionists from following the Chechens' lead. On the first score, it is hard to imagine that Chechnya will ever again, in any meaningful sense, be governed by Moscow. Whether it is too late for Ingushetia, Dagestan, Karachaevo-Cherkessia, and other corners of Russia's North Caucasus that are not yet household words depends on how long Putin's misguided experiment in hyper-centralization lasts.

DESAI: Can external pressure tip the balance in favor of a negotiated settlement of the Chechen problem?

TALBOTT: It could depend, in some measure, on what Putin hears from other leaders, especially fellow members of the Group of Eight—and most of all from his counterpart in the White House. Like most Russians, Putin bristles at Westerners' "preaching." He still wants to be treated as a full member of this club of leading democracies, and he regards the United States as its de facto chairman. Of course, officials in Moscow say that, despite muted criticism from Washington, the policy of the Bush administration is more "understanding" than that of the European Union.

DESAI: Do you think Russia should be expelled from the Group of Eight as Senators John McCain and Joseph Lieberman have suggested?

TALBOTT: Such a move by the United States would backfire. It would only play into the hands of nationalist forces in Russia who believe in their country's uniquely "Eurasian" destiny. They want an authoritarian domestic order and a foreign policy that combines intimidation of other former Soviet republics and xenophobia toward the world at large. A signal that the West is giving up on Russia would also discourage democrats, who are down but not out.

DESAI: Are you suggesting a policy of continuing engagement by the G7 with the Russian president?

TALBOTT: As you know, the group is due to gather in Gleneagles in Scotland next July, followed by a meeting in St. Petersburg in the summer of 2006. Putin's desire for an upbeat meeting gives the other seven some leverage. If they close ranks behind George W. Bush and Tony Blair and acknowledge that the Group of Eight has a Putin problem, they can use the next sixteen months for a campaign of quiet, calibrated diplomacy. If Putin allows adverse trends in Russia to continue, his guests in St. Petersburg will go public with their disappointment. They would provide an incentive for him and his successors to keep Russia on a reformist course.

I believe that the West has a huge stake in how Russian democracy evolves in the coming years. The nature of Russia's internal regime determines its external behavior. A Russia that rules its own people by force and edict rather than by consent and enfranchisement is virtually certain, sooner or later, to intimidate its neighbors. It will also make itself one of the world's problems rather than a contributor to their solution.

NOTES

1. On September 22, 2000, the Cox Commission released its report, "Russia's Road to Corruption: How the Clinton Administration Exported Government Instead of Free Enterprise and Failed the Russian People."

2. The Senate confirmed the appointment of Larry Summers as secretary of the Treasury Department on July 2, 1999; David Lipton was the undersecretary for international affairs at the Department of the Treasury; Carlos Pascual was U.S. ambassador to Ukraine from 2000 to 2003; R. Nicholas Burns was U.S. permanent representative to NATO and also served as U.S. ambassador to Greece from 1997 to 2001; Nancy Lee was the Treasury Department's deputy assistant secretary for Eurasia.

3. Ruslan Khasbulatov, former Yeltsin deputy (1990–1991), together with Vice Pres. Alexander Rutskoi, led Russian legislators in their power struggle with Yeltsin in October 1993.

4. On October 3, 1993, supporters of Khasbulatov and Rutskoi seized Ostankino, the television station, and the office of the mayor of Moscow. The following day, forces loyal to Yeltsin shelled the Russian White House.

5. The Dayton Peace Accords of November 1995 ended the Bosnian war; Slobodan Milosevic, president of Serbia (1989–1997) and Yugoslavia (1997–2000), was arrested in 2001 and turned over to the UN's war crimes tribunal in The Hague.

6. Anatol Lieven, *Chechnya: Tombstone of Russian Power* (New Haven, Conn.: Yale University Press, 1998).

7. In 1999, some three hundred civilians were killed when apartment houses in Moscow, Volgodonsk, and Buinask were bombed. These terrorist acts were immediately viewed as the work of Chechen rebels.

8. Gen. Pavel Grachev was minister of defense and commander of the army from 1992 to 1996.

9. The Bank of New York scandal involved allegations of money laundering and the looting of assets from Russia's Inkombank.

10. In December 1993 Zhirinovsky's Liberal Democratic Party won the largest single bloc of votes—sixty-four seats—in the Russian Parliament; Yeltsin's fiery speech at the Budapest summit in December 1994 warned of a "cold peace," that is, a return to Cold War–like conditions in Europe.

11. Kim Jong-il was the leader of North Korea.

12. Stephen Hadley served as assistant secretary of defense for international security from 1989 to 1993. He held the positions of assistant to the president and deputy national security advisor during Pres. George W. Bush's first term. He is currently director of the National Security Council.

13. Richard Perle was the chair of the Defense Policy Board Advisory Committee during the initial years of the George W. Bush administration.

14. Michael Beschloss, presidential historian, and Talbott coauthored *At the Highest Levels: The Inside Story of the End of the Cold War* (Boston: Little, Brown, 1993).

PART II

Reform Gradualists

CHAPTER 7

The Permanent Oppositionist

MAY 2002

Gorbachev liberated us. He gave freedom to me, my family, my children, my friends, millions of Russians, and the next generation. That was his contribution.

The reform process is missing steps that really belong to the noneconomic sphere. The major problems are elsewhere. In that regard, the process is slow, very slow. . . . There cannot be a market economy without a free press, without the guarantee of basic human rights. Again we need free and fair elections in order to feel part of a liberal, market system.

In Russia, the people can be manipulated and corrupted by the authorities who, in turn, can ignore their welfare. The public feels alienated. There is no mechanism for them to get control of the rulers. None at all.

The Russian government is a technical department of the Kremlin. It is not a political institution.

However, the events of September 11 suggest that we are past the moment of checking our credentials. We must marry and marry now. Alternatively, we can chalk up a long romance lasting more than a century, but the situation we are in rules that out.

MAY 2002

DESAI: Let's start with Mikhail Gorbachev. How do you assess his role in recent Russian history? As a leader who lost control and brought about the demise of the former Soviet Union? Or as a liberator?

YAVLINSKY: One may endlessly explain and discuss his role as a politician, an economic reformer, and a party leader, but I have a different view of him. I see him as a powerful symbol—a man who symbolized freedom and acted upon it. Gorbachev liberated us. He gave freedom to me, my family, my children, my friends, millions of Russians, and the next generation. That was his contribution.

DESAI: Starting from where the Soviet Union was when he became a leader in March 1985, it was a tremendous achievement.

YAVLINSKY: It was not only momentous but also unexpected. Even to this day, it is difficult to explain why he made his choice. You are asking me to assess his role. He was a liberator in a very special sense because he liberated Russians from the system that existed here for more than seventy years.

DESAI: Did you worry about the demise of the Soviet Union, which came about as a result of the liberation?

YAVLINSKY: As an individual, I felt I lost my country, my motherland, but then the Soviet Union had so many parts, the constituent republics, on which Communism was enforced from Moscow. It was important for them also to begin the process of democratization. After all, we Russians imposed Communism on them, so we were responsible for helping them achieve a normal life. At the time of the dissolution of the union, I did not think that Ukraine, Georgia, Belarus, or Uzbekistan should be any different from Russia. They were all part of my original country. Under the old system, we were all together. I had friends everywhere. We had emotional ties. When the union collapsed, I saw that the members of the Politburo simply carved out separate pieces and established their autocratic rule. That for me was the saddest part.

DESAI: In the United States, Gorbachev's contribution is viewed positively. He liberated the Soviet bloc countries in Eastern and Central Europe. The breakup of the Soviet Union was also a desirable outcome.

YAVLINSKY: Naturally. The Americans viewed the Soviet Union as an adversary, so the enemy's disappearance without much effort on their part was clearly a happy event for them. When George Bush Sr. visited Kiev in July 1991 and advised the Ukrainians to proceed slowly and not seek independence without first adopting democratic institutions, I reacted positively. Perhaps we could stay together. I looked toward Europe, which was my model. At that moment Europe was integrating, and we were disintegrating, falling apart. The leaders who launched this disintegration were former members of the Soviet Politburo, among them Boris Yeltsin, Eduard Shevardnadze, Nursultan Nazarbayev, and others.[1] I did not think they were giving genuine independence to their separated countries. It was certainly not democracy. That worried me from the very beginning. Next, the differences, even conflicts, among these leaders could create major problems in the future. As former members of the Politburo, they were a different breed. They came from a special background devoid of democratic impulses and faith in liberal values. Finally, as an advocate of free markets and liberal trade arrangements, I worried about the economic consequences. Instead, we ended up creating customs barriers, separate currencies in a haphazard way, and controls. As a result, we were heading toward major problems.

DESAI: But look, Gorbachev also failed in pushing economic reforms. Neither he nor his reformers understood market reforms. He remained a confirmed Communist even after the failed coup of August 1991.

YAVLINSKY: Yes, he did not understand markets, and he still does not understand them today. But why do you insist on bringing this failing of his to the forefront? He was not an economist. He didn't understand markets, but he couldn't dance, either. Nor did he master literature. He was neither a poet nor a sportsman. Why should one judge him by rules that, in my opinion, are secondary and even irrelevant? He was first and foremost a liberator. He decided once and for all, for reasons unknown to me, that people must have the right to think and say what they want, and that was enough for the system to collapse.

DESAI: But wouldn't you agree that Yeltsin, as a confirmed anti-Communist and a shrewd politician, contributed to the weakening, if not the demise, of the Communist Party and Communist structures in the country? Would you give him that much credit?

YAVLINSKY: I would assign a larger role to Gorbachev. He took initiatives and issued decrees in rapid succession that weakened the Communist administrative apparatus. I think you should compare the progress on this front under Gorbachev with the initial situation, in which the administrative structures under complete Communist Party control managed everything.

DESAI: Is it safe to say that the Communists will never again rule Russia?

YAVLINSKY: What kind of Communists? That is another complicated issue. I was in Luxembourg a few years ago and was told that Parliament had a Communist faction.

DESAI: Well, Communism of the kind that created and ruled the Soviet Union.

YAVLINSKY: This is a complex issue from the perspective of history. We had Communist ideologues. We had Communists who resembled fascists. Then there were Stalinist Communists, Khrushchev-type Communists, and Communists who followed Brezhnev. These groups had their own beliefs and programs as well as strategies for implementing them. Currently we have Gennady Zyuganov and his followers.[2] This crowd is again quite different.

DESAI: I mean Communism as an authoritarian, bureaucratized system. Can it come back in Russia?

YAVLINSKY: In that sense, I agree with you. Gorbachev and Yeltsin changed the old arrangements so radically that there is no chance that the old system will return.

DESAI: What went wrong with the 1992 shock therapy reforms? Would you say that the shock therapists were mere technocrats who failed to understand the political complexities of the reform process? Where did they fail?

YAVLINSKY: I would say that they lacked a consistent and feasible economic policy. The challenge at that time was to liberate the economy from the Soviet-planned arrangements, especially the monopolies. Instead of liberating the economy from the monopolies, the shock therapists liberated the monopolies, which went ahead and charged whatever prices they wanted when prices were freed in early 1992. Inflation shot up to 2,600 percent. So from that perspective, I would not call it a successful economic plan.

DESAI: So you're suggesting that the freeing of the monopolies led to high prices and exorbitant inflation.

YAVLINSKY: Simply put, there was no competition. There was no market infrastructure. The monopolies were free to charge what they wanted. That brought inflation to 2,600 percent at the end of 1992. That was one of the most unsuccessful economic enterprises of all times. That is the simple truth. However, if you will allow me, I will interrupt you for a moment and give you my views of the events of 1991 from a political perspective and explain to you why the economic programs in Poland, Hungary, and the Czech Republic succeeded and those in Russia failed.

Whereas these countries had begun their democratic revolutions before 1990, Russia had its Thermidor in 1991.[3] The Russian Revolution took place on August 19 and 20, 1991, when crowds gathered outside the White House to ward off Soviet tanks that might have appeared to support the Communist-backed putsch. But on August 21 members of the Politburo, led by Yeltsin, assumed power and carried the nomenklatura with them. That was the real Thermidor. Then the "young reformers" were hired, and they launched the reforms with a market orientation, pleasing the West and procuring $40 billion from the international financial institutions. Nevertheless, a genuine democratic transformation was missing. What the so-called reformers managed successfully was a Thermidor. The foundations for genuine democratic changes began earlier in Eastern Europe—in 1956 in Hungary, in 1968 in Czechoslovakia, and in the early 1980s in Poland. Russia began the changes under Gorbachev in 1988 and 1989, much later.

DESAI: So what were the consequences?

YAVLINSKY: There was absolutely no change in the political elite. I believe that Russians wanted to discard Communism, move in a different direction, and opt for a new leadership. The country was ready for that, but the appropriate leadership was missing.

DESAI: In your view, democratic foundations did not begin in Russia because those could have been brought about only by genuine democrats, who were missing in Russia.

YAVLINSKY: Absolutely. In order for a radical change in the political system to take place, 80–90 percent of the people in charge had to be different.

DESAI: They had to think and act like democrats.

YAVLINSKY: They had to be different. For example, take Germany after World War II. It was successful in establishing a liberal democracy because the political leadership wanted it. It couldn't have happened if the Nazis were still at the top. The situation was similar in Japan. In Poland the dissidents under the banner of Solidarity came to power. Of course, later there can be reversals, but a democratic transformation cannot take place without true democrats taking charge of the situation.

DESAI: Let's talk about the role of the International Monetary Fund [IMF] in this process. Do you think that from 1993 to 1998 the government of Viktor Chernomyrdin was excessively influenced by the IMF?

YAVLINSKY: Yes, to the extent that the policy makers in charge here in Moscow lacked ideas and clarity about their positions on Russia's market transition. They were intellectually impotent, so they took their policy prescriptions from the IMF, and the IMF gave bad advice. I also believe that the IMF funding enabled the government to divert its own cash for financing the war in Chechnya. From the very beginning, the IMF supported a corrupt government.

DESAI: You seem to have an extreme position about the IMF's role in Russia. Let me ask you a precise question. Why did the ruble collapse in August 1998?

YAVLINSKY: Because the financial situation was artificial. It lacked solid foundations. The ruble collapsed because of the cash pyramid the government had created.

DESAI: Artificial in what sense? Was the government borrowing too much? Were Russian banks heavily in debt?

YAVLINSKY: The banks borrowed heavily in foreign money at low interest rates and invested in government bonds to earn higher interest rates. The government could not cover its expenses, borrowed heavily for the purpose, and built a pyramid. The bad management of public finances began as early as 1993. The government and the banks were heading toward a debt crisis. That is what happened.

DESAI: Let us turn to politics. Give me an insider's view of the 1999 Duma elections and the campaign leading up to the election outcome. Was it a fair campaign?

YAVLINSKY: The 1999 elections were driven by military hysteria, which in turn was fed by the explosions in the Moscow apartments.[4] The outcome was natural. The groups that supported the criminal war in Chechnya were rewarded with election victories. For example, the Union of Right Forces strongly supported the war and got an extra 3 percent, which pushed them to an 8 percent vote in the election.

DESAI: So the voter support for the Chechen war contributed to the Duma election results.

YAVLINSKY: Definitely. Look at New York. The terrorist attack of 9/11 influenced the position of American voters. Were elections to be held in the United States after September 11, politicians who proposed a conciliatory approach on terrorists and terrorism would have gotten nowhere. They would have gotten few votes. But the situation in Russia was complicated.

Some of us were not sure who was responsible for the Moscow apartment bombings. It was not clear that the Chechen terrorists were the perpetrators. The evidence was missing. In my view, it was wrong to send one hundred thousand Russian soldiers to occupy Chechnya.

Desai: That is a courageous position. Let us move to the March 2000 presidential election. As one of Russia's leading politicians and a presidential hopeful, how do you assess that election?

Yavlinsky: It was the same thing, a continuation of the war hysteria combined with more falsifications.

Desai: But don't you think the public's desire for law and order played a role in the presidential election after the turbulent years under Boris Yeltsin?

Yavlinsky: After Yeltsin, anyone who promised that he would not be in the hospital 80 percent of his working days would be a great improvement. Naturally the public was happy.

Desai: So it was a change for the better. Let's talk about Putin's activist foreign policy before September 11. He traveled to quite a few countries.

Yavlinsky: I can suggest a perfect symbol for Putin's foreign policy before September 11.

Desai: What is that?

Yavlinsky: The bulletproof train in which the chairman of North Korea traveled around Russia for two months. That sums up the pre-9/11 foreign policy. You see, I can give you a precise picture of Russian history for each period that you are quizzing me about. I have a short answer for each phase. Russia's Thermidor was 1991. There was an inflation rate of 2,600 percent for the 1992 shock therapy reform. Now you are asking me about Putin's foreign policy before September 11. The answer is simple. In August 2001, the chairman of North Korea came to Russia and traveled around the country in a special bulletproof train for two months.

Desai: But explain to me and to the American readers who will read your interview how a bulletproof train for the North Korean president represents Putin's foreign policy. How does this relate to Putin's foreign policy?

Yavlinsky: Simple. Putin was trying to revive and restore the old ties that prevailed under the Soviet Union with North Korea, Cuba, and Angola—and Libya by extending an invitation to Colonel Qaddafi to visit Russia.

Desai: Yes, but he also went to Western Europe. He also had a meeting with George Bush.

Yavlinsky: Oh yes, he had a meeting with Bush, who said he looked into Putin's eyes and found his soul.

Desai: So, what now?

Yavlinsky: Since September 11, he has changed his foreign policy dramatically. There is a pro-American, pro-Western leaning.

Desai: Do you agree with that? Your party?

Yavlinsky: Yes, we're supporting him.

Desai: Why?

Yavlinsky: Because it's the right choice for Russia. Because Russia has to answer a three-hundred-year-old question of whether it wants to turn to Europe. My answer is that Russia belongs to Europe, and Putin is taking Russia in that direction. That's why I'm supporting him. You must note that we are talking on May 17 [2002]. This is important because we are in the middle of the Bush-Putin summit.

DESAI: Certainly. I am also watching the unfolding details of the arms control agreement.[5] I think it's a positive step for both sides.

YAVLINSKY: The agreement is only a technical step. It is devoid of politics. It is already a done deal.

DESAI: Wouldn't you regard it as a step forward?

YAVLINSKY: Only as a technical step.

DESAI: But a necessary one.

YAVLINSKY: Certainly. The agreement would not have been possible under Brezhnev.

DESAI: Nevertheless, isn't it more than a technical agreement? Wouldn't it help the Russian economy? I mean, what's the point of maintaining all of those outdated missiles and warheads and spending resources for the purpose?

YAVLINSKY: You see, Russia is going to maintain them because the United States does not want to destroy them, either.

DESAI: So you want parity.

YAVLINSKY: Of course. You said that you are going to store them, so we will store them as well. From that perspective, it is an important technical step.

DESAI: How do you assess Putin's presidency on the economic front? Are the economic reforms that have been legislated so far adequate? What is missing on that front? I think they are moving slowly.

YAVLINSKY: The reform process is missing steps that really belong to the non-economic sphere. The major problems are elsewhere. In that regard, the process is slow, very slow. For example, a market economy cannot function without an independent judiciary. Unless people feel that their rights are protected and their property is secure, they will not take the reform process seriously. There cannot be a market economy without a free press, without the guarantee of basic human rights. Again, we need free and fair elections in order to feel part of a liberal, market system. In my view, a market economy is linked with guaranteed political rights and free choices. I do not think Russia's political elite understands this connection, and I want to tell you that I dislike its members because of their serious failing on this point.

DESAI: But wouldn't you agree that your vision of real choices and guaranteed freedom will take time? Of course, they provide the underpinning of a market system, but they cannot emerge suddenly.

YAVLINSKY: Well, of course, everything takes time. If one wants to have a baby, it takes time, but one has to start.

DESAI: Where would you start with regard to launching a liberal system in Russia? What is the problem?

YAVLINSKY: The problem is the absence of political will. The problem is the inability to change. Look, the Communists are still a dominant political force.

Russians still have the old mentality, the old habit of feeling comfortable with autocratic arrangements. One has to desire freedom strongly in order to be free. If you want to assess the current Russian situation with regard to the progress we have made, look at some of our symbols. They tell you a lot about how strongly we are tied to the past. Take the imperial, tsarist two-headed eagle.

DESAI: The state emblem.

YAVLINSKY: Yes. I have often wondered how a two-headed bird can live so long, but we have it in Russia. Then we have the Soviet anthem. We pretend that we have a democratic flag. In my view, it is not democratic, but we are made to believe that it is. That is my answer to your question. We are unable to break away from the past. It is at best a mixture with a heavy dose of the past, a sort of postmodernism.

DESAI: I have a slightly different view. You know I have been watching the economic and political situation in Russia from the Soviet days for more than three decades. You were probably in high school when I started studying the Soviet Union.

YAVLINSKY: Well, I too began studying the system here thirty years ago, so we are colleagues in the same venture.

DESAI: Perhaps I do not have the historical perspective to link the current Russian situation with symbols of the past. Suffice it to say that, as a liberal politician, you would find it authoritarian, bureaucratized, and corporatist.

YAVLINSKY: Right.

DESAI: The president is authoritarian, the bureaucrats dominate the ministries as well as the regional and local administrations, and the oligarchs control Russia's dominant industrial sector. How can genuine market reforms proceed from this straitjacket?

YAVLINSKY: There is no way. However, I want to share with you my views about the kind of system we have created in Russia. With Yeltsin's election in 1996, we began moving toward a system that I variously call corporatist and criminal, a managed democracy, or a quasi democracy. One may also call it a Potemkin-village democracy.[6] Yet it is different from the arrangements that prevailed under Soviet times. The Soviet system was totalitarian in that it destroyed democratic and civic institutions as they appeared. The prevailing managed democracy is not destroying these institutions, but the major institutions are being controlled to serve the needs of the executive authority. Thus the private TV networks have been abolished; the elections are being manipulated; and the judiciary is subservient to the Kremlin's political authority. The lack of freedom of these three cornerstones of a liberal political system is the chief attribute of the current managed democracy.

DESAI: Let me open up another argument. President Putin complains that the government lacks ambitious goals. He wants it to improve economic performance by changing its policies, whatever they might be. I believe that a large inflow of direct foreign investment can push Russia's economic growth and that Russia's powerful oligarchs, Russia's extensive bureaucracy, and the Russian Left, dominated by the Communists, do not want private foreign investment in the country. The oligarchs think they can undertake the investment activity, and the bureaucrats like the regime of controls. Remember the table you exhibited at the Arden House conference? The Communists everywhere believe that direct foreign investment is exploitative. So even if Russia were to cleanse the system of corruption and establish secure property rights, foreign investment flows would be restricted because of this implicit consensus among these three groups. The president either agrees with them or is unable to fight them. What do you think?

YAVLINSKY: Ah, you remember the table. Marshall Goldman has exhibited it in his book.

DESAI: Yes. In that table you brought out the labyrinthine maze of restrictions faced by small businesses in Russia and contrasted it with the simple German arrangements. I was not aware of the details, but I firmly believe in the collusion against foreign investment among the oligarchs, the bureaucrats, and the Left.

YAVLINSKY: You're absolutely right. I would add a point. The public cannot exercise pressure in favor of foreign investments because Russians have no understanding of them.

DESAI: Why do you think so? Why don't Russians understand and argue in favor of the advantages of a policy change? Every time I visit Russia, I am impressed by the people's energy and vitality. Russians are highly educated and quick learners and can actively influence policymaking.

YAVLINSKY: You know, this is a question of the relationship between people and governmental authority, between people and power. And, if I may, I would say that the Russian government is no worse than the government in the United States or in a European country. The major difference is that, in your country or in Germany or elsewhere in Europe, the people have control over the government. In Russia, the people can be manipulated and corrupted by the authorities who, in turn, can ignore their welfare. The public feels alienated. There is no mechanism for them to get control of the rulers. None at all. You know, I feel that, if you brought the German government to Russia, within six months it would become as indifferent as the one we have here.

DESAI: Nonetheless, you and the other policy analysts and political leaders, whom I know, talk freely and knowledgeably and openly. At the same time, I notice that interaction between the people and the government is missing. There is no public debate under Putin.

YAVLINSKY: You are right. The press is censored. We have no freedom of speech.

DESAI: Is it really that bad?

YAVLINSKY: Absolutely.

DESAI: I hear that television is more controlled than the print media, that the newspapers can write almost anything. This is a vast country, and there are countless newspapers and talented journalists.

YAVLINSKY: These newspapers have little political influence. They inform their readers about a variety of politically neutral subjects and entertain them. They are not actively engaged in educating the public on political issues so that the public can influence political decision making. Putin is not interested in nurturing the press into an active, robust agent for building democracy in Russia. Quite the contrary. He and his team are interested in molding the press to suit their needs. They have established complete censorship and control of the television networks. These channels are not allowed to engage in the discussion of political issues.

DESAI: As a veteran politician on the Russian scene, how do you assess the future of Russian politics? Do you feel hopeful about the political process? Do you feel optimistic or pessimistic?

YAVLINSKY: I have a pessimistic feeling but an optimistic will.

DESAI: In other words, you will continue fighting because you have a strong will, although you are not optimistic about the results.

YAVLINSKY: I would like Russia to be a normal country in a civilized way as part of Europe, but I cannot say when and how we will attain that goal. I am sure about what I want, but I am unsure about how much time it will take. It's a race against time. I am also not sure that it will be a smooth process. It is a complicated issue. I see huge obstacles. Therefore I feel pessimistic.

DESAI: How do you rate your chances of becoming Russia's president down the road? You're still very young.

YAVLINSKY: Well, yes, I have at least fifteen years to go.

DESAI: So you do not rule out your chances.

YAVLINSKY: As you know, the U.S. presidency represents the highest point of a politician's career. In Russia, the highest point of a political career is successful reform. One may be the prime minister or the president, but, in the absence of successful reforms, that means very little. If the Russian president can stop the killings in Chechnya, if he can eliminate corruption, if he can bring Russia into Europe, if my children and grandchildren can enjoy equality with their peers in Europe and the United States, that would mean he has reached the height of his career. The dimension is different. The U.S. president must protect and preserve the system created by the country's forefathers. The Russian president has a different task. He must create a similar system.

DESAI: What do you think is holding Putin back? His background? Because he is a slow mover? Because he does not want to upset the status quo? Will he start big changes if he wins the presidency next spring?

YAVLINSKY: He has the disadvantage of having inherited Yeltsin's men.

DESAI: You mean the cadre at the top has not changed.

YAVLINSKY: Exactly. Yeltsin brought him to power.

DESAI: Yes, but what about the government?

YAVLINSKY: There is no government in Russia. It is a technical department.

DESAI: You mean they are a bunch of managers appointed by the Kremlin?

YAVLINSKY: The Russian government is a technical department of the Kremlin. It is not a political institution.

DESAI: Finally, what is your vision of the future Russia?

YAVLINSKY: I told you. In twenty years I want Russia to be a member of various European institutions: economic, security, and political.

DESAI: Don't you worry about the negative impact of the market system on Russia? Surely some changes will be undesirable. As my husband and I walked along the Tverskaya to the Kremlin, past the statues of Mayakovsky, Dostoevsky, and Pushkin, he asked me whether some of the magnificent poetry and literature would be lost under the banality of market forces.[7] Is that something to worry about?

YAVLINSKY: No.

DESAI: Why not? Wouldn't your culture change or become superficial to some extent?

YAVLINSKY: No, these giants belong to our past, and they will stay with us forever. The question is whether we will manage to create similar ones in the future.

DESAI: Personally, wouldn't you worry about the greater individualism and the looser family ties that the market system will bring in your lifetime?

YAVLINSKY: Perhaps that is the cost we will have to pay in our lifetime to create the market system we want. I will then let my grandchildren worry about the disappearance of close family ties and the loss of Dostoevsky and the rest of them. Look, the Japanese have adopted markets, yet they have preserved their culture.

DESAI: Yes, but the young in Japan are changing.

YAVLINSKY: We will see what happens. In any case, the adoption of some of the social attributes of a liberal market economy is better than the continuing criminalization and corporatization of Russia.

DESAI: On balance, then, you believe you will be better off as a result of market-based changes.

YAVLINSKY: Absolutely, and keep in mind that we are under very heavy pressure. We do not have two hundred years to spare as the Americans had.

DESAI: That's right.

YAVLINSKY: The pressure comes from the fact that we have the longest border with China, a very unstable country. Second, we must not lose control of the enormous stockpile of nuclear, biological, and chemical materials that we created as a former superpower. It must be safeguarded—and fast. Our future will be damaged without an effective control of the arsenal.

DESAI: What are you implying?

YAVLINSKY: I am concerned that, in the current war against terrorism, the terrorists that are thrown out of other countries will make their way into Russia. Russia is the weakest link in the chain. Everything they need is here.

DESAI: Is that why you support a pro-U.S. policy stance?

YAVLINSKY: It's not pro-U.S. It's pro-Russian. Russia will never be pro-U.S. or pro-Chinese or pro-German. Russia will always be pro-Russian. This only implies a sharing of common concerns and common values. That's why I believe that a clear declaration of common goals, common intentions, and shared security guarantees should top the list of the Bush-Putin summit. It would be of the utmost value to sign such a document. This, in my view, is the key, the challenge. If Putin believes that Russia and the United States have common values that we share, here and now, and that we can create a world order on that basis, and if he can manage to convince his U.S. counterpart that we have the same values, that we have the same multiplication tables, that two times two is four for you and two times two is four for me, that would be a genuine breakthrough. Do you understand me? That the two nations have identical values, that we share them here and now in this century, and that we can create a world order on that basis. That is my first point. Next, that we have common threats that require common security guarantees. That would be a breakthrough. Merely counting warheads does not amount to anything. That would be like the Nixon-Brezhnev meeting of the old days, but they were different leaders of different times.

DESAI: You mean two adversaries. But the mistrust still persists.

YAVLINSKY: And you know why: because the common underpinning of values is missing. However, the events of September 11 suggest that we are past the moment of checking our credentials. We must marry and marry now. Alternatively, we can chalk up a long romance lasting more than a century, but the situation we are in rules that out.

DESAI: However, don't you think that Putin must carry with him the conservative factions in the military and in the bureaucracy in order to realize this instant marriage, this bold meeting of values?

YAVLINSKY: But consider his position. If he accepts this triple cornerstone of common values, common enemies, and shared guarantees, he can carry with him a large part of Russian society, all of the democratic and liberal forces, the intelligentsia, and the residents of the big cities. Of course, he will face problems with parts of the military, the security apparatus, the nationalists, and his staff. In that case, he can have an agreement with Bush similar to the Brezhnev-Nixon pact. Of course, Putin may choose to ignore both possibilities, but it would be a pity if he missed the chance to achieve a breakthrough with Bush. Russia would regress into a negative phase, so a big challenge lies ahead.[8]

DESAI: Well, let us hope that the two leaders will rise to that challenge.

NOTES

1. Eduard Shevardnadze, foreign minister of the USSR (1985–1990) and president of the Republic of Georgia from 1992 to 2003, was ousted by Mikheil Saakhashvili, who was elected president of Georgia in January 2004; Nursultan Nazarbayev is a reformist who

championed autonomy for the Soviet republic of Kazakhstan, became the nation's president in 1990, and continues to rule it autocratically.

2. Gennady Zyuganov was a presidential candidate and a powerful figure in the post–Soviet Communist Party.

3. The coup d'état that brought the Reign of Terror to an end in France took place on 9 Thermidor (July 27, 1794). Thermidor is the eleventh month in the French revolutionary calendar.

4. The bombing of Moscow apartment houses was thought to be the work of Chechen rebel terrorists.

5. Presidents Bush and Putin signed a landmark arms treaty in May 2002, which, among other things, provided for a reduction of deployed nuclear warheads to a maximum of twenty-two hundred for each country.

6. Catherine the Great's favorite, Grigory Potemkin (1739–1791), was alleged to have built sham villages along the route of the empress's tour of the Crimea in 1787.

7. Vladimir Mayakovsky (1893–1930) was the leading Soviet poet of the Russian Revolution of 1917. Fyodor Dostoevsky (1821–1881) is the author of *Crime and Punishment* and *The Brothers Karamazov*. Alexander Pushkin, Russia's national poet, is often called the "father of Russian literature" (1799–1837).

8. In a later communication, Yavlinsky emphasized that Putin indeed chose to ignore both possibilities and missed the chance of achieving a breakthrough with Bush.

CHAPTER 8

In Search of Checks and Balances
at Home and Abroad

Sergei Rogov

JUNE 2003

But I believe that the emergence of democracy is inevitable [in Russia]. It will happen sooner or later. However, we must not make the mistake of considering the West as the leader in democracy building or thinking that the West has always been democratic.

Gorbachev is a unique leader in Russian history because he initiated changes at a time when it was possible simply to continue.

We adopted a constitution toward the end of 1993 that gave enormous authority to the executive without appropriate checks and balances. The legislative branch is weak and dominated by the executive authority. The judiciary is not independent.

Yeltsin abandoned the notion of checks and balances and created a democracy for bureaucracy and operated by bureaucracy. The public was sidetracked.

Putin's secret is that he is a political leader who has been acceptable to groups with totally different interests. He came from nowhere at a moment when Russia, after the financial crash of 1998, was paralyzed.

Bureaucratic control is far more extensive in these areas [the outlying regions] than in Moscow. They soon acquired a new brand of criminals and local oligarchs with vested interests, and these people control the regions. . . . [T]his means that the chances of grassroots democracy developing in these areas are slim.

MARCH 2005

[Members of the state department team under Condoleeza Rice] come across as tough, but pragmatic, policy makers rather than ideologues.

[George W. Bush] should not be underestimated merely because his reading is limited.

Rice was explicitly anti-Soviet, but she is not anti-Russian.

In my opinion, the positive impetus in U.S.-Russian relations following September 11 has exhausted itself.

June 2003

Desai: Democracy will not take root in Russia because, from a historical perspective, Russia was autocratic. How would you respond to that statement?

Rogov: I don't buy that argument. Of course, we have limited experience with democracy. For a millennium or more, Russia was an autocratic country with imperial authority or Soviet-style ideology, but I believe that the emergence of democracy is inevitable. It will happen sooner or later. However, we must not make the mistake of considering the West as the leader in democracy building or thinking that the West has always been democratic. If you take the United States, women were given the right to vote only eighty years ago. When I first went to the United States thirty years ago as a postgraduate student, I could see "for blacks only" signs on benches and in buses in the South. Democracy has a long record of step-by-step development in the West. It took centuries to develop and has reached maturity only in the lifetime of the present generation. In the 1950s, U.S. democracy was different from what it was in the 1990s. I am not sure of its status today because I am surprised by the developments in the United States and in the West after 9/11. Sometimes I wonder about the excessive efforts . . .

Desai: To restrict civil liberties.

Rogov: Exactly. Some of these developments really surprise me. I had thought they would never happen in the United States.

Desai: They surprise many Americans, too.

Rogov: It goes to show that the norms of democracy and civil liberties were well established in the United States perhaps a generation ago, but they can also be reversed. By the way, I know a few Russians here who are watching the Ashcroft-style democracy in the United States and declare that perhaps we need something similar in Russia. I think that democracy here will take longer to mature than I would like. I do not know whether it will happen in my lifetime.

Desai: What you're suggesting is that democracy will ultimately prevail in Russia but that it will have a rough-and-tumble trajectory.

Rogov: That is perhaps a more normal pattern than you think. Don't forget that half a century ago Germany was an evil Nazi state and Japan was not any better, but we have seen a major transformation in both. I had thought that the Soviet Union, in which I was growing up, after Stalin's death was already moving into the posttotalitarian phase. I saw the faint beginnings of that transformation under Khrushchev. Unfortunately, that proved short lived. I once again feel that Russia as a polity is less democratic today than ten years ago, but some democratic notions have taken root, especially among the young. I think we will mature into a democracy. There is no turning back. I want to see it happen in my lifetime.

DESAI: What about markets? People say they will not work in Russia because Russia was collectivist, whereas markets depend on individual initiative.

ROGOV: Russia certainly had a long history of the communal tradition, but the communal tradition existed in Europe as well. Of course, U.S. and European traditions emphasize individualism, but the communal elements persist. Some decisions continue to be taken at the community level. The traditions of the town meeting are still alive in the United States. They do not dominate, but they are still important. As a group, Americans are definitely more interested in local affairs than Russians. In my opinion, it is a recognition of the need and the importance of a collectivist, local community approach of solving problems. True, the Russian collectivist tradition lacked voluntary participation. The peasant communes were involuntary associations and were disbanded ninety years ago.

DESAI: Will collective action with free individual participation emerge in Russia?

ROGOV: It's difficult to say. On the one hand, we have the young people, who are more aware of their needs and interests. That is the "me" generation, which comes into conflict with the authoritarian collectivist traditions of Russian and, later, Soviet history. Such tension between individualism and collectivism exists everywhere, but in Russia, the story is complex. Contrary to common impressions in the West, the experience of the 1990s produced a reverse input and popular disengagement that discourage voluntary participation for the common good. Let me explain.

Ten or fifteen years ago, in the early days of Boris Yeltsin, there were enormous expectations. People came out by the thousands in the streets of Moscow, demanding immediate and fundamental changes. Later, people felt that they had been betrayed and manipulated by the government. There was frustration followed by societal fragmentation. Since the expectations were so high, the letdown was massive, too. Most Russians today [mid-2003] do not think they can do anything to bring about a positive turnaround. They have plainly retreated into a do-nothing pessimism. They do not believe the government wants to help them.

Let me give you an example. As you know, in Russia, public reaction to the war in Iraq was no different from that in European countries. If anything, the negative attitude in Russian opinion polls was larger and more widespread than in France, Germany, and other countries. Millions of protestors came out in European cities, in London, and in New York. Nothing like that took place in Moscow or elsewhere in Russia. Why didn't my students go out and demonstrate? In my opinion, this reflects public cynicism and lack of trust in the country's leaders. Why demonstrate against the U.S. administration in the streets of Moscow or, for that matter, on any issue if the leaders will not pay attention and take appropriate action? Russians have retreated into their homes, their family fortresses. "Don't bother us. Leave us alone," they are saying.

Desai: Do you think this is a retreat from an exercise of democratic rights and also from market-based opportunities? People have retreated because the new liberal, democratic arrangements, from which they had hoped to benefit, did not materialize.

Rogov: I think it came from an extreme "here and now" expectation. They hoped for the emergence of total democracy and instant material well-being, so now they have retreated into a "leave us alone" attitude. People do not expect anything positive to come from the government. They do not think it cares about protecting them or providing them with major services. They do not expect the police to protect them from crime. They do not count on the government to pay them their pensions. They do not believe they will receive basic medical services. They have gone from high expectations to massive frustrations.

Desai: When did the process begin? Did it begin with Mikhail Gorbachev, who kindled high hopes of moving away from the Soviet authoritarianism into a new set of arrangements?

Rogov: Gorbachev is a unique leader in Russian history because he initiated changes at a time when it was possible simply to continue. In many ways the Soviet system was perhaps stronger than we were made to believe fifteen years ago. At the same time, the seeds of the catastrophic situation in which we live today were planted a long time ago. Soviet stagnation was a fact. We were going nowhere, and yet we could have continued. We could have stayed like that.

Desai: What in your opinion were the strong points?

Rogov: Science, education, medical services, and the military. The Soviet Union was a superpower, one that was often brutal to its own citizens. At the same time, there was a bargain. If you were loyal, you would be provided for and protected. Until Gorbachev, the majority of Soviet citizens never thought of alternative arrangements. His changes prompted people to start thinking about the possibility of a totally different system. That was a revolutionary move. People began searching for an ideal, transparent system because they knew that the Soviet system was a big lie, but they were in for a crushing disappointment. They did not expect that the seceding governments would, as it were, defect. After the collapse of the Soviet Union, the bureaucracy captured the government, and the oligarchs seized the assets. These guys have been merrily serving their own interests, while ignoring the needs of the people, and the people know that. That's why only 10 to 15 percent of the voters are participating in the elections; they do not think they can change anything. The majority votes by not stepping into the polling booths.

Desai: Let's backtrack a bit. How do you explain the collapse of the Soviet Union? Why did that happen under Gorbachev?

Rogov: Perhaps it's all too close to explain. Under the Soviet system, countless people were unhappy, but there were very few dissidents. In general, people accepted its legitimacy because that was the only system they knew. However, in the post-Stalin, posttotalitarian Soviet phase under Khrushchev, some of us discovered the gap between the big promises, the noble slogans, and the reality of Soviet policies. That—the vast gap—became clear. We lived with two minds. One of our minds yearned for justice and a rosy life, and the other one went to work and managed the daily routines in our workplaces. We worked by rules that had little to do with the slogans. We nevertheless proclaimed the slogans at the top of our lungs, but the arrangements were ready to crumble at a single blow. With Gorbachev's reforms, the legitimacy of the Soviet Union was rejected. Gorbachev began with the idea of slowly transforming the Soviet Union, but soon, in a couple of years, the majority, at least a large plurality of the citizenry, rejected the union. The superpower collapsed for what I consider to be purely domestic reasons. Of course, the containment of the Soviet Union created more problems for the ruling circles. There was continued pressure, but the notion that Star Wars destroyed the Soviet Union was—I beg your pardon—baloney.

DESAI: So the system was rejected from the inside.

ROGOV: Let me illustrate my argument by giving you some numbers, which I may not be quoting correctly. I was discussing them with my students in connection with the allocation of resources on defense, education, health, and so on. We have international comparisons for the last fifty years. In 1950, the Soviet Union was spending as much on defense as the United States relative to GDP but two or three times more on education, health, and social welfare. In 1990, the Soviet Union was spending two or three times less than the United States on welfare-related activities. The irony is that the Stalinist totalitarian arrangements had a firmer grip on resource allocation and dealt effectively with the big issues of social protection of the citizenry. However, during the Cold War, the United States made giant strides in many directions. It matured as a democracy, it overcame McCarthyism, it introduced civil rights legislation to deal with the race issue, and, above all, it offered Medicare and Medicaid to a significant number of Americans. In contrast, by 1990 the post-Stalinist, posttotalitarian Soviet system had lost out to the United States on its single most creditworthy feature, namely, providing social welfare protection. That, in my view, is the most import reason for its rejection, which was epitomized by the disintegration of the Soviet Union.

DESAI: Let's move forward. One view is that the Clinton-Yeltsin chemistry led to the disappearance of the former authoritarian political system and the planned economy.

ROGOV: After the collapse of the Soviet Union, a number of challenges had to be handled, some of them simultaneously. To some extent, they were similar to events in other post-Communist states. Russia had many more, and they appeared simultaneously. Take the transition to a market economy. Russia did not graduate to a market system before the Bolshevik Revolution. Unlike the East Europeans, we lacked the memories of market arrangements.

Political democracy was also absent—not counting Novgorod five centuries ago and the ten months of the provisional government under Kerensky before its overthrow by the Bolsheviks.[1] None of these were robust democracies. The investment process in the Soviet days, regulated by the planners, lacked marked-based incentives. There were no capitalists in Russia, so we had to create them. Markets had to be bred via force-feeding, as it were. Then there were the challenges of establishing a new Russian role in the international sphere. We were a superpower, and we became a second-rate country. The Russian military needs to be completely reorganized.

However, there is another critical issue. Russia needs a national identity as a nation-state. For five centuries it has been first an imperial state and then a Communist state, but we need to become a nation-state with genuine federal political arrangements in which the rights of all ethnic and religious groups are protected. These challenges constituted a formidable task, and we were not ready for it. Perhaps the mistakes we committed in devising our political arrangements and economic reforms were inevitable.

A significant political event that influenced the process could have been avoided. We adopted a constitution toward the end of 1993 that gave enormous authority to the executive without appropriate checks and balances. The legislative branch is weak and is dominated by the executive authority. The judiciary is not independent. The executive branch is divided into the presidential administration, the federal government, and the federal bureaucracies in the regions. Russia today has more bureaucrats than in the pre-Yeltsin days. Yeltsin, the boyar, established democracy via the bureaucrats, who had no control from the legislative branch.[2]

Remember the referendum of April 1993? It was about privatization. The citizens voted for the president and his reforms because they were given vouchers and thought they were going to be instant capitalists. Remember the bombing of the parliament house in October 1993? The legislators wanted to wrest control of the privatization process from Anatoly Chubais and his band. The bureaucrats ultimately succeeded in implementing privatization without grassroots democratic control. The oligarchs grabbed the assets for a pittance because they had good connections with the top bureaucrats. They cornered oil and metals via these contacts, exported them, and acquired cash, which they extended to the cash-starved government in 1995 and 1996 in exchange for some of the best assets as collateral, which they subsequently acquired. Remember the loans-for-shares scheme?

DESAI: Would you suggest an alternative? How could the assets have been privatized?

ROGOV: My point is that the transfer of state assets into private hands in Eastern Europe was managed democratically because those countries did not adopt a constitution that created an all-powerful executive. Their legislatures had power. Yeltsin abandoned the notion of checks and balances and created a democracy for bureaucracy and operated by bureaucracy. The public was sidetracked. Ninety percent of the Russians gained nothing. We now have a societal division in which 1 to 2 percent have become filthy rich, 5 to 7 percent service their businesses, and the remainder eke out a subsistence living. You see these Mercedes cars on Moscow streets? Go outside and you will see the difference.

Let me raise one more point. In its search for an alternative to the Soviet system, the Russian intelligentsia of the 1980s rejected the option of socialism with a human face and embraced Reaganism and Thatcherism.[3] The so-called Yeltsin liberals went for the right-wing conservative ideology of the United States as an alternative to the Communist-planned economy. They exchanged Marxism-Leninism for Friedmanism. For most of the post-Gorbachev period, the [reformist] Russian government was dominated by policy makers who would make the Cato Institute gang look like a Democratic outpost in Washington, D.C. We even have a flat tax! Many members of the Russian intelligentsia absorbed the ideas of the right-wing conservatism of Reagan and Thatcher, and we mistakenly labeled them liberals.

DESAI: Well, the flat tax came under Putin, and we will talk about him later. Returning to Yeltsin, some commentators regard him as a revolutionary, or was he just a blundering *muzhik* (Russian peasant) with solid instincts and good political timing? How do you rate him?

ROGOV: Yeltsin was not a revolutionary. He was certainly hungry for political power—a political animal par excellence. It was quite by accident that he brought about the destruction of the Soviet Union. The only way for him was to become the president, the leader, of Russia because he couldn't be number one in the Soviet Union—Gorbachev occupied that position. Yeltsin was willing to do anything to become the leader, including dissolving the Soviet Union. He could come to power only by riding this massive wave of expectations held by the intelligentsia, which was preaching a neoconservative policy agenda. He made an alliance with them without giving them real power. It was a rather uneasy alliance between the smart part of the Soviet bureaucracy, which abandoned the Communist slogans to maintain power—Yeltsin was one of them—and the neoconservative reformers, who wanted to implement Reaganomics in Russia. While Bill Clinton was reversing Reaganomics in the United States, Larry Summers was implementing Reaganomics in Russia. The last time Clinton was here, I gave him a list of economic measures that his administration was promoting in Russia. I said to him, "What you are doing in Russia is just the opposite of what you would want to accomplish in the United States"—the idea, for example, that our reformers promoted, namely, that there could be no free education and no free medical assistance for the masses. The government followed the advice of Larry Summers and Stanley Fischer. They insisted on small government budget deficits for reining in inflation. How? By simply cutting welfare-related payments. In addition, they created the financial pyramid of the GKOs.

DESAI: The short-term treasury bills to cover part of the deficit.

ROGOV: And financial pyramids invariably crumble, as happened in August 1998. Banks disappeared, small businesses lost heavily, and more people became destitute and retreated from political participation.

DESAI: Why didn't people come out into the streets and protest? That's what would happen in India, for instance.

ROGOV: Or, take Eastern Europe, where people became impoverished, though the situation there was not as bad as in Russia. They responded by turning to liberal democrats or social democrats. That did not happen in Russia. Well, one can put Grigory Yavlinsky's Yabloko group in that category, but it is a small group. There are no social democrats here because the Communists did not change their ideology or offer an alternative program. Why don't the people revolt? I think there are many reasons. I spoke of frustrations earlier but from a psychological perspective. They hoped for everything, and when they got nothing, they did not expect anything anymore. It was like playing a lottery. You know, we Russians also remember the civil war, the gulag, and the turmoil of World War II. We are not enamored of street protests and activism.

There may be other reasons, also. I talked about what they lost, but they also gained something new in return, namely independence, or rather, distance from the government. They created a new bargain and, as it were, wrote a fresh contract. The government, in their view, was not supporting them. So they said, "To hell with the government. We will manage on our own." This attitude relates to the emergence of an underground economy, unreported incomes, nonpayment of taxes, corruption, and criminal activity. However, most people, despite extremely trying circumstances, found a modest way to survive, but not without a cost. Some of them survived, but they have also contributed to the demographic situation. The demographic problem has arisen not only from the high death rate but also from the declining birth rate. Young people cannot afford to have children. As I said earlier, people have responded by retreating into their personal worlds. I must also give credit to the Communist leader, Gennady Zyuganov, for channeling the discontent into a significant electoral vote from election to election.

DESAI: Yes, at about 30 percent for the Communist Party.

ROGOV: I also believe that the radical extremists who might have exploited public frustrations via street protests have remained marginal because Zyuganov provided an alternative.

DESAI: Let's talk about Putin. How is he different? What promise does he hold? Are you hopeful that he can bring Russia out of the chaotic situation you are describing?

ROGOV: Putin's secret is that he is a political leader who has been acceptable to groups with totally different interests. He came from nowhere at a moment when Russia, after the financial crash of August 1998, was paralyzed. The voters also reacted positively to the intensified military action in Chechnya under his watch as prime minister in late 1999. You know the Russians rejected the first Chechen War of 1994–1996 because they believed that Russian tanks should not crush the Chechens' right of self-determination.

But the next war, which began in 1999, was different. The Chechen separatists marched into Dagestan, kidnapped Russian journalists, and demanded a ransom for their release, so Russian public opinion changed in favor of military intervention. It delivered a positive vote for Putin. Right now the public is in a "leave us alone" mood with the Chechen war. "If my family is not serving in Chechnya, then I wake up in the morning, drink my coffee, watch TV, and survive." And you know the TV does not carry any news about Chechnya. However, the most important factor in Putin's favor is that he is totally different from Yeltsin. I think in his second term Yeltsin made most Russians feel deeply ashamed.

DESAI: Why?

ROGOV: Why? That's a strange question. It was so clear. He was not even Brezhnev, under whom living conditions improved. Yeltsin simply did not care about the people. His popularity dropped to 4–5 percent. Once again, people did not want to revolt. They desired stability. After the August 1998 collapse of the ruble and the financial turmoil, Yevgeny Primakov, as prime minister, gave us the first glimpse of stability. Putin combined this urge for stability with the robust image of a young man who walked on his feet, unlike Brezhnev and Yeltsin. In his final days, Brezhnev had to be practically carried up the stairs. Perhaps you know the anecdote about Lenin, too: Владимир Ильич сегодня сощёл с лестницы (Today Vladimir Ilyich walked down the stairs). Putin also presented the image of an ordinary person. And then—surprise, surprise! Yeltsin resigned on December 31, 1999. Nobody believed it was possible. It was such a relief. Then there was another windfall. Yeltsin's resignation and Putin's election as president in April 2000 coincided with burgeoning oil revenues and a reviving Russian economy. So he had luck on his side, too. We have had four years of rising oil prices.

DESAI: So he was a lucky man?

ROGOV: To some extent, yes. As an outsider during the Yeltsin years, he could not be blamed for what had happened. And as the new boy on the block, he could afford to speak honestly about the condition Russia was in. If you look at some of the pictures in his famous Internet article shortly after he was appointed prime minister, he did something rare for an official: He called a spade a spade. That actually helped his credibility. But there is something else. He was acceptable to all of the sectors of Russian bureaucracy—Soviet and post-Soviet, central and regional, Communist and anti-Communist. In this sense, if Yeltsin was the boyars' tsar, Putin is the dvoryanskii tsar, the tsar of the serving nobility.[4] That is not only his strength but also his problem. Apparently he feels that there is no real light at the end of the tunnel.

He also understands that no fundamental changes are taking place in Russia. He certainly is not looking for a revolution. He wants to maintain stability, but he understands that the job requires improving the status quo, rather than managing the transformation of Russia. And you can feel that he's beginning to understand that the bureaucracy says "yes, sir" and does nothing. For instance, if you take his state of the union message this year or last year, he's attacking the bureaucracy, saying it is inefficient. In response, he wants to reform the administrative system. I doubt that he will succeed. The bureaucracy can be reformed only through a change in the relationship between the branches of the government by creating checks and balances and involving the legislative and judicial branches in the process. Currently the executive is all-powerful and can only express hopes and issue decrees. We need a constitutional change.

DESAI: Are you in favor of a parliamentary system in which the executive, say the prime minister and his cabinet, are accountable to the Parliament and can be thrown out of power by a parliamentary vote of no confidence?

ROGOV: Definitely, because the current Russian constitution fails to incorporate the best features of the French or the U.S. presidential arrangements. France is a presidential republic, but its government is responsible to the Parliament. It is formed by the parliamentary majority. The U.S. presidency is perhaps the most powerful in the world, but the presidential appointments need elaborate Senate confirmation. In Russia, the government is responsible to the president and not to Parliament. So we really have neither a parliamentary republic nor a presidential republic with checks and balances similar to that in the United States. The Russian president is the chief of the executive branch, but he is also outside the executive branch because there is a second executive branch called the cabinet. You must have read about Putin blaming the government for the slow growth rate and the pervasive poverty. The dualism of the executive branch arises from the lack of checks and balances or the absence of the government's accountability to Parliament. I believe that, without a constitutional reform, the Russian transition will be directed from the top. The government does not have to respond to the needs of the people. The people understand this, they do not vote, and the president cannot achieve much by pushing from above.

DESAI: What do you think about freedom of the press under Putin ? Do you worry about it? The media? How free is it?

ROGOV: We had a brief span of freedom of the press in Russia in the late 1980s under Gorbachev and early in the 1990s, but, by 1994, it had come to an end. Private interests, especially the oligarchs, began dominating the media. Except during Gorbachev's glasnost and a couple of years under Yeltsin, free mass media did not exist in Russia. A number of oligarchs fought their private wars in the print media, so we subscribed to six or seven newspapers because, if you read one newspaper, it reflected Berezovsky's views, while the next one spoke for Gusinsky.[5]

DESAI: You are talking about the mid-1990s.

ROGOV: Yes. That is more or less the current situation, except that the government is playing a bigger role in controlling the electronic media. But one can argue that the government balances the oligarchic dominance. For example, NTV is now under government control, but it continues to provide a fairly critical view of the government's policies.

DESAI: Even though Boris Jordan was removed?

ROGOV: I think NTV under his management deviated excessively from the party line, more so than the official media. I am not claiming that the Russian media is free. Look, a few policies in the United States after 9/11 make me uneasy. However, I do not think that censorship, or something close to it, can happen in the United States. Currently we have self-censorship in Russia rather than direct government control. Is this different from the self-censorship that the *Washington Post* and the *New York Times* exercise? We do not have only one or two national newspapers in Russia but quite a few. Russians therefore have access to many national newspapers that provide diverse information and shades of opinion of different groups from the Communist to the nationalist to the liberal democratic.

DESAI: As you said, they are controlled by the oligarchs but nevertheless represent different political and ideological positions. What about local control of the printed press?

ROGOV: I have no knowledge of the local press. I focus on the levels of bureaucratic control in Moscow and in the regions and the extent to which they hinder democratic development. In Moscow, the progress in that regard is quite an achievement, in contrast to the lack of it in the outlying regions. Bureaucratic control is far more extensive in these areas than in Moscow. They soon acquired a new brand of criminals and local oligarchs with vested interests, and these people control the regions. This cannot happen in Moscow to the same extent, but this means that the chances of grassroots democracy developing in these areas are slim. There are NGOs [nongovernmental organizations] in the regions, but they have little influence, and they lack national connections. We do not have a Russia-wide ecological or peace movement. This brings me back to my earlier point—that policy initiatives will originate in Moscow, and the regions might provide indirect and secondary input in the process.

DESAI: How would you explain the emergence of the oligarchs?

ROGOV: They emerged from the Chubais-style privatization. His strategy neglected the creation of a middle class in Russia and instead focused on the disposal of the strategic national assets in oil and metals at throwaway prices to a few who could pull the right strings for him or some of the senior bureaucrats. Some, like Vladimir Potanin, who got control of Norilsk Nickel, were former members of the government. So we have a few tycoons, a couple of dozen, maybe two hundred at the lower level, and a thin layer of an emerging middle class. You know, we have fewer private farmers today than a decade ago. Why? We have no agricultural banks that can provide credit for private land ownership, and we had a continuing debate on land privatization. Of course, Russian families have private plots attached to their dachas. That's about all for private land ownership. I have some land with my dacha.

DESAI: How much is that?

ROGOV: Six percent of a hectare. Private farming cannot grow in Russia without the appropriate infrastructure. There is endless discussion and some action. The Duma has passed a law privatizing agricultural land, but it is merely a piece of paper. Nothing much has happened in a dozen or so years. However, beyond agriculture, the positive signs are few. Investment is not picking up rapidly, nor is it spreading beyond the oil sector. Some capital is returning, and we are repaying past debts. About 25–30 percent of federal revenues go into the repayment of foreign debts. As a result, the entitlement obligations to citizens have been increasingly trimmed.

DESAI: Let's turn to noneconomic issues. Do you worry about the Americanization of Russian culture? The Russian poet Yevgeny Yevtushenko spoke about the McDonaldization of Russia.

ROGOV: I'm not so worried about that.

DESAI: Why not? Are they just symbols, for example, the huge DHL billboard right in front of the Kremlin?

ROGOV: I'll give you several reasons. It's clear that U.S. mass culture has an enormous attraction around the world, even in Afghanistan. Russia is no exception. The pop culture of the young—the music, the food, the way they dress—all this is universal. I saw Paul McCartney last month. My generation grew up with the Beatles, and I familiarized my children and my grandchildren with their music. Despite all of that, I am still a good Russian, and I worry about Russia's interests. This kind of Americanization is not threatening to Russia.

I also believe that Russian culture, literature, music, and theater can easily survive the onslaught of McDonaldization. The cinema may prove to be an exception to this rule. We used to make great movies, but we don't anymore. That, too, can change. No, I don't believe that Russian culture is threatened by U.S. culture. Many aspects of the modern, global culture—from rock-and-roll and jeans to the Internet—have their origins in the United States. When I first went to the United States thirty years ago, my wife said that her mother would have a heart attack if she visited a supermarket. Now we are developing supermarkets in Russia. The problem is not the supermarkets; the problem is whether a Russian consumer can afford to buy quality products there.

DESAI: There are other aspects as well, which I realize from having lived in the United States for a number of years. Americans are exceptionally hard working, creative, and energetic. The desire to do something good is also very strong among them. Think of the medical advances taking place in the United States.

ROGOV: You're absolutely correct. They have become leaders in several areas of global development because of these qualities. Many advances in science and technology that have improved the quality of human life have been invented or developed in the United States or copied and stolen by Americans. The United States is a challenge and an example to follow. That does not necessarily mean that we all have to become Americans. The United States is setting a standard that others try to follow, but it can also be a bad example, whether it is foreign policy or human habits. I mentioned the violations of civil liberties in the United States after September 11. That process is being copied elsewhere in Britain, Europe, and Russia. I hope it is temporary and that some of its extreme features are corrected over time.

DESAI: What's going to happen in the elections here?

ROGOV: I have a short answer: Putin will win easily.

DESAI: I mean the Duma elections. What will the configuration be?

ROGOV: That's hard to predict, but I think it will result in a pro-Kremlin majority. The Communists will probably maintain their position. The Duma will continue not to interfere with government policies. It will be a conciliatory Duma.

DESAI: Will Putin fast-forward with reforms?

ROGOV: Oh, that's not clear because that means he will have to move against the bureaucracy—and that's difficult to do. Moreover, I don't see a quick change in the public's mood. Russian society remains fragmented and frustrated. As I mentioned earlier, political authoritarianism has reappeared in Russia. People have become disengaged from public participation. For example, we had a remarkable debate about the monument for celebrating victory, the Victory Square. Frankly, the architecture was bad, and people argued about it. But this kind of public engagement has disappeared. Now the bureaucrats have an upper hand and can get away with bad decisions. This is a setback. In generational terms, the older generation feels that, as a result of the traumatic changes, their lives have been wasted. As for the young—take my students of the last fifteen years—they think that the current chaotic situation is the norm. That's the way it is. Why worry about it? When we were growing up, we sat around the kitchen table and debated the negative aspects. Of course, we could not talk or write openly. Maybe we were unable to change much, but we were engaged in expressing our views to one another that things were not all right. Russian youths today are the "leave me alone" generation, or they are engaged in a cynical way in activities such as creating a youth organization of Putin followers.

DESAI: You're suggesting that the decade of the 1990s failed to bring about positive change.

ROGOV: I'm not suggesting that the transition of that decade could have solved everything, but two major issues remained unresolved. I have in mind the adoption of a constitution that could have created appropriate checks and balances and prevented the emergence of an authoritarian executive at the center. I have in mind the slow creation of a middle class in Russia via the adoption of a well-considered privatization program. Russia would still not be a perfect democracy or a perfect market economy, but we could have begun the process with political arrangements that could have promoted give-and-take between the executive office and the legislature at the center. We could also have avoided both the incredible division between the rich few and the impoverished millions and the resulting alienation that the Chubais-style privatization has left us with. It was a decade of lost opportunities. It will take us a generation before these mistakes can be reversed.

DESAI: I have a final question relating to an issue of your expertise. How do you see the emerging shape of U.S.-Russian relations?

ROGOV: Russia can emerge as a mature democracy and a successful market economy by belonging to the community of similar countries, and the United States is its acknowledged leader. That is Russia's destiny, and we are headed toward it, although in a painfully zigzag fashion. But there is a problem. Our interests overlap as well as diverge, so the building of the partnership will require give-and-take from the Russian side.

DESAI: Give me an example.

ROGOV: Perhaps Russia cannot offer much, but Putin did help Bush after 9/11 by providing assistance for defeating the Taliban. Without U.S. help, it would have been impossible for Russia to contain the Taliban, who are Russia's enemies. That is a clear example of overlapping interests. However, when it relates to Iraq and the war, rightly or wrongly, that equation ceases. The relationship became tense. But look, there is a psychological problem here. I grew up in a generation that felt Russia was second to none. It is difficult for my generation to adjust to being demoted to number fifteen or even worse. Russians would like a relationship of equality with the United States, but who could be an equal partner with the United States? The UK? Germany? Japan? Quite unlikely.

DESAI: But the Europeans and the Japanese share a common set of values with the United States, despite the occasional differences. Wouldn't you agree?

ROGOV: Yes. Nevertheless, the United States has very clearly been demonstrating that it is the leader and that Europe has to follow its lead, which it does after a noisy interval. A few European leaders publicly disagreed, but they came around. So far as Russia is concerned, it cannot be an equal partner with the United States, yet it is difficult for Russians to consider themselves junior partners. You know, in the old days, the Soviet Union was the big brother, and Bulgaria was the junior sibling. Now we feel toward the United States as Ukraine feels toward Russia. It is a new feeling for a country that for five centuries did not feel and behave like a junior partner. The problem also arises from the Bush administration's worldview. I do not think the administration's heavyweights treat Russia any differently from the way they treat other countries. They don't bring NATO into the act anymore because they don't need it. It resembles the scenario in some U.S. films, in which a sheriff sends out his deputies to go after the bad guys.

DESAI: Perhaps Russia can become an equal partner in the future. Russia is large. It stretches from Asia to Europe. It has enormous resources and skilled manpower. Economically Russia will recover in a generation, perhaps a little more. The Russians I meet have a deep patriotic feeling for Russia and for Russian culture. All of this creates a huge potential for Russia to become an equal partner with the United States. Would you agree?

ROGOV: Russia will recover, but it will be a long, tortured process. I don't think our policy makers have a hold on the right strategy. And then there is the looming demographic problem. We cannot hope or plan for a sustained recovery and security if the population is declining. Everything considered, Putin has managed to find a place for Russia in the liberal global community. You know, the transatlantic mud-slinging match between the United States and parts of Europe reminded me of a quarrel among close family members. Perhaps for that reason it was tense and emotional. At some point, Russia joined in the fray as a distant relative, but now we belong in the family as a result of this participation. This is a major development.

Remember, five years ago the war in Kosovo produced a deep rift in U.S.-Russian relations. The relationship remained damaged for almost three years. In contrast, the Iraq war has not reversed the process that Putin and Bush initiated. At the same time, the relationship lacks economic fuel. It is not institutionalized. It is too personal. It's still not clear whether Putin has succeeded in swaying his military and foreign ministry bureaucrats with his pro-U.S. position. That is still the danger. Nevertheless, the prospects for a strong relationship are solid, although it is doubtful that we can be equal partners. I think China—more than Russia—will implement its economic potential and become a solid rival to U.S. superpower status. Who knows, by the middle of the twenty-first century, the United States may cease to be the sole superpower.

DESAI: Because of China?

ROGOV: Yes, China, and the consolidation of the European Union, and the revival of Russia if our leaders avoid making mistakes as in the past. Russia cannot afford that. We may have several major players by the middle of the century. I visualize a diversified configuration and hope that Russia will be part of it. These are my final thoughts.

MARCH 2005

DESAI: What shape will U.S.-Russian relations take in George W. Bush's second term?

ROGOV: It's too early to assess Bush's second administration. As a rule, second administrations differ from the first one. Bush 43 is among the sixteen presidents who were reelected for a second term. For most, the second term was uneventful, except for Richard Nixon, who was not able to see it through. Indeed, eight years in office is a big problem.

That said, I have updated my assessment of U.S.-Russian relations based on my personal meetings and conversations in Washington during the inauguration on January 20, the president's inaugural speech, and his subsequent State of the Union address. Let me begin by assessing his rhetoric. As I said to my U.S. friends, it has been a long time since I last heard the general secretary of the Communist Party of the Soviet Union speak at a party congress promising the inevitable victories of Communism and housing to all Soviet citizens. In a similar vein, the U.S. president's call for promoting democracy around the world in his second term sounded like ideological rhetoric.

I can go a step further by making another provocative comparison. Given the extreme conservative and unified approach of the Bush team, the president's statements reminded me of the pronouncements emerging from the plenary sessions of the Soviet Communist Party Central Committee. It is still possible that Bush will follow through with decisive, even tough, policy measures as the second term unfolds, but the tough words may be just a smokescreen. Perhaps they will be followed by pragmatic policy moves down the road.

Desai: Did you get that signal from Secretary of State Condoleezza Rice's policy pronouncements during her European trip?

Rogov: I have been watching the team she has started forming under her command in the State Department. Are they neoconservatives? Did she invite Richard Pearle? No. Quite the contrary. Rice and Robert Zoellick, now her deputy, dealt with German unification and the end of the Cold War under Bush 41. They come across as tough, but pragmatic, policy makers rather than ideologues. That's quite interesting.

As for her European visit, I think it had a twin agenda. First, relations with Europe must be mended. Why? Because it is necessary to draw NATO and the European Union into Iraq's reconstruction. The United States needs allies for that purpose. While reducing the U.S. military presence, U.S. policy makers realize that they cannot leave a vacuum in Iraq. They do not want a new Vietnam. This means that they need to bring in Europe. The European members can also play a role in mediating the issue of nuclear proliferation in Iran.

Second, as U.S. trade representative, Zoellick managed trade negotiations. He has extensive negotiating experience that goes beyond WTO and NAFTA. It can be put to good use in sorting out differences with Europe. These initial signals suggest that, while the rhetoric has toughened, the actual policies may be milder.

Desai: How do you assess Rice's interview relating to U.S.-Russian relations?

Rogov: Rice's emphasis on democracy in that interview reminded me of something else. Three days before the inauguration address, the *Washington Post* published a substantial interview with Bush in which an interviewer asked about Rice's appointment as secretary of state. He drew the president's attention to an article she and Zoellick had published in *Foreign Affairs* in 2000, in which they defined Republican foreign policy and argued that the goal of U.S. foreign policy consisted in dealing with Russia and China and managing the big power balance rather than employing the U.S. military for promoting democracy and free-market ideology around the world. So the reporter said, "How can you speak about democracy and appoint Rice as secretary of state if she didn't say a word about democracy in her article?" And the president answered, "Do I have to read her articles before making the appointment? I did not read the article." But George W. Bush, in my view, is a special phenomenon. He should not be underestimated merely because his reading is limited. He resembles Ronald Reagan in that respect. The less he reads, the stronger he is as a leader.

However, let us get back to Rice's interview, in which she talked about democracy and U.S.-Russian relations in the same breath. I hope you have read it. Perhaps you noticed a certain asymmetry in the questions and answers. Well, I am exaggerating. But what were the questions? Has Putin established an authoritarian regime in Russia? Has he been following a neoimperialist policy in the neighboring states, which were formerly part of the Soviet Union?

And what were her answers? She suggested that there was a problem in the relationship. The United States, she said, stood for democracy. She mentioned Ukraine, but she emphasized the need for cooperation and partnership between the United States and Russia. She was measured and cautious in her responses. The questions, by contrast, were tough.

DESAI: Do you think the White House policy group is anti-Russian?

ROGOV: Anti-Soviet, yes, but not anti-Russian. Rice was explicitly anti-Soviet, but she is not anti-Russian.

DESAI: Does her guarded approach suggest a lack of momentum in the U.S.-Russian policy dialogue?

ROGOV: I think it reflects a worrisome situation. In my opinion, the positive impetus in U.S.-Russian relations following September 11 has exhausted itself. The situation has come to a standstill. There are two possible scenarios. Let me illustrate my point in terms of an image. Think of a man riding a bicycle. Suppose he stops pedaling and tries hard not to fall. Well, he can stay upright for a minute, maybe three minutes if he is experienced. I believe the record is forty minutes. So either you fall down or you move ahead. Similarly, U.S.-Russian relations will either remain bogged down or move forward, like the bicycle.

DESAI: How do you rate the chances of the relations gaining momentum following the Bratislava summit between Bush and Putin?

ROGOV: Unfortunately, the anti-Russian, anti-Putin consensus in the United States will stand in the way. This consensus stretches from liberal Democrats to right-wing Republicans. They fight over Iraq and Social Security reform and everything else, but they stand united in their view that Putin is authoritarian and is pursuing a neoimperialist policy in the neighboring states. I tell you, I have not seen such a bipartisan consensus over an issue in the United States for a long time, and it extends to the U.S. Congress.

It is good that the Russian and U.S. presidents meet every so often because it shows that there are close contacts between the two leaders. At the same time, it is bad because it means that the strategic partnership, which Bush and Putin declared after September 11, is driven by their personal chemistry. However, given the overall intransigence, personal contacts and meetings between the two presidents cannot be converted into a solid partnership. The declared strategic relationship lacks an interactive mechanism. For example, U.S.-Russian trade and economic ties are meager. They lack a solid legal basis and permanent institutions.

Again, the consensus on the current Russian scene extends across the Atlantic and is embraced by European and U.S. commentators who nevertheless disagree on economic policies and Iraq. So the term that had been moribund since the death of the Cold War, namely, the containment of Russia, has emerged as a policy alternative for U.S. and European policy makers. Build a new fence around Russia, isolate Russia from pressuring Ukraine and Georgia and other former Soviet republics, the chorus goes. The United States and Europe today seem to want a consensus at Russia's expense.

It is clear that Russia is not a superpower now. In the last fifteen years, Russia faced the predicament of a country that had lost a war—the Cold War. Therefore, it must play according to the rules of the victors, we are told. Russia's interests should not be taken into account. Russia is not ready to accept this, however. It does not want to be told, as was the case in the 1990s, what economic policies Russia should adopt and how it should conduct its relations with neighboring states.

At the same time, the internal situation in Russia has become increasingly complex. We are struggling with the historic issue of whether Russia can become a mature liberal state in isolation from other developed democracies. Russia must meet certain norms if it wants to belong to that group, but it cannot accomplish that goal in isolation. I am seriously concerned about the escalating attempts to throw U.S.-Russia relations back to the Cold War days. These voices are vocal not only in the United States and in Europe but in Russia as well. It can become a self-fulfilling prophecy.

A year ago, people said there was a crisis in U.S.-Russia relations. I disagreed then, but I wouldn't now. Call it a crisis, call it a snowdrift, or call it a bicycle stuck in its tracks. It is a serious and complex moment.

DESAI: Nevertheless, you are not suggesting that a second Cold War is in the offing?

ROGOV: Look, a crisis does not necessarily mean that there must be a new Cold War. I think the cyclist can pedal even faster. There are two reasons for that. First, the West's assessment of Russia's domestic situation and of Putin's policies is premature. Second, Bush spoke eloquently about democracy and elections in Iraq, but elections in Iraq made the Chechen elections look fairer and freer.

I want to bring up another fact. Yesterday, the U.S. Senate confirmed Alberto Gonzalez as attorney general. He is the man who provided the legal basis for the torture techniques in Abu Ghraib and Guantanamo, so I have serious reservations about the standards of democracy Bush proclaimed and how he plans to apply them in Saudi Arabia, Pakistan, and Egypt.[6] As I said at the start of my interview, there is a wide gap between the rhetoric and the reality in Bush's position.

DESAI: Despite the gap, aren't there practical issues that the two sides might want to sort out?

ROGOV: Beyond Rice and Bush lecturing Lavrov and Putin on democracy, they may want to seek Russian support on containing nuclear proliferation in Iran and North Korea. Of course, Russia can mediate putting an end to their nuclear programs but not in overthrowing their regimes. That is where Russia will draw the line. It does not want to embark on a messianic mission. Russia can also assist in furthering a possible Israeli–Palestinian accord and keeping peace in the area.

Another issue of mutual interest is the scrapping of nuclear, chemical, and biological weapons stockpiles in Russia. I strongly support an extension of the Nunn–Lugar program for assisting Russia in this task.[7] I believe this item will be part of the future negotiating agenda. As you know, after initial hesitation, Russia has also joined the U.S. Proliferation Security Initiative (PSI) for monitoring aircraft and sea vessels, with a view to intercepting terrorist trafficking in weapons of mass destruction.[8] Over time, our positions have moved closer in counterproliferation.

DESAI: How do you rate the prospects of bilateral progress on cutting back strategic forces?

ROGOV: As before, going back half a century, we are in a state of mutual nuclear deterrence. Both countries have thousands of warheads. Their deployment was inevitable during the Cold War, but it is incompatible with the strategic partnership goal that Bush and Putin have proclaimed.

DESAI: Is there a solution? Are you proposing nuclear disarmament?

ROGOV: Neither Russia nor the United States nor the remaining nuclear states—Britain, France, China, India, Pakistan, and Israel—are ready to abandon nuclear weapons. Therefore, nuclear deterrence is the only feasible option, but I have in mind measures that will make nuclear deterrence more stable. Russian and U.S. negotiators need to abandon the specific confines of the bilateral nuclear deterrence that was designed during the arms race and move forward to a broader arrangement guaranteeing nuclear stability.

DESAI: What do you have in mind?

ROGOV: The U.S.-Russian mutual nuclear deterrence, called MAD and unique between the two nuclear superpowers, does not extend to the other nuclear powers.[9] Only Russia and the United States have nuclear weapons in numbers and quality capable of destroying thousands of targets. Fearing a preemptive strike, only Russia and the United States depend on early warning systems and are poised to launch on warning. Other nuclear nations lack such arrangements.

MAD provides some stability but in a twisted way. The problem is that we keep almost all of our nuclear weapons on high alert. Intercontinental ballistic missiles (ICBMs) can reach their targets in about 30 minutes, while submarine-launched ballistic missiles (SLBMs) fired from submarines on patrol reach theirs in only 10–12 minutes. An early warning system is supposed to determine where the enemy missiles are flying from and to what targets. The military must then report to the political leaders. The president orders a launch, and the decision is conveyed to the launch site.

DESAI: You are outlining a grim scenario.

ROGOV: Of course, mistakes, both political and technical, are possible. So are provocations. The Russian missile authorities once mistook the launch of a Norwegian weather rocket for the launch of a U.S. ICBM. A botched judgment involving a third country is as serious in its consequences as the threat of a U.S. or a Russian missile attack. In my opinion, to design a multilateral nuclear deterrence, U.S.-Russian strategic posturing has to go beyond MAD.

DESAI: What about loose nukes in Russia?

ROGOV: If you ask me, Pakistan poses a clear threat of loose nukes. The world discovered belatedly that Abdul Qadir Khan, the "father" of Pakistan's nuclear bomb, had traded in nuclear components for years. If President Musharraf were to be assassinated, the chances of Islamic fundamentalists taking control of some of the Pakistani nukes could not be ruled out.

No, there are no loose nukes in Russia. Our nuclear systems are under proper control. On the other hand, the storage and transportation of Russian nuclear weapons call for greater security. Every year, the Nunn–Lugar program provides $500 million for eliminating Russian nuclear and chemical weapons. Russia itself spends 10 to 15 billion rubles every year to destroy obsolete weapons (more than one hundred nuclear reactors from old nuclear submarines) and others covered by START I[10] and the Conventional Weapons Convention,[11] but it needs to do a lot more.

As for the operationally deployed nuclear weapons, no nation in the world would permit outsiders to monitor them. Inspections covered under START I are the sole exception. All the same, the two sides can exchange liaison missions at the level of strategic forces command posts. A hotline between Moscow and Washington was established in 1963. This line is for political leaders to use only in emergencies. I believe that the exchange of military representatives who are assigned the task of handling incidents like the one with the Norwegian rocket will reduce serious accidents.

Two years ago, Bush and Putin reached an agreement on ballistic missile deployment cooperation.[12] Comprehensive progress on antimissile defense cooperation between Russia and the United States is both possible and desirable. As a Eurasian power, Russia is seriously concerned about ballistic missile proliferation in its region.

DESAI: What about agreements on nuclear nonproliferation relating to terrorism control?

ROGOV: Putin and Bush agreed in Bratislava to cooperate on preventing nuclear terrorism. They authorized the U.S.-Russian counterterrorism group to expand its plans. They also established a joint U.S.-Russian group on nuclear security (including the processing of fissionable material, which the defense industry considers redundant), chaired by Alexander Rumyantsev, head of the Russian Nuclear Energy Agency, and Samuel Bodman, the U.S. energy secretary.

DESAI: You referred to the danger of ballistic missile proliferation in your region, meaning in China. How would you assess the future course of Russian–Chinese relations?

ROGOV: Neither Russia nor China is a superpower today, but there is a substantial difference in the status of Russia and China. Russia is a nuclear superpower with a larger number of nuclear warheads than the United States. China, on the other hand, ranks ahead of Russia in the economic sphere and is forging ahead as an economic superpower. A recent report of the Central Intelligence Agency considers Russia a potential U.S. and European partner but singles out China as an emerging economic peer competitor. I share the view that, in fifteen to twenty years, China will match the United States in terms of its GDP.

This carries troubling political consequences because China is a Communist country. However, the U.S. administration prefers not to impose sanctions against China, nor does it want a conflict with China. In my view, U.S.-Chinese relations exhibit tensions from three perspectives. China, after all, is a Communist country, and the Chinese Communist Party is not ready to cede power. Second, the Chinese authorities openly stake a claim on Taiwan, but the United States will never let China take control of Taiwan by force. Finally, the United States has a huge trade deficit with China. Given these three elements, China has the potential of becoming a new Soviet Union for U.S. policy makers, especially for the hawks among them.

In contrast, U.S. policy makers do not fear that Russia will turn into a Soviet Union, despite their misgivings about Russia's so-called neoimperialist policy. They realize that this will never happen. This explains their solid interest in promoting U.S.-Russian relations.

DESAI: Let's get back to Russian-Chinese relations. Don't Russian policy makers fear China's growing economic power?

ROGOV: Look, we are neighbors, and we must cooperate and live in peace. Our current trade and economic interaction with China is negligible. That is a shame. Again, from the Russian foreign policy perspective, we agree with both the Chinese and the Europeans that U.S. hegemony should be prevented.

However, we also have differences with China. Some of them arise from the fact that our interests differ. For example, take the Russia-China-India triangle. India and China, both mentioned as the future economic players in the CIA report I mentioned earlier, have been increasingly competitive rivals. In contrast, Indo-Russian relations have been marked by genuine partnership and nonconflicting interests. In our foreign policy management, we try to balance our interests in the context of this complex triangle.

DESAI: You know that the United States is pressuring the European Union to retain its ban on arms sales to China. How will the possible lifting of the ban by the EU affect Russian-Chinese military-technical cooperation?

ROGOV: Thank you for that question because I have everything I need to respond to it. Let us reconsider the purpose of Rice's European visit. She undoubtedly told the European leaders that they should keep the arms embargo in place. The United States has preserved the embargo on military technology trade with Russia just as it used to be during the Cold War. In the military sphere, Russia sells China fourth-generation Soviet technology of the 1980s. We do not produce anything new. But note that Europe doesn't have a lot of new technology, either. Europe lags behind the United States, which spends five times more on military R and D than all of Europe.

Whatever its quality, Russian military hardware is competitive. China and India are our principal markets. We manage to compete effectively with European, Israeli, and U.S. arms suppliers in the Indian market. We don't want to lose that. In contrast, we have almost exclusive access in the Chinese market at present, and we fear competition from the European Union if arms sales to China are opened up. Even if that happens, Russian-Chinese military cooperation will continue. The first Russian-Chinese joint military maneuvers are scheduled for this year.

This does not imply that Russia is ready to sell everything to China, including nuclear and ballistic missile technologies. Note that Europe does not have either the strategic technology to intercept nuclear weapons or a missile defense system. However, Europe, as part of the West, shares technologies and technological advances with the United States, so if the EU lifts the arms embargo, U.S. military technology of the fifth generation can make its way via Europe to China. Rice and Zoellick will bargain hard with the EU on this issue.

DESAI: My final question, and a big one. Do you think that there can be genuine trust between Russia and the United States, who were, until recently, committed Cold War adversaries?

ROGOV: It is currently fashionable among Russian analysts to speculate whether the West, in general, and the United States, in particular, will continue to be Russia's adversaries. In my view, permanent enemies do not exist; for that matter, neither do permanent friends. The United States was our ally in two world wars. We were Cold War enemies for almost four decades. Now our interests are no longer antagonistic. More to the point, our ideologies are no longer conflicting. We face common threats of terrorism and the proliferation of weapons of mass destruction. They provide solid prerequisites for partnership as well. These preconditions, however, will not automatically blossom into a partnership. In any case, it cannot be built on the basis of personal relations, which must overcome significant opposition in Russia and in the United States as well.

From that perspective, the Bratislava summit not only prevented a collapse of the U.S.-Russian partnership but also gave grounds for cautious optimism. The mutual security agreement announced by the two presidents can serve as the launchpad for the legal and institutional process, which can be completed over the next four years. A comprehensive security treaty going beyond the current MAD framework can ultimately transform the U.S.-Russian strategic relationship.

NOTES

1. From July to October 1917, Alexander Kerensky headed the provisional government that came into being after the abdication of Tsar Nicholas II in March of that year.

2. The boyars were the higher nobility from the tenth century through the seventeenth. Peter the Great abolished their rank, privileges, and power.

3. "Thatcherism" is the term for the pro-market policies of conservative politician Margaret Thatcher (b. 1925), who served as British prime minister from 1979 to 1990.

4. The term *dvoryanskii tsar* implies the tsar of the Kremlin "nobility," who are serving Putin.

5. Boris Berezovsky and Vladimir Gusinsky are two of Russia's best-known oligarchs in exile.

6. Converted into a U.S. military prison after Saddam Hussein's removal from power in 2003, Abu Ghraib became notorious for the blatant and sadistic abuses of Iraqi prisoners by U.S. military personnel between October and December 2003; the military base at Guantanamo Bay became controversial because of the detention of hundreds of prisoners of about thirty-five nationalities who had been caught up in the war on terrorism and held without access to a court, legal counsel, or family visits.

7. The Nunn-Lugar program, started in 1991 in cooperation with Soviet and later Russian authorities, helped dismantle Soviet nuclear, chemical, and biological weapons and establish verifiable safeguards against their proliferation. As a result, Ukraine, Belarus, and Kazakhstan transferred their nuclear weapons to Russia.

8. On May 31, 2003, Pres. George W. Bush announced PSI and invited all other countries to join the initiative, which was designed to stop, within the framework of international law, the shipment of weapons of mass destruction. The agreement allows members to search and seize planes and ships carrying suspicious cargo and missile technologies.

9. Mutual assured deterrence (MAD) was developed after the Cuban missile crisis of 1962 to ensure a U.S.-Russian strategic relationship by codifying the rules for managing the nuclear arms race between the two superpowers.

10. The first Strategic Arms Reduction Talks Treaty was signed by Presidents George Bush (Sr.) and Mikhail Gorbachev on July 31, 1991. After the dissolution of the Soviet Union in December 1991, Ukraine, Belarus, and Kazakhstan transferred their nuclear weapons to Russia and also joined the Nuclear Nonproliferation Treaty. The U.S. Senate ratified START I on October 1, 1992.

11. The Conventional Weapons Convention restricts or prohibits the use of conventional weapons such as land mines and cluster bombs, which have an unusually cruel impact and do not discriminate between military and civilian targets.

12. In 2001, the unilateral withdrawal by the United States from the Antiballistic Missile (ABM) Treaty eliminated the restrictions the treaty imposed on U.S. deployment of space weapons such as lasers. Despite the complex technical and cost problems of space missile defense, the program, which gives the United States a civil and military competitive edge, is likely to continue.

CHAPTER 9

Nodari Simonia

The Pro-Putin Vote

Transition, in my view, should imply a change for the better. In contrast, eight years under Yeltsin witnessed a horrific deterioration, a destruction of Russian industry, and the impoverishment of the masses. The reformers destroyed the old structures, hoping that they would automatically discover markets in their place.

There is no point in borrowing the U.S. model of private ownership of oil and not enforcing the U.S. model of tax payment, right? Oil companies here effectively pay a 15–20 percent corporate tax, which is lower than the rates that U.S. corporations pay.

Our faith in state guarantees is stronger than our trust in private business.

OCTOBER 2004

Gubernatorial elections under Yeltsin led to the feudal partitioning of Russia.

A weak, unfocused state cannot fight terrorism.

The Yeltsin years marked a pseudotsarist, authoritarian arrangement—weak, ailing, anarchic, and corrupt.

Gorbachev lost the chance to implant the Chinese model in Russia.

JUNE 2003

DESAI: How did you acquire the varied professional expertise necessary to lead IMEMO, the leading Russian policy institute on international economic and political issues?

Simonia: My biography is simple. I started studying China, got involved with Southeast Asian development experience, and then expanded my professional interest to the economic and political issues of the developing world in the 1960s and beyond. I traveled and stayed in some of these countries, enriching my insights. Finally, I returned to Russia and began interpreting the Soviet and Russian situation in terms of my expertise in developing countries. It turned out to be a challenging research area. I grappled with the issue of the slow pace of reforms in Russia and their spectacular success in China and South Korea, each different from the other, and came up with striking observations.

Desai: So professionally you traveled from the developing countries to Russia and began wrestling with the problem of how it might become a liberal market economy. Usually people with a market economy background try to provide answers for Russia's transition, as they did under President Yeltsin.

Simonia: In my opinion, the Russian situation shared more similarities with the problems of the developing countries.

Desai: From that perspective, how would you assess the economic reforms under Yeltsin?

Simonia: Transition, in my view, should imply a change for the better. In contrast, eight years under Yeltsin witnessed a horrific deterioration, a destruction of Russian industry, and the impoverishment of the masses. The reformers destroyed the old structures, hoping that they would automatically discover markets in their place. They assumed that a new middle class would appear and take charge of economic management. They thought small businesses would spring forth. Official statistics claim that 900,000 small businesses currently operate in Russia. However, Russia is vast and requires a large number of small, independent business units for them to make an impact on growth and employment in its distant regions. Actually, the number of small businesses is declining. We simply do not have energetic, entrepreneurial risk takers who will start small ventures and create new growth opportunities. In fact, people who pass for small business owners from the middle class serve the oligarchs. They are servants of big business. In reality, the assets and the mass of property that were created during the Soviet period were simply divided among a few oligarchs who had connections with the top policy makers in the government. Under the shady loans-for-shares deals, these oligarchs bought the assets for a mere pittance.

Desai: Let me play devil's advocate. Don't you think the privatization of big business, especially in the energy sector—oil and natural gas—has allowed Russia to be an effective player in world markets? That would probably not have happened if they were still state owned.

Simonia: I don't agree. A significant share of the world's oil industry is state owned. Of course, there is the U.S. model of privately owned oil companies, and then there are the rest.

Desai: I don't have the facts with me, but state-owned units in the oil sector operate in an economy that otherwise works under the rules of a market system, so the big, state-owned enterprises function under a market environment. However, in Russia, the situation was the opposite. Everything was state owned. Therefore, it was difficult for some companies to operate efficiently.

SIMONIA: Yes, I understand what you're saying. I'm not against privatization, but you must privatize industries that will really bring better, more effective management. For Russia, oil is important and substantial, unlike in other countries. Gorbachev once said that only oil and vodka were providers of revenue in the state budget. You cannot ruin these pillars overnight, yet this is precisely what Yeltsin and his reformers did. Vodka was gone, and oil was gone, too, from public ownership.

DESAI: But today revenue flows from the oil sector have stabilized the government budget, haven't they?

SIMONIA: A major portion of oil industry profits under Yeltsin was going out of Russia in offshore banks and companies. This, therefore, did not mark an improvement. Only later, revenue flows from the energy sector stabilized the budget under eight months of Yevgeny Primakov's prime ministership and subsequently under President Putin. There was an aggressive rethinking of policies relating to these companies, though not in the sense that they might be nationalized—it is too late now; we do not want a civil war—but to compel them to pay taxes as companies do in the West. There is no point in borrowing the U.S. model of private ownership of oil and not enforcing the U.S. model of tax payment, right? Oil companies here effectively pay a 15 to 20 percent corporate tax, which is lower than the rates that U.S. corporations pay. Of course, they still complain.

DESAI: Let's turn to political issues. Do you think that the positive relationship between Clinton and Yeltsin weakened the authoritarian political system under Communism? Wasn't that a positive outcome? Russia has an electoral democracy today.

SIMONIA: I believe that democracy cannot be built overnight based on a single decision. We do not have democracy. Rather, we have started the process of democratization. That process started not with Yeltsin, but with Gorbachev. There was genuine freedom under Gorbachev. Indeed, critical articles appeared in newspapers against Gorbachev and in media outlets that the government still financed. It was indeed remarkable. Again, small businesses appeared under laws that encouraged cooperative business activity. This process ceased with Yeltsin's appearance. Democratization also came to a halt. Yeltsin gradually began to talk and act like a tsar, so he borrowed from the institutions of democracy, but in reality the essence was a traditionally Russian state of affairs, much as you have in India, where you have elections, parties, and a parliament, but a single party, the Congress Party, which dominated.

DESAI: What years are you referring to?

SIMONIA: Under Nehru and Indira Gandhi. She inherited power. She did not acquire it democratically. It was worse in other countries, including in Russia under Yeltsin. A few people pulled the strings under the guise of elections. There were vote miscounts.

Desai: We will come to this process under Yeltsin and Putin later. Why has the economy revived recently? Which aspects of the recovery bother you?

Simonia: The current recovery must be put in perspective. Primakov and then Putin stabilized the situation politically. Political stability is necessary for economic recovery. Next, the cheap ruble made Russian products competitive. As a result, industry revived in 2000, but the optimistic growth figures since 2001 are based on high oil prices in world markets. True, investment is picking up in the oil sector, in construction, and in machine production, but I also notice that, in the past two years, we have moved into a specific model of development.

Desai: What is that?

Simonia: A big Russian company would invite a foreign partner who would then become dominant. I have nothing against it because, as a consumer, it is important for me to have cheap, better-quality products. And that, too, is happening.

Desai: Give me an example.

Simonia: I heard just recently that Wimm-Bill-Dann, a food and dairy company founded by a Georgian, is likely to be taken over by Danone.[1]

Desai: Why doesn't one of the Russian oligarchs capture Wimm-Bill-Dann? Why aren't they interested in reviving Russian consumer goods?

Simonia: Well, some of the oil oligarchs have recently shown interest in stepping into agricultural activity. Yukos is one of them. And that's new.

Desai: This is in processed foods, isn't it? When you say agriculture?

Simonia: Yes, edible oil is profitable. So is macaroni.

Desai: Tell me, did the economic measures under Putin, among them the simplified tax rate, contribute to the later phase of the recovery in 2002?

Simonia: I think so. It is not enough, but it is the lowest tax, when compared to rates in other countries. The personal tax rate is set at 13 percent, and the corporate profit tax was lowered from 34 percent to 25 percent.

Desai: Is the land reform going to work in improving agriculture and farming?

Simonia: Theoretically, yes, but in Russian conditions, the process will once again be dominated by a few oligarchs. When Yeltsin came to power, the liberal policy makers in the government said, let the peasants do what they want, so the collective farms were converted into joint stock companies. The collective farm households, the *kolkhozniki,* were given the right to sell their share and move off the farm. However, 90 percent of them have stayed put on the farms, most of which are unprofitable. It was not enough to issue a paper decree. The farms, especially the better ones, needed help to retain their workforce. They needed technical input and matching credits. At the same time, some successful farms had their barns burned and their machinery stolen. Overall, the number of farmers has declined to 250,000 in all. Most of them are in unprofitable units. The situation is depressing. The fact is we do not have independent farmers in Russia. We have kolkhozniki, who represent a totally different social phenomenon.

Desai: How is it different?

SIMONIA: It is different because our kolkhoznik is not an Indian or a Chinese peasant. Essentially the product of a modified slavery system, he was dominated by the Communist Party organization in the past. The party bosses said, "You must plant this and harvest now, and here is what you get as a reward from us." But can that psychological makeup change because Yeltsin issued a decree assigning them formal ownership rights? The reality on the farms has not changed. The farm households still feel that it is dangerous for them to contribute to the farm's overall performance. "No, no, it is too dangerous," they claim. "I am better off working on the private plot attached to my dacha, stealing fertilizer and pesticide from the farm stock for the purpose, and selling my products at the nearby city market." These small plots still provide 90 percent of all potatoes and other vegetables and most of the meat to city dwellers. The big corporations have, of course, stepped into profitable ventures such as vegetable oil.

DESAI: Let's go back from edible oil to crude oil. I think the fiscal health of the federal government has improved because of revenue inflows from the booming oil sector. What measures would you suggest for trimming federal outlays so that the budget gets stabilized over the long haul?

SIMONIA: I am afraid federal expenditures will not decline.

DESAI: Why not?

SIMONIA: Why not? Because our current political leadership is concerned about reviving Russia not as a superpower but as a significant power. This means a strong military, a modern army, sophisticated weaponry, and the necessary information technology for the purpose. All of this calls for cash.

DESAI: So you think the military still eats up a substantial portion of the budget?

SIMONIA: Defense outlays in the past two years have gone up.

DESAI: What are they currently in the 2003 state budget? Approximately?

SIMONIA: You know I cannot give you a precise estimate because once again our statistics are not real numbers. Quite a few are unknown. Defense outlays, as in the old days, are hidden in other items in the budget.

DESAI: You mean they are still not transparent?

SIMONIA: Of course not.

DESAI: What about entitlements in the budget outside of the military, the across-the-board housing, education, and other subsidies to the public? Aren't they a big expense?

SIMONIA: The budget has these allocations. For example, the budget allocates 3 percent to science and research. About four years ago, the number was 4 percent. In fact, they never distribute the full amount. I am the director of the largest Russian research institute, with a staff of five hundred people, and I get three thousand rubles as my salary.

DESAI: Three thousand rubles a month?

SIMONIA: That's all. Of course, I manage the institute's finances with different projects funded from other sources.

DESAI: How about your personal finances?

SIMONIA: My wife earns two thousand rubles a month as a senior researcher in the Oriental Institute. We barely make ends meet.

DESAI: What about your personal savings? Your pension?

SIMONIA: That story is one of the state stealing my savings. I had deposited twenty-five thousand rubles in my savings account month after month in the Soviet days. I thought that my savings were safe and that, when I retired, they would supplement my pension. When Gaidar became prime minister, my savings disappeared overnight. Then, when we were given privatization vouchers, we were promised instant wealth via ownership in state assets, but that did not happen. Now I am old and counting on my pension.

DESAI: So privatizing the pension system is dangerous?

SIMONIA: It's a dangerous idea. Few Russians, about 20 percent, believe that it is a better arrangement. Our faith in state guarantees is stronger than our trust in private business.

DESAI: What about introducing a voucher system for higher education? Let's say you have a countrywide qualifying examination, and the best students from small villages to big cities get vouchers that they can use to get into the universities of their choice. That will reduce the current across-the-board budget allocation for the purpose.

SIMONIA: You're not aware that the most promising aspect of the future for our young people, our higher education, is thoroughly tainted. In state universities, teachers demand extra payment on top of their salaries; otherwise, students cannot complete their education and get their degrees. It does not matter how bright they are. A friend in the foreign ministry recently told me that his daughter, a university student, is smart. He was told that she must transfer to another teacher, however, because she was not so bright. So our university professors are transferring boys and girls at will unless they are paid extra, up to $400 a month. The lucky ones escape this extra expense and complete their education. First, it is necessary to weed out this corruption and then think of switching to a voucher system.

DESAI: I will come to the corruption issue later. What are the important economic issues now? For example, take the restructuring of the electric power monopoly, which needs to increase charges for electricity in order to become profitable. But if these prices are liberalized suddenly, so that consumers, households, and industries have to pay higher prices, inflation will go up. If energy prices are liberalized suddenly, inflation control may become unmanageable, and you have parliamentary elections coming up in December. Do you think this is a major issue? How can monopolies, the railways, the natural gas and electric power sectors, be profitable unless they are allowed to raise prices? Isn't there a conflict here?

SIMONIA: There's a conflict here, but it does not arise from local considerations. It comes from outside.

DESAI: How so?

SIMONIA: Members of the European Union demand that we raise energy prices and bring them to world levels before we can be considered for entry into the World Trade Organization (WTO). They insist on this because they want cheaper natural gas from us.

DESAI: How can they get cheaper gas from Russia if the Russian supplier, Gazprom, raises the price of natural gas for domestic consumers?

SIMONIA: The argument is complicated. Currently, Russia charges world prices to European buyers. The question is, can these prices be lowered down the road? As a monopoly supplier of natural gas, Gazprom can charge lower prices by raising supplies via exploration of gas fields in northern Russia that require huge investments of up to $70 billion for extracting them. So the Europeans are telling us, "You raise natural gas prices for domestic consumers and get the cash for these investments." That is unfair.

DESAI: Why is it unfair?

SIMONIA: It's unfair because they need cheap gas for their industries to become competitive against the United States. That is their goal, but they forget that our industries will become noncompetitive if we raise natural gas prices at home. In any case, natural gas and oil prices are high in some European countries not because of foreign delivery prices but because of high taxes on some of these items. Take gasoline prices in Britain. They are inordinately high because of gasoline taxes.

DESAI: So the government raises tax revenues.

SIMONIA: Absolutely. That is why OPEC is telling Western importers, "You reduce your taxes for your consumers and businesses, and everything will be fine. Don't ask us to charge you lower prices."

DESAI: Let's talk about structural reforms. They are essential for promoting stable and high economic growth in Russia. What special changes would you recommend in that regard?

SIMONIA: It is too late to nationalize the companies that are now owned mainly by private business. Putin understands this. He has been telling the oligarchs, "You own these assets. That's history." The first business of the day for him was to make them pay taxes. And we do have companies who run their branches, pay their taxes, and keep away from politics. At a recent conference, he suggested that we stop referring to Russia's big businesses as oligarchs and call them civilized businessmen. His main policy thrust is to make sure that they pay their taxes and stay away from politics. The revenues in the treasury can be used not only for upgrading the military but also for developing the infrastructure and supporting industry. Of course, not to support industry indiscriminately. There is a continuing discussion relating to this issue. Russia is no longer a socialist country in isolation from the world economy. The times have changed. We need to restructure our industrial base in an open, competitive, global economy. There cannot be an all-out support for all industries.

DESAI: Apart from the restructuring of the economy and the industrial sector, there are problems of creating a solid institutional base. You talked earlier about how to deal with corruption, for example, paying higher salaries to judges, removing some bureaucrats, streamlining the bureaucracy, and enforcing laws. This is what I had in mind.

SIMONIA: All of this will take time. It cannot be done in a year or two. It is a long struggle. In fact, this is the real struggle, and it is going on not only between ordinary people and the bureaucrats but also at higher levels—between the president and the government. A little more than a year ago, Putin decided to start the process by having the government work up three antibureaucratic proposals for the Duma's approval. Eight months later, the president asked the prime minister and the first deputy prime minister about the status of his plan and the package of proposals. The government was stalling. At last, three sets of proposals for streamlining the administrative hierarchy from the top down were introduced in March [2003] for legislative action. Soon after, ministers began lobbying against them because their passage would curtail cash allocations from the federal budget for their ministries. They would be forced to reduce the bureaucratic apparatus.

DESAI: It would also cut into their authority and privileges. Bureaucrats do not like to invite such self-destruction.

SIMONIA: Unless this interventionist scourge is removed from the economy, it cannot grow and prosper. Our performance will lag behind that of many developing countries.

DESAI: I believe that substantial direct foreign investment will put Russia in a growth range of maybe 8 percent annually. That will not happen, however, because there is an implicit collusion in Russia among big businesses that says, "We can manage the growth rate; just give us time." The bureaucrats do not want controls to be removed, and the Communists believe that direct foreign investment is exploitative. I feel the president is unable and perhaps unwilling to confront this collusion. As a result, direct foreign investments will flow into Russian manufacturing in small trickles. What do you think?

SIMONIA: You're right. Direct foreign investment flows in Russia are minuscule in contrast to China and Poland because the oligarchs do not want them. The production-sharing arrangements in the oil sector, for example, were debated endlessly in the Duma. When Primakov was prime minister, he proposed twenty-four amendments to the then existing law, and Sakhalin I and Sakhalin II, two of the biggest projects in the oil sector with the direct participation of Exxon Mobil, among several partners, got moving.[2] The Russian oil companies spent money advertising on television and in newspapers, vigorously arguing against production-sharing agreements with foreign investors. They can invest in oil companies—but not in oil and natural gas fields—and recover their investment via a claim on the outputs generated in these fields. The Duma prohibited most of the production-sharing proposals.

DESAI: So you are suggesting that, as prime minister, Primakov pushed production-sharing agreements (PSAs).

SIMONIA: Two PSA packages were passed during his tenure. After that, the anti-PSA campaign was revived and financed by the oil oligarchs.

DESAI: Are you suggesting that the opposition to production-sharing agreements does not come from the Left and the Communists, who argue that foreigners will take over Russia's natural resources, but from Russia's big businesses?

SIMONIA: Yes, from the oligarchs who employ the Communist ideology.

DESAI: Why do you think Russia's entry into the WTO has been delayed?

SIMONIA: Simply because the European Union insists on impossible conditions with respect to energy prices and other issues that are unacceptable to the Russian negotiators.

DESAI: But there are also problems with specific sectors of Russian industry that would like sufficient protection before the economy is liberalized upon Russia's admittance to the WTO.

SIMONIA: You are right. Take the aluminum industry, headed by Oleg Deripaska, who is leading a tough campaign against WTO entry.[3] He is also expanding into the automobile industry, another claimant for protection. In my opinion, it is a despotic way of influencing the entry process.

DESAI: So WTO entry will be delayed until both elections are over?

SIMONIA: I think so.

DESAI: Will the new composition of the Duma, resulting from the December 2003 elections, be more conducive to fast-paced reform?

SIMONIA: The current Duma bends to the wishes of the Kremlin, and the new Duma will also accept the president's reform agenda.

DESAI: But will the composition of the Duma continue to be dominated by the Kremlin-led United Russia group after the elections?

SIMONIA: Yes.

DESAI: You will, therefore, have almost a one-party system with no effective opposition to the president.

SIMONIA: Yes. I predicted such an outcome years ago. I suggested that we were moving toward an Indonesian model of guided democracy. Under Sukarno, they had one party, the Golkar party, which dominated Parliament, and that party was controlled by the president. We are moving toward a similar situation.

DESAI: So what is the alternative? Would you like to have a genuine parliamentary system?

SIMONIA: Not now. A switch to a parliamentary system would require constitutional change. It takes time to create a democratic system. Look at South Korea. They made remarkable economic progress for three decades and developed a middle class. Members of the middle class along with students and workers struggled for the creation of democratic institutions and finally succeeded. Democracy is not something that the U.S. president can hand us in a gift-wrapped package. We have to create it ourselves, and I do not think we are ready for it.

DESAI: Now my final question. How will U.S.-Russian relations develop? In your opinion, what major issues are shaping the relationship?

SIMONIA: We talk a lot about the U.S.-Russian strategic partnership, but we have important partners, among them China, the European Union, and India. Putin is clever enough to say nice things to everybody while defending Russia's interests. At times he is pro-European. Some time later, he meets Bush, and we become friends with the Americans. We need to think differently. Putin first and foremost is pro-Russian, and he leans in the direction that serves Russia's interests.

DESAI: So his ultimate strategy is to protect Russia's interests?

SIMONIA: Protect Russia's interests with the understanding that the world around us is changing and growing and coming closer. This process is not of Russia's choosing. This is an objective reality irrespective of our wishes.

DESAI: But the reality right now is the superpower status of the United States, especially after the Iraq war. Wouldn't you agree?

SIMONIA: I am glad you brought this up. It is a formidable topic. The U.S. share in the world economy has been steadily declining since 1950. It has decreased substantially and will continue to do so because other economic centers, among them the European Union, China, and the East Asian economies, are poised to grow rapidly. I also compared statistics on overseas development assistance. The United States was number one several years ago, followed by Japan.

DESAI: Yes, but U.S. policy makers no longer believe in overseas development assistance. They want to increase the share of American private business in the world economy, where they still dominate.

SIMONIA: In that regard I am also hopeful that multinationals from other countries will compete with U.S. companies in the near future. More players will appear as the global economy opens up. Politically and economically, I visualize a multipolar world.

OCTOBER 2004

DESAI: How do you view the proposal to retain the party slate for the Duma elections and abolish the single-member constituencies?

SIMONIA: Some analysts believe that single-member constituencies promote the election of independent deputies. In fact, that is not true. They are only pseudo-independent. Most of them are linked to criminal groups. Their abolition will reduce corruption in the Duma. As for the formation of a genuine party system, it is an objective process, part of a more fundamental process of the formation of a civil society, which is still beginning in Russia.

DESAI: Will the proposed measure in favor of the president electing the regional governors, whom the regional legislatures will then approve, deprive voters of their right to elect their leaders (i.e., governors) in a federal system?

SIMONIA: My arguments in response to your earlier question are even more relevant in connection with the current method of electing the regional governors. Putin's proposed changes are designed to correct a big mistake made under Yeltsin. Gubernatorial elections under Yeltsin led to the feudal partitioning of Russia. The country was brought to the edge of dissolution.

DESAI: Are these consolidating measures necessary to fight terrorism?

SIMONIA: The connection of these measures to the fight against terrorism is not a direct one. It is general and broader. A weak, unfocused state cannot fight terrorism.

DESAI: Yavlinsky says Putin's proposals smack of "soft Stalinism." What do you think?

SIMONIA: I do not agree with Yavlinsky's description. Stalinism was a ruthless, totalitarian system that Khrushchev tried to dismantle in 1956. That started the slow process of the transformation of Stalinist totalitarianism into the normal Soviet authoritarianism under Brezhnev. The Yeltsin years marked a pseudotsarist authoritarian arrangement—weak, ailing, anarchic, and corrupt. In my view, Putin has begun a soft version of authoritarianism resembling the state capitalism under Lenin from 1921 to 1924.

DESAI: Do you think that Putin regards political consolidation as a necessary precondition for promoting economic reforms?

SIMONIA: In my view, Putin does believe that political stability is absolutely necessary for pushing economic reforms forward.

DESAI: How does this hybrid model differ from that of Pinochet in Chile and of the Communist leadership in China? How would you describe the Putin model? Any other historical parallels?

SIMONIA: Russia under Putin is not Chile. Pinochet's regime was despotic. Russia is different. There are no human rights abuses in Russia. However, it is not China, either. Putin has a more difficult job than Deng Zhao Ping in China, who could rely on the well-organized and accommodating Communist Party. Putin must do everything from scratch and right away, including forming his own team. Gorbachev lost the chance to implant the Chinese model in Russia.

DESAI: Does it make sense to apply the norms of a fully formed U.S.-style liberal order to assess Russia's evolving transition?

SIMONIA: Implanting the Western, especially the U.S., liberal order in Russia does not make sense. Currently, Russia is not ready to absorb it.

DESAI: Despite Putin's illiberal forays, do you think that, from a long-term perspective, the chances of Russia continuing to evolve to a liberal political and economic system remain robust?

Simonia: Russia has a lot of catching up to do in comparison with the developed West. Therefore, for a few decades, the state will play a regulatory role in its socioeconomic development.

Desai: In the old days, Western Sovietologists argued that Soviet foreign policy forays were expansionist and adventurist because the internal political arrangements were ideological and authoritarian. Putin, by contrast, is nonideological and selectively pragmatic in pushing Russia's interests. What is your view?

Simonia: I quite approve of Putin's pragmatic and flexible foreign policy. It focuses on defending Russia's national interests, especially in the neighboring states, which were formerly part of the Soviet Union.

Desai: Will he seek a third presidential term?

Simonia: I think it is too early to talk about a third presidential term for Putin. Let's see how successful the second term is. In theory, a constitutional change is possible. A single individual cannot undertake and accomplish the enormous preparation that such a change requires. He needs an energetic and cohesive team. From 1921 to 1924, Lenin didn't have such a team. Neither did Gorbachev from 1987 to 1990.

Desai: Do you view the proposed Gazprom-Rosneft merger favorably?

Simonia: Even before combining with Rosneft, Gazprom had been attracting foreign investments. Currently it is negotiating joint participation with Shell in large natural gas projects in northern Russia. The government has decided to go ahead with an oil pipeline to Nakhodka, as announced by Energy Minister Khristenko in Beijing. Japanese business suggested last September that a parallel natural gas pipeline from Kovytka in eastern Siberia also be built. Transneft, the state-owned oil pipeline company, has been arguing for these pipelines for quite a while. The government and the president will have the last word on the decision.

Notes

1. Wimm-Bill-Dann, according to their website, wbd.com, is "the market leader among producers of juices, milk products, and baby food in Russia."

2. Having appointed Primakov prime minister in September 1998, Yeltsin fired him in May 1999 for "failing to rescue" the Russian economy, naming Sergei Stepashin acting premier. The timing coincided with the impending hearings mounted by the Communist majority to impeach Yeltsin in the State Duma.

3. Oleg Deripaska is president of Russian Aluminum (Rusal) and one of its controlling shareholders.

CHAPTER 10

George Soros

The Active Philanthropist

Basically the international lenders were not willing to put public resources and real money into the effort. . . . They gave the job of assisting the Soviet Union, and then Russia eventually, to the IMF, which was not the appropriate institution.

Gorbachev counted on the United States to help him initiate economic reforms. He felt that he and his team were incapable of making the transition on their own. . . . Gorbachev visited the United Nations in 1987 and spoke about his new thinking. The U.S. leadership ignored it and instead set conditions, asking him to make concessions. When he made them, they asked for more.

I argued that the same $15 billion [from the IMF] that provided balance of payment and budgetary support could have been earmarked for paying Social Security benefits [to pensioners].

To prove that [direct cash payment] could be done, I established the International Science Foundation, which distributed $500 each to the top thirty thousand Russian scientists. . . . The cash they received is practically the only Western aid that Russians have actually received.

It was convenient for some people in Russia to blame me [for the collapse of the ruble in 1998], saying that I caused the run on the ruble. It would have occurred even if I had not published my opinion.

Yes, I think it is not impossible to do business in Russia, but Western companies have little appetite for investing in Russia, and the government is making very little effort to create a hospitable environment.

I wanted the foundation to lead the way toward an open society in Russia. To some extent, it became embroiled in the transition. . . . We had the August 1991 putsch in Russia. We needed another one to clean the foundation of its Russian corruption. Instead of leading, the foundation became part of the process. That was the painful realization.

DECEMBER 2000

DESAI: Arguing in favor of generous financial support for Russia, you suggested as early as 1992 that the G7 did not come up with a substantial aid package for Russia. However, there were practical considerations against a large aid inflow. Russia could not have absorbed it because of institutional limitations. The U.S. Congress would not approve it because of the adversarial relations with the Soviet Union, which lasted for more than half a century. It seems to me that these practical considerations, rather than opposition to open society as such, dictated the limited financial inflow from the G7 under IMF monitoring. How would you react to that argument?

SOROS: I think that the practical considerations that you mention, namely, the ability of the Soviet Union, and then Russia, to absorb financial aid is correct, and I was acutely aware of it. That is why I felt that the IMF would have to give the aid differently from the way it normally dispenses money. It was absolutely necessary to have a more intrusive approach—not just greater control, but also greater assistance in delivery. Something along the lines of the Marshall Plan after World War II, but even more intrusive than that because, in Western Europe, functioning economies of the past were ruined.[1] In contrast, you didn't have a functioning economy in the Soviet Union, so I was advocating something along the lines of the Marshall Plan, only more intrusive.

But then the idea simply didn't fly. I tried to push it in every way I could. I privately tried to reach Margaret Thatcher, but I never got past Paul, her personal assistant. I tried to reach George Bush [senior] before the Malta conference because I felt it was the last chance.[2] I had been pushing it even earlier. I proposed it publicly at the East-West conference in Potsdam in the spring of 1989, when Potsdam was still in East Germany. I was literally laughed at. It was a rather embarrassing experience. I'd never been publicly laughed at. However, when I said that the Soviet Union needed a Marshall Plan, my copanelist, a minister in the Thatcher government, actually started laughing, and the audience laughed with him. Apparently the idea was simply not acceptable in Western public opinion. Basically the international lenders were not willing to put public resources and real money into the effort. That is why they turned to the IMF—because it had money that didn't belong to anybody. It was sort of "found" money. They gave the job of assisting the Soviet Union, and then Russia eventually, to the IMF, which was not the appropriate institution.

DESAI: I think this is the idea underlying your humanitarian activity, a more detailed, intrusive approach of making sure that the funding you give in a country is appropriately used for a given purpose. But the basic idea of the Marshall Plan, it would seem to me, could not get off the ground with regard to Russia because Germany, for example, which was defeated and received Marshall Plan aid, had to be revived and reconstructed as a bulwark against the emerging threat from Stalin.

SOROS: Yes, but Germany was a defeated country after World War I also and, instead of sending aid to the rebuilding of Germany, the Western powers insisted on a tough peace agreement. You recall Keynes's objection to that arrangement and rightly so.[3] The result was an unfavorable political development, the rise of Nazism and World War II. Having learned from that, the United States, after World War II, had the vision and generosity to engage in the Marshall Plan. However, that vision and that generosity were missing at the collapse of the Soviet Union. The victor can also insist that it has the option to deal with a defeated country differently because it really has the basis for intrusion.

DESAI: Yes, a defeated recipient has limited choice, but the Soviet Union was not defeated on the battlefield.

SOROS: However, I can testify from my personal experience that the Soviet Union would have been very receptive to such an intrusive approach. I proposed to Nikolai Ryzhkov, Gorbachev's prime minister, that he set up a task force in 1988, very early in the game, for creating an open sector in the economy.[4] At that time I was practically a nobody; nevertheless, I got a positive response, and when the Russian authorities were slow and did not include the top people in the task force, I went with the Nobel laureate Wassily Leontief, who, at the age of eighty, became my partner in the enterprise.[5] He came to Moscow, and we went to Ryzhkov, and Leontief insisted that, if the prime minister wanted us to proceed, he must make sure that his top people participated. The prime minister issued an order. They were extremely receptive at the time and remained receptive to this kind of assistance several years later. I realized from my personal conversations that Gorbachev counted on the United States to help him initiate economic reforms. He felt that he and his team were incapable of making the transition on their own. He had a general notion of what he called "new thinking," developed by the foreign ministry, which would reactivate the United Nations and create an alliance between the two superpowers.[6] As part of that alliance, the United States would then assist the Soviet Union in the transition, but we were not at all receptive. Gorbachev visited the United Nations in 1987 and spoke about his new thinking. The U.S. leadership ignored it and instead set conditions, asking him to make concessions. When he made them, they asked for more. In the meantime, the Soviet economy started collapsing. We then treated the Russians like beggars, which they deeply resented. If you interview Alexander Yakovlev [Gorbachev's advisor], he will tell you how resentful he is of the U.S. attitude of those days.

DESAI: So there was a difference of opinion not only about the amount of aid but also its steering. You suggested that the IMF's $15 billion aid package announced in 1993 could have been used for pension payments from the budget, but the IMF wanted to use it for budgetary support for inflation control.

SOROS: Well, as you know, I wrote an article for the *Wall Street Journal,* in which I argued that the same $15 billion [from the IMF] that provided balance of payment and budgetary support could have been earmarked for paying Social Security benefits [to pensioners], which, at the prevailing rate of exchange, were only $8 a month.[7] So the $15 billion could actually have covered the government's Social Security obligations. Of course, had it been paid in dollars, the exchange rate would have changed, but it would have jump-started the economy, people would have received cash in hand, and they would have known where the money came from. Financial benefits for pensioners could have become the mainstay of economic reform. Today the pensioners support the Communist Party.

DESAI: That was a bold suggestion.

SOROS: But, of course, the idea was not seriously considered. To prove that it could be done, I established the International Science Foundation, which distributed $500 each to the top thirty thousand Russian scientists. At the time, the amount was enough for them to live on for a year. The cash they received is practically the only Western aid that Russians have actually received. If you talk to Russians, they are certainly aware of it. It was a practical suggestion, but it did not catch the attention of our leadership.

DESAI: Right before the collapse of the ruble in August 1998, you also suggested that the G7 contribute a $15 billion package to support a currency board for Russia.[8] I doubt that the Russian government or the legislators would have accepted the proposal. Do you have second thoughts about it?

SOROS: I think you're right. They would not have been able to accept the conditions for the currency board.

DESAI: In early 1998 you also suggested in an article in the *Financial Times* that the ruble be devalued.[9] You were subsequently blamed for having brought about its collapse in August 1998.

SOROS: My idea, as the article says, was to offer an alternative to Russian policy makers. Their rejection would make them responsible for the default, so it would have served a political purpose. As you say, my article was misinterpreted because ruble devaluation was part of my scheme, although I had suggested a much smaller devaluation than what actually happened. It was convenient for some people in Russia to blame me, saying that I caused the run on the ruble. It would have occurred even if I had not published my opinion. In fact, I was told that it was a deliberate decision of the Central Bank to blame me in order to deflect the blame from itself.

DESAI: Your views on financial markets are relevant in the context of the meltdown of the ruble. You believe that financial markets by their nature are unpredictable and unstable. Do you think that foreign inflow of short-term capital was opened up prematurely in Russia under IMF monitoring in 1996 so that speculative investors bought short-term government bills and, when the Asian crisis lessened their confidence, they dumped these instruments and walked out?

SOROS: There is no doubt in my mind that it was an unsustainable market access. People were throwing money at Russia. I remember traveling in the Ural Mountains in Yekaterinburg, where they had access to a half billion dollars at 250 basis points above the Euro, and they had absolutely no idea what to do with the money, so they asked me the most ludicrous questions. They were completely unprepared for that loan. It was really forced on them by investment banks that were earning a commission. It was totally unsound.

DESAI: So you would say that free capital mobility in that form was a mistake.

SOROS: It was premature. All together, going back from 1998 to 1992, there was an excessive belief in the virtue and efficacy of market discipline among the Russian reformers and Western advisors. According to MIT economists Rudiger Dornbusch and Stanley Fischer, Gaidar had read their textbook.[10] He actually understood the book's macroeconomic analysis. So, as a worthy disciple, he proceeded to introduce monetary discipline in an economy that didn't obey monetary signals. The fact was that the enterprises continued to function and deliver the goods they were producing according to plan even if they didn't get paid. The monetary discipline that Gaidar tried to impose had no effect. In the process, intercompany debt was ballooning. Gaidar launched his reforms in early January 1992. In April 1992 I was traveling in Russia and noticed the mounting liabilities of Russian companies. When I came back, Gaidar happened to be passing through New York. I called him and drew his attention to this disturbing feature. He said the intercompany debt was only one-twelfth of the GDP. I said it was one-third. The new arrangement had been in effect for only three months, so its impact had to be related to one-quarter of the GDP, not the whole of it. He agreed, but his policies continued. The intercompany debt went out of bounds. There was an excessive reliance on monetary policy and not enough attention to the structural changes that were necessary for enforcing monetary signals on enterprise managers.

DESAI: How would you assess the pluses and minuses of the Russian reform process up to the election of Vladimir Putin as president in March 2000?

SOROS: I think that on the whole it was a failure. The successes were purely superficial. One could get hamburgers at McDonald's in Pushkin Square and Estée Lauder products in GUM, the state department store. A small elite raked off unconscionable profits by carrying out arbitrage between the centrally planned economy and the market economy. One could buy oil at the official price and sell it in the world market at effectively one hundred times the price. The commodity arbitrage produced profits of 90 percent or more. The remainder was mainly bribes, not cost of materials. It was a disastrously unsound situation.

DESAI: So how do you assess the role of the IMF in that context?

SOROS: Well, I do not hold the IMF accountable beyond a point. I blame the Western governments that forced the Fund into this role, but then the IMF exhibited a remarkable ability to deceive itself. I was surprised that the Fund actually tried to defend its performance after the fact. I think that it should have recognized that it was given an impossible task and it failed. However, the Fund regrettably became identified with the process and tried to defend it. It is regrettable because the Fund's involvement in Russia and the other transition economies has damaged its credibility. It pushed the IMF off the rails.

DESAI: The Fund was put in a role that it was traditionally ill equipped to perform.

SOROS: That's right. It operated by signing letters of intent, but when a government cannot actually deliver on its intent, it is effectively guaranteeing failure. That is in fact what happened.

DESAI: Let us take some current issues now. Twenty-five percent of Russia's federal budget goes to foreign debt repayment. Do you think part of Russia's sovereign debt from Soviet days should be written off? How do you react to the idea of converting some of it into foreign equity in Russian companies?

SOROS: You are asking two questions. To answer the first one, there is no question that Russia received great relief from defaulting on its GKOs, its short-term government bills, in August 1998. It would receive further relief if it could default on its euro-denominated and Soviet-era debt. But, you have to ask, how much relief should Russia get? If Russia had an honest, aboveboard, reformed government, maybe it would deserve it, but as it is, it is inappropriate. This is an arcane and obtuse field, and there's certainly room for negotiation and settlement; in effect, Russia is currently not paying that debt but only making partial payments, and the rest has to be rescheduled. And in the context of a settlement, a debt for equity swap would be desirable because it would not only help to regularize the situation but also attract management and investment in some key industries in Russia, so I think it's a promising area.

DESAI: Do you think the oligarchs' influence on government policymaking has been brought somewhat under control since two of Russia's leading oligarchs, Boris Berezovsky and Vladimir Gusinsky, have been reduced to the status of virtual expatriates? Do you think Putin has conveyed effective signals to oligarchic activity?

SOROS: I think the oligarchs are under pressure generally. Putin's attack on them has considerable public support. It is popular. It puts him in a favorable position. In fact, the persecution of Berezovsky and Gusinsky has specific goals and has to do with control of the media as well as bringing oligarchs in general under control. Nevertheless, one should avoid putting them in the same basket. They had very different roles in Russia. Gusinsky is one of the most enlightened Russian entrepreneurs, whereas Berezovsky played a nefarious role in Russian politics.

DESAI: I have a question relating to the inflow of foreign private investment in Russia. I think the Russian president is deliberately soft-pedaling on the issue of foreign private investment flows in Russian industry. In my view, there is an implicit collusion between the Left in the Duma, the lower house of the Parliament, which thinks foreign investment is exploitative—standard Marxist position—and Russian big business, which thinks it can deliver things in Russia without foreign investors on the scene. There was a similar implicit collusion between the Left and private Indian businesses for almost half a century. Putin is unwilling to confront and override this hurdle via a major decision on foreign private investment. How do you view the situation?

SOROS: I agree with your view. There's also considerable popular xenophobia. At the same time, Putin fully recognizes that Russia has to be part of the global economy, and that means bringing in Western technology and Western management. Direct investment flows are limited. However, there is progress in inviting Western management. Some of the leading oil companies are actually using Westerners in key management positions. Yukos, Russia's largest oil company, and the oil companies generally are leading examples.

DESAI: Yes, but there cannot be a breakthrough without management control by Western companies, which can come with substantial equity and investment by Western groups. That they do not want.

SOROS: Yes, I think it is not impossible to do business in Russia, but Western companies have little appetite for investing in Russia, and the government is making very little effort to create a hospitable environment.

DESAI: Let's take a specific example. I have in mind Anatoly Chubais's scheme for restructuring the giant electric power company. I think the plan would pave the way for inflow of the necessary foreign investment by Western companies. What is your reaction?

SOROS: I am also puzzled because Chubais is a capable manager, but he has certainly veered away from relying on foreign investment as a driving force for the company. His plan did not take foreign investors' interests properly into account. He is now behaving much like an oligarch, except that he doesn't actually own or control any of the shares. He is an oligarch at the whim of the central government.

DESAI: There is something I do not understand here. As a financier and investor, you can explain it to me. The foreign minority shareholders are worried that, if a number of power-generating companies are put up for sale, they may sell for peanuts.

SOROS: And that their assets will be dissipated and given away at throwaway prices.

DESAI: But if there is open tendering, if anyone can—if you and I can—acquire these companies in an open bid, what is the harm? Because as foreign investors acquire the assets, their prospects will improve.

SOROS: Yes, but the conditions are not such as to attract foreigners to be active bidders. Take the example of AES, the American company that has bought control of the Georgian power company.[11] AES is in charge of electricity distribution in Tbilisi. Just today the newspapers reported that Chubais threatened to cut off oil and gas supplies to the company from Russia unless it exported electricity to Turkey. So, if a foreign unit is embedded in a distribution system controlled by AES, it is at the mercy of the local producer. Thus foreigners have a different perception of the market value they can actually realize from such investments.

DESAI: How do you rate your investment in Svyazinvest, the Russian telecommunications company?[12]

SOROS: I am moderately optimistic about it, in part because the company's management is improving and in part because the transition to some form of legitimate

capitalism is under way. Hopefully I can realize a part of the value of my investment. As you point out, a decisive push from the Kremlin to encourage foreign
investment is not in sight. Otherwise, Svyazinvest could be a showcase for attracting foreign investment in the Russian telecommunications sector, which needs
substantial inflows from outside.

Desai: How do you feel about your philanthropic activities in Russia?

Soros: As far as the foundation is concerned, I am quite upbeat. The foundation is genuinely nurturing among Russians the aspiration toward an open society.
It is a genuine aspiration among Russians, and the foundation can help them in that
endeavor. I think that it is a worthwhile and, in my judgment, a successful effort.

Desai: How did your philanthropic experience in Russia differ from that in
other countries? Can you pinpoint some differences?

Soros: I wanted the foundation to lead the way toward an open society in
Russia. To some extent, it became embroiled in the transition; it was itself a transitional institution and faced the same problems as the rest of society. We had the
August 1991 putsch in Russia. We needed another one to clean the foundation of
its Russian corruption. Instead of leading, the foundation became part of the process. That was the painful realization.

Desai: So in other countries you were ahead of the process?

Soros: In Russia, the idea was to be ahead and to lead. The [International]
Science Foundation attempted to do that as a separate organization. Of course, the
foundation did not accomplish its purpose early on, but, in the last four years, it has
managed to develop an organization that is appropriate to the conception of an open
society. Now it is a strong organization and is recognized as such in Russia. We
started in 1987, and we lost valuable time that cannot be recaptured. In July 1991,
we had a putsch in the foundation before the August putsch. When the foundation
was captured by corrupt influences, we had to remove the management. We lost a
number of years.

Desai: How do you rate the prospects for the Russian economy in the next
three to five years?

Soros: Three to five years? In this case, it is clear that the economy has strong
dynamism, but it is not clear whether this dynamism can be maintained for three to
five years. This is partly because it is dependent on the price of oil and partly because there is no investment. As the existing capacity is fully utilized, it is not clear
where the new capacity will come from.

Desai: I think Bill Clinton and Boris Yeltsin bonded as leaders with the common goal of doing away with the Communist authoritarian system. Do you think
that the identification in terms of the personalized bilateral deal making in the interest of a common objective is now weakened under the Bush-Putin regime?

Soros: I think it will be a very different relationship. I think that Bush and
Putin like to engage in geopolitical give-and-take. They love each other, actually.

DESAI: From that perspective, do you think we will be in a different environment?

SOROS: Very different. I think we will be back to geopolitics.

DESAI: Does that worry you?

SOROS: I do not worry excessively because I do not think Russia can present a geopolitical threat for *many* years to come. It can, however, create some problems.

NOTES

1. Formally the European Recovery Program, the Marshall Plan was advanced by U.S. Secretary of State George C. Marshall and sponsored by the United States in 1947 to rehabilitate the economies of seventeen Western and Southern European countries (1948–1951).

2. The Malta Conference (December 2–3, 1989) was the first meeting between George Bush (Sr.) and Mikhail Gorbachev to take place after Bush's inauguration.

3. John Maynard Keynes, perhaps the greatest economist of all times, provided a coherent model in his *General Theory of Employment, Interest, and Money,* arguing for an active role for government intervention during economic downturns.

4. Nikolai Ryzhkov served as Gorbachev's prime minister from 1985 to 1990.

5. Wassily Leontief (1906–1999), Russian-born economist and the "father" of input-output analysis, was awarded the Nobel prize in economics in 1973. He taught at Harvard University (1931–1975) and then at New York University until his death.

6. Gorbachev's "new thinking" signaled the abandonment of Marxism-Leninism and military intervention as the guiding principles in foreign policy and the ascendancy of shared moral and ethical concerns.

7. George Soros, "Can the Soviet Economy Be Saved? Not Without U.S. Aid," Op-Ed, *Wall Street Journal,* 7 December 1989.

8. A pure currency board is a strict monetary arrangement in which currency emission depends exclusively on the economy's foreign exchange earnings. By contrast, a central bank has discretionary powers to vary the money supply, depending on the level of economic activity.

9. George Soros, "A G7–Backed $50bn Currency Board Is the Only Way for Russia to End Its Crisis," Letters to the Editor, *Financial Times,* 13 August 1998.

10. Rudiger Dornbusch and Stanley Fischer, *Macro-Economics* (New York: McGraw-Hill, 1989).

11. With businesses in twenty-seven countries, AES is one of the world's leading power companies.

12. Svyazinvest is Russia's biggest telecommunications holding company, in which Soros and other foreign investors have acquired a 25 percent stake.

PART III

Five Policy Perspectives

CHAPTER II

Sergei Dubinin

Monopoly Sector Reform in Progress

MAY 2000

The problem with the budget was lagging tax collections rather than cuts in expenditures.

The joint decision of the government and the Central Bank was that we must continue our anti-inflation monetary policy and move forward on budgetary policy and structural reform, but every year we saw that progress in the latter sphere was missing. The gap grew wider and wider.

It is possible to play against the market, but it is impossible to play against an entire population.

[T]here were a number of mistakes. For example, the government attempted to handle the tax situation by trying to push the tax code, a massive document, in the Duma. It required a lot of time—months—to get it approved. We needed changes in the tax system and the appropriate legislation in perhaps two months. The government worked on the tax code rather than on the concrete problems of taxation.

The problem is how to define what is good for Gazprom.

JUNE 2003

Whatever our evolving arrangements, they are going to be identical for both Russian and foreign investors. There will be no special privileges for the latter. That is the difference between Russia and China.

OCTOBER 2004

[S]tate power should be consolidated not only "vertically" but also "horizontally." We need independent courts and democratically elected municipal and regional administrations with adequate powers and responsibilities.

Similar centralized arrangements led to the crisis and breakup of the Soviet Union twenty years ago.

We need to diversify production and revenue sources by improving the investment climate. From that perspective, the prolonged episode of the Yukos litigation has caused tangible harm to the economy by creating massive uncertainties in investment decision making.

MARCH 2005

The investment climate must now improve.

State activism is a Russian tradition.

We have experienced momentous changes. We have become a free people.

MAY 2000

DESAI: In view of the unsustainable budgetary situation, do you think that inflation control in Russia was attempted too rapidly from 1995 on via a prolonged real appreciation of the ruble? Could it have been done more slowly?

DUBININ: Looking back, I think that we moved too quickly in that direction. It was, however, a broad program that the Russian government adopted in consultation with the IMF. Budgetary measures were coordinated with structural changes and institutional reforms in order to create a more favorable investment climate in Russia. However, money supply, inflation control, and the exchange rate policy were better managed than structural and institutional reforms. We did not create a solid base for economic growth, tax collection, or budget management. The gap between the two directions—anti-inflation policy based on monetary control and exchange rate policy—and the broader microeconomic and structural reforms widened over time. The problem with the budget was lagging tax collections rather than cuts in expenditures. The ministry of finance cut budget outlays dramatically, but tax collection continued to be the main problem. After the 1996 presidential elections, the political risks diminished, but we failed to put measures in place to guarantee genuine economic stabilization and growth for the country. In that situation, the Central Bank had the daily problem of managing the money supply. Furthermore, the joint decision of the government and the Central Bank was that we must continue our anti-inflation monetary policy and move forward on budgetary policy and structural reform. But every year we saw that progress in the latter sphere was missing. The gap grew wider and wider.

DESAI: The next question relates to what you have already said, namely, the decision to allow foreigners to buy Russian government GKOs [treasury bonds] contributed to the already shaky budgetary management.[1] In my view, it was not a sensible decision because it opened the door for speculative inflow of capital into Russia.

DUBININ: That really became a risky decision, but our government insisted on it.

DESAI: Meaning against it or for it?

DUBININ: For it. Yes, that was not a decision made by the Central Bank, but one made by the government. They insisted that we open the market for foreign cash. Perhaps it was essentially a political decision on the eve of the 1996 presidential elections: The government needed cash for making budget payments in the social sphere.

DESAI: The Central Bank and the Treasury do not always agree on policy decisions, do they?

DUBININ: Oh, most certainly not, as in many countries. In the Russian situation, the board of directors of the Central Bank of Russia backed the government, and I personally supported the idea. We thought it was not a big risk, but it turned out to be a mistake.

DESAI: Let us turn to the collapse of the ruble in August 1998. A Russian newspaper suggested that, as you watched the long lines of people trying to exchange rubles for dollars, you felt that the situation was hopeless.

DUBININ: That was probably an anecdote. In reality, I faced a situation in which everybody wanted to buy dollars and nobody wanted to hold on to rubles. The situation in the early evening of Friday, August 15, was critical. It is possible to play against the market, but it is impossible to play against an entire population. But we got there because, between the 1996 presidential elections and the summer of 1998, the government was unable to boost tax collection. They made real efforts to raise taxes, but even the special commission under Anatoly Chubais failed to get genuine results. The ruble was under pressure in the autumn of 1997. At that time, we in the Central Bank thought we might consider devaluing the currency, but then we considered the possibility that it might collapse. As the crisis intensified, it was impossible to undertake a soft devaluation of the ruble.

DESAI: I agree with you completely.

DUBININ: Later, in January 1998, the Central Bank decided to widen the ruble's band, but the market panic worsened, so we stopped the soft devaluation. This was the peak of the crisis, and as it escalated, we wondered whether we had the resources to stop the currency's decline. We informed the government, the presidential administration, and President Yeltsin personally that the situation was critical, but the president decided to change the government. Perhaps he made that decision on the basis of the information we gave him. He removed Viktor Chernomyrdin in March. Even today, I think the decision to remove him was a mistake. I liked Sergei Kiriyenko [the new prime minister] very much, but that was no time to be changing the government and wasting several months in forming a new one. It was necessary to take real measures. Instead, a lot of time was wasted.

DESAI: Yes, but the IMF was not coming up with substantial and timely help, so there was no chance to save the ruble, right? The final question here is, when you look back at the time when you were in charge of the Central Bank of Russia, is there anything that you think you would like to have done differently?

DUBININ: That's a good question for someone in a similar situation. I think perhaps sometime in 1997 the Central Bank authorities should have been able to explain to people the critical nature of the situation—the interdependence between budget deficit control and exchange rate management. We certainly cooperated with the government without creating political problems for it. It was a professional cooperation, and the Central Bank has no public role in this sphere. For example, I did not publicly state in 1996 that the situation was becoming somewhat critical. Certainly before the presidential election, it would have been unwise to participate in political games. However, after the elections, I think I ought to have talked openly to the public about the problem.

DESAI: I think what you have in mind in this regard is a role for the chair of the Russian Central Bank similar to that of Federal Reserve chairman Alan Greenspan. He testifies before Senate committees and even gives public speeches, telling the American people and American businesses his view of the U.S. economy. That sends signals to the public, doesn't it? You, however, didn't have that opportunity.

DUBININ: That was a real challenge—how to steer a critical situation—but in Russia the political context was certainly different. We had a strong left wing in the State Duma, for example. Social groups could use open declarations about the dangerous economic situation to politically pressure the government to change its policy, and that was certainly not the Central Bank's aim. Instead, we informed select professional groups about the unfolding situation. For example, in late December 1996, there was a big conference in which Oleg Vyugin, the deputy finance minister, gave an analysis of the situation, arguing that we had about a year and a half to control the budget deficit and improve tax collection. After that, we would not be able to meet our obligations and pay off the government debt. Several participants and journalists asked me whether that was true. I told them it was absolutely correct. The newspapers wrote a piece on it and then went about discussing other issues. Even Vladimir Potanin, first deputy prime minister in the government, asked me during this conference whether that was accurate, and I told him that we had a year to bring the situation under control. Nevertheless, there were no changes and no results. Prime Minister Chernomyrdin removed Potanin and brought in Chubais in 1997 to help him improve tax collection, but the results did not fulfill our expectations. There were a number of mistakes. For example, the government attempted to handle the tax situation by trying to push the tax code, a massive document, in the Duma. It required a lot of time—months—to get it approved. We needed changes in the tax system and the appropriate legislation in perhaps two months. The government worked on the tax code rather than on the concrete problems of taxation.

DESAI: What do you have in mind when you say "concrete" problems? Do you mean tax rates, tax collection methods, or some practical problems?

DUBININ: Yes, practical problems and tax rates, certainly.

DESAI: But not the whole tax code. That was time consuming.

DUBININ: Right. Since it was a huge document, it was not possible to adopt it quickly.

DESAI: I think you are making two points with regard to budgetary management. There should be greater transparency via open dialogue with the public about the real situation, and government policy makers should focus on the right priorities. Let us now turn to the IMF, which some analysts and policy makers in the United States continue to view negatively. Congress, swayed by the Republicans, is set on limiting its role. How do you assess it based on your experience?

DUBININ: I cooperated with colleagues from the IMF for a long time, and I esteem their expertise and advice. However, they experienced numerous problems of a similar kind in different countries, and they used standard models to resolve them. Often they could not figure out the actual situation in a country. Perhaps that was inevitable. As a result, their decision was based on simple rules. When the IMF favored a country, it wanted to do more for it than was possible. When it disliked a country, less was done.

DESAI: Do you think the IMF liked Russia?

DUBININ: The top-level IMF command team liked Russia. That was helpful, but it applied the same model in Russia as in other countries. For example, it insisted that we open up the market to foreign capital. When we decided to do so, it said the opening ought to be full and free, without restrictions.

DESAI: Exactly. That's my point. When I talk with some of the IMF policy makers, I wonder why they didn't allow a few temporary restrictions.

DUBININ: At the same time, in their assessment of the IMF, the U.S. Congress and the administration were influenced by political and even personal considerations. For example, it was absolutely clear to everybody that there was tension between the Fund and the U.S. Treasury. At the same time, the Treasury had a concrete role in negotiating a program for Russia. It insisted that our anti-inflation program, tax collection effort, and bankruptcy implementation be more severe. It blamed the Fund for being too soft on Russia.

DESAI: I am hoping to interview Camdessus, also. Now that he has left the IMF, he should be able to talk frankly about the situation. The $4.8 billion funding that Russia received from the IMF in July 1998 was debated in the United States. Now, I want you to say, "I don't think it was inappropriately used by the Central Bank of Russia. It was used in a way any central bank would use it in a similar situation." That's my view of the decision. What's yours?

DUBININ: This money was used in an appropriate manner. In this context, we have the Russian press and our prosecutor general's office as watchdogs. We also have a system of regulations in place with regard to the disposal of such IMF funding. Currently, nobody in Russia thinks that the funds were used inappropriately. At the same time, it is not pleasant for me to continue answering these questions, but it was an inevitable consequence of the political situation after the August crisis. Some politicians of the Left blamed the government, calling the Yeltsin presidency a criminal regime. The prosecutor general's office claimed that it noted signs of criminal activity in the Central Bank's operations. It was all a political game. However, it did not find evidence of rule breaking or criminal activity in the Central Bank's operations during my tenure. On the contrary, it found details of the real use of the funds by the Central Bank. The bank transferred $1 billion of the $4.8 billion to the government, which used it for its budget outlays. The remaining $3.8 billion became part of the Central Bank's reserves, along with its gold and foreign exchange reserves. During the crisis weeks, these reserves, which we used for supporting the ruble, decreased dramatically, but the Central Bank did not move the funds outside the country. However, the IMF funding was not sufficient to prevent the crisis.

DESAI: Let us turn to FIMACO.[2] Did it misuse IMF funding?

DUBININ: FIMACO was also investigated by the auditors of the Central Bank, the prosecutor general's office, and other regulatory agencies. They did not uncover evidence of criminal activity on FIMACO's part. There was no evidence that the Central Bank or anyone used FIMACO for money-laundering activity or as a political front. Marshall Goldman wrote in one of his articles that FIMACO was a front for the 1996 presidential campaign.

DESAI: My understanding of the FIMACO episode is that the Russian Central Bank transferred some cash, perhaps $1.6 billion of its reserves, to FIMACO's offshore branch, which, of course, any central bank can do if it finds such a transaction profitable. That in itself was not wrong, but two things resulted from the transfer. First, the Central Bank's Moscow reserves appeared smaller as a result. Next, the Central Bank used FIMACO's reserves to buy government securities, which it was not supposed to do as part of its agreement with the IMF.

DUBININ: I can frankly comment on both of these. FIMACO was started toward the end of the Soviet period by Viktor Gerashchenko [former chair of the Russian Central Bank] as a daughter company of the European Bank in Paris, which in turn was a daughter company of the Vneshekonom Bank.[3] At that time, FIMACO was under government control. Subsequently, Vneshekonom Bank transferred all of the Paris Bank shares to the Central Bank of Russia, so FIMACO became a granddaughter of the Russian Central Bank. However, the Central Bank had no mechanism at that time for managing currency reserves, so it asked the European Bank, the Bank in London, and other Russian banks abroad to manage its reserves. FIMACO was operated as a company bound by French laws. It was impossible for the European Bank to directly invest in U.S. government bonds, but it was possible to do so through FIMACO. In my view, there was nothing objectionable in this activity.

Gradually, before my time, when we changed the system of foreign exchange reserve management by directly using our reserves from Moscow to invest in U.S.

government bonds, we reduced the role of the European Bank, FIMACO, and others for the purpose. I developed the system rapidly. Then, when we opened our market to foreign investors, the government asked us to stimulate investments in Russian government bonds by showing their low risk. So we decided to use FIMACO as an investor in the Russian government bond market for about two months, if I remember correctly. Thus, a fraction of FIMACO's reserves was used for investing in the official bond market.

We examined the plan carefully to determine whether it involved a formal breaking of any rules. There were no formal restrictions in our view. It implied that we put some of the reserves in a foreign bank, which we showed as part of our currency reserves, and we used them to invest in government bonds. When our IMF colleagues saw these transactions in the summer of 1996, they said, "We see there are no formal restrictions here, but it's not a good maneuver, so stop it." The government paid the debt and returned the cash, and we stopped investing in the government bond market. There were no dramatic discussions over the issue. The IMF told us it was not a good practice, so we stopped it. There was no high-level drama about the situation at that time.

DESAI: It seems to me that, later on, after the events of August 1998, everything became so politicized that these events were brought out in the open, which did a lot of damage on both sides. The IMF was made out by some to be the U.S. Treasury's whipping boy, the мальчик для бцтья.

DUBININ: Not only the IMF, but the Central Bank of Russia as well.

DESAI: In your case, you felt that you were your government's whipping boy.

DUBININ: Yes, it's part of our political culture.

DESAI: That's very well put. In my opinion, there are very few central banks that are truly independent. Maybe the Federal Reserve, maybe the Bank of England and the former Bundesbank in West Germany. However, I was thinking about the IMF being the whipping boy of the U.S. Treasury and the Western powers.

DUBININ: Yes, I agree, but the problem is that nobody currently has a genuine solution for organizing the global financial system. Neither the IMF nor the U.S. Treasury nor anyone else can suggest how to perfect such a complicated system and reduce the high volatility of the market in a specific segment. It is dangerously unstable for the emerging market economies, so it is a huge problem not only for the reform of the IMF but also for the globalizing world economy.

DESAI: Your remark about the globalizing world economy brings me to my next question. There are some differences between the Central Bank of Russia and the Russian government on the continuation of exchange controls in Russia. So far as I know, the Central Bank has brought back some exchange control measures. Has the IMF voiced opposition to this policy reversal?

DUBININ: As far as I know, the IMF has opposed these measures—strongly. In fact, there was a real possibility under Yevgeny Primakov [who became the prime minister after the August 1998 debt default] and Gerashchenko [the Central Bank chair] of the reappearance of such restrictions and the reversal of the earlier liberal policy. They wanted to close the Russian economy. That was part of their program, although they did not declare it openly. Had Primakov become president of Russia, we would have seen the closing of the Russian economy and the appearance of strict exchange controls.

DESAI: But you wouldn't be in favor of those, is that right?

DUBININ: Absolutely not. During this period, they needed to negotiate such measures with the IMF but decided to avoid direct conflict with the Fund on these issues, so they postponed the decision. However, in one of the government meetings, Gerashchenko openly declared that we needed two things in our economy: the recentralization of the oil and gas sector and the control of the foreign trade and exchange rate systems. That was his real program. You can ask him directly about it.

DESAI: Yes. So that, in your opinion, is the basis of the disagreement between the government and the Central Bank under Gerashchenko.

DUBININ: Yes, that is a strategic difference.

DESAI: Yes, but he seems to be continuing with some of the control measures.

DUBININ: Not very many, but some. Look, a government needs to prevent money laundering, but that is not the same as controlling capital flight. There's a difference. Capital flight arises as a result of a country's poor investment climate. Only genuine economic development can change it, but we do need to investigate and punish criminal activity.

DESAI: This brings me to the next question. Do you think the extent of money laundering by Russian agents is exaggerated in the U.S. press? In my view, Russia's capital flight is largely the result of the policies in place here.

DUBININ: It's only partly the result of policies, but there is some money laundering. I think that this is not the result of the operations of the Kremlin family or a specific individual. That is too politicized a picture. It's part of so-called big business in Russia. A large number of business operators wanted to stash money abroad, and they used the available mechanisms for the purpose. It's as simple as that. For example, a group of businessmen controlled the sources and prices of oil products for a long time. They supplied these products to their own offshore companies at prices lower than the market prices and then charged higher prices to the end users. They pocketed the difference and deposited it in their accounts in foreign banks. And the corruption in our system—for example, of the customs services—contributed to the practice.

DESAI: So the exporters showed lower values to the customs agencies of their export earnings, the so-called underinvoicing of exports.

DUBININ: Yes.

DESAI: To avoid paying taxes on their oil revenue profits. However, they are not breaking any U.S. laws. U.S. policy makers and bank regulators worry about money laundering through drug money or illegal arms sales.

DUBININ: The illegal operators can subsequently use their corresponding accounts in U.S. banks, in which case it becomes a problem for the U.S. banking system.

DESAI: Let us turn to the current economic recovery in Russia. Is it going to continue?

DUBININ: Yes, the devaluation of the ruble has contributed to it, but in Russia we also have a more market-oriented economy with a large number of small and medium-sized companies—some new, others part of the old enterprises. They can produce items for the Russian markets at lower costs, in particular, low labor costs. Before the crisis, the nominal labor cost was high, but, for the most part, workers did not receive their wages. Now even the official wage rate is lower, so the competition and the possibilities for reviving Russian companies in the domestic market have improved significantly.

DESAI: Yes, but what about demand?

DUBININ: This certainly restricts the recovery, but it will continue for some time. The basic problem arises from the limited investments in the economy. Part of the current recovery took place with limited investments. Now is the time for huge investments for the recovery to continue—for investments that can plow domestic savings and the capital that has flown abroad back into the economy. In my view, the problem is more juridical than economic. It consists in implementing bankruptcies, in recovering the capital outflow, and in protecting business property in Russia. We can then have sustained economic recovery.

DESAI: Let's talk about foreign investment, especially in Gazprom. What are the chances?

DUBININ: The scope is limited, perhaps very limited. According to the current law, the foreign shareholder stake in Gazprom is limited to 20 percent. The actual quota is about 5 percent.

DESAI: Is there a strong feeling within the company that foreign investments should be restricted?

Dubinin. We feel that 20 percent foreign participation is a good target for us. This year the Gazprom board of directors supported the idea of the participation of Burckhard Bergmann, the chairman of Rurhgas, as a member, so there's no opposition to foreign presence. However, our government's policy, which Gazprom supports, is to control the participation of foreign capital. There are two issues here. The first is to prevent conflict of interest. Rurhgas buys gas from Gazprom, so it is interested in a lower market price. At the same time, Rurhgas is one of our shareholders, so there is a conflict of interest here. The other issue is that the price of Gazprom shares in the domestic market is so low that you need very little cash to control Gazprom, and the government wants to prevent this situation from happening.

DESAI: There's a lot of discussion on dividing the company into production and distribution units. That should be possible down the road, shouldn't it?

DUBININ: I don't really think it's a productive idea.

DESAI: Why not? From an economic point of view it makes sense, doesn't it?

DUBININ: I don't agree. The only idea underlying the suggestion was to promote the export of gas to European markets from independent Russian producers. They do not want to supply domestic consumers. So from our point of view, the economic argument does not make sense.

DESAI: You are saying that private producers want to use the pipelines for supplying gas to foreigners and earning foreign exchange in the process.

DUBININ: And this will create a serious balance-of-payments problem. The consequences of such a liberalization could be dramatic for the Russian economy.

DESAI: Why?

DUBININ: Gas prices could collapse.

DESAI: Don't you have a serious payment problem for gas supplied to CIS countries and to Russian domestic consumers?

DUBININ: It's a huge problem for one buyer in particular. Ukraine is about $2 billion in debt to Gazprom. Nobody really knows how to resolve this problem.

DESAI: So it's going to remain. How about the domestic consumers, households, for example?

DUBININ: In Russia, the situation is better than with respect to Ukraine and Moldova. The payment record is better. It's a problem even in Russia, but Ukraine and Moldova made no payments for purchases of Gazprom gas the whole of last year.

DESAI: Finally, the big question. Gazprom is identified with Russia and its destiny. In the old days, we used to say, "What's good for General Motors is good for America." So would you say, "What's good for Gazprom is good for Russia"?

DUBININ: I read somewhere that the CEO of General Motors said just the opposite, "What's good for America is good for General Motors," but the journalists changed it and used the quote for their own purposes. Nevertheless, it's a good slogan. The problem is how to define what is good for Gazprom.

JUNE 2003

DESAI: When I interviewed you last, you were the deputy CEO of Gazprom. Now you are the deputy CEO of UES, United Energy Systems, the electric power company. Let us begin the interview update with Russia's entry into the World Trade Organization, the European Union's position on Russian energy prices in that context, and the restructuring of the energy sector. The EU argues that low energy prices give an unfair advantage to Russia's manufacturing sector and that they should therefore be brought up to world levels. How would you respond?

DUBININ: European Union policy makers are concerned about the advantage conferred by low natural gas and power prices to Russian manufacturing, the oil companies, and the metals sector. Natural gas is critical in the first stage of ferrous metals processing. Low gas prices also benefit our power sector, which is the main consumer of natural gas. In my opinion, it is not a problem of pricing but rather of the use of a market or nonmarket mechanism to set these prices. Ultimately, our enormous natural advantages in contrast to those in the European Union will prevail in our oil and natural gas production.

DESAI: You are suggesting that, when the restructuring takes place in the natural gas and power sectors, these prices will come down because they have a natural advantage.

DUBININ: I definitely believe that to be the case. We are gradually moving to market-determined prices of electric power. Natural gas prices, on the other hand, will remain under governmental control and will be administratively determined for several years. I hope that the natural gas sector will move rapidly toward a market orientation.

DESAI: The Duma has adopted legislation for restructuring the power sector. What is the law?

DUBININ: The principal idea is to separate the monopoly part of the system from the competitive, or market-oriented, sector. The former is the transmission of power, and the latter is power production. The law recognized this separation. It also accepted the principle that marginal pricing was possible in power production and set up an administrative, noncommercial organization consisting of three partners: the government, the power company itself, and consumers. It will organize the marketing procedures and rules in the power sector.

DESAI: How will the power-producing units be reorganized?

DUBININ: More than half—60 percent—of power production is in federal power plants, which consist of thermal and hydroelectric stations. These are to be organized in ten wholesale generating units, six thermal and four hydro. Originally the hydro units were to be set up on a territorial basis, one each in Siberia, in the Volga region, in the North Caucasus, and a special one near Moscow. Subsequently the decision was changed: All hydropower units were consolidated into a single unit. The six thermal units are to be structured as interregional companies. They do not completely cover a district or region. The Siberian plants will be included in separate wholesale companies. The same will be the case for the units located in the Ural region and in central and southern Russia.

DESAI: This concerns the restructuring of the power company. Who will own the separate units? Will foreigners be allowed to participate?

DUBININ: Yes, some foreign shareholders are minority participants in United Energy Systems, the present energy company, which will be restructured. Others participate in the regional units. For example, foreigners hold equity in the Kostromsky power-generating unit. There are a few more as well.

DESAI: How far would you let the foreign shares go? Up to 49 percent? Would there be a limit?

DUBININ: There would be no limits in wholesale power-generating units and in independent producers. Foreigners can own them completely.

DESAI: As a fully owned subsidiary of a foreign company?

DUBININ: They will be Russian, but with foreign capital.

DESAI: Let us go back to Russia's admission to the WTO. It is being delayed because foreign financial groups want entry into the Russian banking and insurance business. When I wrote an article in the *Financial Times* on Russian entry into the WTO, arguing for easing up on this issue, I was attacked by financial groups who would have the Russian financial sector fully opened up. Do you feel that Russia's WTO admission will be delayed unless there is full liberalization of the financial sector?

DUBININ: According to a Central Bank decree, foreign investment in Russian banks is limited to 20 percent. In actual practice, their participation is much less, so there is scope for more foreign investment. At the same time, it is possible to operate a fully owned foreign bank in Russia if a foreign investor or group is ready to take the risk. That decision is not limited by any Central Bank regulation, but rather by the risk evaluation of foreign investors. In the insurance business, foreigners can team up with Russian groups, according to prescribed limits. Given the nature of the business, Russian companies, in my opinion, have a slight advantage.

DESAI: In your view, foreign investors should evaluate the risk, size up the opportunity, and step into Russia. Is that right?

DUBININ: My position is absolutely clear. They should evaluate the risk and then participate in any activity.

DESAI: The other day I learned that Russian households pay their utility bills to their suppliers via their banks. Citibank would like to provide that service, but they have found it difficult to make headway because they must team up with the utility suppliers. In that regard, Sberbank, Russia's state-owned savings bank, is at an advantage.[4] It has all the connections.

DUBININ: That's normal. When foreign operators enter a new market, they have to make new connections, learn new ways of doing business, and struggle for market share. People do not roll out the red carpet for Citibank in other countries. It must survive and succeed on its own.

DESAI: So foreign businesses must fight in order to succeed in Russia.

DUBININ: Absolutely.

DESAI: You mentioned that Russia's trade penetration—exports plus imports as a share of GDP—has reached 35–40 percent of GDP. But the pattern, in my opinion, is skewed. The exports consist largely of oil and metals from natural resources; imports, on the other hand, are largely manufactured items. Do you think the trade opening up is unbalanced? Chinese trade liberalization, by contrast, is more diversified.

DUBININ: It doesn't make sense to compare the Russian economy with the Chinese. China is still planned and controlled. It has cheap labor, which is used in manufacturing, giving it a tremendous cost advantage across the board. Wages, which are under government control, are still very low.

DESAI: Your remarks raise the issue of direct foreign investment. The Chinese leadership took a giant leap by inviting foreign investors and giving them favorable treatment. In 2002, direct foreign investment in China was $50 billion. In Russia, by contrast, there is an implicit collusion between the Kremlin, big business, the Russian bureaucracy, and the Left against direct foreign investment. Doesn't that represent a major difference?

DUBININ: On the basis of my considerable experience in the Russian energy sector, I would disagree. When we tried to negotiate a deal with a potential partner in the power sector, the company estimated the returns, and the proposal was turned down. I will not name the company. In all emerging market economies, policy makers regulate foreign investment flows. We in the power sector have our own policies with regard to pricing, and we are not ready to liberalize the arrangements yet and create market conditions of merchant plans.

DESAI: What is a merchant plan?

DUBININ: Investment decisions by foreign participants in most European countries are based on liberal market-pricing policies and the associated risks. Electric power markets in France, Germany, and Italy are fairly liberalized. Foreign companies are ready to invest there but not in Russia.

DESAI: Why not?

DUBININ: Because the risk estimates are too high. They also demand guaranteed long-term contracts. These are difficult [to obtain] in the Russian power sector.

DESAI: How so?

DUBININ: They want guarantees. They want Gazprom to supply natural gas as fuel to a power plant under their consideration for as long as twelve years, in some cases for the life of the plant.

DESAI: You don't think that is feasible.

DUBININ: Such guarantees are difficult to incorporate in contracts via our legislation. But potential foreign partners say to us, "Why doesn't your government give us guarantees for our very nice project?" The fact is they do not want to play by the same rules as Russian investors, who do not get such guarantees. We tell them that we understand the problems that arise as a result of our administered prices, but we are ready to work up estimates based on alternative tariff projections, which will give them better returns. After all, our tariffs are set for gradual liberalization. However, they want our future arrangements implemented right now. Whatever our evolving arrangements, they are going to be identical for both Russian and foreign investors. There will be no special privileges for the latter. That is the difference between Russia and China. Chinese policy makers are ready to give special advantages to foreign investors. They have not reorganized their gigantic public sector. Moreover, they have not privatized their state-owned enterprises, which are a drain on their economy. At the same time, they subsidize foreign investors via special concessions. Foreigners like these arrangements.

DESAI: Your comments are insightful.

DUBININ: The risks and the transition costs for foreign investors here in Russia are high. The best way to reduce them is to move to a market economy rather than partition our investment sectors for different groups of investors.

DESAI: Do you think that the recent BP-TNK joint deal in the oil sector will serve as a model?[5]

DUBININ: I think so. It was a smart move on the part of the Russian oil company to team up with a foreign partner for the entire production and distribution of oil and oil products. It is a solid example.

DESAI: I believe that TNK proved its case because of its proper governance, its effective cost reduction, and transparent accounting. It signaled that it was an ideal candidate for BP to team up with. These improvements have to become widespread in order for foreign investors to pursue business in Russia, and that will take time.

DUBININ: Yes, these improvements are valued highly and pay off. However, there are exceptions even in the oil sector. Yukos has also improved its management, bookkeeping, and cost efficiency. It has foreign managers and a couple of Americans on its board of directors, but it has so far refused to have a foreign partner.

DESAI: Outside of the oil sector, how can small and medium-sized businesses grow in Russia unless banks multiply, despite the monopoly of Sberbank, which has cornered deposit banking in Russia?

DUBININ: There are no administrative limits on foreign banks operating in Russia. Citibank and Deutsche Bank have banking operations in Moscow, but they have self-imposed limits on their clients' deposits—no less than $5,000—and the interest they pay is low. Foreign banks do not want to operate in Russia or team up with Russian banks. The banking business is risky or too expensive. They are extra careful after the August 1998 default, during which quite a few banks collapsed. However, these are administrative decisions on the part of foreign banks. As far as Russian banking is concerned, it's lopsided. Sberbank holds almost 65 percent of public deposits, and the small and medium-sized banks find it difficult to attract public savings without guaranteed deposits. If the guarantees were legislated, the small banks could attract deposits and even offer higher interest rates to depositors and win them away from Sberbank.

DESAI: That will happen when the law is enacted. You said that a strong ruble is good for Russia. You remind me of U.S. Treasury secretaries from Robert Rubin to Larry Summers to Paul O'Neill, who have argued in favor of a strong dollar. However, Russia is not the United States.

DUBININ: Only a strong ruble can provide momentum to the investment process in Russia, not only from foreigners but also from Russians. These investors do not want to earn high, uncertain, speculative returns. They want to earn the stable incomes that only a strong currency can provide.

DESAI: But the strong ruble also creates problems for the manufacturing sector. You mentioned that the real problem in the Russian economy is the low productivity of its manufacturing. Unless manufacturing productivity improves, the current oil- and metal-based recovery will remain lopsided, and the strong ruble will make Russian manufactured items noncompetitive.

DUBININ: The productivity is low, and without investment flows in manufacturing and services, it will remain so. On the other hand, investors do not move into manufacturing because the returns are low, so we are caught in a vicious circle. It will take time.

DESAI: How firm are the figures coming from the Central Bank of Russia that suggest that there is currently a net inflow of capital? Do the numbers include illegal capital flight? You were once the chairman of the Central Bank. Perhaps we can talk about inflows and outflows qualitatively. Has the capital outflow from Russia diminished?

DUBININ: I cannot give concrete numbers today.

DESAI: But tell us about the method of tracking the numbers, the process.

DUBININ: The method is the same for every country. The numbers are based on estimates of the current and capital accounts. We have noticed a change in the direction in the past two years. Russian capital that moved out in the early years is returning to Russia, improving the capital account in the balance of payments. Often it is not long-term investment but placements in bonds, equities, and real estate, not only in Moscow but also in other places such as St. Petersburg and Samara.

DESAI: So Russian capital is acquiring real estate in the provinces.

DUBININ: Yes.

DESAI: And the capital accounts in the balance of payments reveal a net positive entry, confirming a net capital inflow.

DUBININ: That is the result of the stable ruble.

DESAI: My final question relates to the role of the IMF. The Fund tells countries around the world to "Keep your inflation low, your budget surplus high, and your exchange rate afloat." Yesterday I heard that Anne Krueger, the first deputy managing director of the IMF, is happy with the Central Bank's monetary policy but would like the finance ministry to create a larger budget surplus. Has the IMF finally been marginalized in Russia?

DUBININ: The IMF's role from the start was designed to manage the Russian transition via inflation control and budget management. The cooperation had positive results, but I believe that we need to cooperate with the IMF on a completely different level. The Fund needs to rethink its policy stance in Russia's posttransition phase.

DESAI: In what way?

DUBININ: The people in charge of the Central Bank of Russia and the finance ministry are now well versed in economic policy management—in tracking the economic aggregates and steering them in the right direction. All of this is routine. We need the Fund as a consultant for the next phase of the transition.

DESAI: Give me an example. What is it that you cannot do on your own that the IMF can help you sort out?

DUBININ: Take the leading policy makers in the current administration: finance minister Alexei Kudrin, trade and development minister German Gref, presidential advisor Andrei Illarionov, and several others. Occasionally they have different positions on growth rates, tax burden, budget deficits, monopoly restructuring, energy pricing, and the like. It is important for the IMF to study these varying positions, come up with its own judgments, and in the process reconcile them. This might require a broader role, a wider commitment, and more frequent visits from the IMF. However, in the process, the IMF would cease being a narrow, strict auditor as it was in the old days and become a more effective consultant by examining policy alternatives emanating from the top levels of the government and presidential administration.

DESAI: Let us end on that note. I am grateful to you for finding the time for me in the midst of your busy schedule.

OCTOBER 2004

DESAI: How do you assess President Putin's recent proposals aimed at consolidating presidential powers?

DUBININ: It is absolutely necessary to consolidate the institutions of state power in Russia, and Russians supported this idea in the recent elections. President Putin got a green light from the people in that undertaking. The problem arises with respect to the choice of the methods and the specific solutions for fulfilling the mission.

DESAI: What do you have in mind?

DUBININ: The program of President Putin and the [pro-Kremlin] United Russia party leading up to the Duma elections of December 2003 consisted of not only more state power to fight terrorism but also the creation of a common Russia–European Union undertaking marked by an economic union; a legal, humanitarian, and cultural union implying freedom of information; and finally a joint framework of security provision.

The electorate believed that together these features would strengthen Russia. We want Russia to be a strong democratic state, not a state with an authoritarian rule by bureaucrats. With that in mind, state power should be consolidated not only "vertically" but also "horizontally." We need independent courts and democratically elected municipal and regional administrations with adequate powers and responsibilities.

The president's proposals suggest that he is ready to take on the responsibility of appointing the governors and their future decision making. Boldness is a solid quality of our president. But in my view, these steps represent a faulty orientation.

DESAI: Why do you think so?

DUBININ: Under the proposed arrangements, the resolution of specific decisions, big and small, will take a long time. We will lose flexibility. Regional populations will feel that nothing depends on them. "Everything is decided in Moscow," [they will say]. Nor will central decisions be democratically vetted by regional participation. Similar centralized arrangements led to the crisis and breakup of the Soviet Union twenty years ago. Nor is it clear how they will fight corruption and terrorism.

DESAI: You were once deputy chairman of Gazprom. How do you view the proposed formation of Gazprom and the state oil company Rosneft as a single unit?

DUBININ: I view the formation positively. The state will own a 51 percent stake in the combined unit, but the rest will be opened up for foreign participation. This marks the genuine liberalization of the investment regime for foreign participants. The sale of 7 percent of Lukoil stock to ConocoPhillips, the U.S. company, is also good news because it suggests that attractive opportunities exist in the Russian energy sector for foreign investors.

I would, however, like to add a word of caution here. I am not sure whether these developments will change critical decision making with regard to the use of investment resources in the Russian energy sector.

DESAI: What do you have in mind?

DUBININ: Gazprom and Rosneft have colossal investment resources. They had them in the past, and they have them today. They will possess them in the future, too. The question is whether these will be used effectively according to market rules. More to the point, will the combined unit serve as a model of efficiency for the privatized companies in the energy sector?

DESAI: What kind of a role? Give me some concrete examples.

DUBININ: Will the tax contribution of the unified company in the federal budget increase significantly? Analysts have not touched this issue. The company after all will be headed and run by public sector officials. Will Gazpromrosneft be a model taxpayer? Will it serve as an example to demonstrate how private companies cheat on their tax obligations? Will Gazpromrosneft compete with domestic private companies and thus weaken their plans to work up cartel arrangements? These issues have been ignored.

DESAI: But the federal government's current budgetary status is healthy, isn't it?

DUBININ: Of course, with an oil price exceeding $40 a barrel, we have a surplus budget. However, we need to look beyond that. If the price declines to $25, tax revenues will plummet. If the oil price drops to $10, we will have a budget crisis. Moreover, there is another feature linked with this volatility. If the U.S. Federal Reserve continues lifting the interest rate to, say, 2 percent and above, cash will flow from the Russian oil market to U.S. securities.

Currently, the government is focused in a major way on setting aside part of the budget surplus for future contingencies. The oil-based economic recovery, export earnings, tax revenues, and positive budgetary situation have created a policy myopia.

We need to diversify production and revenue sources by improving the investment climate. From that perspective, the prolonged episode of the Yukos litigation has caused tangible harm to the economy by creating massive uncertainties in investment decision making.

I hope that we will continue openly discussing the economic and political situation in Russia in the future.

MARCH 2005

DESAI: How would you describe the current state of the Russian economy?

DUBININ: Currently, the federal budget is healthy because of strong revenue inflows from the oil companies. These inflows clearly depend on high oil prices in world markets. That can change and damage macroeconomic stability. Consumer spending has picked up, and that can create a steady growth momentum. However, the declining investment is a cause for concern. Right now we have built sufficient capacities in recent years to meet growing consumer demand, but by 2007 and early 2008, as the parliamentary and presidential election campaigns pick up momentum, the shortages could become serious political issues. The investment climate must now improve. We need a stable legal environment and predictable tax claims for that to happen.

DESAI: What measures would you suggest?

DUBININ: The government must regulate the activities of the tax authorities. The formation of a new government in early 2004 led to the entry of a new team in the tax bodies with a fresh mandate. They started collecting taxes with a heavy hand. The prosecution of Yukos represents the tax authorities' excessive zeal for tax collection. Some of them carved out a new career in the process. Yukos is also an extreme example of the government's unpredictability, which in turn has negatively affected investment in the economy. Potential investors are holding back.

DESAI: I read that the finance ministry will introduce a bill that will regulate the tax authorities' powers.

DUBININ: I hope the law will soon pass and succeed in regulating the revenue-collecting authorities.

DESAI: Let's move on to the next urgent issue. Do you think the conversion of Soviet-era welfare entitlements into cash payments and public protests over the inadequate compensation will create a serious problem for the government?

DUBININ: Even during Soviet days, the state did not have real money to meet these obligations in full. Over time, the provision of subsidies for housing, utilities, and medical benefits was slowed down. I understand the current government had incomplete information about the coverage of the eligible population and the support it could claim. In any case, it is a complicated situation. How can one work up an ideal payment in lieu of free transportation? Where would the cash come from? Can the government dip into the stabilization fund, which was created out of the budget surpluses, to cover the payments? If it uses the stabilization fund for the payments, it will add to inflationary pressures. If it continues making the payments year after year, it must find the cash. You see, monetization of the real benefits is neither a one-day nor a one-year decision. At the very least, it will imply cutbacks in real benefits. From a wider perspective, it is also a serious problem in the West—the European Union and the United States. Policy makers must fulfill obligations they assumed in the past.

The Russian situation is very complex. The ratio of working men to retirees is declining, and we cannot fix it by attracting immigrants, as the United States successfully manages to do. We have to learn how to accept people from other parts of the world. We have very little experience in this.

DESAI: You mentioned the uncertain investment climate in Russia. Can the government undertake a proactive investment policy?

DUBININ: The government needs to balance its commitments for the monetization of welfare benefits on the one hand and projects for upgrading the country's infrastructure, among them the ports, bridges, roads, and the railroads, on the other. We will also need fresh infusion of funds in power generation and transmission networks. That is an area I am concerned with.

DESAI: How about the claims of the military?

DUBININ: Of course, the military tries its best to get a share of the budget pie, especially in view of the continuing military operation in Chechnya.

DESAI: I hear complaints that the restructuring of the power company, United Energy Systems, of which you are the deputy chairman, has stalled. Is that correct?

DUBININ: The challenge is how to continue the process and keep it on track. It is a complex problem. However, we are trying to resolve it systematically. The transmission system will be retained as a state-owned holding company. It is a natural monopoly all over the world. As for the generating units, we are separating them into thermal and hydro units. Some of these will remain huge, interregional units with enormous capacities. In the next step, we intend to liberalize the wholesale energy market, perhaps at the end of the year. Right now, 5 to 15 percent of the power is supplied via auction. We plan to free it up. We will also steadily privatize the generating units.

DESAI: Do you think you have an excess supply of power right now at current pricing? I mean, too much capacity was built during the Soviet period.

DUBININ: That is not correct. As the economy continues to grow, we will have reached the power consumption levels of 1990, the peak of the Soviet period, sometime in 2007 or 2008. We will then require additional generating capacities and new investment in the power sector.

DESAI: How do you assess the proposed formation of Gazpromrosneft? Will it attract foreign investment?

Dubinin: The answer is "yes." Definitely. But first, the state wants to establish majority control at 51 percent, not only directly in Gazprom but also in the combined unit. Its current share in Gazprom is less than 50 percent. The dual strategy is to increase the state's direct stake in Gazprom to 51 percent by bringing in a few daughter companies under Gazprom's control. It will raise state ownership in Gazpromrosneft as well to 51 percent by combining the state-owned oil company Rosneft with Gazprom.

This is not a bad idea because the formation of the unit with majority state ownership is to be combined with the freeing of trade in Gazprom shares. As you know, currently Gazprom shares are traded in two separate markets. Foreigners can buy American Depository Receipts (ADRs), which are traded in foreign markets. They cannot acquire the lower-priced domestic shares of the company, which only Russian buyers can claim. Of course, foreign traders can corner them via complicated, nontransparent deals with Russian partners. The formation of Gazpromrosneft will also mark the abolition of this "ring fence." This has been officially and publicly announced. It is a decisive step that will attract foreign capital to the combined unit.

Desai: Has a date been announced for the removal of this dual pricing system?

Dubinin: It will be removed after the formation of the new combined unit. Currently, Gazprom ADRs are twice as costly as their domestic Russian counterparts.

Desai: I am hopeful that European and Asian investors will buy Gazpromrosneft shares. However, the question that we discussed in your office last summer is whether this will promote Gazprom's efficiency.

Dubinin: Yes, that's really the main question. It is relevant with respect to the current deal. In fact, it has persisted throughout Gazprom's history. Here is my personal opinion. Gazprom's production efficiency is low because the domestic price of gas is low in Russia. It is based on the exorbitantly low, Soviet-era price of the company's old paper assets. However, when Gazprom invests in a new gas field, the production costs are higher than in the old fields. We need to increase the domestic price of natural gas, which is set at $30 for 1,000 cubic meters. Yesterday I heard an estimate of $60 for 1,000 cubic meters. We hope to eventually raise the domestic price step by step to $60 for 1,000 cubic meters.

Desai: You are suggesting that the price of natural gas for domestic consumption by households and businesses in Russia itself will gradually be raised in the course of the next few years. That will improve the company's efficiency.

Dubinin: Certainly. Another way of managing it would be cost control.

Desai: In Gazprom itself?

Dubinin: In Gazprom itself.

Desai: I would like your reaction to a broad policy issue. I believe Russian policy makers at the highest level face the challenge of designing a balanced relationship between state authority and big business under conditions of weak law enforcement. What is your view?

DUBININ: I agree. This has been a perennial problem in Russia's political and economic history. In that respect, the historical tradition from the days of the tsars has been unfavorable. State activism is a Russian tradition. Throughout Russian history, it has influenced the lives of ordinary citizens. Russian bureaucrats believe that they have the right to control specific economic decisions. On the other hand, Russian entrepreneurs routinely seek state support via budget subsidies or higher import duties. You know that imported cars are prohibitively expensive in Russia. So the question is, how does one change this pattern?

Fifteen years ago, we started the process of building a market economy. Instead, we ended up creating powerful lobbies of big business, linked with top-level policy makers and bureaucrats who began to influence economic policies and political decisions. One of the first steps of the Putin presidency was to sever this link between business and politics by creating an equal distance between the two. That was an excellent idea. However, when the regime encountered a real problem, it failed to depart from the traditional practice. It used the justice system to punish specific people. That is not a positive development. So the search for an appropriate balance between state authority and business lobbies is the critical issue of the current political situation in Russia.

DESAI: You are right. How the state can be prevented from becoming too autocratic and using the legal system, weak as it is, for its selective goals is the main issue.

DUBININ: There is also the related problem of corruption. We really need genuine changes, a "clean hands" policy, as it were, in our political life, in our business practices, and in the way elections are managed in the country. I believe that the reformist groups, the liberal parties, need to make a beginning by giving their own recommendations, their anticorruption blueprints for the election campaign, for example. There is a real danger that Russia can turn nondemocratic.

DESAI: How does President Putin figure in the unfolding situation? He seems to have his finger on the pulse of the Russian people. He worries about his popularity rating. Wouldn't that prevent him from going overboard?

DUBININ: I think so. I cannot answer the question on the basis of direct contact with the president. It is, however, a sensitive issue with him, both the public support and the media reaction. He enjoys this support and obviously likes it.

DESAI: My final question: As a Russian, how do you think Russia has changed in the last fifteen years? Of course, there is a continuing problem between state authority and Russian big business. Nevertheless, hasn't the country changed?

DUBININ: We have experienced momentous changes. We have become a free people—the result of fifteen years of reform. But the work is not over. We need to develop as a democracy. The economy needs to be freed of monopolies. These are the challenges for the policy makers. As for the actual changes, the contrast with the Soviet situation is difficult to comprehend. It is a different civilization.

DESAI: We'll have a few questions from the audience.

QUESTION: My question is related to Gazprom as a traditional natural gas provider to Ukraine and Turkmenistan as a new supplier on the scene. Do you think that, in light of recent political developments in Ukraine, Turkmenistan will deal directly with Ukraine and bypass Gazprom?

DUBININ: I do not have enough information about the details of the agreement between Ukraine and Turkmenistan. Of course, they negotiated directly without Gazprom's participation. Gazprom provides only pipeline services for transporting Turkmeni gas to Ukraine. When the Turkmeni suppliers asked for higher gas prices, the Ukrainian government agreed. As for the supply of Gazprom gas to Ukraine, we are still supplying gas to Ukraine at the old prices.

QUESTION: What progress have you made in synchronizing the Russian power transmission grid with the European UCT grid? Aren't a few former Soviet Union republics still part of the Russian power transmission system?

DUBININ: You are right. All of the former Soviet Union republics, including the current Baltic states, are part of the united energy network of the former Soviet Union. We have just begun the process of synchronizing the former Soviet energy system with the European system, which is different. It is a complicated technical and physical challenge. The European Union supports the idea. It is, however, an enormous headache for the technical and engineering specialists because it cannot be implemented as readily as the political players want.

Of course, we want to prevent the separation of the Baltic transmission system from the Russian grid. It is enormously costly to set up a new system between, say, Lithuania and Poland. There is also the problem of the Kaliningrad enclave, which is part of the Russian Federation but is separated physically from Russian territory. Will Kaliningrad end up in the non-Russian grid? In that case, how can Russia guarantee a power supply to Kaliningrad?

QUESTION: If the Russian and European grids are integrated, how much power can Russia supply to Europe?

DUBININ: We can export Russian electricity only to Finland and the Baltic countries. It will depend on which countries need additional power. For example, Poland has an excess power-generating capacity. There has to be a solid economic basis for such a transaction, and that can happen if it is mutually profitable.

QUESTION: This has been an interesting talk. Democratization as a historical process emerges from below as a result of the formation of new social groups and politically active parties. The Communist Party has been a dominant party in Russia. How can a significant middle class, an active civil society, and a free media develop in Russia? That is the only way in which democracy can emerge from the bottom up. Wouldn't you agree?

DUBININ: Of course. You will be surprised to learn that our social scientists are discovering an active educated, urban middle class in Russia in response to their questionnaires. Perhaps they are the Russian elite, most of them in financial services, not only in Moscow, although the Moscow region has more than 10 percent of Russia's population. At the same time, political groups have participated in Russian parliamentary elections. In the December 2003 Duma elections, the pro-Kremlin Unity group received 37 percent, the Communist Party 12 percent, and the nationalists from the "Motherland" group 9 percent of the electoral vote. These groups represent different strands of Russian society.

NOTES

1. GKOs are the bills and bonds of the Russian government.

2. FIMACO was registered as an offshore branch of the Central Bank of Russia (via Eurobank, another branch of the Russian Central Bank) on November 27, 1990, on Jersey Island (across the English channel) during the tenure of Viktor Gerashchenko as chair of the Central Bank.

3. Vneshekonom Bank is the Soviet-era foreign bank that handles the country's foreign financial transactions.

4. Sberbank , the Soviet-era savings bank, with 65 percent of public deposits, is owned by the Central Bank of Russia.

5. BP-TNK, Russia's third largest oil company, was established in September 2003 as a result of the merger of two Russian companies, TNK (Tyumen Oil Company) and SIDANCO, with the majority of BP's Russian oil assets. The company is 50 percent owned by British Petroleum and 50 percent by a group of prominent Russian investors, among them Alfa Group and Access Industries.

CHAPTER 12

Monetary Policy in Action

To some extent, yes [there is a conflict between controlling inflation and maintaining growth]. However, inflation expectations are positive. Public expectation is for inflation to steadily come down. People expect it to be lower in the foreseeable future.

Shopping malls are spreading everywhere. They're becoming infectious.

Because the budget is a political vehicle. It is the subject of many battles. We see the entire political process of Russia played out in the federal budget.

Politically, the situation is totally under presidential control.

We need laws to initiate real changes in the banking sector. . . . We want to raise transparency in the banking sector, identify the genuine owners of the banks, and remove fake capital from their balance sheets. . . . We try our best to make Russian banking business transparent, healthy, and honest.

Yes, we are independent. We have only one requirement. We must report to Parliament once a year. As far as the government is concerned, the Duma can pass a no-confidence motion. With us, it requires that we report to it once a year.

JUNE 2003

DESAI: Let's begin with the functions of the Russian Central Bank.

VYUGIN: The Central Bank performs three functions. It manages monetary policy, supervises and regulates banks in the country, and settles claims arising from banking-sector transactions. It gets involved in clearing these claims because we still do not have a RTGS clearing system.

DESAI: You mean through electronic transactions?

VYUGIN: We have electronic clearance, but we do not have an online system.

DESAI: What does that involve?

VYUGIN: With a RTGS system, banks can clear payments in real time. That is still impossible in Russia. They have to wait for a day or more.

DESAI: If the Central Bank extends a loan to a commercial bank, it takes that much time to clear the transaction?

VYUGIN: No, our settlements with the commercial banks are perfect. We can transact them quickly. I mean settlements among banking-sector clients that have to go through the Central Bank.

DESAI: Let's talk about the management of monetary policy.

VYUGIN: Monetary policy is completely different.

DESAI: Your monetary management consists in tracking the growth rate of money supply, doesn't it?

VYUGIN: We have a monetary policy committee and a Board of Directors similar to the U.S. Federal Open Markets Committee, which is responsible for all of the decisions concerning monetary targets, reserve ratios of the commercial banks, interest rate changes, and open market operations. We also have a separate exchange rate department in the bank that tracks and manages the movement of the ruble.

DESAI: Is it correct to say that the board targets the growth rate of the money supply and lets the exchange rate take its value?

VYUGIN: Right now we are not in a position to target the monetary aggregate. We have an overall monetary program, but we do not let it freely determine the exchange rate because that is not a market-determined rate. We are continuing the policy of a managed exchange rate.

DESAI: As in the old days.

VYUGIN: Yes. The reasons are clear. The ruble has been appreciating, and we cannot let it appreciate excessively because many households in Russia have dollar savings. If the ruble becomes too strong, their dollars are worth less in rubles. Politically and even morally, we cannot let the ruble appreciate by, say, 20 percent over a year because the public will say, "What have you done to our savings?" We have to give households time to adjust to our policy. It is better to switch the rules by having a dialogue with the people. You have to give them time. For that reason, the nominal appreciation of the ruble is small.

Our monetary policy choices are complicated. The Central Bank accumulates foreign exchange reserves and prints currency in the process. The accumulation of reserves is not negative, but printing currency is a negative outcome. Again, the Central Bank is not totally free in regulating currency emission. Everyone in Russia has a right to freely sell dollars and buy rubles and vice versa. The decision belongs to households and businesses. A company sells dollars in order to get the rubles it needs. This means there is a demand for rubles. Currently, many businesses and individuals have tight budgets because the ruble is strong. They get fewer rubles for their dollars. If the ruble were lower in relation to the dollar, the Central Bank would have an easier time controlling currency emission. We would be in a better position to manage the money supply absolutely and control inflation at a level we would like. Our policy is an accommodative one. The Central Bank watches the demand for rubles and adjusts the supply accordingly. Our inflation rate is declining, but our inflation target is not ambitious. The Central Bank and the government together have set the 2003–2004 annual targets at 8–10 percent. Actually, that is quite high, but it is the best we can manage. Nor can we let the ruble float freely.

DESAI: Like the U.S. dollar?

VYUGIN: Exactly. But we are getting there.

DESAI: How is the current policy management different from the one in place before 1998? Beginning in 1993, the managed float of the ruble was tilted in the direction of its appreciation. The ruble is currently appreciating in real terms, as in the old days. How is the policy management different? Less difficult?

VYUGIN: To some extent, yes. We are able to better manipulate interest rates to control the money supply. We know that, in view of the appreciation of the ruble, short-term capital is moving in Russia. In early 2003, we decided to lower interest rates to the levels of comparable dollar assets. As a result, hot money inflows are restricted. We are at least able to regulate the money supply growth that way.

DESAI: What is the short-term nominal interest rate right now?

VYUGIN: Between 0.5 and 1.5 percent.

DESAI: Is that so? Medium- and long-term interest rates?

VYUGIN: Medium- and long-term interest rates are, of course, measured as yields on state bonds, depending on their maturity. They are 7 to 8 percent on ten-year bonds and about 4 percent on one-year bonds.

DESAI: I think interest rates have come down dramatically from the old days. Nevertheless, the money supply growth rate resulting from the accumulation of foreign exchange reserves and the pressure on the inflation rate creates a conflict between controlling inflation and maintaining growth. Is Russia in that situation currently, especially when it really needs to grow substantially?

VYUGIN: To some extent, yes. However, inflation expectations are positive. Public expectation is for inflation to steadily come down. People expect it to be lower in the foreseeable future.

DESAI: Why is the expectation positive? Is it because people expect the economy to be productive and to grow from month to month?

VYUGIN: Productivity is definitely growing. Investments in the economy are picking up, too. Investments went up by 12 percent in the first half of 2003, up from a substantial fall in the period following the crisis of August 1998. Output growth in the first half of 2003 was close to an annual 7 percent. Inflation is at less than 1 percent per month.

DESAI: Are investment and output growths becoming widespread or restricted to the energy sector? Are they spreading in manufacturing?

VYUGIN: Investment is growing in all sectors, but, of course, the highest growth is in oil and energy in general. It is also growing rapidly in trading.

DESAI: In retail trading?

VYUGIN: Yes. Domestic trading. It is new investment. Department stores are creating more stores down the chain. Look around Moscow. Shopping malls are spreading everywhere. They're becoming infectious. Russians love to shop in these malls in and around Moscow.

DESAI: But people say this is concentrated in Moscow.

VYUGIN: Not quite. IKEA, the Swedish furniture conglomerate, and Metro, another German outlet, are building department stores in major Russian cities. Fresh investment is also spreading in processed food. Construction materials and chemicals are advancing, too. This is less so in light manufacturing and machine building.

DESAI: The Russian processed food and dairy unit, Wimm-Bill-Dann, is much in the news.[1] Danone, the French company, seems to be interested in buying it.[2] Why wouldn't an oil company oligarch acquire it? Do you think Russian oil businesses do not want to step into manufacturing, especially in consumer goods or processed food?

VYUGIN: Russian oil companies would like to be international oil giants similar to Exxon Mobil, BP, or Shell. Their strategy is similar to that of the global oil companies. They aim at increasing their own capitalization by expanding their oil business. They might sell their businesses, pocket billions of dollars, and venture into new activities later, but right now they want to boost their capitalization. With this strategy in mind, they will continue expanding their oil ventures. But look, BP has few investments outside of oil. It is the same story in Russia. As for Wimm-Bill-Dann, they are pursuing a similar trajectory of building their capitalization, selling the company at an opportune moment, pocketing the cash, and moving into another activity.

DESAI: Let me turn to other issues. How do you coordinate policymaking with the finance ministry? I think a large budget surplus, given everything else, will keep inflation and real exchange rate appreciation lower.

VYUGIN: Of course, accumulation of financial reserves as part of government revenues is positive for inflation control. We have good relations with the finance ministry. We meet regularly with the finance minister and his deputy. Problems arise because the finance ministry's policymaking tends to be unpredictable.

DESAI: Why is it unpredictable?

VYUGIN: Because the budget is a political vehicle. It is the subject of many battles. We see the entire political process of Russia played out in the federal budget. Of course, the finance minister is committed to keeping the actual expenditures within the projections. However, look at the current situation. There are pressures to raise the current allocations, and the final outlays will be higher than those actually approved.

DESAI: This is because of the upcoming Duma elections of December 2003?

VYUGIN: Yes, mostly because of the elections.

DESAI: What kind of expenditures?

VYUGIN: To increase the wages of state-sector employees by transferring additional funds to the regions for the purpose. As of October 1, 2003, the wages of all employees in the budget sector will go up by 33 percent. Local budgets cannot finance these extra charges that suddenly appeared. The finance ministry has to be ready to find the cash and transfer it to them. They must cover all of the wages in full or else face a negative vote from state employees in the December elections. This is an additional charge in the budget.

DESAI: What about pension payments?

VYUGIN: Pension payments are separate. The pension fund is in good health because it has managed to collect funding since the August crisis.

DESAI: With regard to the interaction between the Central Bank and the ministry, can the Central Bank tell the finance ministry that it must trim budgetary entitlements to the public, such as subsidies on utilities?

VYUGIN: No, that's government policy. We cannot intervene. Of course, we discuss and debate these issues in broad terms and express our opinion in favor of a healthy budget, which is a key to investor confidence.

DESAI: Can the Central Bank chairman, for example, make a broad policy judgment or statement like the U.S. Federal Reserve chairman, who is on record saying that rising U.S. federal budget deficits drain liquidity from the private sector, push up interest rates, and in the process damage the task of the U.S. central bank for reviving the U.S. economy? Such policy pronouncements are common in the United States but are probably absent in Russia.

VYUGIN: The chairman of the Central Bank of Russia does not like to make pronouncements that appear to be policy interventions or possible changes. He rarely does so.

DESAI: Does the finance ministry have to be brought in on the decision making?

VYUGIN: No, we have a representative from the finance ministry on the board of the Central Bank. The finance minister as that member can participate in some of these decisions.

DESAI: What about the IMF? Is the IMF active at all in Russia, or is it on the sidelines?

VYUGIN: At present we have no programs with the IMF. A Fund mission visits Russia once a year and monitors the economy's performance, pays special attention to policy changes, and prepares a report based on extensive discussions with officials at this end. The report is published as an IMF document and is available on the Internet. It is a pronouncement by Fund experts on the state of the Russian economy. We also have a separate program representing a new IMF approach to analyzing the effectiveness of financial institutions and markets. The Fund issues a separate report on that aspect.

DESAI: Has Russia been successfully paying off IMF credits?

VYUGIN: Yes, we have. We have only $6 billion left to pay back.

DESAI: I saw a news item reporting that the IMF would like the Russian finance ministry to create a larger budget surplus.

VYUGIN: Yes. The IMF first deputy managing director, Ms. Anne Krueger, recently met with us at the Central Bank and with officials of the finance ministry. She noted that the Central Bank's policies were well established but that the ministry of finance was well advised to maintain a tight control over its budgetary policy and not let it slide. That is my view, also, because a sound budgetary policy inspires confidence in the economy. Nevertheless, opinions differ inside the finance ministry. Some think that the tax burden should be reduced further so that economic growth can take off as in the United States. This may reduce the budget surplus and even push the budget into a deficit if expenditures cannot be cut back.

Desai. So you have supply side economists in the finance ministry as in the United States.

Vyugin. The Russian economy is vastly different from that of the United States, which, in my view, is very flexible in its response to policy signals.

DESAI: You also need strong institutional underpinning for the supply side stimulus to work. I am doubtful whether it works even in the United States.

VYUGIN: Yes, perhaps. One might want to check to what extent. In any case, the United States has a robust economy.

DESAI: An important issue I am interested in is monopoly restructuring. If electric power, natural gas, and railroad charges were raised for households and industry, inflation would go up, wouldn't it? Does the bank have a position on this issue?

VYUGIN: Of course. The government is aware of the Central Bank's position on this issue. This is a complicated process involving a center-regional demarcation of regulatory authority and parliamentary legislation. Utility charges on water and natural gas and rents on apartments are under regional control. The federal authorities set electricity and railroad rates. Of late we have been noticing that most of these charges have increased substantially. Of course, the regional bosses, including the governors, have to be careful about pushing up the rates indiscriminately because social unrest and a political backlash may result. However, central control is ineffective, with the result that most of these rates have gone up without matching improvements in the provision of the services.

DESAI: Why do governors and local authorities undertake the hikes? Are they desperate for revenues?

VYUGIN: Yes, they try to cover losses in their budgets. Local sources of revenue are limited, so they are under pressure to increase these charges. Actually, we need to reform—in fact, completely overhaul—the center-regional arrangements in this regard.

DESAI: What kind of reform?

VYUGIN: We need to create competition in the provision of all services and utilities by bringing in private providers as in many countries. The choices are unlimited, but no one in Russia is ready to take the initiative. It is a massive restructuring job, of which changing the tariff schedules is but one aspect. A restructuring plan for the electric power company, United Energy Systems, was finally approved by the Duma last spring. That was a landmark decision. It took full three years for the measure to be completed.

DESAI: The law has been passed.

VYUGIN: Yes, but the government has not acted on the legislative mandate, and that's a disappointment. On the other hand, the railroad monopoly is not so crucial with regard to competitive restructuring. The railroad system is completely owned and managed by the state. Recently, however, a state commercial company, altogether separate from the ministry of railways, was set up to operate and regulate the entire system. This company will be privatized in due course. That blueprint has almost been completed. We have to watch and see how fast the government will proceed with that decision. The government is slow. And then we have the oligarchs to deal with. Fortunately, the situation has changed in that regard. Today they are not in a position to dictate as before. They have to make requests. They may also buy political power. However, there is a difference. And sometimes they succeed in doing so.

DESAI: Give me an example.

VYUGIN: The easiest example is the taxation of oil. It is hardly a tax burden for them. They have tax privileges because oil is a specific business.

DESAI: What kind of privileges?

VYUGIN: Effectively, they pay lower taxes.

DESAI: Less than the rest of the corporate sector?

VYUGIN: Yes. At the same time, the government is not in a position to impose windfall taxes on their profits. I am talking about windfall taxation. They have the same profit tax rate, but they have specific businesses in the natural resource sector that should be taxed additionally via windfall taxation. The government made two attempts without success. Why? Because some oil companies actively worked against the adoption of these bills by the Duma. This is one example. It is possible to find others as well.

DESAI: Does the Central Bank have a position on Russia's joining the World Trade Organization?

VYUGIN: We are involved in the process in a limited way, relating to the activities of foreign banks in Russia and currency regulations currently operating in Russia. As far as foreign banks are concerned, we decided against imposing restrictions on their activities. From our perspective, we would like to encourage competition because two state banks, Sberbank and Vneshekonombank, are still not privatized, and competition from foreign banks will exert the necessary pressure on them.[3] However, foreign banks are not interested in stepping into Russia. Perhaps it is a matter of time. Of course, we do have certain norms for the activities of foreign banks operating in Russia. We would like them to open branches and invest substantially in order for them to provide banking and other financial services. But they prefer to open offices without backing them up with adequate capital.

DESAI: Why wouldn't Citibank, for example, open a branch, a commercial bank branch, in Moscow and other cities?

VYUGIN: As a matter of fact, Citibank would like to capture 10 percent of the Russian retail deposit market, and it has a specific plan for undertaking the project in Russia. Citibank has branches in eighty countries, and they wanted to participate in Russia also. Finally, we managed to get them to open a branch in Moscow. In fact, the branch offers attractive services besides receiving household deposits. They manage accounts and make investments for account holders via their accounts in specific instruments such as company bonds and equity. It is a flexible, profit-oriented institution.

DESAI: I would have imagined that various foreign banks would open branches like that all over Russia, but that is missing. Are there some local obstacles?

VYUGIN: Again it is a problem of overcoming local competition, and these problems can arise from unexpected sources. For example, Citibank would like to clear payments of utility charges on behalf of its depositors. Banks are responsible for ensuring that these bills are paid to utility providers, but they need to sign agreements with the utility companies for undertaking this service. Citibank may be denied access because a utility provider may say, "We do not need you. We already have a bank with which we have a contract." Of course, Citibank may offer a competitive contract to the utility company, but it may still not succeed because the utility providers are not interested in competitive proposals. They are used to the old ways of doing business, and they do not think it is necessary to look at a competitive offer from another bank. The system of payments for utility services was completely a state prerogative, and it is difficult for a newcomer, even with Citibank's versatility and resourcefulness, to break through and make headway. This is but one example. You can find other examples of diehard attitudes at state and local levels. They continue to control and manage numerous economic activities.

DESAI: What about a bank like Alpha Bank, which is Russia's leading commercial bank? Would it like competition from foreign banks?

VYUGIN: I hope it would. The same goes for Sberbank, a savings bank that dates from Soviet times. Alpha Bank is privately owned. Sberbank, believe it or not, is owned by the Central Bank of Russia. The Central Bank favors the adoption of the deposit insurance law, and Sberbank opposes it.

DESAI: The law for guaranteeing deposits?

VYUGIN: Yes.

DESAI: Why does Sberbank oppose this legislation? Does it fear the potential competition? That people will make their deposits in other banks if they are guaranteed by law? What is the government's position concerning the law?

VYUGIN: The government is worried as well because the law will require that adequate resources be put in the deposit insurance fund to guard against massive withdrawals of deposits in an unpredictable crisis. If there is a shortage, it will have to be covered from the federal budget. The government understands the need for guaranteeing public deposits but feels uncomfortable about it.

DESAI: The United States has a properly funded Federal Deposit Insurance Corporation to cover sudden and massive withdrawals of deposits. Public deposits, in other words, are protected by law.

VYUGIN: That is absolutely necessary for promoting confidence in the banking system. The insurance system should be adequately funded. Beyond that, the government has to take the final responsibility written into the law. Otherwise, it is just a vague promise rather than a foolproof guarantee.

DESAI: President Putin recently announced that the ruble should be made fully convertible. What is the current situation in regard to convertibility?

VYUGIN: Our currency regulation laws are complicated. They prohibit cash transfers abroad from being freely undertaken.

DESAI: Cash transfers by businesses.

VYUGIN: Businesses and individuals. They cannot transfer cash and invest it abroad without clearing it with the Central Bank. Such cash may be used for financing education or covering health expenses but not for acquiring an investment instrument. The control regime is not tough or literally imposed, but permission must be applied for, and that will continue.

DESAI: So the ruble is not fully convertible.

VYUGIN: True, but the system is implemented somewhat flexibly. The Central Bank is ready to give the green light in many cases, as long as the applicants refrain from money-laundering activities. However, restrictions will continue.

DESAI: Some Russian banks had licenses to operate in foreign exchange transactions even before the August 1998 financial crisis. Thus, corporations that held ruble deposits in these licensed banks could convert them into foreign exchange and transfer them abroad, couldn't they? I mean, it was always possible in the old days. So this loophole continues, doesn't it?

VYUGIN: Formally, yes, but in order to convert rubles into dollars, businesses and individuals require a contract for such a transfer. Of course, they can buy and sell dollars in the Russian foreign exchange market, but they need a contract to whisk the dollars abroad out of their bank accounts. They have to specify a purpose.

DESAI: They may need to withdraw dollars from their accounts to pay for imports, for example.

VYUGIN: Yes, our control mechanism is somewhat complicated but workable.

DESAI: But it also existed before the crisis?

VYUGIN: Yes, and afterward as well. However, a new set of liberal laws has been passed by the Duma, approved by the upper house, and signed by the president. The controls we have talked about are set to go. The Central Bank may impose restrictions in specific cases. We reserve that right.

DESAI: I read this morning that companies that had earned foreign exchange were required to bring 50 percent back into Russia. That requirement has been brought down to 30 percent.

VYUGIN: Yes, the Central Bank can adjust this requirement to zero if it sees fit. We plan to slash it to zero because it is not necessary. The currency market, based on the supply and demand of foreign exchange, is working, so this restriction is redundant.

DESAI: From the very beginning, Russian citizens have been allowed to convert rubles into dollars in the exchange bureaus and keep the dollars in a bank here or at home—wherever they pleased. Can they acquire assets abroad? Can a Russian household acquire IBM or Microsoft stock?

VYUGIN: The law distinguishes between carrying dollars abroad in cash and converting these dollars into an asset.

DESAI: How does that work?

VYUGIN: Citizens can take $10,000 with them without securing permission. If they want to take out more cash, they need to apply to the Central Bank for permission.

DESAI: But can they buy Microsoft shares?

VYUGIN: That is an investment. Russian citizens can transfer up to $75,000 abroad in order to acquire an asset, but no more than $75,000.

DESAI: So they can purchase a little house in the United States? Or perhaps use it to raise a mortgage for a bigger house?

VYUGIN: Yes, they can.

DESAI: That's progress, isn't it?

VYUGIN: Of course. Our foreign exchange regulatory system is liberalizing step by step. That is the Central Bank's policy. We have made significant changes in the past year and given more opportunities to companies and individuals to invest abroad. Some controls exist, and we would like to remove them.

DESAI: Right now it makes sense to liberalize because the Central Bank is accumulating foreign exchange reserves, and they are pressing on the money supply.

VYUGIN: Yes, the Central Bank's foreign exchange reserves exceed $60 billion. Besides, the federal budget has a surplus.

DESAI: Do you think the situation might suddenly deteriorate?

VYUGIN: No, not suddenly. We have accumulated foreign exchange reserves because capital flows have stabilized. A serious problem may arise if our trade balance deteriorates or turns negative and capital flows out of the country. In that case, the bank's policy response will be clear: Reduce money supply growth because capital is flowing out. The liquidity squeeze will create problems for our banks, but perhaps not as serious as those in 1998. The liquidity squeeze in the banking sector may lead to bankruptcies among small banks, but that may not be so bad. The banking sector will get a shakeout and come out better.

DESAI: But you do not expect such a sudden reversal of fortune?

VYUGIN: I do not foresee an unexpected financial crisis. That could happen as the result of a sudden turnaround in investor confidence, which is unlikely, or it could happen as the result of political instability. However, that is well nigh impossible. Politically, the situation is totally under presidential control.

DESAI: When I track Russia's economic performance in some detail, I do not feel that the economic recovery is sufficiently widespread, for example, in manufacturing and the consumer goods sector. In that context, I do not think of Russia as Saudi Arabia. Russia has always had a huge industrial base, and that should also revive. Second, progress in corporate governance is not widespread enough for it to inspire confidence internally and externally. As a result, the economic performance will be slow.

VYUGIN: Perhaps, but the economy has become open. The share of foreign trade in the GDP is more than 40 percent.

DESAI: Exports and imports combined in relation to the GDP.

VYUGIN: Yes. It has become an open economy in a short period, which means that it depends on foreign demand and has become vulnerable to external influences. It requires that our policy responses be flexible and continuously adjusted to ward off external shocks. The government should create a stabilization fund, and the Central Bank should maintain substantial reserves.

DESAI: What sort of stabilization fund?

VYUGIN: To accumulate substantial budgetary revenues. That is critical with regard to conserving investor confidence in the economy and preventing an impact from external shocks. The only question, then, is the extent to which Russia's private businesses will take advantage of the market economy stability and political consensus. It's a question of the performance of our private businesses.

DESAI: In that context, do you feel hopeful about banking-sector reform under the Central Bank's leadership?

VYUGIN: I am not positive. We need laws to initiate real changes in the banking sector. We talked about the urgent need for deposit insurance legislation, without which the Russian public will not deposit its savings in the banks. We also need laws to launch revisions in banking-sector licensing procedures. We have made changes on the basis of the regulatory authority available to us under current laws. We want to raise transparency in the banking sector, identify the genuine owners of the banks, and remove fake capital from their balance sheets. We published special instructions to combat this problem and found that some of the biggest Russian banks have fake capital. They get around this requirement via innovative schemes. We instruct them to show their genuine capital, to fill the gap if necessary, and in some cases to reveal in their published balance sheets that they have hardly any capital to back their assets. It is a serious problem and occasionally leads to tough fights. We try our best to make the Russian banking business transparent, healthy, and honest.

Desai: Can commercial banking be actively promoted in Russia? Would the Central Bank be in favor of giving special guarantees to foreign banks?

Vyugin: I do not see any grounds for giving special guarantees or concessions to foreign banks. Politically, it would be dangerous. As we discussed, the environment is not conducive to the entry of foreign banks. Commercial banking activity is dominated by Sberbank, which opposes entry into the banking business. This is the reality. We need to resolve this situation internally via new regulations.

Desai: Can Russia's entry into the WTO [World Trade Organization] help?

Vyugin: Psychologically, yes. WTO membership is useful in creating psychological confidence at various levels. Foreign investors know that a WTO member must follow internationally accepted norms and rules. They may not be stringent, but a member country has accepted established codes of conduct in foreign trade, global finance, and the like. It may not produce tangible results right away, but outside investors feel that a WTO member will not suddenly go off a policy track. From that perspective it is useful.

Desai: Unless that happens, I think, Sberbank and Alpha Bank will be the dominant players in commercial banking.

Vyugin: Alpha Bank will cease to be important. Actually, it has less than 2 percent of retail deposits. Sberbank has 65 percent, but their share is declining because of the newcomers in the banking business.

Desai: A few mid-sized Russian banks are coming up in the regions, right?

Vyugin: The problem is that mid-sized banks are undercapitalized. It is difficult to make an accurate assessment on the basis of the information supplied by the banks. We, however, believe that a Russian bank with a capital of less than 50 million euros or dollars will not survive because its margin will be inadequate to cover its fixed costs. With a small capital base, a bank cannot expand its business by lending to numerous companies, make up for the low margins, and earn adequate returns. If the margins were high, it would be less difficult to stay in business despite a small capital base.

Desai: You mean the margin between what the banks pay their depositors and what they earn on their lending?

Vyugin: Yes. In the old days, banks mushroomed with low capital backing. Inflation and domestic interest rates were high. Banks borrowed at low interest rates often from outside and lent at high rates at home. Now the situation is different. We have a monetary policy in place. Inflation is low, and the margins are low as well. Banks must now undertake their business in the context of these new circumstances. Only banks with genuine and substantial capital backing can flourish in this environment.

DESAI: I have a final question. Federal Reserve chairman Alan Greenspan gives congressional testimony, often makes public speeches, and occasionally provides signals about forthcoming monetary policy changes contemplated by the Federal Reserve. The Federal Open Markets Committee is meeting tomorrow, June 25, and the financial market, based on the committee's last assessment of the economy, is expecting a further cut in the short-term interest rate. Can the Central Bank's chairman assume such a public role in Russia?

VYUGIN: No, because our policymaking is not as transparent as it is in the United States. For example, it is difficult for us to publicly explain our decisions if there is a setback in monetary aggregates or the exchange rate of the ruble. We try our best, but our policy is not perfect. We have to let the ruble progressively decline from its high value, and we manage the exchange rate with that end in view. It reacts to market forces, and we frequently intervene. I also explained to you earlier that we cannot target either our monetary aggregates perfectly or the interest rate, for that matter. Our interest rate management is also connected with the policies of the Fed because, if the Fed favors low interest rates, so must we. Otherwise, short-term capital will move into Russia and push up our inflation.

DESAI: I see that your task of monetary and exchange rate management is tricky and that it's still taking shape, so the Central Bank chairman cannot go around making statements that might destabilize the situation.

VYUGIN: We are, of course, obliged to explain our policy. We cannot escape that altogether.

DESAI: How do you do that?

VYUGIN: Through the mass media and in occasional briefings. Sometimes I talk with a representative of Reuters or give a short speech or supply a piece of information to the press, which is then published.

DESAI: But you do not appear before a parliamentary committee.

VYUGIN: Not formally. I do go to Parliament and meet with groups of deputies who may be members of the Duma banking or budget committees. They ask me to talk with them about specific issues. For example, this month I was asked to explain to them our exchange rate policy. What is its purpose? What might it look like in the future? I discussed this with a small group of deputies who are interested in the issue, but it is not publicly disseminated. It is private. These are useful interactions that are kept quiet. They know it and do not raise questions in public.

DESAI: What is the legal position of the Central Bank? Is it independent by law?

VYUGIN: Yes, we are independent. We have only one requirement. We must report to Parliament once a year. As far as the government is concerned, the Duma can pass a no-confidence motion. With us, it requires that we report to it once a year.

DESAI: Who nominates the chair?

VYUGIN: The president nominates the chair, and the Duma must approve the nomination. A National Banking Council, created by law and appointed jointly by the president, the government, and Parliament, is responsible for supervising the expenses of the Central Bank—the cost of our activities, staff, overhead, and investment decisions. In every country, the central bank needs such supervision because it can print currency, some of which it can use for itself. Someone must enforce limits.

DESAI: So are your assets and liabilities monitored by this council?

VYUGIN: No, [they are monitored] by the accounting chamber of the Duma and an audit body appointed by the National Banking Council. The audit body checks the accounts of the Central Bank. The Central Bank cannot appoint its own body to keep its accounts under cover. Public accountability is therefore necessary to prevent possible concealment. This is all normal. However, monetary policy is the total responsibility of the Central Bank. Nobody can intervene or apply political pressure.

DESAI: Do you have a committee similar to the Federal Open Market Committee, which meets, deliberates, and announces the short-term interest rate? What is the arrangement?

VYUGIN: We have a monetary policy committee that makes the necessary policy decisions inside the Central Bank. The Central Bank chairman is the head of the committee. The Central Bank board regularly assesses the committee's activity.

DESAI: Are there regional representatives on that committee?

VYUGIN: No, it is completely internal to the Central Bank.

DESAI: The Central Bank of Russia, therefore, is the critical instrument in setting monetary policy. Thank you very much for finding the time for the interview in the middle of your hectic schedule. I have learned a lot from our conversation.

NOTES

1. Wimm-Bill-Dann is a market leader in dairy and juice products in Russia.

2. The Groupe Danone in France leads in dairy products and bottled water.

3. Sberbank, the Soviet-era savings bank, with 65 percent of public deposits, is owned by the Central Bank of Russia. Vneshekonom Bank is the Soviet-era foreign bank that handles the country's foreign financial transactions.

CHAPTER 13

Boris Jordan

Media Man and Investor

[Anatoly Chubais's] idea of returning the assets to the people was absolutely brilliant.

Russians are only now beginning to understand the meaning of a stock, a bond, equity, and asset ownership. This is a long process. It was unrealistic to think that 145 million vouchers would translate into 145 million shareholders.

I ran it [NTV] as a business. The people in charge before me ran it as a political outfit.

I think [Putin] wants the media to be responsible. I am also in favor of a responsible media, but the process of legislating against a free media is a slippery one. Once you start, there's no end in sight. I believe that the media should be self-regulated. It must find its limits via self-censorship. The European tradition favors media regulation. The American practice leaves it free to regulate itself. I prefer that.

I have a high opinion of Russian journalists. They are good and articulate, but there are occasional problems with TV and print journalists: They can be bought.

Putin wants businessmen to do business and politicians to handle politics.

OCTOBER 2004

The biggest threat to Russia's security is corruption.

Many in the West simply do not understand the scope of the changes that have occurred in this country.

The president's lack of control of the bureaucracy . . . is another reason this president could never become a Stalin, even if he wanted to.

The words "politics" and "businessman" will not take on their genuine English meanings in Russia until corruption is significantly reduced.

The Yeltsin-era freedoms did not bring forth a democratic political system in Russia.

I think Putin's cleverness consists in identifying common interests with potential foreign partners and implementing them selectively.

American policy makers will find him a tough negotiator in the energy field because Russians are capable of thinking long term.

June 2003

DESAI: You grew up in the United States. When and how did you become interested in operating in Russia?

JORDAN: I think I have always had a fascination with Russia because of my strong Russian background. My grandparents from both sides of the family participated in the civil war as White Russians. They emigrated with General Wrangel.[1]

DESAI: Who was he?

JORDAN: General Wrangel was the commander of the southern forces of the White Army.[2] My grandparents emigrated to Yugoslavia, where my parents were born, my father in 1923 and my mother in 1935. They spent time in camps for displaced people in occupied Germany, but on the Slavic rather than the Jewish side. They luckily ended up on the U.S. side of the occupation in these camps and finally received U.S. exit visas. Had they ended up with the British or the Russian side, they would have been sent back to Russia to face a perilous end. They migrated to the United States and settled in New York. From the time I was a boy, I spoke Russian at home and spent Saturdays in a Russian school learning the language and its grammar, as well as Russian history and geography, and participated in the activities of the Russian Orthodox Church. My family spoke only Russian at home. Our strong sense of Russian patriotism was combined with a strong anti-Communist position, one that in retrospect was probably exaggerated. As a graduate student, I specialized in U.S.-Soviet studies.

DESAI: That was at New York University?

JORDAN: Yes, at NYU. McGeorge Bundy was head of the international affairs program in the School of Foreign Services.

DESAI: About what time?

JORDAN: During the years from 1984 to 1988. I wanted to become a diplomat with the U.S. State Department. I was a Reagan Republican—extremely conservative in my youth.

DESAI: Are you still?

JORDAN: I have probably become more liberal as I have gotten older. You know, I practically framed Reagan's "evil empire" speech. I interviewed with the State Department but gradually came to believe that I would not have been sent to Russia.

So I gave up the idea of becoming a diplomat. I did not want to end up in Latin America or Asia. Soon after that, my father, a banker by profession, helped me get my first job, and before long I found myself in Russia.

DESAI: How did you start your banking career?

JORDAN: Around 1989 I started working for Kidder Peabody, an investment bank founded in 1926 by the Gordon family. Perhaps you know that they are benefactors of Harvard. I think Al Gordon is still alive, around one hundred years old. I then worked for an Irish company and traveled quite a bit in Mexico, Brazil, Argentina, and Chile, managing asset financing.

DESAI: How did you end up in Russia?

JORDAN: In 1991, while I was working for an airline leasing firm based in Ireland, I was asked to speak on the North American Free Trade Agreement (NAFTA). Awaiting my turn, I picked up a newspaper and read about the August putsch in Moscow. I decided there and then to go to Moscow, flew to London, and visited many banks, trying to locate one that was interested in Russia. As luck would have it, I was offered a job in the London office of Credit Suisse First Boston [CSFB]. There I and met an extraordinary visionary, a Swiss German in charge of CSFB in Europe. He was the first person to believe in banking prospects in Eastern Europe and Russia. By 1991, he had offices in Prague, Budapest, and Warsaw and was just opening an office in Moscow. In 1930 a Russian émigré was the CEO of CSFB. When the Glass Steagall Act of 1926 required that commercial banking be separated from investment banking, the First National Bank of Boston was split into First Boston and CSFB.

DESAI: So you set up the Moscow office of Credit Suisse First Boston?

JORDAN: Yes.

DESAI: In the early 1990s.

JORDAN: My first visit was in April of 1992. I permanently moved to Moscow on July 1, 1992.

DESAI: Did you help them launch voucher privatization of Russian companies?

JORDAN: Yes. We at CSFB wrote the voucher plan. In 1992, Anatoly Chubais faced a major dilemma. His idea of returning the assets to the people was absolutely brilliant.

However, we did not have the time to organize big sales as was done in Hungary, for example. The Communists were still strong in Russia, unlike in Eastern Europe, where the public swiftly rejected them. In Russia they were still a major threat. The asset base of the country had to be moved out of state ownership into people's hands. You know that Yeltsin's strategy was to break the totalitarian system. The only way to succeed in that goal was to free prices, transfer the assets to the public, release market forces, and then make sure that the process was irreversible. However, the Congress of People's Deputies, dominated by the Communists, was scheduled to meet on December 9, 1992, and was bent on vetoing any privatization. So Chubais approached me in late September with a three month timetable to outwit the Communists via a fast-track privatization program.

A group of us, my partner Steven Jennings and I, began devising a plan. We hired accountants and lawyers. We worked free of charge for the government, promising to ready the program in three months. We worked day and night, literally day and night, sleeping in our offices a few hours a night and working frantically. A young banker sat next to us and recorded everything that happened during those three hectic months. We might even publish a book in the future and give our account of the events. Some day they will prove of interest as history in the making. We launched voucher privatization on December 8, a day before the meeting of the Congress of People's Deputies. What my grandfather could not achieve during the civil war between the White Army and the Communists, we were able to manage by getting the state out of property ownership. The Moscow office of CSFB handled the auctions of the first companies put up for privatization.

DESAI: The purpose of voucher privatization, in my view and you have hinted at it, was political. It was aimed at getting the state out of the ownership and control of productive assets. In fact, Yeltsin's reformers used economic measures, such as privatization, price decontrol, and trade liberalization, to serve the political purpose of retiring the Communist authoritarian bureaucracy. As for the voucher holders, they thought they were about to become instant capitalists.

JORDAN: Russians had not owned property for eighty years. Many voucher holders sold their vouchers for vodka and the like. They did not understand auctions; they did not know the meaning of a company share and what they were going to own. It was total confusion for about six months. However, soon after, people started buying and selling vouchers, and a market was created. I realized that something incredible was happening in Russia. In the first CSFB auction, we put up a big stake in the Bolshevik Biscuit Factory, a prestigious confectionery company. When the auction was completed at the end of three days, I calculated the amount for which 50–60 percent of the company was sold in exchange for the vouchers. Considering the street value of a voucher and the number of vouchers offered, the stake went for $680,000. Several months earlier, a colleague in the Polish privatization office had sold an equivalent stake for $80 million. I then realized the power of what we were accomplishing.

DESAI: In what sense?

JORDAN: In the sense that we were releasing market forces and creating wealth for the people. Foreigners also had access to vouchers. Although the assets were selling cheaply, the risks were high. We started the process in 1992, and today, thirteen years later, Russia has a burgeoning stock market in stocks of companies that are now worth $25 to $30 billion. Some of these companies were being sold back then for a couple of hundred million dollars.

DESAI: How much is the Bolshevik Biscuit Factory worth now?

JORDAN: We sold it to Groupe Danone, I think, for $50 million. People who bought the company's shares gained by several thousand percent. And there were many factory workers who bought shares.

DESAI: Insiders?

JORDAN: Yes, insiders. Employees who bought the company equity made a lot of money.

DESAI: What you are suggesting is that the plan was hastily prepared and put into place, but the results were all right.

JORDAN: We had a time constraint. We had to complete it before December 9. Otherwise, we ran the risk of having the whole process of privatization halted. Russians are only now beginning to understand the meaning of a stock, a bond, equity, and asset ownership. This is a long process. It was unrealistic to think that 145 million vouchers would translate into 145 million shareholders. The United States, with a population of about 300 million, has 8 million shareholders. Voucher privatization, at the very least, gave everyone a chance. Then market forces took over, and things started to consolidate. We have brokers, traders, and investors today. Company shares have been consolidated and valued in separate groups.

DESAI: In the early days, did you have a connection with the Harvard group at all?

JORDAN: Harvard University?

DESAI: The Harvard Institute for International Development.

JORDAN: Yes, I did. Andrei Shleifer and Jonathan Hay worked with me back then when they were writing the laws. Jonathan worked in the ministry, and I used to visit him in his office. I noticed he hardly ever slept or ate. He wrote all the laws for creating a securities market in Russia. The work those people put in and the debt this country owes them are immeasurable.

DESAI: You helped Credit Suisse First Boston acquire the vouchers and invest them in Russian companies. When did your association with the bank end?

JORDAN: April 1995.

DESAI: What happened?

JORDAN: It was obvious to me that Russia was a satellite operation for CSFB, only an office, one office in a network of hundreds of offices. Russia was never going to be a top priority for them. I wanted to start on my own, be my own boss, and build my own business.

DESAI: So then you founded Renaissance Capital?

JORDAN: Yes.

DESAI: That was an investment bank?

JORDAN: It is the biggest investment bank in Russia today.

DESAI: How did you calculate the risks of starting out on your own? It was a huge step.

JORDAN: I felt I was ready for it. By 1995, I had begun to understand the Russian scene and had made several important contacts. I felt I could strike out on my own. Ultimately, my success or failure as an entrepreneur depends totally on me. I like the risk—I like that feeling.

DESAI: Yes, but it involves raising capital and seeking reliable partners.

JORDAN: Four people who worked at First Boston joined me in the new venture. I found an investor who put up $20 million for 20 percent of the business. Together we founded Renaissance Capital.

DESAI: Renaissance is still very active.

JORDAN: Renaissance today is the largest investment bank in Russia. It undertakes strategic investment banking, Russian and international, fund management, and market research, among its activities.

DESAI: Explain something to me. I was reading the other day about Gazprom and its equity, which is divided in two categories, American Depositary Receipts (ADRs) for investment by foreigners on the New York Stock Exchange and the rest for trading in Russia by Renaissance Capital, among others. The two types are not interchangeable. Why this segmentation?

JORDAN: Gazprom's equity structure is unique, the only one of its kind in Russia, but it will be unified soon.

DESAI: Yes, that is what I hear.

JORDAN: It is a deliberately partitioned market. Basically, the Russian government is worried that, by opening Gazprom shares fully to the public, it will lose control of the company. Therefore, they have a two-tier market. The Russian government is set to own 51 percent of the company, so there is no reason for the ring fence to continue. Ultimately, Gazprom will be revalued on the basis of its true market value.

DESAI: When do you expect this division between the domestic and foreign equity to end?

JORDAN: Within a year.

DESAI: And the government won't worry that Gazprom will be, say, 40 percent owned by foreigners as a result of this freeing up?

JORDAN: I think they might limit it to 25 percent.

DESAI: So they are still in the world of ratios.

JORDAN: They are exceptionally concerned about Gazprom. Of course, they have restrictions on foreign investment in some media concerns, too, but Gazprom is special. It contributes substantially to Russia's GDP because of its sheer size. It supplies gas to European countries, so there are strategic considerations. The government does not want it to fall into the wrong hands.

DESAI: What is Ruhrgas's share in Gazprom's equity?

JORDAN: Only 4.5 percent.

DESAI: So foreigners have scope for advancing into Gazprom ownership. I read the other day about Deutsche Bank wanting to acquire a stake in United Financial Group.

JORDAN: United Financial Group is a small brokerage outfit. It's significantly smaller in that regard than Renaissance or other groups—more of a boutique operation. It's a good firm. Deutsche Bank is looking for entry in the Russian market.

So I think it would be a smart move. Deutsche Bank operations in this part of the world are run by my brother, so I know.

DESAI: Do you think they will go through with it? After all, Deutsche Bank left Russia about two years ago, right?

JORDAN: Yes, because they suffered big losses. Today, however, Russia's prospects and the potential deals are promising. Foreign banks, including European banks, are ready to make Russia a priority again. They are more interested than U.S. banks because Russia is next door. It is natural for them to want to be active here in Russia. Citibank and Chase have offices in Moscow. Deutsche Bank would also like to get back in Russia. Raiffeisen Bank from Austria is also interested.

DESAI: You envisage significant operations by foreign banks. Russian groups will also actively explore banking, financial, and investment opportunities in Russia. In that context, I would like you to discuss the regulatory environment in Russia. Recently there have been financial, insider stock-trading scandals in the United States. Based on your personal experience, how would you contrast the situation in Russia?

JORDAN: The Russian financial sector is far removed from the regulations that prevail in the United States. Insider trading in Russia is not illegal. It is largely unregulated. It is comparable to the conditions in Germany five years ago. The Russian regulatory environment clearly needs to be upgraded. The process of writing new laws has begun, but enforcement is difficult because many stocks are traded over the counter without much monitoring. It will take time. They need an effective regulatory system, but one can't create it in five years or less. Ten years ago Russia did not have a functioning stock market, and trading in the market was in the range of a few hundred million a day. Today it approaches hundreds of billions. Bringing it to U.S. standards will take time.

DESAI: The other day I read that Sibneft, the oil company, declared dividends for Russian majority owners but not for minority foreign owners.[3]

JORDAN: I heard about that, too. However I don't think it was dividends. It was a bonus.

DESAI: Whatever it was, the minority shareholders were excluded from the award.

JORDAN: That is an issue of corporate governance. I do not want to comment on the Sibneft situation because I do not know the details. Russia has made significant progress in improving corporate governance, but problems persist. That, too, will take time. The Securities and Exchange Commission is making strong efforts in bringing offenders to court trials. The other enforcer is the market itself. Everyone wants to make money here. Companies know that, if they break the rules, their stocks will trade at a discount. Many Russian companies are straightening out because they want their shares to trade at a premium price. The movement is in the right direction.

DESAI: Nevertheless, corporate governance, in my opinion, is not widespread.

JORDAN: All right, let's take an example from the United States. The United States has presumably an exceptionally developed corporate governance regime. From that perspective, the violations by Enron, Tyco, and Worldcom are more serious. In many ways, the United States is a world leader, and yet the monitoring and enforcement are far from perfect. This was troubling to my Russian acquaintances, who brought up the issue of lax corporate governance in the United States. That is worrisome because the world looks up to the United States as an example, and, if it fails, the rest may follow suit.

DESAI: I think these were a few bad apples. The U.S. corporate sector as a whole follows the rules. Wouldn't you agree?

JORDAN: But look, $70 billion worth of Enron stock vanished in two weeks, followed by $100 billion of Worldcom equity. That's the entire capitalization of the Russian equity market. Investors took massive losses based on fraud. Bringing the wrongdoers to justice will send a correct message all around, including in Russia.

DESAI: Let's talk about the BP-TNK deal in the oil sector. It's enormous, isn't it?

JORDAN: Yes, it's about $6.7 billion. You know some domestic deals are even bigger.

DESAI: Can you give me an example?

JORDAN: The proposed Yukos-Sibneft transaction is close to $36 billion.[4] In any case, it is good to see foreigners bringing significant amounts of cash into Russia.

DESAI: I still think they are only tiptoeing into the Russian market.

JORDAN: The Shell deal in Sakhalin is still bigger—at $40 billion.

DESAI: I think Russian companies have to start setting an example in terms of cost cutting, efficient management, proper accounting, and all of that for facilitating foreign investment flows.

JORDAN: Russian companies right now are not rushing out in search of foreign investors. They are looking for cash at home from prospective Russian partners.

DESAI: I know that some Russian companies in the oil and metals sectors are bursting with cash, but are they ready to invest in Russia?

JORDAN: They are. Just look at the patterns of investment. It's all Russian money. The Western participation in the Russian equity market is small, very small, about 20 percent. The remaining 80 percent is Russian owned.

DESAI: What is the market capitalization?

JORDAN: I have to check the recent numbers. The index went up from 500 to 615 yesterday. In 1997, it was down at 50; at its best it was 100.

DESAI: It's still a thin market.

JORDAN: It's growing. I can easily move a couple of hundred million dollars a day in and out of the market.

DESAI: And you feel good about it?

JORDAN: Of course. It's stressful, but I do it. On any given day, we have close to $100 million invested in the Russian bond market, which is highly liquid. It's bigger than the equity market.

DESAI: I still feel you may be overdoing the role of domestic investors investing in Russian markets. I read the other day that the Groupe Danone was interested in acquiring a stake in Wimm-Bill-Dann, the dairy company.

JORDAN: I think the Groupe Danone wants to buy the whole company. It's a $5 billion deal. It's the largest food products business in Russia.

DESAI: Why wouldn't a domestic player be interested in buying it?

JORDAN: I think some are. There will be a counterbid.

DESAI: Let us talk about something else: your media experience. In 2001, you became the general director of the television station NTV.[5] You took charge of the network with the intention of reviving it financially and keeping it independent. How well did you succeed?

JORDAN: It was a total success. We turned the company around. I had two positions. I was chairman of Gazprom Media, the holding company, which has several media interests.

DESAI: That came a little later, right?

JORDAN: In November, they fired the previous head, and they hired me because I had worked earlier for Gazprom Media, the holding company. When I became chairman of NTV television, it was already owned by Gazprom Media. We turned NTV around financially, so I was asked to take over the entire Gazprom Media business. I was appointed chairman of the entire group. When I took over as chairman of Gazprom Media, it was in debt to the tune of more than a billion dollars. None of its companies made money.

DESAI: How large was Gazprom Media?

JORDAN: It was in charge of NTV, the global network; NTV Plus, satellite TV; TNT, an affiliate network; Seven Days, a publishing house; and five radio stations, of which only two were in operation and both were losing money. [At the time,] NTV was $150 million in debt. It never made a penny in the eight years of its existence. In the final two years before I took charge, it lost $25 to $26 million a year. [In addition,] NTV Plus was losing $3 million a month, had most of its channels turned off by foreign creditors, and was on the brink of collapse. [Finally,] TNT had a national rating of 1 percent and a huge debt. When I left, each business was making money. In the last two years of my tenure, NTV made $27 million. Overall, we increased revenues by 150 percent in two years and raised profitability. I can't say by how much because the group did not make any profit before I came in.

DESAI: So financially you really turned around the whole group of media companies. However, did you feel that you were also making it independent?

JORDAN: I ran it independently. That is probably the reason I ended up losing my job. I joined Gazprom Media on the condition that I would run its editorial policies totally independently of the shareholders and Gazprom. Those were the terms of the deal. The shareholders may exercise control, but the editorial policy of the media group has to be left to the company's editorial staff. Two years later, after I had turned everything around, I think Gazprom's decision changed. Gazprom, the major shareholder of Gazprom Media, wanted to have greater control over the editorial policies. We could not agree, so they got rid of me.

DESAI: Give me an example of the differences in editorial policy. Something concrete.

JORDAN: They just wanted to have a lot more control. I prefer not to go into details. It was political. And I plan to operate in Russia for a long time. As you know, parliamentary elections are coming up in December 2003. As a natural gas supplier, Gazprom operates all over Russia, and it wanted to steer the election process. Gazprom's management wanted to use the NTV station for influencing the process. I was against it because I believed it would affect the reputation of the network.

DESAI: Did your removal have anything to do with NTV's coverage of the hostage crisis in the Moscow theater?[6] That was the story in the U.S. press.

JORDAN: Gazprom's management was not happy that NTV covered the hostage crisis in depth, twenty-four hours. But more to the point, members of the television community were against me and lobbied for my removal. When NTV started making profits, they began worrying about their future. A growing, profitable company was dangerous for their prospects. They are a tight, exclusive group, and I was an outsider. I introduced market practices in Russian TV. They lobbied aggressively with the powers that be to have me removed.

DESAI: How did you convert NTV into a profitable TV network? Did you earn revenues from advertising?

JORDAN: I ran it as a business. The people in charge before me ran it as a political outfit. One makes money in media the classic way—by successful advertising and sponsorship. That was beyond them. They relied on politicians, but I kept politics out. I cut costs, brought [in] professional managers to run all parts of the business, and created transparency at all levels so that the day-to-day financial performance of the company was carefully monitored and the cash flow systematically watched. I created a sales division and developed good relations with advertisers. The advertising revenue grew steadily.

DESAI: When you say they made money out of politics, what do you mean?

JORDAN: Politicians and businesses that support politicians pay cash to get TV time. I am against that. I do not play that game.

DESAI: Let us talk about media freedom. How do you assess President Putin's attitude regarding media freedom?

JORDAN: I think that he, like any head of state, wants the media and the press to support him. I would like to discuss the issue from a general perspective. In my opinion, the situation in the United States right now is worrisome, too. If you speak out against the administration or against the war in Iraq, you may be seen as unpatriotic. In Russia, too, you are unpatriotic if you criticize the state. I think the freedom guaranteed by the First Amendment rights in the United States is like the oxygen we breathe. It is absolutely necessary in the United States and elsewhere.

DESAI: I do not want to play devil's advocate. I think President Putin needs the press. Elections are drawing closer. He is a popular leader, and his rating is high. I recall that, after the siege at the theater, the Duma and the upper house together passed a strict law restricting the freedom of the media to report such events. Putin vetoed it and suggested amendments to the legislation.

JORDAN: Yes, he vetoed it and came up with amendments, but that was staged. It seemed a positive step on his part, so the Duma made a few changes and brought it back for his approval. The new law is marginally better, but it is still highly restrictive.

DESAI: You don't think he was trying to strike a balance between the media's responsibility and freedom?

JORDAN: I think he wants the media to be responsible. I am also in favor of a responsible media, but the process of legislating against a free media is a slippery one. Once you start, there's no end in sight. I believe that the media should be self-regulated. It must find its limits via self-censorship. The European tradition favors media regulation. The American practice leaves it free to regulate itself. I prefer that.

DESAI: Yes, and financial independence.

JORDAN: Exactly. That is the problem in Russia. I am opposed to the European regulatory system, via significant legislation, which exists in England, France, Germany, and elsewhere in Europe. I favor the U.S. arrangements. I spoke out against the law adopted by Parliament after the Moscow theater siege. That may be another reason for my removal.

DESAI: Putin is also on record as having said that the Russian media cannot be politically independent unless it is financially independent. He expresses views that suggest he may be thinking in the right direction.

JORDAN: But then why are half of the TV networks owned by the state? I showed that NTV can be financially independent. The minute I proved it, I was removed.

DESAI: How do you assess Russian television's cultural and informational role?

JORDAN: It is extremely important. The networks do an excellent job. I think the quality is substantially better than in the United States.

DESAI: In terms of . . .

JORDAN: Documentaries and films. Of course, they are getting an influx of serials, sitcoms, and talk shows, but, in general, the quality is better.

DESAI: Is it more Moscow centered, though? After all, this is a huge country.

JORDAN: Well, there are three national networks, and there are thousands of affiliate stations. The former provide national coverage, and the local units focus on local items. The problems are essentially technical.

DESAI: What sort of technical problems?

JORDAN: The entire system is ancient. There are problems everywhere—with the satellites, with the towers. They need billions of dollars to renovate them. They need to upgrade the system to the analog and digital mode. I do not want to bore you with the technical details.

DESAI: What about the quality of the journalists?

JORDAN: I have a high opinion of Russian journalists. They are good and articulate, but there are occasional problems with TV and print journalists: They can be bought. Some are corrupt, so a strict code of ethics is absent. We managed to introduce it successfully at NTV. Those who strayed from the ethics code were fired.

DESAI: Give me an example from the ethics code.

JORDAN: Journalists who take money to give a one-sided view of an issue. That's the biggest violation in Russian journalism.

DESAI: A journalist paints a rosy picture of a company because he gets money in return. But isn't there a law prohibiting such activity?

JORDAN: There is a law, but nobody follows it because it is difficult to establish the necessary facts.

DESAI: Do Russian opinion makers worry about the Americanization of Russian TV in terms of explicit sex and violence, for example?

JORDAN: I think everybody worries about it everywhere, but everyone wants more of it.

DESAI: The public wants more and more such material?

JORDAN: Yes, because the ratings go up as a result. The more violence and sex, the higher the ratings.

DESAI: It's a universal phenomenon.

JORDAN: Yes. By the way, are you Indian?

DESAI: Indian by birth but an American citizen.

JORDAN: I am asking because I recently watched an Indian film on Russian TV. It had love and romance, plenty of singing and dancing but no sex or kissing.

DESAI: Yes, the Indian public is awaiting the moment when a man and a woman will actually kiss on screen. But let us get back to Russia. I think the Russian president is a cultural maestro. He goes to the theater every week if he has time time. I read that he admired Valery Gergiev's production of *War and Peace*. His cultural tastes, from the details I've seen, are certainly catholic. I sense that he must disapprove of some of the entertainment on Russian TV.

JORDAN: You're right. He watches TV and comments on it. He appreciates the theater, too. He is a supporter of the arts in Russia. Despite my guarded view of his media policies, I regard him as a singularly positive force on the scene. I think Putin has done an incredible job in four years of transforming Russia into a force to be reckoned with in world affairs. He is actively consulted by all heads of states on major international issues. Russia is being taken seriously. It is an associate member of the Group of Seven. He has moved Russia in the right direction, so I think that he will be remembered as person who really moved Russia in the right direction.

DESAI: Your reference to Putin's media policies brings me back to that issue. Tell me, is the printed media freer than TV?

JORDAN: Yes, much freer.

DESAI: How so?

JORDAN: Because it doesn't have so large an audience.

DESAI: Yes, but isn't it controlled by regional bosses?

JORDAN: Of course, there are massive controls by regional politicians, local bureaucrats, and business groups. But look, there are so many local and regional newspapers and magazines, there is so much written press that news, information, and entertainment get to the public despite the roadblocks. Few of them, however, turn a profit.

DESAI: Name some good ones.

JORDAN: My favorite Russian newspaper is *Kommersant*. It has four sections, consisting of Russian politics, arts, international business, and Russian business. Its editor in chief, in my opinion, is the best in Russia today.

DESAI: Who is he?

JORDAN: Andrei Vasiliev. He's brilliant. He is one of the smartest guys, and the newspaper reflects that.

DESAI: What about *Moscow Times*?

JORDAN: *Moscow Times* works on a small budget. It gives you bits and pieces of information, but it does not represent powerful journalism.

DESAI: *Argumenty i Fakty*?

JORDAN: It has become worse since it was bought from the original publisher.

DESAI: But it deals with a variety of issues and has a solid circulation.

JORDAN: It is not in the class of *Kommersant,* which is quality journalism.

DESAI: What about *Nezavisimaya Gazeta*?

JORDAN: One sided.

DESAI: In what way?

JORDAN: You've heard about Boris Berezovsky.

DESAI: Who hasn't?

JORDAN: Well, Berezovsky owns *Nezavisimaya Gazeta* and *Kommersant*. But the editor in chief of *Kommersant,* whom I mentioned earlier, is his own man, and his agreement with Berezovsky is that he should be left alone to pursue the contents and policies of the newspaper. By contrast, *Nezavisimaya Gazeta* is Berezovsky's outlet. *Kommersant* has incredible value. *Nezavisimaya Gazeta* is Berezovsky's print outpost in Moscow, with limited value.

DESAI: Wouldn't Berezovsky want to call it a day and quit?

JORDAN: I don't know. I think he keeps it to voice his opinions in Russia. Why not? He's a wealthy man. He can afford it.

DESAI: I feel that Berezovsky and Vladimir Gusinsky became politically too meddlesome in wanting to influence the presidential elections.

JORDAN: That's exactly right. That's why Putin got rid of them. Putin wants businessmen to do business and politicians to handle politics. These guys used their business interests and their media empires to control Russian politics.

DESAI: My final question: Are you back in the world of finance and investment?

JORDAN: I am still in the media business. I own a successful publishing company called Afisha. It has a newspaper like the *Village Voice* with the same format. It also publishes a popular magazine twice a month. We have been publishing travel books and are launching a travel magazine in September. It's a very exciting business. I own the second most popular radio station in Russia, Europa Plus.

DESAI: Does it broadcast European news? International news as well?

JORDAN: It is mainly a music station with some news.

DESAI: Is it popular in Russia?

JORDAN: It's number two.

DESAI: Which is number one?

JORDAN: Ruskoe Radio. Mine used to be number one, but the ratings fluctuate. Currently I have several television projects in the pipeline. I also own an insurance company.

DESAI: Is the insurance business developing fast in Russia?

JORDAN: Yes. Right now especially. For many years it was in the doldrums, but it is picking up. We had a long strategy session yesterday. I own a forestry company that manufactures home-building wood products. The housing sector is growing rapidly in Russia, and we want to be a big player in that market. We also have a fund-management vehicle that manages our capital and trades in the equity and bond markets. We are just getting into real estate in Moscow. We are building a large housing complex outside Moscow, about three hundred homes, so we are doing all sorts of things.

DESAI: Do you have Russian partners in these ventures?

JORDAN: I usually own these units myself.

DESAI: And what is the Sputnik Group?

JORDAN: That is just my personal holding company, which I control.

DESAI: So that covers all of the activities you mentioned.

JORDAN: Yes. Well, the holding company, with about forty people, is not large, but the staff and the workforce in all of the ventures run into the thousands.

DESAI: How is the operational context different from what it would be if you were doing similar things in the United States?

JORDAN: In the United States, your returns depend on which business you choose to get into, how well you run it, and the market conditions. All of these factors matter in Russia, plus you must deal with political risks, corruption, massive volatility, total uncertainty, and retraining your staff and workers. People here are not aware of the modern ways of running a business, so one faces the normal risks here plus the uncertainties. One has to work harder [and] risk more, but the returns are higher, too.

DESAI: Do you worry about your personal safety?

JORDAN: Not really.

DESAI: But you have to be careful, don't you?

JORDAN: Well, for twelve years I haven't had much of a problem. Sometimes I worry that some disgruntled person from my numerous companies could go after me and buy me out, so I face risks beyond the normal.

DESAI: You have a Russian wife?

JORDAN: With a background similar to mine. Her grandmother and my grandmother studied together in St. Petersburg at the famous Smolny Institute, so our families have known each other for generations.

DESAI: It almost sounds like an arranged match. Is your principal residence here in Moscow?

JORDAN: Yes. My wife and children go back to the United States on June 1 and return on August 20, when schools reopen here. They go to summer camps and get a taste of American life because they are otherwise totally Russian.

DESAI: Were they all born here?

JORDAN: Yes.

DESAI: Are you a Russian citizen?

JORDAN: No, I am a U.S. citizen.

DESAI: The very last question. Do you now regret not being in the diplomatic or international relations field?

JORDAN: You know, I've had the best of both worlds because of my work in Russia. I have acted as an informal advisor to the Clinton administration. I had meetings with Robert Rubin and Bill Clinton and senior members of the Clinton administration in order to discuss Russian affairs with them, so I had an opportunity to play politics, as it were.

DESAI: But I thought you were a Republican.

JORDAN: Most recently I've had a difficult time with the Republican administration because initially they took a negative view of my activities in Russia. I was persona non grata for a while. However, they have changed their opinion, so I have established contacts with the Bush administration. I feel I have business interests in Russia combined with political entrée in the United States. Who knows, may be in the future, I will drop my business commitments and go into public policy because I enjoy that, too. I also believe that one has an obligation to give something back, not only by way of charity but also in the capacity of using one's expertise for a social purpose, for public service.

DESAI: Do you think about going back sometime?

JORDAN: I don't know, I don't know. I am involved in Russia. But who knows? I try to not look too far into the future.

DESAI: Do you get tired sometimes?

JORDAN: I was exceptionally tired in February, but I took three months off for the first time in my life for health reasons after I left NTV. I've recuperated. I feel a lot better. I spent time in the sun [and] slept a lot, and I am just getting back into an active routine.

DESAI: I caught you at the right moment. I wish you good luck.

JORDAN: Thank you.

OCTOBER 2004

DESAI: Will the proposed change to retain the party slate for the Duma elections and abolish the single-member constituencies eventually lead to the development of a party system in Russia?

JORDAN: In my view, the proposal is sincere and is aimed at developing a viable and genuine party system. It is not a grab for further power, as some have portrayed it. The current pro-Kremlin parties in the Duma give Putin sufficient clout to get his legislation passed without touching the structure of the Duma. If adopted, however, the proposed changes will not change the Duma composition until early 2008, in the very last months of Putin's term.

The question is whether the proposals represent the best way to help develop the political system. That is difficult to judge. They are calculated to initiate political parties. Despite my laissez faire convictions, I do see the need for active measures to jump-start the party system. Russians tend to be cynical about parties because apart from, ironically, the Communist Party, they find it difficult to recognize the current parties as broad-based political organizations.

As for single-mandate candidates, several among them enjoy genuine political support and represent significant diversity in the Duma. On the other hand, individual first-past-the-post contests to the Duma have been financed by questionable means. Putin's initiative, therefore, has a clear anticorruption motivation.

DESAI: Will the proposed measures of electing governors deprive voters of their presumed rights in a federal system to elect their regional leaders?

JORDAN: In this regard as well, the proposal from the president is sincere in intent. I cannot say what percentage of the governors are oligarchs or directly wrapped up in the interests of Russia's big business groups, but this is clearly the case in several regions. It would be hard to call the process by which this situation came about a democracy. I do not have a democracy meter, so I cannot say to what extent poorly contested elections, resulting in the empowering of corrupt governors who then trample on the democratic rights of citizens, are better than no elections. Unfortunately, this proposal does look like a rollback for the right to vote. This is probably not a good signal to send, regardless of the practical, short-term changes or even benefits that it might bring about.

DESAI: Are these consolidating measures necessary to fight terrorism?

JORDAN: I am hard pressed to find a direct connection between these measures and terrorism. The biggest threat to Russia's security is corruption. No security policy will protect the country if it is undermined by corruption. This is also the biggest limit on the president's power. Despite talk of authoritarianism, presidential authority in Russia is severely undercut by corruption. This is perhaps the link between the proposed measures and Russia's security. However, more direct measures to reform the police, the military, and the intelligence agencies should form the bulk of reforms aimed at improving security.

DESAI: Yavlinsky says the proposals smack of "soft Stalinism." Do you agree?

JORDAN: I respect Grigory Yavlinsky, and I hope—and am confident—that he will remain prominent on the political scene in Russia for a long time. I understand his comment to mean that the current administration is seeking to reassert the president's power over the bureaucracy and that these attempts smack of an authoritarian approach in the public sphere. As I have said, I believe that the president is sincerely trying to foster the rule of law and conditions for democracy, but I would agree that micromanaging the situation may not be the most successful strategy. I would call it micromanagement rather than authoritarianism.

In any case, I do not think comparisons to Stalin are an effective way to make this point. The current Russian situation certainly does not remotely resemble Stalinism. Comparisons with Stalinist horror should not be made lightly. The phrase "soft Stalinism" is, in any event, unclear. What is Stalinism without terror, cruelty, and murder directed at total control of society? I think Russians who hear Yavlinsky's comments may interpret them in a somewhat abstract manner. However, such comments may create a serious misunderstanding among Americans and Europeans who are more familiar with Soviet history than contemporary Russians. Many in the West simply do not understand the scope of the changes that have occurred in this country. Westerners will react to Yavlinsky's comment with alarm. I do not think that he intends to create such a misperception. At least I hope he does not.

DESAI: It would seem that Putin regards the consolidation of political power as a necessary precondition for promoting economic reforms. Do you agree?

JORDAN: I'm not sure that Putin views the consolidation of political power as necessary for promoting economic reform. I think he views the consolidation of control over his own bureaucracy as vital to promoting economic reforms. In fact, short of abolishing interventionist bureaucrats, control over the bureaucracy is vital to enforcing any policy whatsoever. The president's lack of control of the bureaucracy, by the way, is another reason this president can never become a Stalin, even if he wanted to. The ground under him is very soft—wherever he steps, it gives way under corruption. I often tell Westerners that a great deal of misunderstanding about the current situation in Russia arises from the mistranslation of two words that are basically the same in Russian and English—these words are "politics" and "businessman." When Russians use the word "politika" these days, they usually mean something far more cynical and sinister than what we mean by "politics." Politics for us is ultimately tied to the interests of groups in society and broad government policies. In contemporary Russia, "politika" simply means the process by which a small elite uses the offices of government to directly divide the nation's wealth among its members.

When Russians talk about a "biznesman," they do not mean a person who founds, manages, or invests in businesses. They simply mean a crook. When Russians hear the phrase "a businessman who got involved in politics," they do not refer to a person, successful in building a business, who wants to share his expertise with the rest of the country by helping form national policies. They understand the phrase to mean "a crook whose ambitions involve schemes to get richer through cutting deals with officials at the highest levels of government." The words "politics" and "businessman" will not take on their genuine English meanings in Russia until corruption is significantly reduced. Politics is dysfunctional if the government lacks the clout to choose and implement policies. The ground gives way under the weight of corruption.

DESAI: Does Putin's model differ from that of Pinochet in Chile and of the Communist leadership in China? Are there any other historical parallels?

JORDAN: These analogies are, at best, general. Politically, I think that the human rights violations that occurred in Chile are simply not happening here, with the exception of Chechnya and the Caucasus. However, Pinochet did not face anything like Chechnya. Again, the Chinese state retains far more control over the economy than the Russian. Current moves to impose state policy on Russian big business is perhaps an attempt to move in the Chinese direction. Even if successful, it will not bring Russia closer to the controlled regime that exists in China. Perhaps we can compare and contrast, but I cannot come up with specific parallels or models for Russia. As always, Russia remains exceptional!

DESAI: Does it make sense to apply the norms of a fully formed U.S.-style liberal order for assessing Russia's evolving transition, as Western analysts are doing?

JORDAN: I believe in the norms of American liberal democracy, and I am not comfortable with applying them selectively. I definitely apply these norms to Russia when I think about the current Russian situation. Norms, however, are not particular rules or structures but principles to be lived up to. The problem is not whether to apply these norms to Russia, but rather the difficulty in determining what constitutes progress toward these norms.

I think the current popular view in the West—that Russia is backsliding—is based on a misperception of what Russia looked like in the nineties. The freedom achieved under Yeltsin, compared to what existed under the Soviet Union, was one of the major social transitions in history. I think you would be hard pressed to name a more significant social transition that occurred without a violent revolution, mass murders, repression, or famine. Under Yeltsin, and one must credit

Gorbachev, too. Political repression, although not eliminated, became marginal. Freedom of speech and conscience became broadly acceptable.

A free, independent, and responsible press, however, is another matter. The free flow of ideas and people in and out of the country became a right that has entirely changed Russian society. Property rights, previously almost nonexistent, were firmly if imperfectly enshrined. Many other areas of freedom that we take lightly, such as the right to choose one's career or occupation, were opened up. They say that, once you have free speech, the "cat is out of the bag," but so many cats are out of the bag that no one here seriously thinks that they can be put back in.

While these freedoms certainly exist, they can be encroached upon by the state or other citizens exercising their freedoms. The Yeltsin-era freedoms did not bring forth a democratic political system in Russia. I think the West saw several likable faces, heard familiar pronouncements, witnessed seemingly positive events, and took them as signs of a more developed democracy than actually existed—features such as elections, political parties, democratic rhetoric from businessmen and officials, massive privatization, a vocal private interest, and an outrageously open and bold press. A closer examination suggests that these were marks of a Potemkin democracy. They did not represent genuine public involvement and resulted in policies that most of the people strongly opposed.

The most telling misperception centered around Yeltsin's 1996 election. It was hailed in the West as a major coup for democracy, although he and his policies had become unpopular by the time of the election, and the balloting process was acknowledged as flawed. On the other hand, Putin's successful election in May 2000 was decried as undemocratic, despite his clear popularity with the electorate and the confirmation by Western observers that the balloting process was significantly less flawed.

DESAI: Despite Putin's illiberal forays, do you think that, from a long-term perspective, the chances of Russia continuing to evolve to a liberal political and economic system remain robust?

JORDAN: Based on what I have said, I believe that Russia is moving ahead in terms of developing the rule of law and democratic institutions—at a pace that may disappoint distant observers, but one that still seems pretty fast when you watch it up close.

DESAI: In the old days, Western Sovietologists argued that Soviet foreign policy was expansionist and adventurist because the internal political arrangements were ideological and authoritarian. Putin, by contrast, comes across as nonideological and selectively pragmatic. What is your view?

JORDAN: I think Putin's cleverness consists in identifying common interests with potential foreign partners and implementing them selectively. That has perhaps surprised several skeptics, given his KGB background. I think his policy stance is beneficial for U.S.-Russia relations. Of course, competition will still continue, and

Putin will remain a strong competitor in the economic field. American policy makers will find him a tough negotiator in the energy field because Russians are capable of thinking long term. They are good at chess. Russia's natural resources represent such a game. If Putin manages to get sufficient control of the bureaucracy so that he can begin to formulate long-term policies, the U.S. administration will have to undertake more long-term planning than it has been doing to protect U.S. interests.

DESAI: As a seasoned investor in Russia, how do you assess the proposed formation of Gazpromrosneft?[7]

JORDAN: I view it positively. The merger will allow the new company to efficiently negotiate natural gas pricing vis-à-vis the European Union, attract direct foreign investment in the combined unit, and maneuver foreign-policy-related objectives, such as whether an oil pipeline should be built from eastern Siberia to China or alternatively to Japan. It will enable the Kremlin to kill several birds with one stone. The move is part of the Kremlin's long-term thinking I mentioned earlier.

DESAI: Will Putin seek a third presidential term?

JORDAN: That would be inconsistent with what he has said on the topic so far.

NOTES

1. Baron Pyotr Wrangel led the White Army, the anti-Bolshevik forces, in the civil war that followed the Russian Revolution.

2. The White Army, consisting of forces loyal to the Russian tsarist regime, fought the Bolshevik Red Army, which was composed of revolutionary forces that were hostile to the monarchy and everything associated with it.

3. Sibneft is a vertically integrated Russian oil company with extensive interests in finding, producing, refining, and marketing oil.

4. The on-again, off-again merger between Sibneft and Yukos, Russia's best-managed company, which was prosecuted on charges of tax evasion and fraud in 2003 and 2004, ultimately did not take place. Yukos-Sibneft was to have been the name of the proposed new company.

5. NTV is a Russian television company that was brought under state ownership and control in 2003.

6. On October 23, 2002, forty-one Chechen separatists seized the Dubrokva Theater in Moscow, taking more than 800 theatergoers hostage. The standoff was brought to an end when authorities pumped a strong anesthetic gas into the theater. When the gas proved to have a stronger effect than anticipated, 129 hostages and all forty-one terrorists died.

7. In the final act of the unification drama, calculated to raise state control of Gazprom to 51 percent, Gazprom was set to acquire the private oil company Sibneft instead of the state-owned Rosneft.

CHAPTER 14

Anatoly Vishnevsky

Demographic Dilemmas

In the last twenty-five years of its existence, the Soviet Union lagged behind the rest of the developed world in enforcing measures for fighting mortality. As a result, Russia began its transition in 1992 as a laggard. That was its Soviet heritage. To this day, no changes have occurred to alter the situation, so high mortality and low life expectancy continue to be predetermined by the strong inertia of the Soviet days.

Excessive mortality due to external causes is a Russian problem, but it is also an old problem. The gap between Russia and the Western countries has been increasing for decades.

The current contraction [of population], the fourth since 1913, differs significantly from the previous three, which were caused by extreme social shocks—World War I and the civil war, famine, the repressions and purges of the thirties, and World War II. In contrast, the current loss is conditioned by stable changes in the demographic behavior of Russians. That is why one should not expect that it will be transitional and that a positive natural growth in population will be reestablished in the near future, leading to an increase in the number of the country's residents. The Russian population will continue to decline in the future. All of the demographers agree on this prediction.

[Russia] needs immigrants. Its demographic situation with the continuing population loss is extreme. It is also experiencing migratory pressure from the outside. Its labor market does not welcome foreigners. . . . The immigrants feel excluded and unassimilated.

DECEMBER 2003

DESAI: How serious, in your view, is the Russian demographic situation, which analysts attribute to a sharp rise in the mortality rate and a decline in the birthrate in the nineties?

VISHNEVSKY: Russia began the twenty-first century with a difficult demographic situation. I will address the exact details of this complex legacy as we talk, but I'll confine myself to a single comment for now. If I were to explain the current demographic situation solely in terms of the events of the 1990s, I would end up sounding like the man on the street or the quasi-literate journalist or the political agitator who is seized by nostalgia—all those who view the recent demographic situation as an inevitable negative part of all that is new in Russia. By tracing the origins of Russia's demographic problem to its Soviet past, I will attempt to put it into its proper perspective.

DESAI: Let's begin with the mortality rate. It is abnormally high among men of working age. What special factors contributed to this statistic in the nineties?

VISHNEVSKY: In Russia and beyond its borders as well, everyone is convinced that a huge, "unheard-of-in-peaceful-times" rise in mortality occurred in Russia in the 1990s. Even Yeltsin's opponents used this as grounds for impeaching him, saying that he was guilty of "the genocide of the Russian people." In reality, the situation is not that simple.

It is true that in the early 1990s the mortality rate among men as well as women increased in all age groups. Overall, 22 percent more deaths occurred in the five years from 1990 to 1994 than in the preceding five years. The increase in the mortality rate for men was 32 percent. Life expectancy, which reached its historical maximum in 1987 at 65 years for men and 74.6 years for women, declined in 1994 to numbers unseen since the end of the fifties, when these numbers began to be regularly reported. In 1994, life expectancy had slumped to 57.5 years for men and 71 years for women. All of these indicators, however, are a matter of coincidence and reflect the situation in particular calendar years.

DESAI: What do you mean?

VISHNEVSKY: These numbers are the result of extraordinary economic and political factors that contributed to the distortion of the mortality calendar, making the number of deaths in one year either "denser" or "thinner" than in another. Precisely such changes were taking place in Russia between 1985 and 1995. Gorbachev's antialcohol campaign, which began in 1985, sharply altered the evolving mortality dynamics. A temporary improvement set in, annual deaths decreased, and generational extinction slowed down, but this improvement did not last long. The first half of the nineties witnessed a significant rise in the deaths "delayed" from the late 1980s. As a result, the total number of deaths became "denser," resulting in a dramatic worsening of the mortality numbers.

I say all of this not with a view to justifying the rise in the mortality rate indicators in the first half of the nineties or for absolving Yeltsin of the accusations of "genocide." These accusations, in effect, did not amount to much. The problem, however, is different.

DESAI: How is it different?

VISHNEVSKY: Let me first separate the short-term, temporary influences on mortality from its long-term trend. At the very outset, the "mythology" of an unforeseen rise in mortality as a reaction to an overall deterioration of the situation in the country and as proof of such a deterioration can be used for political purposes. It certainly deflects attention from an understanding of what, in reality, was happening with mortality in Russia. In fact, long-term mortality indicators had been deteriorating for the past forty years.

DESAI: You mean for most of the Soviet period?

VISHNEVSKY: In the last twenty-five years of its existence, the Soviet Union lagged behind the rest of the developed world in enforcing measures for fighting mortality. As a result, Russia began its transition in 1992 as a laggard. That was its Soviet heritage. To this day, no changes have occurred to alter the situation, so high mortality and low life expectancy continue to be predetermined by the strong inertia of the Soviet days. The current low life expectancy for Russian men—less than 59 in 2001—is on the trajectory that developed in the sixties and the seventies and around which the sharp fluctuations of the 1980s and 1990s occurred.

Thus the real challenge is to get Russia off the well-traveled track of worsening mortality that it has been riding for several decades, rather than focus on the "imagined" mortality crisis of the 1990s. Russian mortality indicators have been moving in completely different directions from those in other developed countries. Russia, a nonparticipant in the improving performance, is paying a heavy price.

DESAI: What price do you have in mind?

VISHNEVSKY: Let me give you some numbers to illustrate my point. Suppose Russian mortality, starting in 1966, decreased on average at the same rate as in the United States, Japan, and member nations of the European Union from 1961 and 1966. In that case, the number of deaths in Russia during the thirty-five years of the last century, although higher than the rates for the set used for comparison, would have been 14.2 million fewer than in reality. In other words, the population would be 14.2 million larger. These losses can be considered excessive. More than half of these consisted of middle-aged men—it's as if the country were in a constant state of war.

DESAI: Which specific causes contribute to these higher deaths in Russia?

VISHNEVSKY: If you consider the entire population, the excessive mortality rate among Russians, when compared to their Western counterparts, arises from the diseases of the respiratory and circulatory systems. This is not because Russians are more prone throughout their lives to die from diseases of these types, but because they die from them at a much younger age than the Europeans, the Americans, and the Japanese.

If, however, we focus on the group at extreme risk of mortality, namely middle-aged men, then the primary causes are external: accident, poisoning, injury, murder, and suicide. Excessive mortality due to external causes is a Russian problem, but it is also an old problem. The gap between Russia and the Western countries has been increasing for decades. The numbers tell the story. In 1960, the standardized coefficient for deaths due to these causes in Russia was 1.5 times higher than in the United States; in 1970, the difference was 1.9; in 1980, 2.8; in 1984, on the eve of Gorbachev's antialcohol campaign, 3.1. In 1994, it was unprecedented at 5.2. Later it declined a little but still remained high.

The antialcohol campaign highlighted the well-established connection between high mortality and alcoholism in Russia. Perhaps there is a similar link between other specific factors and high mortality in Russia in the 1990s and even earlier. I would attribute this high mortality not to specific factors but to the long-term tendencies of Russia's failure to reach the advanced stages of epidemiological transition.

DESAI: The general impression was that the Soviet Union was quite advanced in providing health services to the population.

VISHNEVSKY: The Soviet health care system more or less successfully managed the early stages of combating mortality when the state could successfully use paternalistic means such as mass prophylactic campaigns, obligatory vaccinations, and improved living conditions. These paternalistic methods, however, were deficient when it came to strong activism on the part of the population itself.

By the midsixties, the opportunities for combating mortality through this strategy were exhausted. Western countries had moved to the next stage of transition by developing a new strategy, a new type of preventive approach aimed at lowering the risks of mortality from noninfectious diseases, among them heart disease and cancer. The new strategy extended to combating other causes, such as accidents and violence, unrelated to these diseases. This strategy demanded active and informed participation by the public in dealing with health problems. It was also matched by more government spending. The process was interactive.

DESAI: In your view, the Soviet health care system was lagging behind as far back as the early 1980s.

VISHNEVSKY: Absolutely. The new response was missing. As the 1970s ended, Soviet nonparticipation in this novel approach of fighting mortality created the widening gap I mentioned earlier. This was not an accidental, temporary episode, but rather pointed to a deep crisis in the system. The inadequate financing of the health care system contributed to the gap with the West. Along with other "nonproductive" sectors, the health care system received the meager cash left over after the militarized "productive" industries had been abundantly provided for. This residual funding was not adequate for safeguarding and rehabilitating public health. Compared to the resources devoted in the West for the purpose, it was skimpy. By some accounts, the average provision per capita in 1990 was 124 rubles. In the United States, it was a high $2,600.

DESAI: And, as you mentioned, individual initiative was also missing.

VISHNEVSKY: Absolutely. Growing social apathy and disappointment in the unrealized common ideals of socialism contributed to the malaise. The new strategy of fighting mortality demanded that the public adopt an active role rather than passively accept the standard provisions of the health service organizations. Neither before nor after the fall of the Soviet Union was the Russian public able to alter its lifestyle, to care for its health, or to discard bad and adopt good habits. Meanwhile, the majority of the population was marginalized by decades of Brezhnev-era stagnation. It found itself in a cultural and ideological void. It lacked the drive to actively fight for its health—for life itself. Alcoholism and the related high mortality from accidents, poisoning, and injuries are the direct results of this general social malaise.

These are the objective conditions that led to the current redoubling of the mortality rate in Russia. As of this date, nothing has changed. Russia is still stuck somewhere in the early stages of the epidemiological transformation.

DESAI: Let's move from the mortality problems to the fertility picture. Is the decline in the fertility rate contributing abnormally to a lower birthrate in Russia? How would you compare it with trends in the world's developed economies?

VISHNEVSKY: The number of annual births between 1973 and 1999 [twenty-six years comprise a mean interval between successive generations] declined by roughly eight hundred thousand, not an insignificant number. The fertility level, measured in terms of the total fertility rate, really plummeted in the nineties.

The public associates the resulting population decline, which began in 1992, with the socioeconomic crisis of the "transition period." Therefore, it hopes that, as soon as the crisis ends, births will start to increase. The actual situation, unfortunately, is more complicated. There is little room for optimism.

DESAI: Why are you pessimistic about a rebound in the fertility rate?

VISHNEVSKY: Birthrates in Russia have been declining throughout the twentieth century. In the midsixties, the birthrate for the first time fell below the replacement level. It has continued to fall ever since. Russia, in fact, was increasingly moving toward the pattern of urbanized and industrialized countries, which, by and large, are marked by low, and recently very low, fertility levels. The Russian fertility level, following its decline in the 1990s, was not lower than that in many European countries. Therefore, the excessively low Russian fertility, as an indicator of the overall systemic crisis at the end of the twentieth century, has no basis. Even if one views the low Russian fertility as a crisis, its extensive presence in all industrial, urbanized societies does not make it a specifically Russian malaise. It is more likely a common crisis of the entire modern, postindustrial West.

DESAI: So declining birthrates, in your opinion, are a common crisis of postindustrial societies.

VISHNEVSKY: I am not sure that one necessarily has to view them as a crisis. We know that declining birthrates in postindustrial societies accompany the changes that are usually interpreted as positive attributes of modernization: the almost complete elimination of child mortality, the emancipation and self-fulfillment of women and an increased freedom of choice for them, the increase in per capita investment in children, higher levels of education, and so on. These changes in mass procreation behavior and their consequences, therefore, do not necessarily represent a crisis but instead underscore the internal contradictions of the modernization process. Perhaps modernization changes social life from mere quantities to better quality.

DESAI: In your belief, the fall in fertility in Russia cannot be considered in isolation from similar processes in developed countries.

VISHNEVSKY: Lately I have increasingly come to believe that this decline can and should be viewed in a wider, more global, context. It can be seen as a systemic reaction to a worldwide demographic crisis created by a global demographic explosion pressing on the planet's limited resources. Declining fertility on a global scale below the level of simple reproduction for a sustained period is therefore a boon. The decline in births in Russia and in the West is simply one episode in this global transformation. Viewed in this light, the low Western birthrate is by no means proof of the negative propensity of Western civilization, but rather evidence of its immense adaptive ability.

All of this does not rule out the fact that low fertility and the consequent slowing or halting of the population growth of the developed world is harmful, even dangerous. However, nothing can be done about this because the interests of the survival of all countries together outweigh the interests of a particular country.

DESAI: So you do not think that specific policies can raise the birthrate in Russia.

VISHNEVSKY: Let me backtrack a little. As far back as a hundred years ago, public opinion, backed by demographics researchers, sought to explain low fertility in terms of a variety of factors, including a low standard of living, which prompted families to raise consumption levels that conflicted with the costs of having more children, which in turn contributed to parents' lack of interest in having children, unemployment, excessive labor force participation by women, uncertainty about the future, women's desire for self-fulfillment, and the list goes on. However, these factors, multifaceted and interacting with one another in a variety of ways in different countries, have continually led to the same result—declining fertility. One can hardly expect to produce a large effect on the birthrate by influencing a single factor, yet that is exactly what demographic policies are expected to do.

DESAI: So you do not believe that the Russian health care system can cope with the problems of high mortality and low birthrates?

VISHNEVSKY: The potential of the health care system for influencing mortality, and more so fertility, is limited. Mortality and fertility tendencies are formed under the influence of diverse economic, social, and cultural factors. A few of them are or can be under the control of the health care system.

Of course, I would not want to diminish the ability of health care to influence the situation, but declining fertility is not a medical problem at all. Furthermore, the overly high Russian mortality is primarily mortality from external causes of absolutely healthy men. Here, preventive measures may deflect dangerous behavior and lower mortality from accidents and injuries, but they cannot eliminate the root of the evil.

DESAI: Does Russia face a drastic population decline from the current level of about 145 million as a result of these demographic factors? Is it possible that the improving economic situation will lower the mortality rate, lift the birthrate, and help arrest the population decline?

VISHNEVSKY: Let me respond by giving you a historical perspective. In 1913, the population of Russia in its present borders was ninety million. Russia experienced a demographic transition in the twentieth century, which was generally accompanied by accelerated population growth around the globe. But in Russia, the potential demographic expansion was cancelled out by the immense human losses suffered during the catastrophes of the first half of the century. The chance to appreciably increase the population was permanently lost. However, the natural growth in population, which remained high despite the many catastrophes the country faced, helped close several demographic gaps. As a result, the country survived the demographic crisis caused by World War II. In 1955, we reached the prewar levels of population. During the next ten years, through the second half of the 1960s, natural growth increased the population, allowing some people to migrate to other Soviet republics.

DESAI: When did the impact of the declining birthrate actually begin?

VISHNEVSKY: Soon thereafter. The natural increase weakened under the combined impact of diminishing fertility, the end of the declining mortality rate, and an aging population. In 1964, the crude rate of the natural increase of the population of Russia fell below 10 per thousand for the first time, reaching 7 per thousand in 1967; it never again reached that level, fluctuating from 5.5 to 6.5 per thousand—rarely outside that range. These numbers fell rapidly at the end of the eighties. From 1992, when the Russian population was historically at its highest with 148.7 million people, the natural increase became negative, leading to an overall decline of the country's population by more than 5.2 million people, or 3.5 percent in 2003. In contrast, Russia's population had increased by 8.7 million people, or 6.2 percent, in the preceding decade.

DESAI: How does the recent continuing decline differ from the earlier pattern in the first half of the last century?

VISHNEVSKY: The current contraction, the fourth since 1913, differs significantly from the previous three, which were caused by extreme social shocks—World War I and the civil war, famine, the repressions and purges of the thirties, and World War II. In contrast, the current loss is conditioned by stable changes in the demographic behavior of Russians. That is why one should not expect that it will be transitional and that a positive natural population growth will be reestablished in the near future, leading to an increase in the number of the country's residents. The Russian population will continue to decline in the future. All of the demographers agree on this prediction. According to the 2002 forecast by the United Nations, in 2050 the population of Russia will be 101.5 million people, which represents a decline of about 30 percent from 2000 levels. Russian forecasts suggest similar numbers.

DESAI: What consequences will result from such a sharp population decline?

VISHNEVSKY: Of course, population does not have to increase always and everywhere. Declining population is not always a problem, nor is growth always a benefit. However, considering the specific conditions in Russia, this loss in population is unquestionably damaging.

Although Russia ranks among the more populated countries of the world, serious inconsistencies prevail between its population and the size of its territory, the length of its borders, the vastness of its territory that needs exploration, and the lack of a developed settlement network. Russia has always had a lot of poorly utilized land with low population density. These features were gravely distorted after the collapse of the Soviet Union in 1991, when Russia inherited three-fourths of the territory but only half of the population.

The European part of Russia has a population density that is comparable to that of the United States, with 27 people per square kilometer, compared to 29 in the United States. However, in comparison to the industrial countries of Western Europe, Russia's historical center is thinly populated. More than a quarter of Russians are concentrated in the central federal districts, which constitute less than 4 percent of the territory. However, even here, the density of the population—more than 58 people per square kilometer—is thinner, by half, than that of the European Union, at 119 people per square kilometer.

DESAI: Isn't the situation much worse—actually a demographic disaster—in the Asian part of Russia?

VISHNEVSKY: Exactly. The Asian territory, which represents 75 percent of the country's landmass, accounts for only 21 percent of the population—a density of 2.5 inhabitants per square kilometer. The demographic potential of Siberia and the Russian Far East is totally inadequate in relation to their natural resources, not only for their exploration but also for the creation of a settlement structure that could more or less cover these territories.

However, there is another problem. In addition to the mismatch between the country's demographic potential and resource endowment, Russia's urban settlements are few in number and underdeveloped. Let me explain. The fraction of Russia's urban population at 73 percent matches that in the European Union and in the United States at 75 percent and in Japan at 77 percent. Overall, Russia is as urbanized as these countries. However, its urban population is spread out over a large number of settlements with a thoroughly underdeveloped network of large cities.

DESAI: You mean Russia has very few large cities.

VISHNEVSKY: Yes. With the dissolution of the Soviet Union, Russia acquired thirteen of the twenty-four Soviet cities with a population of a million people. The current census puts them at ten at the start of 2002, only two of which are west of the Urals. Only two Russian cities have more than 2 million residents. The United States has fourteen cities with a population of more than 2 million, eight of which exceed 3 million.

DESAI: What are the specific disadvantages of having fewer large cities?

VISHNEVSKY: This underdevelopment of large cities attests to Russia's regional underdevelopment and its failure to generate a large number of regional and inter-regional capitals. The urban population, in conditions of limited demographic resources, moved to the few sizeable centers. This process prevented the growth of large regional metropolises, which in turn could provide an impulse for the development of their regions.

These internal complications, which Russia faces as a result of the current population shortfall, will intensify as the numbers decline. Then again, the decline creates external difficulties relating to Russia's place in the world community.

DESAI: What do you have in mind?

VISHNEVSKY: The country is rapidly losing its place in the world demographic hierarchy. In 1913, the Russian Empire had about 8 percent of the world's population, 4.4 percent of which lived in Russia proper. Even in 1950, the territory of Russia, though it had not yet reached its prewar population level, had more than 4 percent and the Soviet Union 7.1 percent of the global population. Russia's current share—2.4 percent—of the global population is falling rapidly. According to the UN report I mentioned earlier, it will be a mere 1.1 percent in 2050.

In 1913 and 1950, the Russian Empire and the Soviet Union ranked behind China and India in population. However, Russia's present borders would put it in fourth place—after China, India, and the United States in 1950. Currently, it is in eighth place, having been overtaken by Indonesia, Brazil, Pakistan, and Bangladesh. In 2050, it will move to eighteenth place, having been surpassed by several African and developing countries, including Mexico, Egypt, the Philippines, Vietnam, Japan, and Iran.

DESAI: Why are you concerned about this global ranking?

VISHNEVSKY: It is important because, even though Russia is sliding in the global population hierarchy, it composes almost 13 percent of the global territory—the largest in the world, rich in natural resources but poorly settled. Its neighbors, by contrast, are densely populated states that from time to time announce claims on Russian territory.

Thus, the population loss has internal economic and external geopolitical consequences that are contrary to Russia's interests. A larger, even a stable, population would prove beneficial, but is that possible?

Clearly Russia went down in the global ranking because of internal and external factors. The former arose from the low fertility and the high mortality, which we talked about earlier. The external factors relate to the demographic explosion in the developing countries, which are clearly surpassing Russia and the developed nations. Both of these factors are beyond Russia's control. Perhaps arresting the rise in mortality can be managed. The experience of the developed countries provides an answer for Russian policy makers, but raising the fertility rate is next to impossible. Russia is stuck with low fertility, a negative natural population growth, and an aging population. It is well nigh impossible to find a solution out of this situation without creating new problems.

DESAI: Can immigration from the outside, as in the United States, help, or would it create new problems? Is that what you have in mind?

VISHNEVSKY: In principle, immigration can at least partially counter the contraction and the aging of populations in the industrial countries and posttransition economies, including Russia. However, Russia is currently unprepared to accept a large number of immigrants.

In order to keep the population at 146 million people, the count at the turn of the current century, Russia would need to accept, on average, more than 700,000 immigrants on a net basis and gradually increase the inflow to 1.2 to 1.3 million by 2035. These are, of course, ballpark figures.

DESAI: These are awesome numbers.

VISHNEVSKY: Right now, these numbers fly in the face of reality. In fact, net immigration into Russia is declining. From 1981 to 1990, 8.9 million people arrived in Russia from the former Soviet republics; only 6.9 million people did so between 1991 and 2000. However, Russia has been losing people to out-migration; as a result, the net addition to its population in the last decade due to migration was only 3.3 million, less than Germany's 3.8 million during the same period. Even if one adjusts the interstate migration numbers in the 1990s for their inaccuracy, it is difficult to argue against the net contraction (as against net expansion, as is often believed) of the immigrant flow into Russia.

DESAI: Why do you think that Russia is not prepared to accept significant immigrant flows?

VISHNEVSKY: Countering population decline through immigration requires an active strategy for the purpose. The Russian public, however, does not support such a strategy. Anti-immigrant attitudes exist in many European countries, but they emerged over time as a result of the presence of a significant number of migrants in these countries. Russians, in contrast, displayed a negative attitude toward immigrants long before immigration inflows began. Most Russians believed that there were already far too many immigrants, although, in reality, their numbers were declining. They also believed that the presence of immigrants inevitably entailed negative consequences. In fact, Russians currently exhibit a negative attitude toward Russian and Russian-speaking immigrants from the former Soviet republics.

DESAI: You mean that Russians in Russia are opposed to the migration of ethnic Russians from outside? Why?

VISHNEVSKY: The locals see the outsiders as potential competitors in the labor market. Perhaps reflecting public sentiment, the Law on Citizenship passed on May

31, 2002, [and] imposed severe restrictions on applications for Russian citizenship. It was amended on November 11, 2003, and restored fairness with regard to former citizens of the Soviet Union. In reality, though, it acknowledges only that they can serve as stopgap additions for countering the shortages inherited from the breakup of the Soviet Union. Nothing more.

DESAI: You mean the law does not have a long-term perspective.

VISHNEVSKY: The law does not recognize migration as a strategically important process for correcting the effects of the declining population on Russian life both today and in the coming years. More important, it does not deal with the potential role in that regard of non-Slavic immigrants and migrants with other religions, toward whom "migrantophobia" is magnified into xenophobia. These prejudices are so widespread that an aggressive proimmigration policy is politically risky.

Shutting the doors to immigrants would mean that the population will continue to contract and age, the mismatch between human resources and territory will grow worse, and Russia's place in the global demographic hierarchy will further deteriorate.

DESAI: Do you not think that Russian policy makers will act before the situation gets out of control?

VISHNEVSKY: You are assuming that the inflow of immigrants into Russia depends on the decisions of the Russian government and that the government can fully control the situation. Such logical thinking rests on the possibility of a smooth migratory interaction between the developed and developing worlds, which has already ended. In the initial, benign stage of international migration, the engine of migratory flows was controlled by the recipient countries. However, as soon as these flows developed, they created their own momentum, increasingly reflecting the situation in the countries that were supplying migrants. The developed minority, "the golden billion," is losing the initiative to withstand the push of the surrounding billions of the Third World. Some time ago there were 2 billion, then there were 3 billion, now there are already 5 billion, and there will be more.

DESAI: Are you suggesting that policy makers in the developed countries are increasingly unable to manage the pressures of illegal migration from outside?

VISHNEVSKY: Yes. When the legal routes for migration provided by the recipient countries became too narrow, illegal channels developed. We can see that ourselves. Exact information in Russia is hard to come by, but illegal immigrants are reported to number in the millions. The problem of illegal migration is becoming acute and is of serious concern to politicians and public opinion in recipient countries. The demographic pressure of the overpopulated Third World will only continue to grow. For a time, improving migration control in the recipient countries will prevail, but it will eventually be overtaken by the ability of illegal migrants to circumvent controls. I believe that the population transfer from the overpopulated to the depopulating countries provides an answer to demographic problems of the twenty-first century. It will probably be the most critical challenge of the new century.

DESAI: What forms might this challenge take?

VISHNEVSKY: Today's migration pressure may turn out to be only the distant thunder of a coming storm. Given the presence of certain critical conditions, the demographic pressure of the south on the north could escalate into military and political pressures, leading to a large-scale redistribution of the global political map. In view of that possibility, it might be prudent to let off some of that steam by allowing economic immigration from the South, despite some of its negative consequences.

DESAI: What are the negative consequences?

VISHNEVSKY: These negative implications arise from economic and cultural incongruities. The demographic masses of the two worlds are numerically incomparable. The potential supply of cheap labor from developing countries is practically limitless, whereas the needs of the developed countries are limited. These immigrants face problems of social adaptation in the recipient countries, which have different cultural traditions. In any case, as long as the scale of immigration is limited, immigrants assimilate rather quickly, almost dissolving into the local environment without creating intercultural issues. However, when the absolute and relative numbers of immigrants become significant and, more important, when they multiply rapidly and create compact sociocultural enclaves in the recipient countries, the assimilation process slows down, generating intercultural tensions, which increase objectively as a result of the growing social and economic inequality of the "local" and the "foreign" populations. These "outsiders," settled in immigrant enclaves, battle marginalization and cultural duality by keeping in touch with their home countries, often turning to their traditional practices and simplified "fundamentalist" ideas, which help them retain their whole "I." Meanwhile, the process of assimilation is blocked, and many—not all, of course—immigrants find themselves maladjusted in their adopted lands.

DESAI: That is a pretty negative picture.

VISHNEVSKY: The host countries that use foreign labor begin to feel the limitations of their immigrant capacity, and the impact of the competition between "us" and "them" in the labor force gradually escalates into debates over immigration policies, which turn into a major playing card in political battles. Anti-immigration sentiments arise in the public, and stereotypes are created, which often attract the intellectual elite. All of this is on the same level as the discontent harbored by the semiliterate, marginalized immigrants.

DESAI: I wonder whether the rather polarized picture that you have presented relates to the Russian situation.

VISHNEVSKY: All of this applies to Russia in full measure. It needs immigrants. Its demographic situation with the continuing population loss is extreme. It is also experiencing migratory pressure from the outside. Its labor market does not welcome foreigners. It is aware of its limitations to absorb and assimilate immigrants. The immigrants feel excluded and unassimilated, but Russia's special features render its situation more complex.

DESAI: What special features do you have in mind?

VISHNEVSKY: These include vast, sparsely populated, and resource-rich territories, arable land, fresh water, and energy, all critical attributes for this century. These factors not only create demand for more workers in Russia but also attract migrant workers from the overpopulated South. However, from a geopolitical perspective, the migration outlook for Russia is not altogether benign. In particular, the massive inflow of the Chinese into the Russian Far East, if it were to take place, would not only leave them culturally separate because of the proximity of their massive homeland next door but also activate territorial claims by China sooner or later. Obviously, limits of immigration capacity should not be seen as totally airtight. Russia's migratory capacity can be increased via special policies aimed at widening the narrow corridors of opportunities as in other countries. Such policies, however active, can only expand the boundaries of Russia's migratory capacity; they cannot eliminate the problems I have outlined.

DESAI: If the labor force cannot be replenished by immigrants, Russia will experience a serious decline in the ratio of working-age people to retirees. This will have serious consequences for the Russian pension system. Are suitable reforms of the pension system being considered?

VISHNEVSKY: Let us consider a few numbers. The proportion of elderly people in Russia who are at least sixty years old grew from 6.7 percent in 1939 to 11.9 percent in 1970, to 18.7 percent in 2001, and it will continue to grow. Currently, their share in several countries (exceeding 20 percent) is 21.5 percent in the European Union and 23.7 percent in Japan. The same future awaits Russia. Because of decreasing mortality, the age pyramid changes inexorably: The years lived by each cohort in the middle- and older-age brackets increase, thereby contributing to an increase in the combined lifetime of each generation.

DESAI: So most developed countries face the negative consequences of a changing age pyramid. What is new?

VISHNEVSKY: For decades, demographers have discussed the negative economic and social consequences of an aging population. The biggest concern arises from the fast growth in the numbers and the proportion of pensioners relative to active wage earners. There are other problems, too, among them the aging of the labor force itself, the slowdown in the renewal of knowledge and ideas, the weakening of generational pressure for such renewal, and, above all, the impact of gerontocracy itself. The negative burden of an aging population and the social dynamic of the "shabbying" of nations diminish the benefits of democratic modernization.

DESAI: What is the answer to the burdens of an aging population?

VISHNEVSKY: As with all changes, social institutions must adapt to the new demographic realities. The creation of the pension system provided the answer to the fast-emerging proportion of seniors in the twentieth century. The current growth of the "senior citizen load" is unquestionable, but why should it arouse such concerns, as if society is powerless to rise to the challenge? What is wrong with redistributing the common pool of society's resources in favor of later and later generations? Having extended the lives of the majority to truly old age, why must we express concern about having to provide for elderly people until they pass away?

DESAI: What are the answers?

VISHNEVSKY: In fact, the demographic changes have created an economic opportunity and provided an answer. Along with declining mortality, the number of total human years is growing in terms of not only consumption but production as well. The relationship between the years of "dependency" [in childhood and old age] and the "period of production" has remained practically unchanged. Viewed in this way, the problem of aging ceases to be a demographic problem. Dependent children act as consumer borrowers until they start producing. By contrast, the elderly revert to a dependent status after their working life is over, and their consumption is then paid for by labor they contributed earlier.

DESAI: Are you suggesting that in Russia the financing of pension payments to retirees is manageable?

VISHNEVSKY: Currently, the issue of the destructive influence of aging on senior citizens and on the overall economic conditions in the country is widely debated in Russia. Note that the extreme changes in the Russian age structure did not occur until the end of the twentieth century. The population, of course, got older, but one should not forget that workers in the "active phase of production" provide for the "free-ride periods" of old age and childhood as well.

DESAI: I do not understand the relevance of introducing the double burden of providing for the very young and the retirees in your argument.

VISHNEVSKY: In postwar Russia, the total burden of providing for children and seniors moved in waves as a result of the special features of the age pyramid formed under the double impact of the natural evolutionary process and the destructive traumas of the first half of the century. However, despite impressions to the contrary, the Russian population had a favorable age composition at the end of the last century, almost the best in the entire postwar period. The burden of supporting senior citizens continued to rise, but the combined burden of supporting young dependents and the elderly was falling and was unusually low by the end of the century.

DESAI: So you see a silver lining in the emerging age composition of the population.

VISHNEVSKY: Obviously the age structure of the Russian population will continue changing; in the absence of the damaging traumas of the first half of the last century, the evolutionary component will dominate. Therefore, Russia's population will get older. However, in my view, the effects of the aging population, including economic ones, are not as threatening as the current demographic stereotypes occasionally make them out to be. The presence of more seniors comes hand in hand with a variety of demographic and other changes that create genuine opportunities for neutralizing the negative consequences of aging. Let me give you the view of the distinguished American demographer and economist Richard Easterlin:[1] "The real issue to be faced is largely political, namely, how to capture via taxation the savings of households from supporting fewer younger dependents, so that these funds can be used to meet the rise in public expenditures needed to support older dependents. The question of political feasibility is a serious one, but it does not seem insurmountable, given that the workers to be taxed would themselves eventually be beneficiaries of such taxation."[2]

DESAI: Easterlin is suggesting a redistributive tilt via taxation for supporting the older generation.

VISHNEVSKY: Yes. We need an appropriate social philosophy that will enable us to redistribute resources in favor of the later phase of generational life in the context of the new demographic realities. Currently, this approach is missing, but it will emerge in the developed world when it reaches a stable age pyramid with a narrow base and a wide top. Until then, in the absence of the necessary policy drive, the increase in the share of the elderly every ten years will aggravate their situation and create new economic pressures.

I also want to inject a note of caution from a global perspective. Developed countries, preoccupied with their own problems, clearly underestimate the dangers of the massively young age structure of the poor countries. Taken together, children and the elderly in developed countries number 800 per thousand people aged 20–59 years in contrast to 1,000 or more for the developing countries with rapidly growing populations. That number is 1,450 per 1,000 for Nigeria, which will soon surpass Russia in population.

DESAI: What is the reason for such divergence?

VISHNEVSKY: The contrast results from their rapidly growing populations with large numbers of children in relation to people aged 20–59 years. These ratios are only 464 per 1,000 for Russia, in contrast to 585 for China, 723 for Brazil, 872 for India, and 1,339 for Nigeria. The immeasurable difficulties of providing for the children of these poor lands are far more serious than the problem of the aging in the developed countries.

Second, viewed in the context of world realities, the challenge of aging is more than just economic.

DESAI: What is that challenge?

VISHNEVSKY: I mentioned earlier that, for every developed-country resident, the developing world has five. But for people under 20, the ratio is one to seven. The developing countries have 2.1 billion children and youth under 20 in contrast to 300 million in the developed nations. I wonder whether the wealthy, aging, tired North can successfully handle the impact of this imbalance in the twenty-first century. Russia's task in managing that challenge will be no less difficult.

Note

Mariya Konovalova translated the interview from Russian into English.

1. Richard A. Easterlin, professor of economics at the University of Southern California and member of the National Academy of Sciences and the American Academy of Arts and Sciences, combines the various disciplines of economics, economic history, sociology, and psychology in his research. His pathbreaking contributions include an analysis of worldwide transitions from high to low fertility and mortality.

2. Richard A. Easterlin, *Growth Triumphant: The Twenty-First Century in Historical Perspective* (Ann Arbor: University of Michigan Press, 1996), 123.

CHAPTER 15

Jack Matlock Jr.

The Road Ahead

Russia's history does not prevent Russia from being a democracy any more than Bourbon autocracy deprived France of the possibility.

Gorbachev was the more systematic political reformer. . . . Yeltsin was not so much a systematic reformer as a master politician.

The elements of electoral democracy are not perfect but are far more extensive than they have ever been in Russian history.

Putin has brought a sense of stability to the Russian populace, which explains his current popularity.

I believe he [Putin] has a better understanding of Russia's interests than Yeltsin. The danger is that he will go too far in recentralizing political authority and rely too heavily on police methods.

Putin now has television tamed, in the sense that it will not report negative stories about topics that could be politically damaging to him—in particular, the war in Chechnya is not reported objectively.

Soviet mass culture was even more banal than quick food and Hollywood and was often imposed by police methods.

I believe that, ideologically and in spirit, the Cold War ended at the end of 1988, certainly not with the collapse of the Soviet Union but before that.

The end of the Cold War gave the Soviet leadership an opportunity to reform without the pressures of an adversarial U.S.-Soviet relationship.

During the Bush Sr. administration, the Cold War confrontation had practically disappeared.

While Russia under Putin is regressing in terms of democracy, I never really understood why some thought it would be easy or automatic for Russia to suddenly become a democracy.

Russia will not be able to deal with terrorism effectively until it greatly reduces the corruption of its security organs.

February 2004

DESAI: How would you counter the argument that democracy will not take root in Russia because, from a historical perspective, Russia was autocratic?

MATLOCK: Viewed historically, democracy in its modern form is a relatively new political system. It does not exist unblemished anywhere. All current democracies more or less emerged from something else. Most were, at one time or another, autocracies. Russia's history does not prevent it from being a democracy any more than Bourbon autocracy deprived France of the possibility.[1] Nor did flings with fascism—and a history of autocracy somewhat further back—make democracy an unattainable goal for Germany, Italy, and Spain.

DESAI: Do you believe that markets will not work either because Russia was collectivist?

MATLOCK: No. Tsarist Russia had a market economy, even if the peasant *mir* [Russian village community] was a collective structure in some respects. (So were plantations with slave labor in the American South.) Of course, a modern market economy requires an elaborate structure of institutions, laws, and habits that are only partially present in Russia because of the heritage of a command economy.

DESAI: Didn't the Slavophiles argue that the West represented rationality, scientific inquiry, and self-interest, traits that were inimical to the Russian character? Any truth to that blanket judgment?

MATLOCK: The Slavophiles made the argument, but I think they were wrong. Theirs was an emotional reaction to shame over Russia's economic backwardness as compared with Western Europe. Their theories are better seen as sour grapes than a reflection of reality.

DESAI: Gorbachev wanted, somewhat belatedly, the former Soviet Union to be restructured as a voluntary federation of participating units. Was that a feasible proposition?

MATLOCK: Probably not. Too many resentments had developed during the Soviet period. Also, as Gorbachev tried to move away from a command economy, he gave republic party leaders an incentive to break away. By doing so, they could retain control over the economy as well as the political system. When Gorbachev destroyed the direct rule of the Communist Party, there was no force to contain the various centrifugal tendencies in the republics. Also, Gorbachev's feud with

Yeltsin gave the latter an incentive to get back at him by destroying the country Gorbachev headed.

DESAI: How would you explain the disappearance of the Soviet empire?

MATLOCK: Once centralized Communist rule was destroyed, the political elites in most republics felt that they could best retain their power by breaking away from the Soviet Union. The three Baltic countries, western Ukraine, the South Caucasus, and, to a degree, Moldova all had strong nationalist movements, but in the other republics and eastern Ukraine, it was the Communist Party hierarchy that chose independence.

DESAI: How would you contrast Gorbachev and Yeltsin as reformers?

MATLOCK: Gorbachev was the more systematic political reformer. He managed to do what no other person at that time could have done: He weakened Communist rule in the Soviet Union. He did not understand economics very well, however, and bungled his economic policy. Yeltsin was not so much a systematic reformer as a master politician who seems to have had two overriding drives: to put a stake in the heart of the Communist Party so that it could never regain power and to retain power for himself. He was better at destroying the old system than building the new.

DESAI: Why didn't the economic deprivation under Yeltsin's fast-paced reforms, for example, the nonpayment of wages to millions of workers for months on end, lead to a societal breakdown and massive upheavals? Where did the restraint and resilience come from?

MATLOCK: Russians are indeed inured to hardship; they survived the atrocities of Stalinism and the horrors of World War II. What they went through in the 1990s, difficult as it was (and for many still is), was mild compared to the revolution, civil war, Stalinist collectivization, forced labor, and World War II.[2] Furthermore, things were not quite as bad as they may have looked from the outside. For example, even when people were not paid wages for months on end, they were often given payments in kind, free housing, access to garden plots, and other support devices. People were unhappy, certainly, but they knew from experience that uprisings could only make matters worse. So there was a certain rationality behind the restraint.

DESAI: Will the chaotic, even violent, trajectory of Russian history from Lenin to Stalin and from Gorbachev to Yeltsin take a stable course under Putin?

MATLOCK: Time will tell. The "trajectory" since Stalin's death in March 1953 seems to be away from state-sponsored violence. The elements of electoral democracy are not perfect but are far more extensive than they have ever been in Russian history. Of course, Russia has not yet developed democracy to the point that it can install a president who received fewer votes than his opponent. Putin has brought a sense of stability to the Russian populace, which explains his current popularity.

DESAI: In what way is Putin a different leader from his predecessors?

MATLOCK: He seems more calculating. He obviously wants to strengthen the authority of the Russian federal government. I believe he has a better understanding of Russia's interests than Yeltsin. The danger is that he will go too far in recentralizing political authority and rely too heavily on police methods.

DESAI: Do you think that the Russian media is being muzzled under Putin? According to some observers, sophisticated journalists and analysts continue informing and entertaining the public on issues of international, national, and local concern. What is your view?

MATLOCK: Putin now has television tamed, in the sense that it will not report negative stories about topics that could be politically damaging to him—in particular, the war in Chechnya is not reported objectively. The print media, too, is less daring than it used to be. However, on most topics the Russian media are reasonably objective. Russian TV viewers probably get more world news than those Americans who confine themselves to network shows.

Putin's attempts to avoid bad press are dangerous for the future of Russian democracy, but they should not be compared with the sort of total control exercised by the Communist regime in all but Gorbachev's final two years.

DESAI: Putin remarked that the December 2003 Duma elections represented "the current political reality in Russia." What did he have in mind?

MATLOCK: I suppose it was that most Russians are content with Putin's leadership and are willing to elect a Duma that is likely to follow Putin's lead.

DESAI: Do you worry that the Duma election and Putin's reelection as president in April 2004 might lead to a reversal of Russia's fragile democracy?

MATLOCK: Some of Putin's moves, particularly his reliance on former security service colleagues, may erode democratic institutions if certain recent trends are continued. This, of course, is worrisome, but I do not think it is inevitable that these trends will continue. We can still hope that President Putin will be more tolerant of criticism and less inclined to use legal procedures for political purposes during his second term.

DESAI: Do you attribute the appearance of the oligarchs in Russia to specific aspects of Russian culture or history? Or have they emerged because of the chaotic transition?

MATLOCK: I do not believe the appearance of the oligarchs is a specific Russian phenomenon. It is explained by the breakdown of the Soviet system and the lack of restraint in moving to a market economy. For a few years, there seemed to be few, if any, limits on what people could do to obtain economic power. The Russian political leaders of the early 1990s considered privatization of state property an overriding and urgent goal to prevent the return of a Communist system. They felt that privatization had to happen quickly, but there was no substantial legitimate private capital to purchase state assets in an orderly manner. This resulted in a Hobbesian scramble that may not have been inevitable but may have prevented a worse outcome—the victory of the Communist Party leader Zyuganov as president in 1996.

The accumulation of enormous economic power by a few individuals has occurred, of course, in cultures quite different from Russia's. Although the American "robber barons" of the nineteenth century were different from the Russian oligarchs in some important respects—unlike the contemporary Russians, they invested their assets in their own country for the most part—there are similarities. The rapid accumulation of capital under conditions of little governmental interference is common to both.

DESAI: The Russian poet Yevgeny Yevtushenko once complained about the McDonaldization of Russia.[3] Will the culture that produced some of the world's richest literature, music, and ballet survive the onslaught of the cultural banality of Americanization?

MATLOCK: Soviet mass culture was even more banal than quick food and Hollywood and was often imposed by police methods. McDonald's restaurants brought tasty, hygienic food to a city with few decent restaurants—thus the long lines to get into the first U.S.-style restaurants. If this and American mass culture really disturbed Yevtushenko, one wonders why he has chosen to live in Oklahoma for the last decade or so.

Selected Russian classical culture did receive support from the state that has been lacking in post-Communist times, but it will certainly survive since it is now a possession of the whole world. However, the best writers and artists of the Soviet period were either suppressed by the state or required to conform, as Yevtushenko might recall in his more sober moments. If there is a problem today, it is that the enforced conformism of the Soviet period poorly prepared talented writers and artists to compete in an open, commercial market. In addition, the economic disarray of the 1990s limited the number of people who were able to pay decent prices for books, art, and theater tickets. But the writers and artists are not doing too badly, and, like the Russian nation as a whole, genuine art will survive.

DESAI: Do you think that Tolstoy and Dostoevsky have become irrelevant for Russian readers?

MATLOCK: No, of course not. They are relevant for all of us! My happiest moments are spent reading them.

DESAI: Russia stretches from Europe to Asia. Its economy will revive. What kind of challenges will it present to U.S. foreign policy makers?

MATLOCK: I see no fundamental conflicts of national interest between Russia and the United States. Of course, there may well be commercial competition. That would be not only normal but actually a benefit to both countries since competition drives technical development and production efficiency.

DESAI: What is your vision of Russia's future? Do you think that it will acquire sufficient political and institutional resilience of the Anglo-American variety in order to avoid authoritarian outcomes?

MATLOCK: I am not a prophet and would not presume to predict developments in a country as vast and varied as Russia—and with so many contemporary problems. Nevertheless, two thoughts come to mind. One is that there is no reason why Russians should not, over time, develop a humane, productive, modern, and free society. The second is that, if they do, they will do it in their own way. It will not be simply a copy of the "Anglo-American" variety (I would say British and American varieties), nor of the French, German, Italian, or Spanish, none of which are identical to one another.

APRIL 2005

DESAI: I have been reading your fascinating new book, *Reagan and Gorbachev: How the Cold War Ended*.[4] How did the Cold War end?

MATLOCK: I wrote the book because I felt we needed to get some of the recent history right if we want to understand the dynamics of the current situation under Putin.

To begin with, there was a very interesting human story of two leaders, Reagan and Gorbachev, who were totally different and came from opposite points of view in almost every respect. Yet, within the historically short period of three and a half years, having started as antagonists, they left with the feeling that they had a sort of partnership.

DESAI: But you also have a huge political story in the book about how the Cold War and the Soviet Union ended. When did the Cold War end?

MATLOCK: I believe that, ideologically and in spirit, the Cold War ended at the end of 1988, certainly not with the collapse of the Soviet Union but before that, because no matter how you defined the Cold War, it was over before the Soviet Union collapsed. Therefore, the end of the Cold War did not automatically mean the collapse of the Soviet Union. Far from it.

DESAI: Why is this sequencing so critical?

MATLOCK: The end of the Cold War gave the Soviet leadership an opportunity to reform without the pressures of an adversarial U.S.-Soviet relationship. Presidents Reagan and Gorbachev, in effect, cooperated on a scenario, a plan of reforming the Soviet Union, which was defined initially by the United States. The plan was devised by the United States but with the idea that it should not be contrary to the national interests of a peaceful Soviet Union. We didn't really ask them to do anything that wasn't in their own interest if they defined it in a peaceful way.

DESAI: Why would Mikhail Gorbachev agree to such a plan?

MATLOCK: Gorbachev finally began to understand this in 1987. We know from the politburo records that, in effect, he adopted the U.S. agenda, which had been defined in Washington, without attribution, of course, as his own plan. He certainly had his own reasons for doing this when he began to see that the Soviet Union did need reform. As he moved along with these reforms, Reagan supported them. You may recall that, when Reagan went to Moscow in May of 1988, he was asked, "Is this still the Evil Empire?" He said, "No, that was another era, another time."

Then someone asked, "Well, who is responsible?" And he said, "Mr. Gorbachev, of course. He is the leader of this country." One more question [to Reagan]: "Who won?" "Well, certainly, the Cold War ended on terms that had been set by the West, and specifically by the United States, and yet I think both sides won."

This is essentially the position that both Reagan and Gorbachev held—that it was a mutual victory and that what was defeated was the Communist ideology and the Communist system, which was already being modified in the Soviet Union when the Cold War ended.

DESAI: You were U.S. ambassador in Moscow during the Reagan presidency going into that of George Bush Sr. How did you encounter these winds of change?

MATLOCK: As a diplomat, I could certainly feel that we were working with Soviet diplomats. [The years] 1989, 1990, and 1991 were years of important diplomacy that consisted in cleaning up the detritus, the very serious detritus that had been produced by the Cold War and its confrontation. During the Bush Sr. administration, the Cold War confrontation had practically disappeared. Of course, it was changing gradually, but by January 1989, we were working with Soviet diplomats. We were trying to reach a mutually defined goal that was not to the detriment of either side. We were no longer measuring it by the old Cold War yardstick. The zero sum game had ended. The spirit was entirely different. As you know, the two sides concluded several arms control treaties in a remarkably short time.

DESAI: Do you think the end of the Cold War contributed to the end of Communist rule in the Soviet Union?

MATLOCK: Of course it did, but we cannot and should not take credit for that. Gorbachev gets sole credit for that because he was the only person who could have done it. Communist rule could not have been brought down by pressure from the outside. In fact, pressure from the outside tended to accentuate it. When the party apparatus began to object to the reforms that Gorbachev thought were necessary, he decided he had to supercede party control. Systematically, step by step, using a good bit of deceit, he managed to get his own party officials to go along with the process. I think at first they thought he wasn't really serious, but by the time they realized his intention, it was too late to do anything effective about it. So the credit or the blame, if you wish, for the end of the Communist rule in the Soviet Union belongs to Mikhail Gorbachev, not to Reagan or Bush or the United States or the West.

DESAI: Wouldn't you say that, in the end, Gorbachev lost control over the process?

MATLOCK: The Soviet Union was a monolithic structure with internal inconsistencies and pulls and pressures. A fair measure of mistakes was made both by Gorbachev and his enemies, particularly by his enemies in terms of the attempted coup in August 1991. That really was the last nail in the coffin of the Soviet Union. The idea that the United States somehow, by its policies, brought down the Soviet Union and therefore ended the Cold War gets almost everything backward. It simply does not accord with the facts as I saw them.

DESAI: But you don't think that the end of the Cold War and of the Soviet Union was a victory for the United States?

MATLOCK: We often acted in the 1990s as if in fact it was a victory for us not just over the Soviet Union but also over its successor state, Russia. I think that, too, was a wrong way of looking at it. Russia was actually one of the winners of the Cold War. Its end freed the Russians and the Russian leadership so that they could, in effect, become themselves. They would have preferred to keep some sort of a union if Ukraine had stayed in. Once Ukraine decided in 1991 to leave the union, the Russian leadership did not want to hold on to the other republics. It was really the elected Russian leaders, including Yeltsin, that decided to slough off the republics. There were nationalist movements in some of the republics, particularly in the Baltic republics and in Southern Caucasus, but I believe that taking everything into account, the Soviet Union did not fly apart just because of nationalism, as some would have it.

DESAI: In what way does your experience as a diplomat and a scholar of the Soviet Union and Russia help you interpret the evolving domestic situation under Putin?

MATLOCK: I have two broad observations. While Russia under Putin is regressing in terms of democracy, I never really understood why some thought it would be easy or automatic for Russia to suddenly become a democracy. When I was in Moscow in the eighties and nineties, I was asked by Russians how long it was going to take for them to become a normal country. They didn't then say "a democratic country" but rather "a normal country." I would respond by saying, well, at least two generations. They are a little more than halfway through the first. I also think that the United States has very little leverage over the current internal developments in Russia. The Russians themselves will decide how to manage the process.

DESAI: Help me sort out the implications of Putin's regressive steps. Do you think that his measures aimed at consolidating political authority in his hands will help him contain terrorist activity?

MATLOCK: Steps such as appointing governors and abolishing constituency districts for the election of members of the Duma are not necessary to combat terrorism. They seem designed just to enhance his power. Some Russians, however, feel that the only way to end the grip of local mafias on Russian regions is to have the president appoint the governors. Nevertheless, Putin's proposals are definitely a step or two backward in the development of a democratic society.

DESAI: What would you suggest with regard to controlling the situation in Chechnya?

MATLOCK: Russia will not be able to deal with terrorism effectively until it greatly reduces the corruption of its security organs. There is no easy solution, given what has happened [in Belsan] and the culture of revenge that is common in the region. Simply granting Chechnya independence will not work; the result would be more like Afghanistan under the Taliban than Algeria after the French left. It will be a long struggle that Russia can win only if most Chechens are convinced that they must oppose the terrorists.

DESAI: Do you think that, despite the proposed abolition of individual electoral contests and the retention of only party-contested seats for the Duma, the long-term prospects continue to be positive for a liberal political order in Russia?

MATLOCK: The abolition of individual constituency elections for the Duma is, in my opinion, a dangerous step that can lead in practice to a one-party state. It also weakens the local institutions needed in a civil society, but we cannot foresee all of the consequences. Perhaps it will convince the Russian parties seeking democracy that they must cooperate more fully—even, perhaps, to merge—in order to retain influence in the Duma. Also, it will mean that the population will hold the president personally responsible for problems that he might otherwise have dodged.

As for the long-term prospects for a liberal order in Russia, I wish I could comment about the future with confidence, but I have found that many key elements, particularly the effect of political decisions, are not predictable. There are too many unintended consequences in a fluid situation. I used to say (and still do) that I cannot predict what will happen in the future, but when it happens I'll be happy to explain why it was inevitable.

I agree that, for a country in the stage of development in which Russia finds itself, good government is more important than pure democracy. Take Chile, for example. Chile emerged from Pinochet's dictatorship better off than it was before—even though that does not excuse the violence that brought him to power. I find the example of the British in Hong Kong even more persuasive. Until near the end of British tenure, there was little democracy in Hong Kong, but there was a relatively honest government with limited powers, an independent judiciary, respect for property rights, and so on.

If Putin's latest moves give him the authority to improve government efficiency, diminish corruption, and keep economic reforms on track, then they will eventually be seen as justified. If I fail to applaud these moves, on the other hand, it is because I am no longer sure that Putin's ultimate aim is reform. The treatment of Yukos, in particular, leads me to believe that he places his own power and state control over the hurly-burly of a civil society and an economy for which the government sets and enforces rules but refrains from dominating. If Putin's goal is control, the latest moves are unlikely to bring the positive effects we all hope for. Nevertheless, I believe that Russia is too varied and too divided to permit the reestablishment of an autocracy. Therefore, we can hope for the best, and we should reserve final judgment until we see how the changes Putin has proposed really work out.

DESAI: Does it make sense to apply the norms of the full-fledged U.S. democracy to Russia's evolving political transition?

MATLOCK: Of course not. Each country must find its own way, creating institutions consistent with its own culture, but there are certain norms to which all countries must adhere if they are to be considered democracies. President Putin's latest proposals seriously risk undermining some of the foundations of democracy that were built with such pain and effort in the 1990s. Nevertheless, as I said earlier, the outcome is far from clear, and a sympathetic foreign observer can only watch developments and hope that things will not turn out as badly as they look at this moment.

DESAI: As a former diplomat, how do you assess the intensely personal relationship between Bush and Putin?

MATLOCK: I am all for having a good personal relationship between the two presidents. In fact, one of the themes of my book on Reagan and Gorbachev focuses on how each side was able to influence decision making through personal contacts while keeping its own interests in mind. So I would never argue in favor of simply putting policy considerations at the top, entirely above personal relationship. I think that for years our relations with India were plagued by bad personal relations between U.S. presidents and Indian prime ministers. Nehru just seemed to rub American presidents the wrong way, and this had an effect, and not a positive one, on U.S. policies with respect to India.

DESAI: Nevertheless, don't you think the personal aspect can be overdone to the point of being misleading?

MATLOCK: Well, yes, if it sinks to the level of looking into the soul and the eyes of a foreign leader. That kind of rhetoric may be politically self-serving. In my experience, Reagan and Bush Sr. were brutally frank with Gorbachev in private, and this had an effect. Once the relationship developed, they were less so in public, but they refrained from saying anything terribly misleading.

So I think we should encourage our presidents to develop close personal relations. We do not gain anything from open hostility of the kind that occurred between George W. Bush and Jacques Chirac. When things get to that point, they are bad for both countries. At the same time, it is important to define our interests, prioritize them, and trade off a minor concession to protect a critical advantage. Such tradeoffs may offend some bureaucrats who are used to focusing on a specific objective rather than balancing several of them. However, that's what we elect our presidents to do, rightly or wrongly, and that's what we pay them for.

NOTES

1. The Bourbons were a French royal family descended from Louis I, Duke of Bourbon (c. 1270–c. 1342).

2. The October Revolution of 1917 brought Lenin and the Bolsheviks to power; during the civil war (1918–1920), the Red Army defended the new regime; the Stalinist

collectivization of the 1930s sought to establish huge, collective, state-run farms and to exterminate small private farms.

3. The Russian poet Yevgeny Yevtushenko (b. 1933) now teaches at the University of Tulsa. He came to prominence in the 1960s during the post-Stalinist "thaw," which witnessed a lessening of controls on literature and life in general.

4. Jack F. Matlock Jr., *Reagan and Gorbachev: How the Cold War Ended* (New York: Random House, 2004).

Part IV

The Role of History

CHAPTER 16

Martin Malia

History Lessons

APRIL 2000

Like all countries, Russia has never existed in a political or cultural vacuum. It has always had to interact with other, neighboring countries, which, as it turned out from the very beginning, were all much more advanced culturally, economically, and politically than Russia was. In this situation of relative backwardness, therefore, its national character . . . was developed in the interaction with its neighbors.

All Peter [the Great] needed to do in the early eighteenth century to be competitive with the rest of Europe was to create a standing army . . . a navy, and enough education to make these two modern attributes work. Moreover, his Western models in the eighteenth century were almost all absolute monarchies. All he had to do was call himself emperor and create a European, Versailles-like court, and he was modern.

Putin cannot be Peter the Great because the twenty-first century is not the eighteenth. . . . In the twentieth century, modernization, or Westernization means much more than an army or a navy. If Putin wants to make Russia strong, he must make it advanced technologically, and that means fostering education. Advanced technology and education mean an independent-minded, diverse, civil society. You cannot run a modern, technological, and educated society the way you run an eighteenth-century military monarchy. I think that Putin understands this, for he considers himself to be the Petrine tradition. He's from St. Petersburg.

He [Gorbachev] deserves credit for opening the windows, letting in fresh air, and permitting people to speak the truth. It was only this speaking of the truth that destroyed what Solzhenitsyn called "the Lie," the pretension of the system to be rational, just, egalitarian, and not coercive.

Yeltsin's power was based ultimately not on his position as a Party boss, but on winning elections.

He [Yeltsin] did indeed devour Gorbachev, for in the end he drove him from the presidency. Yet comparing Yeltsin to a snake is inappropriate, for it implies a secretiveness and deviousness that are not central to his character. He is more a blustering Russian *muzhik* [peasant].

Nineteen ninety-one [in Russia], therefore, was not a revolution in the same sense as 1789 [the French Revolution] had been.

They [Gaidar and Chubais] were market-oriented ideologues. I think their main prophet was Friedrich Hayek.

His [Putin's] program of Westernization and modernization cannot, under twenty-first century conditions, take extreme authoritarian forms.

He [Putin] cannot be Chilean dictator Gen. Augusto Pinochet, because international conditions do not allow it. At the beginning of the twenty-first century, international norms have changed. . . . There will be some law-and-order tightening—the Giuliani, zero-tolerance effect on a national scale. However, as for real authoritarian restoration—no.

APRIL 2000

DESAI: What is the basis of your argument that the roots of Russia's continuing dilemma are not in some unchanging natural essence pushing it to authoritarianism and expansionism?

MALIA: The roots of my argument are in comparative history. Like all countries, Russia has never existed in a political or cultural vacuum. It has always had to interact with neighboring countries, which, as it turned out from the very beginning, were all much more advanced culturally, economically, and politically than Russia was. In this situation of relative backwardness, therefore, its national character—and it does exist: All states acquire over time a set of cultural norms that count toward their character—was developed in interaction with its neighbors, first, with respect to the Mediterranean world, from which it received Greek Christianity. It was, in ecclesiastical terms, a dependency until the fifteenth century. Second, [it was influenced] in economic terms: The heartland of Russia, the area between the Oka and the Upper Volga rivers, is the easternmost, northernmost, and poorest part of the North European Plain, a plain that, starting in southern England and France from the Pyrenees northward, builds across Germany and Poland into Russia, getting progressively farther away from a warm climate and fertile soil. So not only was it culturally dependent on developed regions farther south, but its basis of natural resources in an agricultural era was also much poorer. Moreover, like Poland or Prussia, it was in a very exposed geopolitical position. To the south, the steppe nomads were a real problem until the eighteenth century, something that did not happen in Western Europe after the eleventh century. Russia had no sea outlet until the eighteenth century, except for Arkhangelsk in the north, that would foster the development of commerce. So, the Russian nucleus of Muscovy developed as a poor frontier zone in a weak defensive position. Its only wealth was land and serfs to work the land.

Hence, the country became a very simple, military, serf-based autocracy. Absolute monarchy and autocracy are military modes in politics, and an army has to have a supreme commander. That is why Europe had absolute monarchies until well into the nineteenth century in some cases and certainly into the eighteenth century in almost all cases. So Russia became a particularly stringent military monarchy or an autocracy, ruling over a very poorly diversified society. Most notably, it was "missing" a middle class—but I don't really like that term because it implies that it is normal to have a middle class, even though many militarized societies do not have one.

To summarize, religious dependency and the fact that Russia was the only European state that did not belong to a major European church made a difference; this, together with a poor economy, an undiversified society, and a military monarchy, creates a certain mindset. Such a heritage is not conducive to the development of representative institutions and sophisticated economic forms. Thus, insofar as there has been continuity of political forms from the mobilizing era of Peter the Great to, say, Stalin, it is because of a continuity of a basic geopolitical situation, not of something innate, something in the Russian genes.[1]

DESAI: But isn't there a continuing Russian-Soviet tradition of a process and a specific leader becoming indistinguishable from the process? Isn't that a danger?

MALIA: To speak only of the past, I think I have already answered that question. Since Russia was always a poor society even when it was a great empire, as under the eighteenth- and nineteenth-century tsars, in an exposed position, its natural form of organization was a monarchy, which means a strong leader. However, if conditions change in the future, there will not necessarily be a need for a strong leader. I think that conditions had changed by the end of the twentieth century: Putin cannot be Peter the Great because the twenty-first century is not the eighteenth. All Peter needed to do in the early eighteenth century to be competitive with the rest of Europe was to create a standing army instead of a seasonal militia, which is what Russia had before; a navy; and enough education to make these two modern attributes work. Moreover, his Western models in the eighteenth century were almost all absolute monarchies. All he had to do was to call himself emperor and create a European, Versailles-like court, and he was modern. In the twentieth century, modernization or Westernization means much more than an army or a navy.

If Putin wants to make Russia strong, he must make it advanced technologically, and that means fostering education. Advanced technology and education mean an independent-minded, diverse, civil society. You cannot run a modern, technological, and educated society the way you run an eighteenth-century military monarchy. I think that Putin understands this, for he considers himself to be in the Petrine tradition. He's from St. Petersburg.

DESAI: What tradition is that?

MALIA: That means a strong state to modernize Russia through Westernization.

DESAI: Petrine?

MALIA: Meaning "like Peter"; it is a historian's word, and it connotes building a strong Russia internationally by creating a strong state internally so as to foster Westernization and modernization from above. But to repeat, Westernization in the twenty-first century does not mean the crude and simple thing it meant at the beginning of the eighteenth. It means creating a sophisticated, modern, technological society and market economy, and Putin understands that.

To speculate a bit on the basis of very little evidence, I would say that one of the traumatic experiences of Putin's life must have been his experience in East Germany, for while there he witnessed the complete collapse of the Soviet system, a system in which he believed when he joined the KGB in 1975. This could only have impressed on him the extraordinary vulnerability of that system and the contrasting dynamism of its rival, which he had always been taught to hate as "capitalism." The shock must have been a bit like what Peter felt when he lost the battle of Narva against the Swedes or what Ivan the Terrible felt when he lost the Livonian War in the same Baltic area.[2] Putin could only have concluded that what he had been brought up to believe was progress for Russia—that is, socialism—was in fact a burden. The corollary of this was that Russia had to chuck the old Muscovite ways of Stalin and adopt the new modern ways of the so-called capitalist world. So, when he returned to St. Petersburg after having lost his job in East Germany, he joined the reformers.

DESAI: So let's talk about the Soviet system, which Putin experienced firsthand. Throughout the Soviet era from Stalin to Brezhnev, the Communist Party of the Soviet Union defined the goals and implemented them ruthlessly. There was no distinction between ends and means. Is that a correct view of Soviet history of seven decades?

MALIA: The goals were defined first not by Stalin. They were defined by Marx. They are right there in part 2 of the *Communist Manifesto*.[3] The proletariat should "seize control of the state and wrest all capital from the bourgeoisie," after which the Communists should introduce a rational "plan" for the economy, including "industrial armies in agriculture." The Second International also had such a program. The difference between the Bolsheviks and the other parties in the Second International was that the Western social democrats never implemented their maximal program because they were waiting for a parliamentary majority that would permit them to combine the Communist goals of Marx with parliamentary democracy. Well, the fact that they thought they could combine such goals with parliamentary democracy meant that they could never implement them. So the social democrats remained nicely democratic, but they never built socialism. What the Communists did, starting with Lenin's "War Communism," but especially under

Stalin, was to carry out the full suppression of capitalism—no private property, no profit, no market, land collectivization. And that's the basic Marxist program.

DESAI: But the means were not in Marx?

MALIA: Not explicitly, for Marx thought that the logic of history would produce a proletarian majority that would automatically want Communism after only a short dictatorship of the proletariat. But, of course, the logic of history never led to such a result. The Marxist belief that history necessarily culminates in the non-capitalism of Communism is an impossible utopia. In fact, as the twentieth century demonstrates, what is required to reach Marx's Communism is the coercive will of a Leninist party to do what history fails to do, that is, suppress capitalism. So, in the real world, the only choice for Marxists was to either give up the Utopia, which is what the Western social democrats did, without admitting it to this day, or use coercion in the conviction that you are expressing the genuine will of the proletariat and that you are on the side of history. And that is why a small minority of Bolsheviks, beginning with Lenin, but especially under Stalin, had the will to coerce an entire society into Communism.

DESAI: Would you give Mikhail Gorbachev some credit for introducing in Russia the winds of change that—through glasnost—gave the Russian people and certainly Russia's intelligentsia the opportunity of distinguishing between ends and means?

MALIA: He deserves credit for opening the windows, letting in fresh air, and permitting people to speak the truth. It was only this speaking of the truth that destroyed what Solzhenitsyn called "the Lie," the pretension of the system to be rational, just, egalitarian, and not coercive. Gorbachev deserves credit for that, but I don't think he deserves credit for the results that he produced because he did not intend to destroy the system and "restore capitalism," to use the Soviets' stock phrase for the designs of their "enemies." Even to this day, Gorbachev's declarations indicate that he felt that the "national choice made in October," as he put it, that is, Marxist socialism, was a viable choice and that the Soviet Union was a viable political entity.

DESAI: The "choice" of October 1917?[4]

MALIA: Yes, October 1917. But that simply means that Gorbachev did not really understand the system he was ruling over.

DESAI: Do you think that under Yeltsin this lack of distinction between means and ends—that is, anything goes for the good of the cause—persisted not only because stable, strong political institutions that foster accountability were not in place but also because of his own view of how politics must be conducted?

MALIA: Well, after all, Yeltsin entered politics as a party secretary, a regional party boss, and party bosses were always little autocrats. Yeltsin was used to mobilizing the people behind whatever program he had in mind and then to giving orders to implement his intentions. As for his goals, he became convinced, through the experience of trying to make the system function, first in Sverdlovsk (now Yekaterin-burg) and then in Moscow, that the system would not work. Consequently, it had to be replaced by the modern Western system of democracy and the market. And here I think that Leon Aron's chapter "America, America" is a very important part of his *Yeltsin: A Revolutionary Life* [New York: St. Martin's Press, 2000]. The spectacle of America's, to him, incredible prosperity finally convinced him that Russia had to get rid of the whole kit and caboodle of "real socialism" and replace it with democracy and the market. To be sure, he went about it in a somewhat Petrine fashion, for example, autocratically deciding that, on January 2, 1992, there would be full liberation of prices and, ultimately, reluctantly deciding in 1993 that you had to use force against the Supreme Soviet's opposition to his program. However, on other occasions, he tried negotiating and cajoling. For instance, in December 1992, when he had to get rid of Gaidar and take on Chernomyrdin [as prime minister], he negotiated long and hard before he gave in. He tried appealing to the people over the head of the Supreme Soviet, as he did in the referendum of April 1993. In 1996, he fought for his reforms by going through an extremely strenuous reelection campaign, even dancing in public to please young voters. So the means he used were a mixture: He was part party boss and part democrat, even at times a demagogic politician, but I don't think that he ever gave up on his new, anti-Communist ends, namely, electoral politics, free markets, and free expression.

DESAI: But don't you think that the Gorbachev-Yeltsin confrontation was a titanic power struggle during which the craftier apparatchik won? After all, the Soviet Union was dissolved as a result of the secret deal that Yeltsin made with the leaders of Ukraine and Belarus. The snake won over the hedgehog, or is that an inapt comparison?

MALIA: I think it is an inapt comparison—and too unkind to Yeltsin. First, he was a craftier politician than Gorbachev, not a craftier apparatchik. Yeltsin's power was based ultimately not on his position as a party boss but on winning elections. And, before the end of the Soviet Union, he ran for election three times and was elected by huge majorities, first from Moscow to the Union Congress of People's Deputies, then from Sverdlovsk to the Russian Congress of People's Deputies, and finally as president of Russia. Thus he really played the democratic card to the hilt, whereas Gorbachev was never willing to run for popular election. As a matter of fact, Yeltsin won five elections, for we must also count the referendum of 1993 and the presidential election of 1996. So Yeltsin was craftier only in the sense that he was a better democratic politician than Gorbachev.

DESAI: Yes, but what about the hedgehog and the snake comparison?

MALIA: He did indeed devour Gorbachev, for in the end he drove him from the presidency. Yet comparing Yeltsin to a snake is inappropriate, for it implies a secretiveness and a deviousness that are not central to his character. He is more a blustering Russian *muzhik* [peasant].

DESAI: In what sense is Yeltsin a revolutionary?

MALIA: That depends on what you mean by "revolution."

DESAI: What is your definition?

MALIA: There is, of course, no one definition, but our great models of revolution are the American Revolution and the French Revolution.

DESAI: What about the Chinese Revolution?

MALIA: That was intended as a second edition of the Russian Revolution of 1917. However, to understand the pair of them, it is necessary to go further back in time. The modern concept of revolution emerged between the American revolt of 1776 and the French upheaval of 1789. What "revolution" has meant since then is a violent change from one historical era to another, leading to the creation of a new society, a new world, and a new man—at least, this is the intended or hoped-for result. This transition is effected, moreover, through the breakthrough of new forces that were previously suppressed: self-governing colonies in America, an educated and wealthy third estate in France.[5]

In Russia there was indeed a transition from one era to another under Yeltsin, but the new era the Russian "democrats" hoped to reach was simply self-government and the market, things that were hardly new in the human experience. They simply marked a return to 1789. Nor was there an organized emerging force in Russia or any analogue of the third estate. The forces that broke through in Russia in 1991 were the intelligentsia and a body of opportunistic apparatchiki that decided it was time to change sides. There was thus no new civil society. And all of these not-very-new people were camped in the midst of the ruins of the old structures.

Nineteen ninety-one, therefore, was not a revolution in the same sense that 1789 had been. With regard to China—and indeed to the whole Communist process that began in 1917 in Russia—this was supposed to be the revolution that goes beyond 1789, the revolution to end all revolutions, the socialist revolution—in sum, the end of history. But, of course, neither in Russia nor in China did the "second 1789" create anything lasting. The Soviet system collapsed completely, and the Chinese had to abandon everything but the party—which is saying a lot, but it is only the shell of socialism. Yet the substance of socialism, the goals of the revolution, and its economic and social program had to be abandoned in China no less than in Russia. In sum, therefore, Yeltsin's revolution marks a return to what Marx had called a "bourgeois revolution," namely, universal suffrage in politics, a market economy, and an independent civil society. That is very new for Russia, and in that sense, Yeltsin was a revolutionary. However, in terms of the world experience, 1991 was not new.

DESAI: Yes, but wiping out seventy years of the Soviet regime?

MALIA: That just brings us back to February 1917, which in the Soviet context is revolutionary enough in the loose sense of that slippery word. So Leon Aron likes to call 1991 the "August Revolution" because he wants to emphasize the new start for Russia. But I do not think the term will stick in the historiography because too many people in the West, if not in Russia, associate revolution with socialism rather than antisocialism.

DESAI: Do you think Gaidar and Chubais, the two architects of Russian reform under Yeltsin's presidency, were market-oriented ideologues determined to decommunize Russia? In my view, they adopted economic measures to weaken the Communist Party and Communist leadership through a frontal attack on Soviet-era structures.

MALIA: I agree with that. They were market-oriented ideologues. I think their main prophet was Friedrich Hayek. While Communism was still in power, they both read Hayek and became converted to what one might call "market fundamentalism." However, they went beyond that to do what you just indicated. They used the market reforms to promote political and social transformation by destroying the party. Since the party was the framework of the whole society, its destruction was necessary to clear the deck for a new society. And that, I think, explains their haste and a lot of their failures because, even though you destroy the party, you have not yet put anything solid in its place. In evaluating the outcome of the reforming effort, we should not forget that, since the party had been everything in the Soviet system, it had not permitted the emergence of new forces, on the model of the third estate, before 1991. Thus, the Yeltsin government inherited only rubble from the past.

DESAI: Is the Yeltsin revolution likely to be followed by a reactionary consolidation under Putin?

MALIA: First, after the fall of the Soviet system, as well as of Communism in other countries, there has been a backlash everywhere because people were used to the social security Communism provided, even though they resented the despotic aspects of the system. Marketization and liberalization are painful for large elements of the population, so there has been a backlash. Both in Hungary and in Poland, therefore, former Communists returned to power, but this "velvet restoration" did not last. In Russia itself there was the constant pressure of what Yeltsin used to call the Red-Browns [Communist nationalists], that is, the desire to return to the Soviet system but with a new nationalism added, though this movement never came to power. And that pressure is still there. It will be felt during Putin's years in power. Nonetheless, his program of Westernization and modernization cannot, under twenty-first-century conditions, take extreme authoritarian forms. Putin wants to make Russia strong internationally, and he also wants to make the Russian state strong internally. In the twentieth century, to be strong internationally, Russia lacks the resources to conduct such an evolution all by itself. It will require massive foreign investment, and this means it has to create circumstances that will favor such investment. This means that Russia is going to have to be respectable internationally, which means that it has to observe certain norms regarding civil and human rights, civil liberties, and so on. In sum, it means that it has to be in some measure democratic. This is indispensable if it is going to attract foreign investment.

These constraints mean that Putin cannot restore an autocracy; he cannot create an authoritarian, right-wing regime; [and] he cannot be Chilean dictator Gen. Augusto Pinochet because international conditions do not allow it. At the beginning of the twenty-first century, international norms have changed. The world accepted brutality much more easily in 1945 than it does in 2000. During World War II, the Western allies bombed German cities to destroy them, killing innocent civilians. And they bombed Tokyo and other Japanese cities to destroy them.

These firebombings killed thousands and thousands of people. Today, a few atrocities in Bosnia and Kosovo get the world up in arms. The world community intervenes. There's a huge outcry over the war in Chechnya. Stalin got away with murder on a mass scale, and there was very little protest. International standards of what constitutes civilized behavior have evolved enormously in the past half century. Russia cannot behave in an old-fashioned, brutal, autocratic, nationalistic way and get away with it. It needs the support of the world community to survive; therefore, it will more or less comply with those norms. For Russia, I think, Chechnya was an exception. Here national honor rather than Russian territorial integrity was at stake. Russia's manhood as a nation was more or less at stake in the eyes not just of its leaders but also of its population. Therefore, the population put up with this, for our age, exceptional brutality.

Now that it is done, Russia does not have to repeat it. So, as the Chechnya war recedes into the past, the pressure on Russia to observe the new higher norms of international and civic morality will prevent Putin from doing anything extreme. He cannot do what the Kuomintang did in Taiwan,[6] or the generals in South Korea, or Lee Kuan Yew in Singapore,[7] or, finally, Pinochet in Chile because similar policies would now cost Russia her international respectability.

At the same time, it should be noted that it is the authoritarian mode of modernization of Taiwan, South Korea, Singapore, Chile, and Brazil that worked most successfully in the twentieth century. Communism was a distinctly less efficient form of authoritarian modernization. It ultimately failed in Russia and in Eastern Europe, and the Chinese have abandoned it de facto.

So, later in the twentieth century, that is, down to the 1980s, authoritarian modernization worked, but, strangely, the fall of Communism has made the world a much softer place. Although the West supported the Kuomintang's and Pinochet's modernization, it would not put up with Putin taking the same route now. The West was hard hearted and hard headed about autocratic modernization only so long as the Communist menace existed. Thus, the fact that Russia is no longer Communist has created a world environment where the constraints on its internal behavior are much greater. And remember how staggering its internal problem is: That huge country is now so poor that its economy is only the size of that of the Netherlands.

DESAI: Nevertheless, short of going to full-blast authoritarianism, can Putin adopt a semiauthoritarian mode?

MALIA: Here, let us make another comparison. I remember in France, after de Gaulle took over, the Left (most of my French friends are socialists) constantly complained about the government's monopoly of information on television and the radio. In fact, it was not a monopoly, though the state did intervene more than it had in the past, but this was enough to generate complaints of a "one-party state."

Of course, the situation in Russia is much more dramatic, and the problems are much greater than they ever were in France. So, yes, there could very well be some tightening of state controls in Russia. There could well be a sort of Giuliani reaction in Russia. This would appeal to the "simple Ivan," the ordinary citizen. There are many of them who would welcome a strong man to bring all of the crooks to justice and restore order, but this reaction would not turn into anything like a police state. Putin cannot push the nationalist impulse too far because, as Aron rightly insists, Yeltsin irrevocably destroyed the Russian Empire. The new government is not going to try to reconquer Ukraine or Belarus. Indeed, Russia does not even want Belarus back under any circumstances because it is a basket case economically. So Putin will no doubt go to military parades and give vigorous speeches. There will be some law-and-order tightening—the Giuliani, zero-tolerance effect on a national scale. However, as for a real authoritarian restoration—no. This is just beyond the capacity of the still very weak Russian state, and it is beyond the toleration of the world community. To emphasize the point, I repeat that Putin does need the world community just to make Russia a viable society—not a superpower, but simply a society that works. Do you agree with that?

DESAI: Yes, I do, but, being a New Yorker, I find your reference to Mayor Rudolph Giuliani a bit alarming.

MALIA: I just thought of it today because we are in New York.

DESAI: Would you go for a right-wing reactionary state in order for the reform momentum to continue?

MALIA: Personally, of course, I would not like to see a right-wing reactionary state in Russia. Still, there are times and situations where choices are very narrow. In retrospect, I think that the Korean generals probably did what needed doing at the time. Even in the case of Chile (though no one is saying this anymore), we should not forget that Salvador Allende was a disaster.[8] He was, in effect, destroying the economy, and the democratic opposition (the Christian Democrats) thought that Pinochet's coup was justified. They also naively thought that, after having gotten rid of Allende, Pinochet would hand the country back to them—even though these democrats had permitted Allende to come to power in the first place. When things get into the kind of impasse they were [experiencing] in Chile in 1973, the real choices are painfully limited. Obviously, of course, Pinochet went much too far; I am not trying to make a hero of him. Someone like de Gaulle, on coming to power when France was at a comparable impasse, did not shoot anybody. Nor do I think that Putin intends, or needs, to do anything drastic. Neither the world community nor the Russian population would support such action, and it would be counter-productive to the end of a revived, strong Russia.

DESAI: Given his KGB background, given statements like "democracy is a dictatorship of laws," "the stronger the state, the freer the individual," what signals do you get as a historian?

MALIA: I don't remember the context in which he made those remarks. "Dictatorship of the law" could be just a strong way of saying "the rule of the law." Or a *Rechtsstaat* (he knows German well).[9] In Russian, the term is *pravovoe gosudarstvo*. "Rechtsstaat" is Hegel's term. It is the general German term because, historically, Europe has often had the rule of law without a parliament. The Germans took the term *état de droit* from Montesquieu and translated it as Rechtsstaat.[10]

DESAI: In other words, the state of law is not the dictatorship of law?

MALIA: For Montesquieu, état de droit means the opposite of despotism. He distinguishes sharply between "despotism," which is the rule of lawless force, and "monarchy," which is founded on the rule of law. Putin no doubt had something like this in mind. Maybe he used the term *pravavaia diktatura* [legal dictatorship, i.e., dictatorship of the law], I don't know, but he certainly did not mean dictatorship in Stalin's sense.

DESAI: What will constrain him? If you agree that the historical record has been one of a failure to distinguish between ends and means, won't the lack of accountability continue under Putin, given his KGB background?

MALIA: His ends, which are a strong, dynamic, and modern Russia, preclude radical authoritarian means. This is the opposite of the situation under Stalin. And the reason is that the Bolshevik Revolution and the resulting civil war had been a disaster for Russia's economic development [and] in fact had set the country back twenty-five years. Stalin's crash industrialization was carried out essentially by the use of military means to achieve economic ends. He called this effort "class struggle," but, in reality, it meant using the party as a kind of political army to collectivize, industrialize, and develop the country. At the low level of Russia's economic development in the 1930s, those means were effective, at least in the short run. Moreover, they were effective for winning the war, but they are not effective for a sophisticated, modem, urban technological transformation of the sort Russia must now make. Therefore, Russia cannot repeat her historic pattern of using a strong military monarchy to remain competitive in the present-day world, no more than Japan could return to Meiji methods after World War II.[11]

DESAI: Is it possible that, given his desire to build a political consensus, he may craft a more legal, law-based state working with the Duma rather than operate via the array of decrees and arbitrary decisions under Yeltsin?

MALIA: He has already started that. First, he is in a situation that Yeltsin never enjoyed. Yeltsin never had a parliamentary majority, either with the Supreme Soviet until 1993 or after it with the Duma. The Russian president has been able to count on a parliamentary majority only since December 1999. Also, it is now clear that Communist support has stabilized at around a third of the vote, so Putin is trying to cut a deal with the Communists, giving them a small share of power, thus mobilizing as much of the nation as possible behind him. In other words, he wants a strong majority. He therefore cut a deal with the Communists to prevent Yevgeny Primakov from becoming the speaker of the Duma,[12] opting instead for Gennady Seleznov, who is a weak figure,[13] and giving the Communists some places on Duma committees. Just as Roosevelt took Republicans into his administration during the war or as de Gaulle debauched the socialist Guy Mollet to help him write the new constitution, many of Mollet's supporters expected that he would treat de Gaulle as a fascist;[14] instead, Mollet went along with the general because he believed France needed a more stable government. So I think Putin will try to be above any one party. Bismarck used to do this.[15] The Italians once called this tactic *trasformismo*.[16] Thus, Prime Minister Giovanni Giolitti governed sometimes with the radicals and sometimes with the conservatives, depending on the issue.[17] Quite probably Putin will try something of the sort.

DESAI: Given Russia's Soviet history of ruthless land collectivization and dekulakization, should the reverse, that is, the breakup of Russia's collective farms, also be forced?[18] That would also be a frontal attack on the most essential pillar of Stalinism. How practical is that?

MALIA: I do not know whether it should be forced because I am not that well acquainted with the situation in the countryside. As I understand it, the rural population is down to less than a third of the total. The people in the kolkhozes, the collective farms, are largely the elderly or the less ambitious, for whom the kolkhoz means security. They do not want to leave the collective. Moreover, the country cannot feed itself anyway. It has to import grain, so the kolkhozes are no longer vital to the nation. Maybe they should just slowly be liquidated. In any event, the peasants clearly do not want to escape from them.

DESAI: The public opinion polls across a wide spectrum consistently oppose rural land privatization.

MALIA: Yes, because of the long peasant tradition that the land is theirs collectively. Since this is so, a certain amount of vigorous action from above may well be necessary to break the impasse in the countryside. However, such action would not be anything on the level of the brutality of Stalin's collectivization, which was a military operation. Perhaps matters can be handled now on the model of Stolypin's reforms in 1905, that is, by legalizing private property in land.[19] Prime Minister Pyotr Stolypin did not require support from the peasants to initiate his reforms. By government fiat, he simply made it possible to legalize private land ownership in the hope that a minority of peasants would be interested and so create farms of their own.

DESAI: Are Russian oligarchs, who are maniacally exploitative, a special Russian phenomenon? Or would they have emerged anywhere given similar circumstances and opportunities?

MALIA: I do not think their emergence was culturally determined. They are not an especially Russian phenomenon, but rather a post-Soviet one. They made their money not by stealing the state, via Chubais's privatization or via his plan of loans for shares. They made it earlier in the Yeltsin years by taking advantage of the difference between artificially low Soviet prices and much higher world prices to sell commodities abroad for hard currency. It is this "accumulation of capital" that permitted them later on to play their political role and to engage in their freewheeling financial speculations. Their fortunes depended on a peculiar conjunction of circumstances that was temporary, specifically post-Soviet. With time, I think, as the economy develops in a more diversified fashion, they will lose their importance. Besides, most of them were bankrupted by the crash of August 1998.

DESAI: Quite a few of them have been finished.

MALIA: Now it is really only Boris Berezovsky and Vladimir Gusinsky who are active.[20]

DESAI: I think Putin can do without them.

MALIA: I think so, too.

DESAI: Should he choose to, could he start legal prosecution against them?

MALIA: He can get rid of them politically. Now that he has four years, he does not need to run for election again. He can sideline them politically.

DESAI: You mean political attrition.

MALIA: He may have to act to curtail their importance in television and the press. They are part owners of the major TV stations, and each one controls a newspaper.

DESAI: As a historian, where do you see Russia ten years from now?

MALIA: Historians normally do not analyze the future. So, speaking as a non-historian, as an ordinary citizen, I rather expect continued halting progress toward a more normal modernity because there are no other forms of modernity than the one we now associate with globalization. Third ways or second ways simply do not exist. I do not see any real possibility of a conservative, nationalist, authoritarian restoration. It may be attempted, but if it were it would not work, and it would not last. However, I do not think it will even be attempted, at least not by the present government. The present government is not going to have an easy time bringing order out of the great chaos that is post–Communist Russia, but I think it will make some progress, nonetheless. Ten years from now, I expect Russia will be further along the process of converging with the rest of the modern world but will not yet have arrived there.

NOTES

1. Peter the Great (1672–1725), remembered as the "westernizing" Russian tsar who built a window onto Europe with the founding of his new capital, Petersburg, is here juxtaposed with Joseph Stalin (1879–1953), the autocratic tyrant of the twentieth century.

2. Charles XII of Sweden defeated Peter the Great in 1700 at Narva, the first major battle of the Great Northern War. Peter, however, recaptured the city a few years later, in 1704. In 1558, Ivan the Terrible began a campaign against Livonia. After initial successes, he was defeated by Stephen Báthory, the king of Poland and Lithuania.

3. The *Communist Manifesto* (1848), written by Marx and Engels, represents a synthesis of German philosophy, British political economy, and French socialism. It became one of the defining texts for the Communist Party in the USSR.

4. The Russian Revolution of October 1917 ushered in the reign of the Bolsheviks, with Lenin at the helm.

5. The first estate comprised the clergy, the second estate was made up of the nobility, and the third estate consisted of the bourgeoisie, or the common people.

6. The National People's Party, or Kuomintang, governed in China from 1928 until 1949; it then ruled in Taiwan under Chiang Kai-shek and his successors.

7. During his thirty-one years as prime minister, from 1959 to 1990, Lee Kuan Yew saw the transformation of Singapore into an affluent and bustling metropolis.

8. Salvador Allende (1908–1973) was Chile's first socialist president.

9. A Rechtsstaat is a constitutional state; an état de droit is a state of law.

10. Montesquieu (1689–1755), French philosopher and author of *The Spirit of Laws* (1748).

11. Meiji (1852–1912), emperor of Japan from 1867 to 1912, transformed Japan into a great, modern power.

12. Having appointed Primakov prime minister in September 1998, Yeltsin fired him in May 1999 for "failing to rescue" the Russian economy and then named Sergei Stepashin acting premier. The timing coincided with the impending hearings mounted by the Communist majority to impeach Yeltsin in the State Duma.

13. Gennady Seleznov, a Communist, was elected speaker of the Duma in January 2000 as a result of an alliance between the Putin-backed Unity bloc and the Communists. In his interview, Gaidar called the move "clever, tough, and cynical but also wrong."

14. Guy Mollet, socialist politician and premier of France (1956–1957), joined de Gaulle's government as minister of state (1958–1959).

15. Otto von Bismarck (1815–1898) was prime minister of Prussia as well as founder and first chancellor (1871–1890) of the German Empire. His name has become synonymous with authoritarian tactics.

16. Trasformismo, the policy of bringing together members of different parties in the same cabinet, was practiced by the Italian politician Agostino Depretis (1813–1887), who served in several cabinet posts from 1862 to 1867. He became premier in 1876 and was the dominant force in Italian politics until 1886.

17. Giovanni Giolitti (1842–1928) served as prime minister of Italy five times.

18. Dekulakization is the brutal campaign that was begun in 1929 to "liquidate the kulak as a class." Kulak, which literally means "fist" in Russian, was a pejorative term for a relatively prosperous peasant. Collective farms were to replace small private farms.

19. By executive order in 1906, Pyotr Stolypin (1862–1911) introduced agrarian reforms that were further elaborated in 1910 and 1911. Stolypin's reforms aimed to alleviate both the plight of the peasant and the economic and political situation in the country in general.

20. Boris Berezovsky and Vladimir Gusinsky, two of Russia's best-known oligarchs, are both in exile.

CHAPTER 17

Richard Pipes

The Past in the Present

Russia basically never had democracy to speak of.

I think Russian presidential elections tend to be volatile because they lack solid voting traditions.

The main thing they [the Russians] regret is the loss of the great power status under the Soviet Union.

Russians know how to cope with hard times. In fact, Russians are more adept at coping with hard times than with good times.

Putin makes it very clear that he does not think Russia is ready for democracy.

In Soviet days, Russians read Pushkin and Tolstoy because there was hardly anything else, but if there are choices, they'll go for something lighter. I don't think you can blame the United States for that.

From the point of view of ethnic roots, American culture is neutral. Therefore, it has universal appeal.

I think Communism is altogether dead in the world. It's utterly discredited.

OCTOBER 2004

The notion that political parties can express the interests of society is alien to Russian political culture.

Putin undoubtedly is a "smart" politician, but what Russia needs is a statesman, and this he is not.

353

APRIL 2003

DESAI: How would you counter the argument that democracy will not take root in Russia because, from a historical perspective, Russia was autocratic?

PIPES: Russia basically never had democracy to speak of. Even in 1917, the provisional government was not elected. An interim government took power with the intention of holding national elections, but by the time the elections could be held, the government was ousted, so the Russians never really had a democratic government. I would not go so far as to say it would never take root. "Never" is a loaded word, and some countries that haven't had democratic traditions have managed to develop them. The problem is that democracy has to come not from above but from below; the pressure has to come from the people. These pressures did not exist in Russia, and to this day, they are very, very weak. Even if the current government under Putin wants to bring in democracy, and I'm skeptical that it does, it will run into difficulties. Two years ago, Putin made a statement to the effect that democracy is fine, but it is not for Russia.

DESAI: Nevertheless, they have had several elections—the elections of the Duma and of the president. Doesn't that count?

PIPES: First of all, democracy requires strong party structures. Russians don't have them. The only real party is the Communist Party, which is not democratic. The other parties are groupings around charismatic figures, but they have no structure. That is one big obstacle. Second, the government has managed in the past two years to control the principal media. Television is the principal medium, and you'll see that next time around, the election campaign will be regulated. Even in Yeltsin's days, rival candidates hardly had genuine opportunities to speak up, so there are serious problems.

DESAI: But democracy takes different forms in different countries, depending on their cultures, their historical traditions, and so on. Are you guarded about its prospects in Russia because, for example, they lack a civil society, a middle class?

PIPES: Of course, these elements are relevant. Western societies developed democratic features early on. Even urban citizens in the Middle Ages had civil rights, political rights, and elected officials. There was a sizeable feudal rural structure. Of course, feudalism was not democracy, but the relationship between the lord and the vassal was a contractual relationship. If one party violated it, the injured could seek recourse in the courts, so the contractual relationships of hundreds of years eventually changed into the rule of law and civil rights under mature democracies. Europe had a rudimentary democracy in the nineteenth century. It began earlier in America. I wonder whether it can be developed overnight in Russia. It would be very difficult.

DESAI: Let's talk about Gorbachev as a democratic leader. Do you think his policies marked a break from the long tsarist and Soviet traditions of authoritarianism?

PIPES: I think his policy of openness, or glasnost, developed over time. Initially he did not intend to bring anything resembling democracy to Russia. He introduced glasnost and voting rights as means of applying pressure on the Communist nomenklatura. Then things began to get out of hand. I once heard Alexander Yakovlev say that by 1988 they had decided that Communism was not reformable.[1] Gorbachev tried these evolutionary reforms for three years, after which he said "enough," and then the situation simply ran away from him. He was here at Harvard a few months ago for a lecture, and we chatted over dinner, and I felt he finally understood genuine democratic processes and the limitations of his policies, but this was not the case when he was in office. At that time, he wanted to bring pressure on the nomenklatura from below because they were an obstacle in the way of the changes he wanted.

DESAI: You know, talking about pressures from below, I am reminded of a conversation I had with him three years ago. I told him that, in early 1990, he was the most popular politician in the Soviet Union; in fact, his popularity rating was ahead of Andrei Sakharov and Boris Yeltsin.[2] I asked him why he did not think of getting elected president via a general election. That way he could have gotten a mandate from the people that would have freed him from the constant fear of being ousted by the party bosses as Khrushchev was. He said he should have considered that.

PIPES: I wonder whether that could have worked in his favor. Election results, after all, depend on established traditions and a mature electorate. In England and here in the United States, the shifts are gradual because of that. Take the 2000 presidential election here: One candidate got a majority of popular votes, whereas another one got a majority of the delegates. In an inexperienced country, the electorate can swing violently from one end to the other. That was noticeable in the elections held in Russian villages before the revolution. People shifted from one extreme to the other. So the fact of his being so popular in early 1990 did not guarantee anything, and today he gets less than 1 percent of the popular rating. I'm surprised it hasn't happened to Putin already. I think Russian presidential elections tend to be volatile because they lack solid voting traditions.

DESAI: But doesn't the volatile public opinion represent something like Ibsen's "Enemy of the People" syndrome? From that perspective, one might want to say that democracy works in Russia. The Russians felt that Gorbachev was responsible for the breakup of the Soviet Union. It was humiliating, so he should be removed.

PIPES: Today, certainly, they blame him for just about everything: the collapse of the Soviet Union, the disintegration of the country, the loss of access to social services. He's immensely unpopular.

DESAI: The sinking star trajectory befell Yeltsin, also. Disorder and corruption became rampant under his watch, and millions were impoverished.

PIPES: There was an interesting public opinion poll published in *Izvestiya* a couple of months ago where they asked people, "What do you consider to be your own власть, your own government, your authority? The majority said the Soviet Union, even though it doesn't exist! Only a minority said the present regime. They are terribly befuddled and confused. I was in Perm recently, a city in the Urals, and all of the streets still have the old names—Leninskaya, Oktyabrskaya, Komsomolskaya, Kuibysheva, and so on—and you get the feeling there is really no break with the past.[3] They don't quite know where they are, as if they are between two worlds, in limbo. I think that was a great mistake on Yeltsin's part. When he first came to power—he was elected with a vast majority—he could have removed Lenin's body from the mausoleum. He could have made these changes. He could have given orders—"within three months all street names in Russia must abandon their Communist origins"—but he didn't do that. Now it's too late. They are in limbo; they don't know where they are or who the authorities are. The main thing they regret is the loss of the great power status under the Soviet Union.

DESAI: Let's talk about the breakup of the Soviet Union. Somewhat belatedly, Gorbachev wanted the former Soviet Union to be restructured as a voluntary federation of participating units. Was that a feasible option?

PIPES: Not at all, because it was not a voluntary union to begin with. I mean, each constituent republic was conquered either right after the revolution or in the course of the deal with Hitler, so the union was not voluntary. I have written quite a bit on this subject. My original doctoral dissertation was on this subject, as was my first book, *The Formation of the Soviet Union* [Cambridge: Harvard University Press, (1954) 1997]. I had no doubt that the union would eventually break up.

DESAI: Because the Communist party, which held it together, was a monolithic organization?

PIPES: The party was not divided into autonomous national units. It was an empire all right, and empires could not last in the twentieth century. It was a fluke it survived so long.

DESAI: Yes, I think all empires eventually disappear—the Ottoman Empire, the British Empire, the Soviet Empire. The surprise was the way it disappeared. It just collapsed.

PIPES: I had predicted that. I had said that, if there was any trouble, any weakening in the center, the whole edifice would disintegrate, fall apart suddenly, because it had nothing to hold it together, really, except force.

DESAI: Where did you say that? Which book?

PIPES: *The Formation of the Soviet Union,* which I wrote in 1954. I ended it with the following words, which are very often quoted:

> From the point of view of self-rule, the Communist government was even less generous with the minorities than the czarist predecessors had been. It destroyed independent party structures and local rule in cultural institutions. It was a unitary centralized authoritarian state such as the czarist state had never been. On the other hand, by granting the minorities extensive linguistic autonomy, and by placing the national territorial principle as the base of the state's political admin-

istration, which it previously was not, the Communists gave constitutional recognition to the multinational structure of the Soviet population. In view of the
importance which language and territory have for the development of national
consciousness, particularly for people who, like the Russian minorities during
the Revolution, have had some experience in self-rule, this purely formal feature of the Soviet constitution may have proven to be historically one of the most
consequential aspects of the formation of the Soviet Union.

What I meant is that, by setting up these essentially spurious republics, they created
a basis for the disintegration of the Union.

DESAI: Your judgment was well founded.

PIPES: I had no doubt about the disintegration of the union, although I did not
predict exactly when it would happen. However, I did know that the moment
something happened at the center, it would fall apart.

DESAI: Occasionally one hears people say that Sovietologists failed to see that
the Soviet Union would fall apart.

PIPES: Some people even objected to the possibility of its disintegration. I remember that the late Hugh Seton-Watson, who was a good friend of mine, at-
tended a conference in Washington, D.C., in the late 1970s, where I said that the
Soviet Union would fall apart one of these days.[4] He was outraged. He came up to
me and said it was nonsense. Of course, I wasn't the only one to come up with that
forecast, but I certainly had no doubts about it.

DESAI: Let us fast-forward in time and talk about Yeltsin. Bill Clinton and Boris
Yeltsin had common objectives of destroying the Communist-planned economy
and the authoritarian political system. Others argued that the process of weakening
the former arrangements with a view to introducing a liberal market system was
destructive. It brought about corruption and impoverished millions. What is your
view?

PIPES: When you have a rigid totalitarian system, such as the Soviet Union or
Iraq under Saddam Hussein, things fly apart. Violence, corruption, and stealing are
inevitable. You cannot have a gradual, peaceful transition. By contrast, the outcome was different in Poland. First of all, Polish patriots were in charge of Poland.
Second, Poland was never fully Communist. Agriculture was primarily in private
hands. Finally, the strong national, religious, and ethnic identities contributed to
the relatively gradual, peaceful process. Russia had little to hold it together, but
there was little violence. It was a bloodless revolution.

DESAI: One criticism of the bonding between the two presidents was that the
process got too personalized. Do you think so?

PIPES: Well, I wasn't there. Someone like Strobe Talbott would be in a better
position to answer your question. I did not agree with Clinton's policies in general, but his approach toward the ex–Soviet Union and the new Russia was correct. He established a warm, personal relationship at the top and welcomed another
member to the free world, and I think this was right.

DESAI: Was Yeltsin a revolutionary?

PIPES: Yes, he came to detest the system and wanted to overthrow it. The trouble was he didn't know what to do with it afterward. He was not an administrator. I think he was essentially—the Germans have a word for it, *Krisenmensch*—a man for crisis situations. He was wonderful, courageous, brave, and imaginative, as he climbed on a tank. But after the battle was won and the situation had calmed down, he had to administer and work with people. He got bored with it. I read his memoirs and reviewed the first one, in which he describes his insomnia and his boredom with routine matters. Those are the situations Putin is good at managing.

DESAI: So he was not just a blustering *muzhik* [peasant] with a sound political instinct.

PIPES: No, no. He prevented the return of Communism. But for him, a return to Communism, another successful coup could have happened. After all, the changes in 1990 and 1991 were weak and could easily have been reversed, and Russia could have returned to the old days. He prevented that. That is his great accomplishment.

DESAI: In early 1996, he considered canceling the presidential election, but ultimately he chose to go ahead with it. Boris Nemtsov talks in his interview about the predicament of having Gennady Zyuganov, the Communist leader, as the president of Russia.

PIPES: There was no chance of that happening.

DESAI: But if Yeltsin had not won?

PIPES: If Zyuganov had won, Russia would perhaps have returned to a modified version of Communism. I talked to Zyuganov when he was here some years ago. He claims to be a nationalist but nevertheless a democratic nationalist. It would certainly have been a different Russia under him. I would say that Gorbachev loosened the system to the point where it was ready to collapse, and then Yeltsin moved in and gave it the *coup de grâce*. It was destroyed, and after that there was no chance of its coming back.

DESAI: There are certain issues that puzzle me. Why didn't the economic deprivations under Yeltsin's fast-paced reforms lead to societal breakdown and a massive upheaval?

PIPES: I think there are two reasons. Russians know how to cope with hard times. In fact, Russians are more adept at coping with hard times than with good times. They have various devices for doing that. It is both a strength and a weakness. The second reason is that, after all the bloodletting under the Communists, they do not want any violence. They have lost a taste for violence of any kind. They also adopt various devices. I rented an apartment in Moscow in 1992. It was full of rice, sugar, and macaroni, and even the balcony and the closets were full of these items. They have learned these survival strategies from long experience and hoard for better times. Peasants used to do it. In medieval and modern Russia until the Communists appeared, Russia had periodic droughts. They knew how to survive those. They have a tremendous talent for coping in hard times.

DESAI: I also notice strong family and intergenerational ties among Russians. Often three generations support one another. I have lived in the United States a long time now, and I notice that, if you're out of a job here, you're out on the street, more or less.

PIPES: Yes, ours is an individualistic society. The Russians are different. You can count their friends on your fingertips, few in fact, but they have strong ties with family and friends. As a result, they manage to survive under unbelievable circumstances. I observe them here in Boston and in Cambridge. I remember when I was director of the Harvard Russian Research Center in the early 1970s, a Russian came to see me because he wanted a fellowship. I said to him, "I'm very sorry, but we have no money." He said, "You have nothing at all?" I said, "Look, I can give you three thousand dollars a year." He said, "I'll take it." How can anyone live on three thousand dollars a year in this country? For him it was enough to buy bread and tea. Perhaps he could count on friends. He could perhaps supplement it with a job. That is their mentality, and they are good at it.

DESAI: Perhaps these are the norms of people from traditional societies. However, let us go back to Putin. Will the violent trajectory of history from Lenin to Stalin and from Gorbachev to Yeltsin take a stable course under Putin?

PIPES: Obviously, he's offering stability, and Russians like that, which is why he is very popular. He is not a man of great vision, but he is a capable administrator; he is level headed; he has his emotions under control, and they like that. But it depends. I would hope for stability there, but Russians, by and large, are skeptical when you talk to them about the future.

DESAI: I'm also thinking about Putin's style of resolving political situations, of resolving political differences with adversaries like Boris Berezovsky who might threaten him. What means will he adopt for the purpose? Has the situation radically changed from the old days in that regard?

PIPES: He is more sensitive to criticism than Yeltsin was, but he will not adopt brutal means. He prefers backstage manipulations, which he employed in order to get rid of Berezovsky and Gusinsky, but he will not resort to violence. He is quite effective at that, the manner in which NTV, the television network, was transferred from private control. Neither Leninist nor Stalinist, but quietly, in an underhanded fashion. Of course, that does not solve the underlying problem, but at least it avoids explosions.

DESAI: Some among the Russian elite think that Yeltsin was a democrat at heart, whereas Putin is not.

PIPES: I think the question is, is Russia ready for democracy? Putin makes it very clear that he does not think Russia is ready for democracy. My view of him is that he believes in the free market. In his view, Communism as a system of running the economy was a fiasco. He believes in the free market but does not believe in democracy for Russia.

DESAI: Early on he talked about *pravovoye gosudarstvo,* a law-based state.

Pipes: He talks about it, but he hasn't done much about it.

Desai: He also talked about *diktatura zakonov,* a dictatorship of laws. Perhaps in the first step he wants to set up a legal infrastructure for bringing in law and order in small steps.

Pipes: Perhaps. In the last couple of years, the courts have occasionally ruled against the government. They favored the defendant, which is unusual in Russian tradition. So perhaps a kind of pravovoye gosudarstvo is slowly emerging. In some ways, Putin is following the Chinese model of economic freedoms and political centralization—of course, not to the same degree as in China. As far as freedom of speech is concerned, he doesn't care if the newspapers disagree with him. They are not read widely. He worries about television. Russia is a vast country, and television is the main medium of information, so he has pretty tight control over that.

Desai: A few journalists and former reporters also gave a similar view, saying that the print media is left largely free.

Pipes: The situation resembles the tsarist regime in the last years of the nineteenth century. Marx's *Das Kapital* was brought out in Russia with the imprimatur of the Russian censor, but the tsar and his underlings were not worried. Who would want to read it anyway? It is a boring economic treatise. That attitude still prevails in Russia. You perhaps do not know that my book *Property and Freedom* [New York: Alfred A. Knopf, 1999] was just published in mainland China. It is totally subversive because it argues that one cannot have freedom without property, and freedom inevitably comes with property. But the Chinese censors doubt that many will read the book. The *tirazh* (print run) is 5,000 copies in a country of more than a billion people, so what harm can the book cause? There is no harm. To some extent, Putin thinks the same way. The tirazh of serious books in Russia is small. I get books with a tirazh of 200, 500, or 1,000 copies. Five thousand is already very large. It doesn't really matter. The only outlets that matter are radio and television. He exerts a lot of pressure on them.

Desai: Let's talk about the oligarchs. Would you attribute their appearance to specific aspects of Russian history or culture?

Pipes: No, I don't think so. We had here the men who carried out Russia's privatization, among them Yegor Gaidar. I asked him to explain how he had managed the speedy privatization of Russian assets and allowed the nomenklatura to grab the best of them and become oligarchs. He said, "We did it to prevent a political revolution. We bought them off. We deprived them of political power and gave them wealth." So that's the price Russia paid for avoiding a political revolution.

Desai: I have always argued that Russian privatization was driven by political motives. It had little to do with promoting corporate governance or the efficient management of companies or the egalitarian distribution of assets. That was not in the works. However, having accumulated massive wealth, the oligarchs might end up by controlling the Kremlin and defeat Gaidar's purpose. Do you think so?

PIPES: Not according to the historical Russian tradition. I will tell you about a famous incident in 1730 that will illustrate my point. Before Peter the Great died in 1725, he passed a law allowing the tsar to nominate anyone he chose as his successor. He was not favorably inclined toward his eldest son and had him killed. His widow, an ordinary peasant woman, took over as Catherine I. During her reign, a *Verkhovny tainyi sovet,* the Supreme Privy Council, was formed in 1726. Originally consisting of five and then eight members, it was run by two families, the Dolgorukys and Golytsins. When Peter II, the successor to the throne suddenly died, they assumed power. They wanted to nominate as successor a woman who was a novice in politics. They picked Anne of Courland and presented her with conditions that allowed them to restrict severely her powers. She could do this, she could not do that, she could not spend money, she could not appoint someone without their approval, she could not declare war, and so on.[5] She accepted their conditions because she wanted to be tsarina. When she came to Moscow for her coronation, the gentry told her to tear up the constitution. The gentry wanted to get even with the two families. She, of course, tore up the "conditions," dissolved the Supreme Privy Council, punished its members, and became an autocrat. The oligarchs of that time could not seize power in this notorious episode of Russian history.

DESAI: And this was in 1730?

PIPES: Yes. Russians would not tolerate oligarchs. They said, "We would rather have one autocrat than eight of them who would divide Mother Russia among them. We would rather have one supreme ruler and be punished by him than have several autocrats ruin the country."

DESAI: So they prefer one supreme leader.

PIPES: Yes, but not an oligarchy. This is their tradition.

DESAI: This throws an interesting historical light on the current situation, but then there are other external factors at work, too. Let's talk about the U.S. influence on Russia, perhaps from a different perspective. Yevgeny Yevtushenko, the Russian poet, once worried about the McDonaldization of Russia. Will the culture that has produced one of the world's richest literatures, music, and ballet survive the onslaught of the cultural banality of Americanization?

PIPES: Every time I go there, I get complaints about American television and movies and how bad they are. That does not mean that they have influenced Russia's high culture. The Russians like the low culture, the mass culture. Of course they resent it, but they like it, too. Recently, when I lectured at Perm University, the students asked me about my opinion of American TV. They said they didn't like it. I said I didn't like it, either. And then I asked, "Why do you buy it?" Obviously, half of the television programs on Russian TV are soap operas, but it is still not widespread enough to affect high culture.

DESAI: I tell my young Russian friends in Moscow, St. Petersburg, and elsewhere that I grew up reading the old masters, Tolstoy, Dostoevsky, Chekhov, and Turgenev. That was the reason I went into studying the Soviet Union and then moved into Russian studies. Any reference to these great masters leaves them cold.

PIPES: It's a worldwide phenomenon. When I was teaching at Harvard, I used to give freshman seminars. They were oversubscribed, 120 applicants for ten places, so I would give them a screening test. I didn't expect them to know anything about Russia or Russian intellectual history, but I expected them to be generally interested in political or literary history. Most of them had read *Crime and Punishment,* but they read it as a thriller. Some who had studied advanced French had read *Madame Bovary* because it's a torrid French classic, but they knew nothing of Emile Zola or Dickens. It's a worldwide phenomenon. Young people today are cut off from classical culture. My grandchildren do not read the classics.

DESAI: What do you think of Boris Akunin? Have you read any of his novels? He seems to be very popular in Russia.

PIPES: I cannot say anything about it, but the classics are not read.

DESAI: But this is not necessarily Americanization.

PIPES: The United States represents mass-produced culture: films, television, and music. The intellectuals are upset by it. Every time I go to Russia, I attend Lena Nimirovskaya's seminars near Moscow.[6] They're usually held in Golytsino, outside Moscow. People in their thirties—journalists, politicians, and academics—participate in the discussions. They are bitter about the influence of U.S. culture. We're not an occupying power there, and we do not force them to look at these films, so obviously there is an appetite for it. In Soviet days, Russians read Pushkin and Tolstoy because there was hardly anything else, but if there are choices, they'll go for something lighter. I don't think you can blame the United States for that.

DESAI: Well, it seems to me that aspects of American culture have spread across the globe, but countries absorb them in their own way.

PIPES: That's right. American culture, after all, lacks strong ethnic roots. From a cultural perspective, we are basically an Anglo-Saxon country. Our literature and our constitutional system come from England. If you compare it to French culture, there is a difference in cultural origins. French culture is grounded in French history. So is the Polish culture. From the point of view of ethnic roots, American culture is neutral. Therefore, it has universal appeal.

DESAI: It has itself absorbed many influences from outside.

PIPES: People do not appreciate that. Think of the Marines in Iraq. It was like a foreign legion. I remember the picture of a Marine hoisting the U.S. flag over Saddam's statue, and he was ethnically Chinese. U.S. culture is open to outside influences, and, therefore, it has global features. People do not think it's tied to any particular ethnic group. That is its strength and its weakness.

DESAI: As a foreigner coming from a different culture, who is now completely and happily settled here, I am amazed not only by its absorptive capacity but also by its capacity to transform those who settle down here.

PIPES: Because it is not ethnic. Anyone who lands here with an immigration visa is considered American and becomes one in due course. If you land in France, you never become French. You are not French unless you go through the French *bachot,* the French high school diploma.

DESAI: What about German culture?

PIPES: Being and becoming German again has a lot to do with ethnic background. Third-generation Turks living in Germany are not recognized as Germans. On the other hand, Germans who went to Russia under Catherine the Great and who do not speak a word of German are returning to Germany and are acknowledged as German. They have the right of free return.

DESAI: If they can prove their parentage.

PIPES: Right. Blood. But we don't have it here. If there is a willingness to be an American, you're an American. That's why American mass culture has such a universal appeal. People acknowledge that it's not specifically English or American. It's international.

DESAI: Let us talk about U.S.-Russian relations down the road. Russia is huge. It will revive economically. It is a dominating nuclear power. It will always have its strategic interests.

PIPES: Its geopolitical location alone, from the Baltic to the Black Sea and the Pacific, gives it a dominant global position.

DESAI: That's right. So what will the future relations be like? Can we ever become partners, for example?

PIPES: Well, it will depend on the Russians. I mean the U.S. policy makers would be more than willing to negotiate. I wrote an article in the *Jerusalem Post* not long ago on the crisis in U.S.-European relations over the war in Iraq. I asked myself, why did Putin ally himself with France and Germany rather than with the United States? I think that the driving force behind Russian foreign policy is the recognition that Russia is no longer a great power. The leadership wants Russia to be a great power. That feature has marked much of Russian history. The polls indicate it, too. Russia is no longer a great power, and the Russians regret it. They're not feared. They're not respected. Russia could have become a U.S. ally only as a junior partner, ranked probably after the United Kingdom. On the other hand, Putin's alliance with the French and the Germans made Russia an equal partner. That plays an enormous role in the Russian psyche.

DESAI: Didn't Putin want to contribute to the creation of a multipolar world?

PIPES: Yes. With the Germans and the French, the Russians can balance the United States. Russia would not be a superpower, but it would be part of a superpower complex. They can be only a junior partner with the United States. I think this is the main obstacle. It's a pity because most Russians consider the United States even more of a model for them than Europe. That was true even in the Soviet days. The United States was in many ways the model despite being an adversary. Like the United States, Russia is a big country, potentially a dynamic one, too.

DESAI: The United States spends more on defense than the rest of the world combined. Its military technology, some of which we watched in Iraq, is advanced. As a result, it will remain a dominant superpower. The European public does not want to spend on defense.

PIPES: Yes, that is why European governments do not want to intervene militarily anywhere.

DESAI: That's right! So how can they provide a balance in global affairs?

PIPES: The European game is to get away from military intervention and into economic and cultural competition. In that respect, they are more or less equal.

DESAI: Do you really think so?

PIPES: Think of the European Union as a single unit. Its GDP could soon be as big as ours.

DESAI: Down the road.

PIPES: Oh, yes. And culturally, the EU countries consider themselves superior anyway. That's why they won't focus on military intervention—because the United States will remain number one. If the French had participated in the Iraq war, the U.S. military would have had linguistic problems integrating them into our forces. We preferred to go alone.

DESAI: As Russia revives economically, it can perhaps compete with the United States in military technology. I think Russia is more poised in that regard than any other country.

PIPES: It might be eventually, but I think Putin realizes that if military spending is revived on a big scale, it could ruin the economy. The Russian military is in bad shape anyway with regard to both hardware and morale. We bring generals here from Russia.

DESAI: To the Kennedy School of Government?

PIPES: Yes. They are angry and bitter. They come here because it's nice to be in the United States. They eat well and drink not vodka but whiskey, but they don't think we have anything to teach them. They're an angry lot.

DESAI: I think the way things look now, Putin will be elected president of Russia. I also believe that the U.S. economy will revive on the eve of our next presidential election, and George W. Bush will be reelected president. Do you think they're both geopolitical animals?

PIPES: I think Bush thinks geopolitically. After 9/11 he decided that terrorism is the real threat to the United States and the world. He is determined during his presidential tenure to wipe it out. I'm not sure that Putin has any such vision.

DESAI: But doesn't he have limited goals, for example, in Iran?

PIPES: Recently I read a record of interviews with him, a book called *First Person*. There's nothing there. No ideas. I do not think he thinks strategically. Perhaps that is not so bad. He is basically an administrator who maintains stability. I doubt that he has a grand vision for Russia. I mean, Russia needs someone with a vision, but right now, the Russians want stability and peace. Does he think geopolitically? I see no evidence of it.

DESAI: Strobe Talbott mentioned in his interview that Putin talks about *zapadnichestvo,* an expression that Gorbachev and Yeltsin never used, an expression that he translated as "Russia's Western vocation." So perhaps one might consider that as Putin's long-term goal.

PIPES: Russia has three basic choices: Russia can turn to the East, but that is not popular. China is not liked and is not a model for Russia. The other is Eurasianism, or isolation. That route is actually quite popular, but it is not feasible. A country with 150 million people and a poor economy cannot be a world unto itself. So the West is the model. But which West? Europe or the United States? It seems Putin is moving toward Europe rather than the United States for the psychological reason I mentioned earlier. He can be an equal partner with Europe.

DESAI: Do the Russians worry about the Chinese? I know they don't like the Chinese, but . . .

PIPES: For a short while they were ideological partners. Currently they do not like the Chinese.

DESAI: Where does the expression "yellow peril" come from?

PIPES: From the philosopher Vladimir Soloviev.[7]

DESAI: Which was when?

PIPES: Late nineteenth century.

DESAI: In what context?

PIPES: He was a strange man who believed that the Mongols would take over the West. In one of his books he referred to the Chinese as the "yellow hordes." That fear also prevailed in Germany and elsewhere after Japan had defeated Russia. An Oriental power had defeated a European power, in turn raising fears that the future belonged to the Orient. One heard of the "yellow peril" during the Soviet period because of the ideological rupture, but one does not hear it now.

DESAI: What is your vision of Russia's future? What about expansionism? Let's take that theme first.

PIPES: I think the leadership might flex its muscles with the independent states that were part of the former Soviet Union. I do not think it wants to be expansionist beyond that.

DESAI: How will Russia relate to the states nearby?

PIPES: Russia will regard them as its sphere of influence, particularly Ukraine. Ukraine's loss is a sore point with the Russians, but they are getting used to it. Initially it was a terrible wound. Once, in the nineties, I was traveling by a night train from Kiev to Moscow. An ex-Russian officer was traveling with me. When the Ukrainian border guards came in and asked him for his passport, he was shaking. He had lost his arm defending the Ukrainians from the Nazis, and now the Ukrainians were treating him like a foreigner. Such experiences bother them, but less so now. They will continue to regard the Central Asian states, the Caucasus, and Ukraine as their sphere of influence. They have written off Eastern Europe completely.

DESAI: Is there a chance for the revival of Communism?

PIPES: No, I think Communism is altogether dead in the world. It's utterly discredited.

DESAI: But the Communist Party has a steady electoral support of 30 percent.

PIPES: In Russia? Oh yes, but because it is the only organized party. Five years ago I saw a poll on this question: "Is your standard of living better or worse than it was in the Soviet days?" About 30 percent said it was worse. The next question was this: "Would you like the Soviet government to come back?" Fifty percent of the worse off said yes, and the other half said no.

DESAI: How will the December 2003 Duma elections turn out? The oligarchs are providing cash to all of the parties, including the Communists.

PIPES: For the sake of insurance. The rich provide support to all of the parties almost everywhere. Here they support the Democrats and the Republicans.

DESAI: In Russia they are spreading their cash with a view to counterbalancing Putin's United Russia group.

PIPES: Boris Nemtsov was here and talked about his unsuccessful efforts to combine all of the liberal factions. They refused. Russia needs a strong, liberal, pro-Western party. They just cannot want to get together. It's terrible. You know the situation was similar before the revolution. The opposition parties were splintered. I am a firm believer in a two-party system for a very simple reason: Nuanced programs do not appeal to most people because they cannot distinguish one program from another. However, it is simple in a two-party system. The voters are asked, "Are you satisfied with those in power?" If the answer is no, then vote the rascals out. I think that is the basis of democracy. Of course, there can be more than two parties, but then they need a party structure and a solid organization. The Russians are unable to discipline themselves.

DESAI: Tell us about the need for a party structure in Russia from a historical perspective.

PIPES: The Bolsheviks took power after the revolution because they were the only disciplined party.[8] They had a structure, they had discipline, orders flowed from top to bottom, and they were followed. The other parties were loose organizations with broad programs.

DESAI: For example?

PIPES: The Mensheviks. The Kadets were well organized, but they were basically an urban party in a country that was overwhelmingly rural, so they were very easily eliminated.[9]

DESAI: So it's going to take a while before they stabilize the parties.

PIPES: That's what Nemtsov said. He tried to get the liberal parties together, but they wouldn't agree to it.

DESAI: I think it is probably off the mark to talk about national temperament, but I do find the Americans more pragmatic, more accommodating, and more in the give-and-take mode, quite ready for horse trading in politics. The Russians seem to be different.

PIPES: In the Russian vocabulary, compromise is a bad word because it implies opportunism. The tradition before the revolution was to stick to one's guns and to believe strongly in something. It still survives, perhaps less so. The politicians realize that politics can't be run that way. You know, even the Communists are ready to compromise now. Three or four years ago we had Zyuganov here for a lecture. Somebody asked, "Do you, Mr. Zyuganov, believe in private property?" He said, "Certainly, the Communists also believe in free speech and free elections." They would pronounce any slogans to get power. That, of course, does not make them pragmatic.

DESAI: I think it's going to take time before party politics gets stabilized in Russia.

PIPES: Certainly. If you give Russia fifty years of peace and prosperity, it will become like a European country, but that is a lot of time. It is asking for too much. As someone said, "Time is something history never grants."

DESAI: How do you see its relationship with Europe? What is the European view, for example, about Russia's joining the European Union?

PIPES: They will never allow them in.

DESAI: Why not?

PIPES: Because Russia is too large. Too populous. Europe has always had a balance of power. There was a dominant power and the other powers to balance it. Already in the seventeenth century, the French said to the Russians, "Go to India. Go to China. Leave us alone." A hundred and fifty million people? That's more people than the population in France and Germany combined.

DESAI: And enormous resources?

PIPES: Potentially, yes. Russia certainly has mineral resources, but its tradition is hardly European, no matter what people say. The Europeans will never let Russia into Europe.

DESAI: You can't imagine Russia becoming a member of the European Union?

PIPES: No, not at all.

DESAI: Down the road?

PIPES: No, the Europeans would never let them in because it would upset the balance of power. Europe always wanted Russia to be outside of Europe.

DESAI: Are there strong views by some famous Europeans in the past on this issue?

PIPES: There was a Frenchman in the seventeenth century—I have him quoted somewhere—who said, "Russia does not belong in Europe. Russia belongs in Asia." When Napoleon marched into Russia in 1812, he gave a speech in which he said that Russia is not Europe. It is a different country, a different civilization. There are a lot of views like that.

Desai: Nevertheless, if you ask Russians, they are quite eager to join Europe. The Russians' view of themselves is that they are Europeans.

Pipes: In her famous *zakaz* [instruction], article 10, Catherine the Great said, "*Rossiya evropeiskaya derzhava*" (Russia is a European power), but then Pushkin said, "Russia has nothing nor ever had anything in common with Europe." So at the cultural level, these two views are opposite. At the political level, one cannot even imagine Russia being admitted because the differences are so profound. Take the religious differences. Russia is Orthodox Christian. There are no Orthodox Christians in Europe except in the Balkans. Then take the enormous size and the despotic tradition.

Desai: Wouldn't it be tempered over time by the emergence of democracy, free elections, and a free press?

Pipes: Its very size alone will prevent Russia from becoming a part of Europe. The entry of such a giant would upset the balance of power.

Desai: But could you see Europe and Russia joining forces to contend with the United States?

Pipes: They can do that, and they're doing it right now. This morning's papers report that Russia and France oppose the lifting of sanctions against Iraq, which the United States wants. Yes, they can play these games. They can merge for convenience. But a regular marriage? No, I am quite confident of that.

October 2004

Desai: How do you assess the prospects for the emergence of party politics under Putin?

Pipes: In a recent interview, a politician who is close to Putin said that political parties are fine as long as they cooperate with the government. This is the old tsarist mentality resurfacing: Tsarist statesmen like Pyotr Stolypin would have understood and concurred. The notion that political parties can express the interests of society is alien to Russian political culture. I don't see how you will develop parties unless you give them the maximum opportunity to act as a loyal opposition by giving them access to the media and so on.

Desai: Can you draw some parallels that might give us a comparative perspective on Putin's consolidating impetus?

Pipes: Of course, a lot has changed since 1991, but pre-Soviet mentalities remain embedded. I need not compare Putin to Pinochet or the Chinese leadership: He is acting as would Nicholas I or Alexander III, showing essential respect for property (up to the point when it meddles with politics) and little respect for political or civil rights.

Desai: Don't you think Putin is a pragmatic policy maker?

PIPES: Putin undoubtedly is a smart politician, but what Russia needs is a states-man, and this he is not. He has no vision; at least, he has not articulated one. His alli-ance with the United States in fighting terrorism is phony because he is fighting a movement for national independence that has limited aims, whereas our Muslim en-emies want to destroy our civilization. He could easily resolve the Chechen conflict.

DESAI: How would you rate the steady economic growth under his leadership?

PIPES: You know more about this than I, but to my mind economic progress requires full respect for private property and an independent judiciary, neither of which exists in today's Russia. The economic stability we are witnessing there is surely the byproduct of high oil prices; if they drop to, say, $20 per barrel, the situ-ation will change drastically. Why is there a steady outflow of capital from Russia? It is estimated at $17 billion this year. Russian businessmen seem to have little con-fidence in their country's future.

NOTES

1. Alexander Yakovlev was the principal architect of Mikhail Gorbachev's policies of perestroika (restructuring) and glasnost (openness).

2. Andrei Sakharov (1921–1989), Soviet nuclear physicist and human rights advo-cate, received the Nobel Peace Prize in 1975.

3. Streets named after Lenin, the October Revolution, the Young Pioneers, and V. V. Kuibyshev, an early Soviet leader.

4. Hugh Seton-Watson, Russian historian. His many books include *Decline of Impe-rial Russia, 1855–1914* (London: Methuen, 1952), *Russian Empire, 1801–1917* (Oxford: Oxford University Press, 1967), and *Nationalism and Communism: Essays 1946–1963* (New York: Praeger, 1964).

5. Empress Anna, the niece of Peter the Great and the widowed duchess of Courland, reigned from 1730 to 1740.

6. Elena Nemirovskaya, founder and director of the Moscow School of Political Studies.

7. Vladimir Soloviev (1853–1900) was a Russian philosopher, writer, and poet.

8. Lenin's party, the Bolsheviks (literally, the party of the majority), came to power after the revolution.

9. The Bolsheviks had been opposed by the Mensheviks (literally, the party of the minority), followers of Plekhanov, and the Kadets, the Constitutional Democrats.

Index